Refugees and Asylum Seekers

Refugees and Asylum Seekers

Interdisciplinary and Comparative Perspectives

S. Megan Berthold and Kathryn R. Libal, Editors

Foreword by Richard F. Mollica

 PRAEGER™

An Imprint of ABC-CLIO, LLC

Santa Barbara, California • Denver, Colorado

Library of Congress Cataloging in Publication Control Number: 2019941201

ISBN: 978-1-4408-5495-8 (print)
       978-1-4408-5496-5 (ebook)

23 22 21 20 19   1 2 3 4 5

This book is also available as an eBook.

Praeger
An Imprint of ABC-CLIO, LLC

ABC-CLIO, LLC
147 Castilian Drive
Santa Barbara, California 93117
www.abc-clio.com

This book is printed on acid-free paper ∞

Manufactured in the United States of America

Dedicated to Craig and Scott

Contents

Foreword: Violence toward Immigrants as the "Other"   ix
   Richard F. Mollica

Chapter 1   Supporting Refugees and Asylum Seekers in
                an Era of Backlash: An Introduction   1
                Kathryn R. Libal and S. Megan Berthold

Part 1   **Legal and Social Policy Perspectives on Refugee
          and Asylum Seeker Systems**   15

Chapter 2   Evolution of Refugee and Asylum Law in
                the United States   17
                Karen Musalo

Chapter 3   Locked Up and Kicked Out: Detention and
                Deportation in the United States and
                the United Kingdom   44
                Carol Bohmer and Amy Shuman

Chapter 4   Refugee Resettlement in the United States:
                The Central Role of Voluntarism in a
                Time of Backlash   74
                Kathryn R. Libal, Grace Felten, and Scott Harding

Chapter 5   Migration Policies in Europe and the United
                States: Securitization, Safety, and the
                Paradox of Human Rights   100
                Marciana Popescu

Part 2   Health and Well-Being of Refugees   129

Chapter 6   An Integrated Model of Interdisciplinary
                   Care for Refugees   131
                   J. David Kinzie and Crystal Riley

Chapter 7   Refugee Resilience and Spirituality: Harnessing
                   Social and Cultural Coping Strategies   159
                   *Linda Piwowarczyk, Kathleen Flinton, and
                   Fernando Ona*

Chapter 8   Re-creating Family and Community Networks:
                   Group Interventions with Forced Migrants   182
                   *Adeyinka M. Akinsulure-Smith and
                   Hawthorne E. Smith*

Chapter 9   Child Migrants in the United States: Challenges
                   to the Promotion of Their Rights and Best Interests   202
                   S. Megan Berthold and Alysse M. Loomis

Chapter 10   Promoting the Health and Well-Being of Child
                   Migrants in the United States through
                   Holistic Practice   231
                   Alysse M. Loomis and S. Megan Berthold

**Part 3   Cultural Considerations and Refugee-Informed
            Perspectives**   259

Chapter 11   Transcultural Mental Health Services for Refugees:
                   Two Service Models from Montreal, Canada   261
                   *Toby Measham, Jaswant Guzder, G. Eric Jarvis,
                   Rayanne Elias, Cécile Rousseau, Lucie Nadeau,
                   and Ghayda Hassan*

Chapter 12   "We're Not Asking for Handouts!" Voices of
                   Women Refugees from Africa on Rapid
                   Economic Self-Sufficiency in the United States   290
                   Badiah Haffejee and Jean F. East

Chapter 13   Creative Arts Therapies with Refugees   314
                   Amber Elizabeth L. Gray

Chapter 14   Future Directions to Promote the Rights of
                   Refugees and Asylum Seekers   337
                   S. Megan Berthold and Kathryn R. Libal

Index   347

About the Editors and Contributors   373

Foreword: Violence toward Immigrants as the "Other"

Richard F. Mollica

The largest mass lynching in American history took place in New Orleans, Louisiana, on March 14, 1891. The following day, a *New York Times* editorial supported these public executions:

> These sneaking and cowardly Sicilians, the descendants of bandits and assassins, who have transported to this country the lawless passions, the cut-throat practices, and the oath-bound societies of their native country, are to us a pest without mitigation. Our own rattlesnakes are as good citizens as they . . . Lynch law was the only course open to the people of New Orleans. (The New Orleans Affair 1891, 4)

The lynch mob had murdered nine Italian American immigrants. These Italian immigrants had been found to be not guilty of the murder of Police Chief David Hennessy. Despite their innocence, they were killed by an angry mob that was strongly supported by the general public and prominent local politicians. Attorney William S. Parkerson rallied the support of community members and decried the jury's decision, denouncing them as perjurers and scoundrels. The angry mob then marched to the jailhouse. Among the participants were John M. Parker and Walter C. Flower. Each would go on to hold gubernatorial positions in Louisiana. Parker, who would go on to become Louisiana's 37th governor, famously stated as follows in 1911 about Italians: "just a little bit worse than the Negroes, being if anything filthier in [their] habits, lawless, and treacherous" (Falco 2012, 2).

In 1899, in Tallulah, Louisiana, three Italian American shopkeepers were lynched because they had treated black customers the same as white customers. The lynch mob hung five members in total related to this event—the three shopkeepers and two bystanders (Schoener 1987).

These events marked the beginnings of America's public acceptance of Italian Americans as a race of ambiguous color (i.e., neither white nor black) and as people of intrinsic criminality and inferior mental intelligence.

While America has a proud immigrant history, it also has a strong element of debasing and dehumanizing the "other," including violent hostility and even death (Falco 2012). I would like to briefly focus on the historical racial prejudices directed toward Italian Americans to illuminate a model similar to current sociopolitical factors and trends that impact modern-day immigrant groups entering (or trying to enter) the United States. It would then be helpful to examine the theoretical principles that might explain America's long-standing racial hatred of refugees and immigrants and finally to suggest possible social solutions to this problem of inflicting pain and suffering on the "other." I have chosen to use Italian Americans as an example of our country's stigmatization and ostracism of the "other" because of my firsthand experiences as an Italian American child growing up in the urban ghetto of the South Bronx. My family was no stranger to the systemic forces of acculturation and institutionalized racism. I was the son of two parents who were orphaned by tragic events related to racism. When I was a student, I was subject to the micro-aggressions of the institutions where I sought my education. These forces were not merely artifacts of the past, but to this day, I have worked in environments that continue to make slights toward Italian Americans.

When Italian Americans Were the "Other"

Clearly, no discussion of racial oppression and exploitation can begin without acknowledging the enormous suffering of the African American communities, which had experienced slavery, and the genocide of the Native Americans. The intergenerational impact of violence on these communities continues to this day from generation to generation. Individuals and families from many countries in Asia, Latin America, Africa, and the Middle East have faced significant oppression and violence as well in the United States and other countries they have immigrated to. Having spent the past four decades working with survivors of mass violence and torture, I have seen the ripple effects violence can have on a community. Violence leads to a serious impact on the health and well-being of survivors decades after the major events have occurred and continues to affect the health and well-being of each new generation. Post-traumatic stress disorder (PTSD) is never "post"; it is always ongoing.

Racial prejudice toward Italian Americans is embedded in the long-standing racial slang Americans have used to describe an entire group of immigrant peoples. The word *Guinea* was used as a derogatory word for "an Italian" and is derived from the term *Guinea Negro*, which referred to black persons of mixed ancestry. The Italians were considered "black" people or people of "ambiguous color" but certainly not "white people." Another racially charged ethnic slur for Italians is the term *Wop*. *Merriam-Webster* dictionary says it was first used in America in 1908 and originates from the Italian word *guappo*. In Southern Italian dialect, *guappo* is a friendly term broadly meaning "dandy," "dude," or "stud." Unfortunately, Americans transformed this into a derogatory term for Italians.

Each of these terms would be and still are considered by Italian Americans as the equivalent of the *N*-word for African Americans. The discrimination toward Italian Americans hit a high point in the 1920s. The Immigration Act of 1924 or *Johnson-Reed Act* included the *National Origins Act* and the *Asian Exclusion Act*. These actions by Congress, signed into law by President Coolidge on May 24, 1924, strongly restricted the immigration of Italians (among many other races) into the United States. The proponents of this act, strongly supported by Congress, used the following arguments to legislate fewer admissions by certain countries. Arguments that favored Northern European immigrants as opposed to Southern European immigrants included "maintaining the racial preponderance of the basic strain of our people and hereby stabilize the ethnic composition of the population" (U.S. Immigration and Migration Reference Library 2004). The supporters of the bill believed that Italians (and similar races) were sickly, disease ridden, and mentally feeble, incapable of contributing and adjusting to American culture. The people who supported these laws used eugenics (Galton 1904; Gould 1981) as a justification for restrictions on entering into America because they feared Italians would marry healthy, white non-Italian-American women and produce mentally limited children—and the latter would threaten our democracy.

Immediately after this law was passed, American prejudice toward Italian Americans heightened, and it led to the public execution of Bartolomeo Vanzetti and Nicola Sacco in the electric chair on August 23, 1927. These men living in Boston were Italian American anarchists who were convicted of murdering a guard in an armed robbery. This execution was internationally followed and universally condemned outside of America. On April 9, 1927, several months before his execution, Vanzetti gave a moving speech summarizing for history the great injustice perpetuated by American society:

I would not wish to a dog or to a snake, to the most low and misfortunate creature of the earth—I would not wish to any of them what I have had to suffer for things that I am not guilty of. But my conviction is that I have suffered for things I am guilty of. I am suffering because I am a radical and indeed I am a radical; I have suffered because I was an Italian, and indeed I am an Italian; I have suffered more for my family and for my beloved than for myself; but I am so convinced to be right that if you could execute me two times, and if I could be reborn two other times, I would live again to do what I have done already. (Vanzetti 1927, para. 4)

On the 50th anniversary of their execution, Massachusetts governor Michael Dukakis issued a proclamation that these men had been unfairly convicted. The dark side of Italian American social history in America resonates strongly with our current events manifested toward immigrants and migrants. The terms used at the highest level of government and supported by millions of Americans are familiar and terrifying. Crude and violent terms are used to describe immigrants:

1. They are infestations.
2. "These aren't people. These are animals."
3. Why not immigration from Norway? "Why are we housing these people from shithole countries?"
4. "Drug dealers, criminals and rapists." (Korte and Gomez 2018)

President Trump, after a white nationalist rally in Charlottesville, Virginia, went on to defend the racially charged bigotry of this group by casting aspersions on all parties involved (Shear and Haberman 2017)—despite the death of a woman protesting the white nationalists, who was hit by a car driven by a nationalist supporter. The fear of the immigrant as the "other," who will infect our society, bring in criminal elements, steal our jobs, and have babies with pure white American women, is linked to increasing incarceration and deportation practices and calls for the building of a border wall. This fear is at a fever pitch. The horrible story of America's degradation of Italian Americans is being repeated with large support from many mainstream Americans.

Repetition of Oppression and Exploitation

As the chapters in this book make clear, we are repeating our oppression, exploitations, and violence to our immigrant communities, despite our great history as a nation founded by immigration. There are many great traditions in our country beginning with the U.S. Constitution and the Declaration of Independence. The Statue of Liberty stands heroically in New York Harbor with the date of the U.S. Declaration of Independence inscribed in Roman numerals, intended to be a symbol of freedom to welcome immigrants arriving from abroad. Our immigrant tradition of pride and merit is expressed in the 1883 poem "The New Colossus," by Emma Lazarus, later added on a bronze tablet mounted in the Statue of Liberty pedestal (and currently in the statute's museum). It is one of the greatest expressions of a welcoming for immigrants leaving their motherlands. The full poem is a beautiful expression of American generosity and hospitality.

The New Colossus

Not like the brazen giant of Greek fame/With conquering limbs astide from land to land;/Here at our sea-washed, sunset gates shall stand/A mighty woman with a torch, whose flame/Is the imprisoned lightning, and her name Mother of Exiles./From her beacon-hand glows world-wide welcome; her mild eyes command/The air-bridged harbor that twin cities frame./"Keep, ancient lands, your storied pomp!" cries she with silent lips/"Give me your tired, your poor, your huddled masses yearning to breathe free,/The wretched refuse of your teeming shore,/Send these, the homeless, tempest-tost to me, I lift my lamp beside the golden door!" (Lazarus [1883] 2005)

So it is very difficult to understand the two opposing forces in American immigration: thought and policies.

Paradoxically, we can turn to certain philosophers in Europe who can lend us a hand in understanding our current immigration crisis. Antonio Gramsci, Italy's leading political theorist and revolutionary thinker, was arrested by Mussolini and was subsequently sentenced to 20 years in prison by the fascist state. His prison confinement ended with his death in 1937. During his incarceration, he wrote the most important political theory since Machiavelli, the *Quaderni del Carcere* (Prison Notebook) (Gramsci 1975). Gramsci's theory of *Hegemony* was groundbreaking. Gramsci defined *hegemony* as the "spontaneous" consent given by the masses of the population to the general direction imposed on social life by the dominant fundamental group. Their consent is historically caused by the prestige (and consequent confidence) which the dominant group enjoys because of its position and function in the world of production (Gramsci 1971). Hegemony is much more than a society's social consensus. It is those historically based practices (sometimes referred to as "articulations" or "discursive practices") that reveal the meanings and values society assigns individuals and institutions.

The late French philosopher Michel Foucault further elaborated upon a description of *discursive formations* (Foucault 1970) as those historical forms of social behavior and institutions constructed by language, rules, laws, and customs. All elements—rules, regulations, practices, and routines—are part of the complex web that makes up a *discursive formation* (i.e., empirical phenomena situated within a field of complex social forces). For example, some of those factors that constitute immigration's discursive formation are rooted in America's history toward the "other," including slavery, genocide of Native Americans, the American Dream, "pulling yourself up by your bootstraps," and the self-made man. While these social practices reveal their historical foundations, they may be in conflict and are not easily understood by policy planners, the general public, and immigrants themselves. The hard work and commitment by immigrants and refugees in building and maintaining our modern society is deeply appreciated by most American citizens. However, the fear of the "other" is equally strong.

Hegel (1977), Sartre (1964), and others help us appreciate the ontological human forces creating the master-slave relationship, with the "other" as a victim of human aggression, oppression, and exploitation. It seems the need to affirm our identity by oppression of "others" is well established philosophically. But a human need to turn away from this domination of the "other" is not an easy task. Renowned French philosopher Jean-Paul Sartre embraced the power of our "freedom" to empower our positive "authentic" actions in the world. For these existentialist philosophers, a true confrontation with our own identity is a confrontation with our "nothingness" and an assertion of our need to make something out of our identity (Sartre 1964).

Fortunately, modern humanistic psychology find more than nothingness and freedom that binds us all together. Maslow discovered the universal need in all human beings to find meaning in their lives through "self-actualization" (Maslow 1943). His famous expression holds true: "What a man can be, he must be" (Maslow 1954, 93). The discovery of the "mirror" neurons in all human beings and life itself places all of us in a historically shared, common experience (Winerman 2005). These mirror neurons have hardwired all of us for empathy. It is a biological miracle that all living beings can empathically relate and share love and affection with every other being on the planet. But unfortunately, fear, greed, and envy can override human empathy (Ammaniti and Gallese 2014). So this is the crisis of our moment on immigration. Can our empathic-self overcome the violent and hateful policies of racist immigration attitudes, policies, and practices?

Transforming Old Wine in New Bottles

Our current immigration crisis is a case of transforming "old wine in new bottles." To the Italian Americans, Native Americans, and other oppressed, marginalized groups in American society, the current violent and racist immigration policies are painful to witness. Those who have been oppressed by our previous immigration laws and policies need to speak out publicly and support current victims of violence.

During my father and mother's generation, Italian Americans moved politically to the right in order to "fit in." They gave their children anglicized names and forbid them to speak Italian. The overcoming of tragedies by my Italian parents was never articulated and their story never told. The incredible silence of immigrants/asylum seekers is loud. Their stories too need to be told with their permission in the media, town/community meetings, and in local storytelling sessions. They are being told in the chapters in this volume that present the "shadow-side" of American immigration policy and practices currently manifesting here in our country. These stories of resilience and oppression need to appear in local communities, so that immigrants and asylum seekers become known to other Americans as decent, hardworking human beings. We can only overcome our fear when we disclose the humanity of another.

In looking more deeply into the historical oppression faced by Italian Americans in the United States, I felt great sadness in learning of the lynching of Italian immigrants in Louisiana; the 1924 Congressional Act, which did not allow my family reunification; and the murder of Sacco and Vanzetti. The public lynching of the "other" is over. Embracing the diversity of immigrants and asylum seekers and all the richness they have to offer our society is what is needed now.

References

Ammaniti, Massimo, and Vittorio Gallese. 2014. *The Birth of Intersubjectivity: Psychodynamics, Neurobiology, and the Self (The Norton Series on Interpersonal Neurobiology)*. New York: W.W. Norton.

Falco, Ed. 2012. "When Italian Immigrants Were 'the Other.'" *CNN*, July 10, 2012. http://www.cnn.com/2012/07/10/opinion/falco-italian-immigrants/index.html.

Foucault, Michel. 1970. *The Order of Things: An Archaeology of the Human Sciences*. New York: Pantheon Books.

Galton, Francis. 1904. "Eugenics: Its Definition, Scope, and Aims." *American Journal of Sociology* 10, no. 1: 1–25.

Gould, Stephen Jay. 1981. *The Mismeasure of Man*. New York: W.W. Norton.

Gramsci, Antonio. 1971. *Selections from the "Prison Notebooks."* Edited and translated by Quentin Hoare and Geoffrey Nowell Smith. London: Lawrence and Wishart.

Gramsci, Antonio. 1975. *Quaderni del Carcere*. Vols. 1–4. Edited by Valentino Gerratana. Torino: Eiunaldi.

Hegel, Georg Wilhelm Friedrich. 1977. *Phenomenology of Spirit*. Oxford: Clarendon Press.

Korte, Gregory, and Alan Gomez. 2018. "Trump Ramps Up Rhetoric on Undocumented Immigrants: 'These Aren't People. These are Animals.'" *USA Today*, May 16, 2018. https://www.usatoday.com/story/news/politics/2018/05/16/trump-immigrants-animals-mexico-democrats-sanctuary-cities/617252002/.

Lazarus, Emma. 2005. "The New Colossus." In *Emma Lazarus: Selected Poems: (American Poets Project #13)*, edited by John Hollander, 58. New York: The Library of America.

Maslow, Abraham H. 1943. "A Theory of Human Motivation." *Psychological Review* 50, no. 382: 370–396.

Maslow, Abraham H. 1954. *Motivation and Personality*. New York: Harper.

"The New Orleans Affair." 1891. *The New York Times*, March 16, 1891, 4. https://timesmachine.nytimes.com/timesmachine/1891/03/16/103299119.pdf.

Sartre, Jean Paul. 1964. *Being and Nothingness: An Essay in Phenomenological Ontology*. Secaucus, NJ: Citadel Press.

Schoener, Allon. 1987. *The Italian Americans*. London, UK: Macmillan Publishing Company.

Shear, Michael D., and Maggie Haberman. 2017. "Trump Defends Initial Remarks on Charlottesville; Again Blames 'Both Sides.'" *The New York Times*, August 15, 2017. https://www.nytimes.com/2017/08/15/us/politics/trump-press-conference-charlottesville.html.

U.S. Immigration and Migration Reference Library. 1st ed. 2004. Farmington Hills, MI: The Gale Group Incorporated.

Vanzetti, Bartolomeo. 1927. Court Statement. http://wps.prenhall.com/wps/media/objects/172/177076/23_court.HTM.

Winerman, Lea. 2005. "The Mind's Mirror: A New Type of Neuron—Called a Mirror Neuron—Could Help Explain How We Learn through Mimicry and Why We Empathize with Others." *APA Monitor on Psychology* 36, no. 9: 48. https://www.apa.org/monitor/oct05/mirror.aspx.

CHAPTER ONE

Supporting Refugees and Asylum Seekers in an Era of Backlash

An Introduction

Kathryn R. Libal and S. Megan Berthold

The Precarious Quest to Support Refugees and Asylum Seekers

One of the most profound aspects of globalization in the early 21st century has been efforts of individuals and families to migrate across borders seeking refuge, safety, and corresponding economic stability. The "Global North," or the so-called receiving countries of this migration, continues to dominate the formal politics of opening or closing borders and defining the rules for who can be admitted or excluded. Since what is known as the "European migration crisis" began in 2015, European states, the United States, and other countries have vacillated between welcoming and exclusionary policies, increasingly shaped by public attitudes toward immigrants and refugees (Vollmer and Karakayali 2018). Images of refugees, asylum seekers, and migrants are deployed in mainstream media outlets and on Facebook and Twitter, both by those who support developing strong humanitarian and human rights–based responses to forced migration and by those who oppose admissions (Krzyżanowski, Triandafyllidou, and Wodak 2018).

It is challenging to stay abreast of the global politics of migration—the scale of political reaction in many countries is profound and rapidly

evolving. During one week in mid-December 2018, global news was dominated by the politics of migration at local, national, and global scales. Several
events punctuating the news landscape are illustrative of the tension between
the efforts to support those forced to migrate and those seeking to exclude
them from crossing national borders in search of refuge. In Europe, *Médicins
Sans Frontières* decommissioned its humanitarian rescue ship, the *Aquarius*,
due to severe pressure from EU governments and lack of protection on the
Mediterranean during refugee rescue missions (Brabant 2018). In Belgium,
the liberal premier Charles Michel attended a UN forum in Marrakesh, signing the UN Global Compact on Safe, Orderly, and Regular Migration. In
doing so, he lost coalition support of a major conservative party and tendered
his resignation (BBC 2018).

In the United States, where immigration has become a flashpoint for President Trump's administration and a significant part of the electorate, officials
for the Department of Homeland Security and immigrant rights groups
debate who is responsible for the death of Jakelin Amei Rosmery Caal
Maquin, a seven-year-old Guatemalan girl who died of exposure less than a
day after being taken into custody by the U.S. Immigration and Customs
Enforcement. Nearly 2,400 children and youth were interned at a closed
camp in Tornillo, Texas (Associated Press 2018), and 14,000 children were
in immigrant custody, despite pressure by those in the health and social
professions, children's rights advocates, and legal action groups like the
American Civil Liberties Union (Kopan 2018). In the same week, a group of
interfaith clergy members was arrested for protesting the treatment of a
migrant "caravan" of more than 6,000 asylum seekers from Central America,
who have been unable to approach the U.S.–Mexico border and claim asylum and face harsh living conditions in Tijuana, Mexico (Jenkins 2018).
Hussam Ayloush, executive director of the Council on Arab and Islamic
Relations in Los Angeles, wrote in an e-mail of the protest that "it was my
faith, love and passion for dignity, respect of human rights for all people,
including our brothers and sisters from Central America seeking asylum and
refuge, that led me to protest and get detained in order to help raise awareness about this injustice" (Kuruvilla 2018). And Stephen Miller, architect of
many of the new highly restrictive policies and proposals for U.S. immigration, gave an interview on a leading news program, in which he asserted that
the rise in border crossings by asylum seekers and migrants at the U.S.–
Mexico border was due to "illegal immigration" that was "incentivized by
loopholes in our laws and loopholes created by activist, left-wing judges"
(Kragie 2018).

The question of how to foster global support for refugees and asylum
seekers in the early 21st century has intensified, particularly in the context
of rising nationalism, xenophobia, and anti-immigrant sentiments in the so-
called receiving countries (Ife 2018; Newland 2018). Many governments
have revised migration policies to restrict eligibility for immigration. As

Popescu and Libal note, "Exclusionary asylum policies have become increasingly shaped by discretionary national political decisions rather than norms of international humanitarian and human rights standards" (2018, ii). Despite global pressure from the United Nations and some political leaders, such as Angela Merkel, Justin Trudeau, and Barack Obama in 2015–2017, quotas for resettlements dropped by more than half between 2016 and October 2018 (UNHCR n.d.). Increasingly restrictive immigration policies continue to threaten resettlement programs as an option for refugees.

Immigration policy broadly and policy related to refugees and asylum seekers more narrowly have become centerpieces of everyday politics in the West (Polakaw-Suransky 2017). In 2015, in response to the mass migration of Syrians, Afghans, Iraqis, and others to Europe, forced migration became a lightning rod. Initially, many European states, under pressure from their citizens, expressed commitment to providing refuge in EU member countries. Germany led this initial opening, by committing to take in one million refugees (De La Baume 2017). Yet, almost immediately, building on an earlier legacy to restrict irregular migration and stymie asylum seekers' efforts, a rhetoric of xenophobic, ultra-nationalist backlash occurred. The United States, long considered a leader in refugee resettlement, reversed long-standing refugee admissions practices; President Donald Trump ran his election on an anti-immigrant platform and, since taking office in 2017, has radically curtailed pathways for immigrants, asylum seekers, and refugees seeking entry into the United States (Pierce, Bolter, and Selee 2018). The Trump administration has also accelerated processes of deporting immigrants, including those with permanent resident status, for even minor criminal offenses. For example, his administration has renewed its attempts to deport Vietnamese immigrants who came to the United States by mid-1995 and who, under a 2008 agreement that restored U.S.–Vietnam diplomatic relations, are specifically barred from deportation (Dunst and Calamur 2018).

Anti-immigrant and anti-refugee sentiment formed the backbone of President Trump's 2016 U.S. presidential campaign and the Brexit vote in the United Kingdom. Some prominent analysts argue that Angela Merkel of Germany will step down as head of the center-right Christian Democratic Union in 2021 due to growing opposition to policies related to refugees and asylum seekers within her own party and the gradual empowerment of the right-wing *Alternative für Deutschland* (AFD, Alternative for Germany), a staunchly anti-immigrant party. Indeed, former U.S. secretary of state, Hillary Clinton, pinned the rise of right-wing nationalism in Europe on governments, such as Germany, being too responsive to refugees and migrants:

> I admire the very generous and compassionate approaches that were taken particularly by leaders like Angela Merkel, but I think it is fair to say Europe has done its part, and must send a very clear message—"we are not

going to be able to continue to provide refuge and support"—because if we don't deal with the migration issue it will continue to roil the body politic. (as cited in Wintour 2018)

Kathleen Newland, senior fellow and cofounder of the U.S.-based Migration Policy Institute, underscored that the recent "retreat" of a number of key countries from signing the UN Global Compact on Safe, Orderly, and Regular Migration was marked by a purposeful "mis-reading" of the compact by right-wing conservatives across Europe and the United States. Newland (2018) notes:

Over the course of the late summer and autumn, the Compact was taken up as another weapon in the arsenal of anti-immigration, anti-globalization forces on the European right. On far-right websites such as Breitbart and Rebel Media, a drumroll of denunciation gathered strength, painting the Compact as a nefarious attempt to deny states their sovereign right to make decisions about their migration policies (never mind that the Compact clearly states it is based on respect for national sovereignty). (para. 9)

The UN Global Compact on Refugees, endorsed by members of the General Assembly in late December 2018, aims to establish "a stronger, fairer response to large refugee movements" (UN News 2018). The Global Compact on Refugees has four objectives: to (1) "ease the pressures on host countries," (2) "enhance refugee self-reliance," (3) "expand access to third-country solutions," and (4) "support conditions in countries of origin for return in safety and dignity" (UN Refugees and Migrants n.d.). These objectives resemble the long-standing principles of UNHCR to support durable solutions of voluntary repatriation, resettlement, and integration (UNHCR USA n.d.). The Global Compact on Refugees and a related Global Compact for Safe, Orderly, and Regular Migration have been developed at the same time that skepticism about the effectiveness of UN mechanisms to realize humanitarian and human rights ideals is on the rise (DeGooyer, Hunt, Maxwell, and Moyn 2018; Moyn 2018).

Twenty-First-Century Challenges: Forced Migration and Human Rights

Hannah Arendt's often-cited critique of the Universal Declaration of Human Rights and its premise that rights would be realized through individuals making claims within the political boundaries of their own nation-states is as relevant today as it was in post–World War II Europe. She wrote, "The right to have rights, or the right of every individual to belong to humanity, should be guaranteed by humanity itself" (as cited in Gessen 2018).

Today it is clear that the humanitarian and human rights systems supported by the United Nations and its member states are unable to effectively and justly meet the challenges of mass forced migration.

The responsibility does not rest with the United Nations as a supranational body alone, however. Some of the most powerful global actors arguably are responsible for a significant proportion of mass forced migration. This has included the United States and allies who waged wars in Vietnam, Cambodia, and Laos in the 1950s–1970s; in Iraq in the early 1990s; and in Iraq and Afghanistan since the early 2000s. Ostensibly, the destabilization of Central America and the mass migration of asylum seekers and refugees from Guatemala, El Salvador, Nicaragua, and Mexico owe much to the U.S. support for military dictators and the "War on Drugs" waged for many decades. The consequences of these foreign policy decisions by the United States, coupled with destabilizing trade agreements and failure to support the reconstruction of countries crippled by decades of externally supported civil wars, have fostered a climate of violence and fear that impels tens of thousands to flee Central America annually. Yet many U.S. politicians and citizens are ignorant of or deny any responsibility for large-scale migration to the United States.

And, while the "refugee crisis" may appear to be most significant in Europe and the United States, in reality, countries in the Global South, particularly those that border regions where war or armed conflict has occurred, bear the disproportionate responsibility of providing refuge (Parekh 2016). Nearly three million refugees currently reside in Turkey, in and out of formal camps. Forced migration due to the ongoing conflict in the Democratic Republic of Congo gains scant attention in global news, though the scale of displacement rivals that of refugees from Syria (Staedicke 2018). Venezuela figures as one of the top-ten "silent" refugee crises in 2018; the International Organization of Migration estimated 1.6 million people left the country in 2017 (Norwegian Refugee Council 2018). While migration by asylum seekers and migrants to Europe and the United States dominates news media in the Global North, 85 percent of refugees are in developing countries (Staedicke 2018).

The United Nations High Commissioner for Refugees (UNHCR) has been a critical institution in monitoring and managing refugee challenges since its formation in December 1950 (Loescher 2017). Yet at no point in its history has UNHCR had the institutional capacity or license to enforce global participation in addressing forced migration. The United Nations Convention Related to the Status of Refugees (1951) entails the strongest legal responsibilities for securing the rights of asylum seekers (Parekh 2016). Yet, as Parekh points out, there is no widely held sense of moral responsibility or legal basis for resettling refugees or providing aid to refugees through UNCHR. She notes, "Any aid states give to refugees abroad, either through financial contributions or by agreeing to resettle them, is considered a matter of gener-osity and good will, rather than the fulfillment of a moral or legal norm. States consider aid to refugees and the UNHCR to be more or less discretion-ary" (2016, para. 5). Parekh argues for a robust recognition of the rights of refugees and for the moral obligations that countries of the Global North have toward refugees and asylum seekers.

> It's crucial that we move away from thinking of our obligations solely in terms of resettlement and take seriously the moral obligations we have to the forcibly displaced while they are between homes, that is, between the initial displacement from their home states and either returning to or find-ing a new one. This is the space where the vast majority of displaced peo-ple will spend their lives. (2016, para. 15)

Parekh points to the robust moral obligations that states in the Global North have: to not only provide places of refuge (asylum and resettlement) within their own borders, but also to support refugees in all sites of disloca-tion and along their journeys. These are the ideas that animated the New York Summit on Refugees and negotiations between 2016 and 2018 for two global compacts related to refugees and migrants.

On September 20, 2016, President Barack Obama spoke at the United Nations during a Leaders' Summit on Refugees. In a speech marked by simultaneous calls for action and reflections on the impacts of war on ordinary people, Obama noted that he had called for the summit "because this crisis is one of the most urgent tests of our time—our capacity for collective action." He continued, "It's a test of our international system where all nations ought to share in our collective responsibilities, because the vast majority of refugees are hosted by just 10 countries who are bearing a very heavy burden—among them Turkey, Pakistan, Lebanon, Iran, Ethiopia" (Obama 2016).

Yet, even in the face of such international efforts to provide new standards not currently outlined in international human rights and humanitarian law, scholars and advocates are increasingly alarmed by the isolationist, nationalist rhetoric that pervades national and international discourses on migration. Months after the Leaders' Summit on Refugees—in a stark reversal of course—the newly elected president Donald Trump imposed several executive orders asserting the primacy of restrictive immigration and refugee policies as a core part of his platform. Legal scholar Jacqueline Bhabha recently underscored the scope of human rights violations for refugees and migrants in the United States:

> In less than two years, the administration has promulgated a visa ban that critics say targets Muslims, including those fleeing war zones; it has can-celled a policy designed to regularize the status of more than 700,000 undocumented but law-abiding young people brought to the United States

as children, including those who have no recollection of any other home; it has prosecuted, arrested and detained adult refugees and migrants entering the country without prior authority, even those applying for asylum; it has separated parents and children traveling together in search of safety, even when the latter are babies and toddlers; and it has announced its intention to reverse the law and exclude survivors of domestic abuse and gang violence from eligibility for refugee protection, even where no protection is available for them in their countries of origin. (Bhabha 2018)

Executive orders expanding efforts to detain and deport undocumented migrants and restrict access to refugees were followed with a cascade of changes to administrative guidelines and rules that impact not only refugees and asylum seekers but also other noncitizen groups, including those with permanent residence in the United States (Pierce, Bolter, and Selee 2018). In late 2018, the president opined that the executive branch could administratively reverse the Fourteenth Amendment to the Constitution (Jadwat 2018). While such a move would be unlikely to hold up in U.S. courts, it signals substantial pressure to reverse a long-standing legal norm that grants citizenship to all born within the United States. And, in a troubling example of nondemocratic, executive rule, the Trump administration recently moved to "radically broaden the scope of the 'public charge' grounds for inadmissibility and deportation" from the United States (University of Minnesota Law Clinics 2018, 2). Departing from past practice in which only "noncitizens primarily dependent on cash assistance can be considered public charges," the new rule, if implemented as proposed, expands current law to include those receiving noncash benefits, affecting nearly 50 percent of noncitizens (all except refugees and those granted asylum) in the United States (University of Minnesota Law Clinics 2018, 2; Capps, Greenberg, Fix, and Zong 2018).

Yet, in the United States, there are substantial signs of a countermovement to support immigrants and refugees. Following President Trump's executive order that banned admission of immigrants and refugees from several countries, spontaneous protests took place across the country (Bacon and Gomez 2017). Organizations like the American Civil Liberties Union rapidly garnered millions of dollars in donations to mount legal battles on a range of anti-immigrant and anti-refugee policies (Stack 2017). Levels of citizen voluntarism to support refugees, asylum seekers, and migrants went up, and a number of cities took stances to be recognized as "welcoming" or "sanctuary" cities (see Chapter 4). In spring and summer 2018, there was widespread reaction to the "zero tolerance" policy that entailed family separation and a recognition that such policies intentionally cause indelible harm (see Chapters 3 and 9). In the coming years there is no doubt that immigration and refugee policy will continue to be deeply politicized in the United States and other parts of the world. The role of refugee and immigrant rights advocates, social workers, mental health and health providers, lawyers, educators, and faith leaders takes on greater significance in this context.

This book addresses many of the themes raised in the introduction, as well as provides insights into interdisciplinary clinical and community-based practice to foster healing and social inclusion for refugees and asylum seekers. Often lost in the political debates of how to address migration policy broadly, and the rights of refugees and asylum seekers more narrowly, are the lived experiences of refugees and asylum seekers themselves. This book thus draws attention to the experiences and voices of forced migrants, but also highlights the work of mental health and social service providers in developing innovative programs and approaches to fostering the well-being and social inclusion of refugees and asylum seekers. The conclusion illuminates how such practitioners, as allies, may help build more effective national and international advocacy on immigration and refugee policy.

Organization of the Book

This book brings together experts from a range of fields—law, anthropology, sociology, political science, psychology, transcultural psychiatry, social work, theology, creative arts therapy, public health, and folklore and narrative—to provide insights into the legal and policy developments and challenges related to migrants as well as their impact on migrants' psychosocial, physical, and spiritual well-being. Contributors provide rich insights on institutional perspectives critical to understanding U.S., European, and Canadian politics, laws, and practices of refugee resettlement and asylum processes and coverage of relevant international human rights and humanitarian law. They also address contextual factors linked to global forced migration and conditions that shape the lives of refugees at multiple stages of migration. Richard F. Mollica reflects on the current global realities faced by refugees and asylum seekers in the foreword, tracing how migrants have been treated as "others" over generations and making a case for the timeliness and importance of this book.

The book includes three parts. The first part focuses on legal and social policy perspectives on refugee and asylum seekers in the United States and Europe. Contributors engage the heated global policy debates in politics and society regarding the admission of refugees, policies toward asylum seekers, and related immigration policies. They tackle questions about what refugee policy should be in the United States and in Europe and analyze the human rights implications of various options. Chapter 2, by Karen Musalo, provides a valuable framework for understanding the status of refugees and asylum seekers in the United States and internationally and details the evolution of U.S. immigration law and policy over the past 50 years. A comparative analysis of detention and deportation practices in the United States and the United Kingdom is provided by Carol Bohmer and Amy Shuman. The authors illuminate the effects of such practices through legal and historical research, coupled with reports from human rights and nongovernmental organizations, the media, and detainees themselves. Kathryn Libal, Grace Felten, and Scott Harding address refugee resettlement in the United States following the U.S. Refugee Act of 1980. In particular, they address approaches to engaging voluntarism in resettlement efforts in Utah, Kentucky, and Connecticut and outline policy developments and strategies to advance the well-being and social inclusion of refugees in the United States. Marciana Popescu examines migration policies in Europe with a focus on factors that challenge a rights-based approach to migration. She examines international and regional legal standards to protect the rights of asylum seekers and refugees and discusses two cases of positive approaches to addressing the rights of forced migrants in Germany and Austria.

The second part focuses on the health and well-being of migrants. Contributors examine models of care provided to refugees in the United States to address bio-psycho-social-spiritual domains of their lives and examine to what extent the treatment of child migrants promote or threaten their rights. The first three chapters in this part focus on different specialized torture treatment programs in the United States. J. David Kinzie and Crystal Riley present their pioneering interdisciplinary model of psychiatric treatment for refugees and asylum seekers, including those who have experienced torture. The Intercultural Psychiatric Program, founded by Kinzie in 1977 at Oregon Health and Science University, provides continuity of care in a culturally acceptable manner through teams of psychiatrists and ethnic mental health counselors who are interpreters and case managers for patients from their own cultures. Linda Piwowarczyk, Kathleen Flinton, and Fernando Ona address the important potential role of spirituality in supporting resilience and recovery from refugee trauma and torture. They outline the benefits of incorporating spirituality as a valuable dimension in treatment and provide a detailed case example of the individual psychotherapy treatment of a woman from Africa who was tortured because of her activism as a member of a political opposition party. The authors also address the impact of this work on and challenges faced by clinicians. Drawing on their work at the Bellevue/NYU Program for Survivors of Torture, Adeyinka M. Akinsulure-Smith and Hawthorne E. Smith present considerations for the psychosocial treatment of forced migrants and discuss the curative factors associated with group therapy. They draw on case examples from their experience in conducting diverse types of groups with survivors of torture and refugee trauma (e.g., psycho-educational orientation groups; therapy groups with Francophone African men, Tibetan-speaking survivors, and those who survived homophobic persecution; and nonverbally based art therapy and trauma-informed yoga groups) to illustrate challenges faced and lessons learned. They emphasize the contribution of group therapy to recreating family and community networks lost by migrants who were forced to flee their homelands.

The last two chapters of this part, by S. Megan Berthold and Alysse M. Loomis, attend to the situation of child migrants in the United States, drawing on empirical investigative testimony, court findings, and news reports to illustrate widespread human rights violations and failures to promote the best interests of these children. Analysis of the impact of migration-related traumas on child development and health and well-being is given based on the clinical and research literature and holistic practice and policy recommendations are provided.

Attention to cultural considerations in mental health treatment, the voice of refugee women regarding the U.S. government mandate for them to become rapidly economically self-sufficient, the use of creative arts to promote healing, and the empowerment of refugees are covered in the third part. The authors examine key intersectional factors, such as how culture, racism, sexism, and classism affect refugees. Toby Measham and colleagues discuss two transcultural refugee mental health service models developed within the McGill University Division of Social and Transcultural Psychiatry and related community health networks in Montreal, Quebec, Canada. These service models provide a cultural orientation to mental health care services while addressing the particular needs of patients from refugee and minority backgrounds. Clinical vignettes illustrate the application of culturally informed and responsive mental health principles to treatment in both models of care: a child- and family-oriented cultural psychiatry service working with community-based primary health care services in a collaborative care setting; and in a tertiary care regional hospital-based psychiatry cultural consultation service that provides psychiatric consultation and treatment planning for children, adults, and their families. The authors describe the Canadian context of refugee and mental health policies in relation to the impact on the mental health care of traumatized migrants. Badiah Haffejee and Jean F. East weave voices from qualitative interviews of African refugee women living in Colorado to examine their lived experiences with resettlement and efforts to become economically self-sufficient. The authors identify key barriers to achieving self-sufficiency such as ongoing emotional and cognitive challenges associated with their traumatic experiences, navigating difficult resettlement and social service systems, and work place and policy barriers. They discuss the promising practice of a cultural navigator model to address some of these barriers and recommend a revised welfare policy that more adequately supports women refugees. The benefits of creative arts therapies— art therapy, dance movement therapy, drama therapy, music therapy, and poetry therapy—for refugees who largely come from sociocentric cultures are elaborated by Amber Elizabeth L. Gray. She argues that sociocultural processes (e.g., rituals and rites of passages) utilized in creative arts therapies are considerably more commonplace than psychotherapy in the cultures where the majority of refugees come from. Case examples illustrate the application of these approaches with refugees.

The conclusion provides a synthesis of key points covered in the book within a broader human rights framework. It makes the case for sustained advocacy and underscores how diverse voices acting together matter in promoting the rights of refugees and asylum seekers and combating inhumane and illegal policies and practices that harm them and society at large. At its core, the conclusion is a call to action, highlighting some of the many ways concerned individuals and organizations can engage in and make a difference at local, regional, national, and international levels.

Significance of the Book

This book is timely given the recent developments in policies and practices toward refugees and migrants in the United States and globally. As lawmakers, heads of state, governmental and nongovernmental actors, and the public seek to respond to the situation of refugees and migrants crossing their borders, it is vital that they understand the human rights implications of their actions. The contributors to this book critically examine the impact of legislation to restrict the resettlement of refugees and bar access to applying for asylum and offer creative solutions for reform that protect the legitimate security and safety concerns of states while promoting the rights and well-being of refugees.

Fostering a better understanding of the politics and history of resettlement, relevant laws and social policies, as well as experiences of refugees themselves is a valuable contribution of this collection. This book differs from previously published books by its specific comparative focus on migration to the United States, Canada, and Europe among those with varied legal status (i.e., the undocumented, but also refugees and asylum seekers). Significant attention is given to the impact of culture on the well-being of and appropriate services for refugees and other migrants and in-depth examination of integrated health and mental health responses to the situation of refugees in the United States and Canada. The book also foregrounds the voices of migrants themselves, where possible, in the analysis. Throughout the book, a human rights lens is used to frame the discussion and analyze the strengths and limitations of the efforts to realize the rights of refugees.

References

Associated Press. 2018. "Tornillo Detention Camp for Migrant Kids Still Growing." *AP*, November 27, 2018. https://www.ktsm.com/immigration/tornillo-detention-camp-for-migrant-kids-still-growing/1622020682?apt_credirect=1.

Bacon, John, and Alan Gomez. 2017. "Protests against Trump's Immigration Plan Rolling in More Than 30 Cities." *USA Today*, January 27, 2017. https://www.usatoday.com/story/news/nation/2017/01/29/homeland-security-judges-stay-has-little-impact-travel-ban/97211720/.

BBC. 2018. "Belgium's PM Charles Michel Submits Resignation amid Migration Row." *BBC*, December 17, 2018. https://www.bbc.com/news/world-europe-46611320.

Bhabha, Jacqueline. 2018. "America's Treatment of Migrants Is Sending the Country Back to the Dark Ages." *Globe and Mail*, June 29, 2018. https://www.theglobeandmail.com/opinion/article-americas-treatment-of-migrants-is-sending-the-country-back-to-the/.

Brabant, Malcolm. 2018. "How Anti-Immigrant Politics Forced Rescue Ship Aquarius off the Mediterranean." *PBS*, December 13, 2018. https://www.pbs.org/newshour/show/how-anti-immigrant-politics-forced-rescue-ship-aquarius-off-the-mediterranean.

Capps, Randy, Mark Greenberg, Michael Fix, and Jie Zong. 2018. "Gauging the Impact of DHS' Proposed Public-Charge Rule on U.S. Immigration." Migration Policy Institute. https://www.migrationpolicy.org/research/impact-dhs-public-charge-rule-immigration.

De La Baume, Maïa. 2017. "Angela Merkel Defends Open Border Migration Policy." *Politico*, August 27, 2017. https://www.politico.eu/article/angela-merkel-defends-open-border-migration-refugee-policy-germany/.

DeGooyer, Stephanie, Alistair Hunt, Lida Maxwell, and Samuel Moyn. 2018. *The Right to Have Rights*. Brooklyn, NY: Verso.

Dunst, Charles, and Krishnadev Calamur. 2018. "Trump Moves to Deport Vietnam War Refugees." *The Atlantic*, December 12, 2018. https://www.theatlantic.com/international/archive/2018/12/donald-trump-deport-vietnam-war-refugees/577993/.

Gessen, Masha. 2018. "'The Right to Have Rights' and the Plight of the Stateless." *The New Yorker*, May 3, 2018. https://www.newyorker.com/news/our-columnists/the-right-to-have-rights-and-the-plight-of-the-stateless.

Ife, James. 2018. "Right Wing Populism and Social Work: Contrasting Ambivalences about Modernity." *Journal of Human Rights and Social Work* 3, no. 3: 121–127.

Jadwat, Omar. 2018. "No Mr. President. You Can't Change the Constitution by Executive Order." *American Civil Liberties Union*, October 30, 2018. https://www.aclu.org/blog/immigrants-rights/road-citizenship/no-mr-president-you-cant-change-constitution-executive-order.

Jenkins, Jack. 2018. "At Least 30 Faith Leaders Arrested in Border Protest." *National Catholic Reporter*, December 11, 2018. https://www.ncronline.org/news/justice/least-30-faith-leaders-arrested-border-protest.

Kopan, Tal. 2018. "More Than 14,000 Immigrant Children Are in U.S. Custody, an All-Time High." *San Francisco Chronicle*, November 16, 2018. https://www.sfchronicle.com/nation/article/More-than-14-000-immigrant-children-are-in-U-S-13399510.php.

Kragie, Andrew. 2018. "Stephen Miller as MAGA's Angry ID." *The Atlantic*, December 17, 2018. https://www.theatlantic.com/politics/archive/2018/12/stephen-miller-appeared-scripted-and-angry-sunday/578293/.

Krzyżanowski, Michal, Anna Triandafyllidou, and Ruth Wodak. 2018. "The Mediatization and Politicization of the 'Refugee Crisis' in Europe." *Journal of Immigrant and Refugee Studies* 16, no. 1–2: 1–14.

Kuruvilla, Carol. 2018. "Quakers, Rabbis, Imams Protest for Migrant Rights Because 'Love Knows No Borders.'" *Huffington Post*, December 12, 2018. https://www.huffingtonpost.com/entry/interfaith-border-protest-migrants_us_5c112943e4b0ac53717af2ce.

Loescher, Gil. 2017. "UNHCR's Origins and Early History: Agency, Influence, and Power in Global Refugee Policy." *Refuge* 33, no. 1: 77–86.

Moyn, Samuel. 2018. *Not Enough: Human Rights in an Unequal World*. Cambridge, MA: Harvard University Press.

Newland, Kathleen. 2018. "An Overheated Narrative Unanswered: How the Global Compact for Migration Became Controversial." Migration Policy Institute. https://www.migrationpolicy.org/news/overheated-narrative-unanswered-how-global-compact-became-controversial.

Norwegian Refugee Council. 2018. *The World's Most Neglected Displacement Crises*. https://www.nrc.no/globalassets/images/fr-2018/neglisjert/eng/the-worlds-most-neglected-displacement-crises.

Obama, Barack. 2016. "Remarks by President Obama at the Leaders' Summit of Refugees." https://obamawhitehouse.archives.gov/the-press-office/2016/09/20/remarks-president-obama-leaders-summit-refugees.

Parekh, Serena. 2016. "Moral Obligations to Refugees: Theory, Practice and Aspiration." *The Critique*, January 6, 2016. http://www.thecritique.com/articles/moral-obligations-to-refugees-theory-practice-aspira-tion-2/.

Pierce, Sarah, Jessica Bolter, and Andrew Selee. 2018. "U.S. Immigration Policy under Trump: Deep Changes and Lasting Impacts." Migration Policy Institute. https://www.migrationpolicy.org/research/us-immigration-policy-trump-deep-changes-impactshttps://www.migrationpolicy.org/research/us-immigration-policy-trump-deep-changes-impacts.

Polakaw-Suransky, Sasha. 2017. *Go Back to Where You Came From: The Backlash against Immigration and the Fate of Western Democracy*. New York: Nation Books.

Popescu, Marciana, and Kathryn Libal. 2018. "Social Work with Migrants and Refugees: Challenges, Best Practices, and Future Directions." *Advances in Social Work* 18, no. 3 (Spring): i–x.

Stack, Liam. 2017. "Donations to A.C.L.U. and Other Organizations Surge after Trump's Orders." *The New York Times*, January 30, 2017. https://www.nytimes.com/2017/01/30/us/aclu-fund-raising-trump-travel-ban.html.

Staedicke, Sara. 2018. "Top 10 of 2018—Issue Number 10: 'Silent Refugee Crises' Get Limited International Attention." Migration Policy Institute, December 10, 2018. https://www.migrationpolicy.org/article/top-10-2018-issue-10-silent-refugee-crises.

UN Global Compact on Refugees. 2018. https://www.unhcr.org/events/conferences/5b3295167/official-version-final-draft-global-compact-refugees.html.

UN Global Compact on Safe, Orderly, and Regular Migration. 2018. https://www.un.org/pga/72/wp-content/uploads/sites/51/2018/07/migration.pdf.

UN High Commissioner for Refugees. n.d. Resettlement Data. https://www.unhcr.org/resettlement-data.html.

UN High Commissioner for Refugees USA. 2018. "Solutions." https://www.unhcr.org/solutions.html.

UN News. 2018. "Global Compact on Refugees: How Different Is This from the Migrants' Pact and How Will It Help." https://news.un.org/en/story/2018/12/1028641.

UN Refugees and Migrants. n.d. "Global Compact on Refugees." https://refugeesmigrants.un.org/refugees-compact.

University of Minnesota Immigration and Human Rights Clinic. 2018. "Analysis of DHS Proposed Rule on Public Charges Prepared for the International Refugee Assistance Program." October 29, 2018.

Vollmer, Bastian, and Serhat Karakayali. 2018. "The Volatility of the Discourse on Refugees in Germany." *Journal of Immigrant and Refugee Studies* 16, no. 1–2: 118–139.

Wintour, Patrick. 2018. "Hillary Clinton: Europe Must Curb Immigration to Stop Right-Wing Populists." *The Guardian*, November 22, 2018. https://www.theguardian.com/world/2018/nov/22/hillary-clinton-europe-must-curb-immigration-stop-populists-trump-brexit.

PART 1

Legal and Social Policy Perspectives on Refugee and Asylum Seeker Systems

CHAPTER TWO

Evolution of Refugee and Asylum Law in the United States

Karen Musalo

Introduction

Migration, the movement of people within countries as well as across borders, is a global phenomenon. Thousands of people are on the move at any given point in time. The term "immigrants" is frequently used to describe individuals who have left their home countries and are sojourning—either on a permanent or a temporary basis—in a foreign country.

An immigrant may enter a country with legal permission to do so. She may have temporary permission to remain, tied to a specific purpose. An example of this would be an individual who has a tourist visa allowing a limited visit or a student visa allowing presence throughout a course of study. Many immigrants have legal permission to permanently reside, which they may have obtained through a family relationship to a U.S. citizen (USC) or Lawful Permanent Resident (LPR), or through the possession of skills that can lead to obtaining permanent legal status.

Some immigrants enter or remain in the United States without legal documentation. They may have crossed the border without a visa or other permission, or they may have entered with legal permission, but overstayed the permitted stay, or violated the terms of their presence.

In the United States, as well as in many other countries, national policy toward immigrants can be a highly controversial issue. Although the question of temporary entry can be an issue of dispute, there is even more disagreement around the granting of permanent legal status, which puts one on a path to citizenship. Contested issues include: Who should be permitted to immigrate? Should there be a preference for family members of USCs and LPRs? Should there be an upper limit on how many are permitted to immigrate and, if so, how is that to be determined? Is it ever proper or appropriate to favor—or to disfavor—certain nationalities or ethnic groups?

The U.S. government has answered these questions in different ways throughout its history and has often engaged in shameful discrimination against certain ethnic groups, such as when it upheld the exclusion of Chinese immigrants—a policy affirmed by the U.S. Supreme Court in the *Chinese Exclusion Case* in 1889.[1] Many see the January 2017 Presidential Executive Order[2] to prohibit the entry of individuals from Muslim majority countries as being a similarly lamentable discriminatory policy. Individuals who defend such policies often attempt to justify them by arguing that every sovereign nation has the right to decide whom to admit and whom to exclude. However, even if that is true, such policies cannot be made in violation of bedrock principles of the U.S. Constitution.

The preceding discussion has focused on the broad category of immigrants, that is, all of those who enter the United States with intent to remain temporarily or permanently. However, this book, and indeed this chapter, addresses a particular subset of immigrants—namely, *refugees and asylum seekers*. This distinction is significant because, unlike other immigrants, refugees and asylum seekers are the subjects and beneficiaries of commitments the United States has made under international law and has implemented through the enactment of domestic law.

In the national debate, refugees and asylum seekers are often seen as undifferentiated from other immigrants and, therefore, subject to whatever restrictions and harsh enforcement measures are being advocated. This represents a fundamental misunderstanding of who they are and what legal protections should accrue to them. This chapter provides a framework for understanding the status of refugees and asylum seekers in the United States as well as internationally and details the evolution of law and policy toward them over the past 50 years.

International Origins of Contemporary Refugee Protections

Although the tradition of protecting the "stranger" goes back to early Arab-Islamic as well as Judeo-Christian times,[3] the modern refugee protection regime has its origins in the post–World War II period. The international community came together in the aftermath of its collective failure to protect Jews and other persecuted populations during the Holocaust. Under the aegis of the United Nations, the 1951 Convention Relating to the Status of Refugees[4] was drafted. In relevant part, it defines a refugee as an individual who, "owing to a well-founded fear of being persecuted for reasons of race, religion, nationality, membership of a particular social group or political opinion, is outside the country of his nationality and is unable or owing to such fear is unwilling to avail himself of the protection of that country[.]"[5]

The Convention includes numerous articles providing for substantive and procedural rights for those fleeing persecution. One of the Convention's central provisions is Article 33, which prohibits the return of refugees to countries of persecution. This prohibition on return is so widely accepted that it has become recognized as a norm of customary international law referred to as the right to *nonrefoulement* (nonreturn). Its status as a customary international law norm means that even countries that are not parties to the Convention are obligated to comply with the prohibition. A second central provision of the Convention is Article 34, which encourages state parties to the Convention to "as far as possible facilitate the assimilation and naturalization of refugees."[6] This is understood to mean that in addition to not returning refugees to persecution, countries should attempt to give them a regular permanent status, including citizenship. Also of significance is Article 31, which provides that states should not punish refugees fleeing persecution who enter or are present without legal authorization.[7]

The Refugee Convention was drafted with World War II refugees in mind. For that reason, it included geographic and date restrictions, limiting its application to individuals who became refugees as a "result of events occurring before January 1951"[8] and states that ratified it could further limit it to events occurring only in Europe.[9]

Shortly after the Convention came into force, there was recognition of the need for an international treaty to deal not only with past refugee crises but for prospective ones as well. This led to the drafting of the 1967 Protocol relating to the Status of Refugees.[10] The 1967 Refugee Protocol is virtually identical to the 1951 Convention, incorporating its Articles 2–34, but notably omitting the Convention's geographic and temporal restrictions. As of April 2015, 145 states were parties to the Refugee Convention, 146 were parties to the Refugee Protocol, and 142 states were parties to both.[11] The United States is one of the three countries that is a party to the Refugee Protocol, but not the Convention. (The other two countries are Cabo Verde and Venezuela.)

As discussed earlier, two of the most significant articles of the Refugee Convention/Protocol are Article 1.A(2), defining a refugee (using the "well-founded fear" standard), and Article 33, prohibiting his or her return to persecution. Although the United States became a party to the Refugee Protocol in November 1968,[12] it was not until 1980 that Congress enacted legislation—the Refugee Act[13]—intended to align domestic law with these international obligations. Many commentators have observed that U.S. law was not in compliance with international obligations in this interim time period (1968–1980), and although the Refugee Act brought the United States closer in some respects, it diverged in others. Unfortunately, as this chapter will detail, over the years, the gap between U.S. law and the letter and spirit of the Convention and its Protocol has only grown wider.

U.S. Refugee Law and Policy—1980 to the End of the Obama Administration (January 2017)

Overview of the 1980 Refugee Act—U.S. Refugee Admissions Program and Applications at the Border

The 1980 Refugee Act adopted virtually verbatim the Refugee Protocol's definition of a refugee as an individual with a "well-founded fear of persecution" on account of race, religion, nationality, political opinion, and membership in a particular social group (referred to as the "enumerated grounds"). The Act created two distinct procedures by which individuals fleeing persecution could seek protection in the United States.

First, under the U.S. Refugee Admissions Program (USRAP),[14] individuals may apply for protection from outside the United States and, if approved, enter the country as refugees. There are numerical and geographical limits applicable to the USRAP. Second, there is a procedure allowing applications for protection to be made by individuals arriving to the U.S. border or already present within the United States.[15] The following sections discuss these two routes to protection, analyzing the evolution of the processes from 1980 through the end of the Obama administration. The chapter's conclusion addresses proposed as well as implemented changes during the early months of the Trump administration.

The U.S. Refugee Admissions Program

The USRAP gives the president, in consultation with Congress, the authority to determine the number of refugees to be resettled in the United States annually (referred to as the "admissions ceiling"), as well as the global regions from which they are to come. The numbers and regional allocations are to be informed by "humanitarian concerns," as well as "national interest." The statute also permits the president, after consultation, to adjust the number in cases of "unforeseen emergency refugee" situations.

Within this framework of numbers and regions, there are also "priority" processing categories; an individual must come within a priority area in order to be considered for refugee resettlement. Currently, priority one is for individuals referred by the United Nations High Commissioner for Refugees

(UNHCR), U.S. embassies or designated nongovernmental organizations; priority two is for groups of special humanitarian concern; and priority three is for family reunification (specified relatives of those already granted protection in the United States).[16]

Applicants who come within these categories are interviewed abroad by an officer of the United States Citizenship and Immigration Services (USCIS) to determine if they meet the refugee definition. Contrary to assertions made by Donald Trump,[17] those individuals found to be refugees go through a very extensive security check before they are approved for entry. The security check involves UNHCR and multiple U.S. security agencies (National Counterterrorism Center, the Federal Bureau of Investigation, the Department of Homeland Security, and the State Department) and can take up to two years.[18] The Obama administration also instituted additional, enhanced review of Syrian cases.

Although it is laudable that the United States resettles refugees, there have been many criticisms of the USRAP over the years. Some scholars have noted that its design—with decision making in the hands of the president, in consultation with Congress—increases the likelihood that foreign policy, rather than humanitarian considerations, will influence the numbers and regional allocations. Foreign policy would militate toward extending refugee protection to those fleeing enemy regimes of the United States, rather than those fleeing authoritarian governments with which the United States maintains friendly relations. In fact, this tilt was especially notable throughout the first 20 years of the USRAP, when a high percentage of refugee numbers went to those fleeing the Union of Soviet Socialist Republics (USSR) and Cuba, while there was minimal allocation to the entire African continent, or to Latin America and the Caribbean, notwithstanding alarming levels of human rights abuses in these regions. The abuses in a number of Latin American and Caribbean countries, such as El Salvador, Guatemala, and Haiti, were committed by governments that the United States supported, and/or funded in some way, which clearly affected decisions regarding refugees from those countries.

Criticisms have also been made regarding the overall numbers of refugees admitted through the USRAP. UNHCR has reported that "wars and persecution have driven more people from their homes than at any time since" UNHCR began keeping records.[19] A total of 65.3 million individuals are currently displaced worldwide.[20] Taken together, Syria, Afghanistan, and Somalia account for half the world's refugees, with Syria at 4.9 million, Afghanistan at 2.7 million, and Somalia at 1.1 million.[21]

Given the resources of the United States, many argue that it should resettle significantly more refugees than it currently does. Although in some years, admissions were slightly over 200,000 (1980 and 1981) and in 1993, as a result of the Balkan Wars, reached 142,000,[22] in most years, they have been substantially less. From 2008 to 2011 the ceiling was set at 80,000, in 2012 at 76,000, and it remained at 70,000 from 2013 to 2015. It was only during his last years in office that President Obama increased the ceiling, raising it to 85,000 in 2016 and to 110,000 in 2017.

U.S. policy toward Syrian refugees is illustrative of a failure to carry its fair share. From fiscal year 2011 through fiscal year 2014, the United States only resettled 211 Syrian refugees. The number increased in fiscal year 2015, rising to 1,682, but that was a paltry response when one considers the need (with five million Syrian refugees and six million internally displaced within Syria), as well as the refuge extended by other countries. For example, to date Canada has resettled slightly more than 40,000 Syrians, and although it is hard to calculate the exact number that Germany has accepted, it has been in the hundreds of thousands. Toward the end of his administration, Obama did change course in a positive direction, with the fiscal year 2016 allocation of 10,000 slots to Syrians, and the fiscal year 2017 goal of matching or exceeding 10,000.

However, all of this came to a crashing halt with the Trump administration. As will be discussed in the section focusing on policies from January 2017 to present, one of Trump's first Executive Orders attempted to place an indefinite ban on the entry of all Syrian refugees, to suspend refugee admissions for six months, and to slash the annual admission number by more than half. Whatever criticism one might have for the Obama administration's failure to accept its fair share of refugees in general, and of Syrian refugees in particular, pales in light of Trump's policies.

Applications at the Border or from within the United States

Two Remedies—Asylum and Withholding

Whereas the 1980 Refugee Act, through its establishment of the USRAP, gave the president and Congress authority to set the numbers, countries of origin of refugees, and priorities, the Act created a second procedure intended to be independent of political or foreign policy considerations. It did so by providing that any individual at the border, or physically present in the United States, "irrespective" of that person's status (meaning they could be undocumented) could apply for protection. The Act created two forms of relief: individuals who meet the refugee definition of a "well-founded fear" may be granted asylum (analogous to refugee status), while individuals who demonstrate that their "life or freedom would be threatened" are to be granted "withholding of removal," which prohibits their return to the country of feared harm.

Although it is beyond the scope of this chapter to go into an extensive discussion of the differences between asylum and withholding, it is important to make a few points as regards these forms of relief. Asylum is far preferable to withholding. Individuals granted asylum can apply to become LPRs after one year and can apply for citizenship five years later. They can also bring their spouses or minor children to join them. In contrast, the status of withholding does not lead to any permanent status, nor does it allow its recipients to bring other family members. It does, however, prevent the individual's return to the country of feared persecution, which can obviously be a life-saving benefit.

Paradoxically, asylum, which is clearly more desirable, has a lower burden of proof than withholding. The well-founded fear standard for asylum is understood to require a showing of a one-in-ten likelihood of persecution, while the language "life or freedom would be threatened," which is the standard for withholding, has been interpreted to require a showing that the harm is more likely than not—that is—a greater than 50 percent probability. This would not make sense (i.e., why would the better remedy of asylum be easier to obtain?) were it not for two factors that actually make a grant of asylum more tenuous. First, a grant of asylum is "discretionary," meaning that a decision maker may still deny relief to an individual who has met her burden of proof if certain adverse factors are present. Second, there are statutory bars to asylum that do not apply to withholding, putting asylum out of reach for many individuals. For example, individuals who do not apply for asylum within a year of entering the United States are barred, unless they fit within the narrow exceptions to this rule. Such persons would have to meet the higher standard of withholding in order to avoid return to their home country.

Adjudicatory Structure for Asylum and Withholding Applications

There are four decision-making levels in asylum and withholding cases; they are asylum offices, immigration courts, the Board of Immigration Appeals, and the U.S. circuit courts of appeals. The following discussion will provide an overview of these decision-making fora.

Asylum Office—Affirmative Applications

Individuals who are legally present in the United States, or who are undocumented but have not come to the attention of the immigration authorities (i.e., have not been arrested), may come forward and apply at asylum offices, which are within the USCIS branch of the Department of Homeland Security (DHS). There are eight asylum offices throughout the country.[23] Because these individuals come forward voluntarily to apply, their claims are referred to as "affirmative" applications.

Proceedings at the asylum office are "nonadversarial," meaning that they are not structured like a trial (such as those that take place in immigration courts, discussed later), in which an applicant is examined by counsel and cross-examined by opposing counsel in front of a judge. Instead, the information is elicited in an interview format, conducted by a specially trained asylum officer. Because of the less stressful, nonadversarial nature of asylum office adjudications, all unaccompanied child asylum seekers have their cases initially heard there.

Asylum officers can dispose of cases in two ways. They can grant relief, or if they rule that an individual does not meet the legal standard or fails to merit asylum in the exercise of discretion, they will "refer" them to immigration court. The word "refer" in this context is euphemistic; in reality, the individual is being placed in immigration court removal proceedings and can only avoid being sent to her home country by prevailing on her claim for protection.

Immigration Court—Defensive Applications

Asylum and withholding claims presented in immigration court are referred to as "defensive" applications because they are raised as a defense against being removed. In addition to hearing the claims of individuals with failed affirmative applications, immigration courts adjudicate claims for protection brought by any individual placed in removal. Individuals can be subject to removal for a range of reasons—from lacking legal documents to having committed a crime that is a basis for potential loss of existing legal status.

Proceedings in immigration court are adversarial; the decision maker is an immigration judge, within the Executive Office of Immigration Review (EOIR) of the Department of Justice (DOJ). The U.S. government, which has brought the removal proceedings against the individual, and is therefore the opposing party, is represented by an attorney with the office of Immigration and Customs Enforcement (ICE), which is within DHS. Although the asylum seeker has the right to be represented, there is no representation at government expense, so that if an asylum seeker does not have the resources to pay for private counsel, or is not fortunate enough to secure *pro bono* (free) representation, she will proceed in court unrepresented. As discussed next, this puts the asylum seeker at a great disadvantage.

Board of Immigration Appeals and Federal Courts of Appeal

Grants or denials by immigration judges can be appealed to the Board of Immigration Appeals (BIA), an administrative appeals body also within the EOIR of the DOJ. The BIA is located in Falls Church, Virginia, and has nationwide jurisdiction, meaning that it can hear cases arising in any geographic region of the United States and its rulings apply throughout the country. BIA decisions are appealable to the federal circuit courts of appeals. On issues of importance, the U.S. Supreme Court may grant *certiorari* [24] and hear a case. Although the Supreme Court only takes a very small percentage of cases in which review is sought, a number of very significant issues involving the requirements for asylum and withholding have been decided by the Supreme Court over the years since the 1980 Refugee Act came into existence.[25]

Disparities in Decision Making

In their seminal book, *Refugee Roulette*,[26] analyzing disparities in asylum decision making, Jaya Ramji-Nogales, Andrew Schoenholtz, and Philip Schrag quote former attorney general Robert Jackson as follows: "It is obviously repugnant to one's sense of justice that the justice meted out . . . should depend in large part on a purely fortuitous circumstance; namely the personality of the particular judge before whom the case happens to come for disposition." Yet this appears to be exactly the case in asylum adjudication.

Based on an extensive analysis of 133,000 decisions at the four levels of adjudication described earlier, Ramji-Nogales, Schoenholtz, and Schrag documented pervasive disparities that cannot be explained by differences in the cases, and that bring into serious question the quality of justice in an area of law with life or death consequences. The disparities were both between regional asylum offices or courts, as well as between decision makers in the same asylum office or court.

The authors of *Refugee Roulette* concluded that a range of factors—including the background and philosophy of the adjudicators, as opposed to the merits of the cases—were causing these disparities. Ramji-Nogales, Schoenholtz, and Schrag made extensive policy recommendations aimed at addressing what they characterize as a fundamental lack of due process. Unfortunately, the majority of their recommendations have not been implemented, and striking disparities at the asylum office and immigration courts have continued to the present.[27]

The persistence of disparities is highly troubling to those who believe in fairness and justice. As the late Senator Edward Kennedy, who was a key force behind the 1980 Refugee Act, wrote in his foreword to *Refugee Roulette*, the granting of protection to an individual fleeing persecution "should not rest on the random assignment of the case. . . . There is far too much at stake in these cases."[28]

Barriers to Protection and Critiques of the Process for Those Who Apply at the Border or from within the United States

"Access to the Territory" of Asylum: Haitian Interdiction and the Law of Expedited Removal

When the 1980 Refugee Act first went into effect, it provided that any individual who arrived at the United States had the right to request asylum and withholding, and if denied, to appeal at the administrative (BIA) and federal court levels. However, over the years, the right to apply for protection and access to the courts has been drastically curtailed, so that many individuals seeking asylum and withholding do not have the opportunity to even file a claim, much less to challenge a denial through the U.S. court system.

The first significant limitation on access to protection in the United States occurred in response to Haitian asylum seekers. Haitians have long been subject to discriminatory policies in the United States.[29] Shortly after the enactment of the 1980 Refugee Act, then president Ronald Reagan entered into an agreement with Haitian dictator Jean-Claude Duvalier, allowing the U.S. Coast Guard to board Haitian craft in international waters and to return Haitian nationals to their home country. Notwithstanding this agreement, Haitians who expressed a fear of persecution were to be screened, and if they expressed a fear that could be the basis for an asylum claim, they were to be permitted entry to the United States to apply for asylum. Between 1981 and 1991, 23,000 Haitians were stopped at sea, and only 28 passed the screening procedure and were permitted to apply for asylum. Given the repressive human rights conditions in Haiti during this time period, those numbers are universally seen as demonstrative of bias toward Haitians.

On September 30, 1991, a violent coup in Haiti overthrew Jean Bertrand Aristide, that country's first democratically elected president. In the aftermath of the coup, his supporters faced brutal repression, and it was undisputed that "hundreds of Haitians [were] killed, tortured, detained without a warrant, or subjected to violence . . . because of their political beliefs."[30] Haitians who could flee, did so, many of them taking to small boats with the intention of making it to the United States, where they could seek protection.

For a short period after the coup—until November 18, 1991—former president George H.W. Bush suspended screening and repatriation of Haitians. When screening resumed, large numbers of Haitians were found to have valid claims, and they were brought to the U.S. Naval Base in Guantanamo, Cuba, to pursue their claims.[31] Once Guantanamo filled up, the choice was whether to allow those with legitimate claims entry to the United States so they could apply for protection or to return them directly to Haiti without screening. President Bush opted for the latter, issuing an Executive Order in May 1992 that all Haitians stopped at sea were to be returned without being screened. The consensus of legal scholars is that this policy violated international obligations, as well as the 1980 Refugee Act.[32] Unfortunately, the Executive Order was upheld in 1993 by a near-unanimous decision of the U.S. Supreme Court.[33]

U.S. policy toward Haitians—limiting their access to the territory where they could seek protection under the Refugee Act—has been seen as a precursor to restrictive 1996 legislation, referred to as "expedited removal,"[34] that requires *all* undocumented asylum seekers (not just Haitians) to establish the strength of their claims in order to be permitted to apply for asylum.

Pursuant to expedited removal, individuals whom U.S. Customs and Border Protection (CBP) officers deem lack proper documents to enter or be present in the United States can be immediately removed without a hearing. The law is supposed to protect bona fide asylum seekers through a screening process. The first step of the process is for the CBP officer to inform the individual that U.S. law "provides protection to certain persons who face persecution, harm or torture upon return to their home country," and to ask three questions to determine if the individual may have such a fear. The questions are as follows:

1) Why did you leave your home country or country of last residence?
2) Do you have any fear or concern about being returned to your home country or being removed from the United States?
3) Would you be harmed if you are returned to your home country or country of last residence?[35]

Individuals who express a fear are supposed to be detained and referred to an asylum officer for a "credible fear interview," in which it is to be determined whether their claims have sufficient legitimacy such that they should be permitted to apply. However, the CBP officer's decision whether to refer for a credible fear interview or to remove the individual is subject only to his or her supervisor's review. The individual seeking entry has no access to counsel, or to the courts, and can be immediately removed based on CBP's determination.

Governmental and NGO reports have documented numerous instances of improper removal at this stage. There are multiple reasons for the erroneous removal of bona fide asylum seekers. The process itself is flawed in that it does not take sufficiently into consideration the vulnerable state of asylum seekers and the difficulty they may have in expressing their fears immediately upon arrival. In addition, CBP officers may fail to apply the law as written and order the removal of individuals who have expressed a fear. The result has been the wrongful removal of legitimate asylum seekers.

As discussed in the section focusing on Trump administration actions, the January 2017 Executive Orders on immigration worsen this situation by calling for the procedure of expedited removal to be more broadly applied and for the credible fear standard to be heightened so that it would be harder to meet the standard.

Adjudicatory Bias As mentioned earlier, while the USRAP permits the president, in consultation with Congress, to allocate refugee slots based on nationality, and to take foreign policy objectives into consideration, grants of protection to individuals who apply at the border or from within the United States are not supposed to be subject to any such preferences. The refugee definition applied to them is a neutral one, and congressional intent was to apply it without regard to ideology, religion, nationality, U.S. foreign policy objectives, or other considerations.

However, it became apparent almost immediately after the 1980 Refugee Act was passed that bias was infecting the adjudication of asylum claims. Credible studies[36] documented that different standards were being applied to claims depending on the United States' relationship with the applicants' countries of origin.

During the 1980s, the Cold War was still a powerful factor in international relations, and this improperly influenced asylum decisions. The United States had a clear foreign policy interest in granting asylum to individuals fleeing communism; such individuals were sometimes referred to as "trophy refugees" because they could be pointed to as living examples of how bad conditions were in communist countries. In that same vein, the United States had little interest in granting asylum to those fleeing countries it supported, even if those countries persecuted their citizenry. Internal U.S. government memos confirmed this bias, with one document stating that "different levels of proof are required of different asylum applicants," with Polish applicants having "extremely weak" cases being granted, while Salvadorans needing to have a "classic textbook case" before they would be granted asylum.[37]

During this time period, brutal civil wars raged in El Salvador and Guatemala, with their respective governments receiving U.S. support. Consistent with the pattern described earlier, the grant rates for these nationalities was extremely low (2.6% for Salvadorans and 0.9% for Guatemalans) and class action litigation, *American Baptist Churches v. Thornburgh*,[38] was brought on their behalf, arguing that there was impermissible adjudicatory bias.

While the case was being litigated, the government agreed to settle, a move that was seen as implicit acknowledgment of the lawsuit's validity. The settlement agreement explicitly stated that

> foreign policy and border enforcement considerations are not relevant to the determination of whether an applicant for asylum has a well-founded fear of persecution; the fact that an individual is from a country whose government the United States supports or with which it has favorable relations is not relevant to the determination of whether an applicant for asylum has a well-founded fear of persecution; whether or not the United States Government agrees with the political or ideological beliefs of the individual is not relevant to the determination of whether an applicant for asylum has a well-founded fear of persecution; the same standard for

determining whether or not an applicant has a well-founded fear of persecution applies to Salvadorans and Guatemalans as applies to all other
nationalities[.][39]

As part of the settlement agreement bringing an end to the litigation, the U.S.
government agreed to readjudicate the case of every Salvadoran and Guatemalan that it had previously denied.

The settlement agreement in *ABC v. Thornburgh* was important for
vindicating the principle that a neutral standard is to be applied and that bias
has no place in asylum adjudication. However, trends in asylum grants and
denials indicate that impermissible factors continue to impact decision
making to this day. For example, U.S. policy makers and adjudicators fought
long and hard—from 1996 to 2014—against recognizing that women who
flee gender-related persecution, such as domestic violence, should be
recognized as refugees.[40] There are numerous indications that the resistance
was not on a principled basis, but on "border enforcement considerations,"
namely the fear that the recognition of asylum in these cases would lead to a
"flood" of women seeking asylum in the United States.[41]

Bias has also been evident in the adjudication of the claims of Guatemalans,
Salvadorans, and Hondurans (often referred to as the "northern triangle" countries) fleeing the rising violence of gangs and organized crime in their countries. The interpretation of applicable law has shifted in a manner calculated to
exclude these individuals from protection.[42] Of course, this bias is carried out
in a more subtle way than the favoritism for Polish sailors over Salvadoran
asylum seekers, discussed earlier, that resulted in the application of a different
standard to one group than the other. However, it constitutes bias nonetheless,
because it permits impermissible factors, such as fear of floodgates, to influence what should be a fair, unbiased interpretation of the law.

Procedural Barriers to Protection

The preceding sections have discussed obstacles to exercising the right to
request asylum (such as interdiction at sea and expedited removal) and troubling
disparities and bias, which draw the fairness of the process into serious question.
However, a discussion of barriers to protection would not be complete without
focusing on U.S. law and policy regarding detention and legal representation.

Detention   The position of the UNHCR is that "as seeking asylum is not
an unlawful act, any restrictions on liberty imposed on persons exercising
this right need to be provided for in law, carefully circumscribed and subject
to prompt review."[43] Detention should be resorted to only when necessary for
public safety or national security.

U.S. law gives lip service to the principle that detention should be limited,
and DHS has set forth criteria for determining if an individual is a security

or flight risk such that detention is justified. However, the reality is that the criteria for release are often ignored, decisions on detention are made arbitrarily, and asylum seekers meeting the release criteria are often held for long periods, or their release is conditioned on unreasonable conditions— such as the payment of bonds in exorbitant amounts, which they cannot afford.

In many circumstances, it is evident that detention is being used for an improper and unlawful purpose—that is, to deter asylum seekers. The response to the so-called 2014 "surge"[44] of Central American women and children fleeing escalating violence provides an example of detention as deterrence.[45] Prior to the surge, in recognition of its deleterious effects, the detention of families (women and children) had all but been discontinued. There was only one family detention facility in the entire country—a 94-bed facility in Berks County, Pennsylvania.

However, as the number of families arriving at the U.S. border seeking asylum increased, the Obama administration adopted a policy of blanket family detention. It first jailed women and children in a makeshift facility in Artesia, New Mexico, and then shortly after opened two massive detention centers in Texas, one in Dilley, with a 2,400-bed capacity, and the other in Karnes City, with a 532-bed capacity. Both facilities are run by private companies; Dilley is administered by Corrections Corporation of America, and Karnes by GEO Group. The Obama administration failed to release any of these detained families, leading to a lawsuit. A district court in the District of Colombia ruled that detention for purposes of deterrence would likely violate constitutional principles.[46]

As numerous studies and reports have confirmed, the detention of asylum seekers is highly damaging and prejudicial in a multitude of ways. Many—if not the majority of—asylum seekers have suffered persecution and horror in their home countries, and their detention is deeply retraumatizing.[47] The detention of mothers with their children is especially egregious as the mothers suffer a double anguish: their own trauma from the conditions of detention, along with the feeling that their decision to flee subjected their children to imprisonment. The remote location of detention centers also presents a barrier for asylum seekers to obtain the assistance of medical or mental health professionals who may provide expertise in support of their cases. As discussed next, it also has an extremely adverse impact on access to legal representation. Trump administration policies on detention are leading to sharp increases in the use of detention and even greater limits on release.

Legal Representation   In a number of Western, industrialized countries, the government provides legal representation to asylum seekers. However, that is not the case in the United States. U.S. law provides that although asylum seekers "have the privilege of being represented," it is not to be at the expense of the government.[48] Many asylum seekers do not have the resources to pay for private counsel and must secure *pro bono* representation or go unrepresented. As noted earlier, it is more difficult for detained individuals to obtain representation because detention centers are often far from major population centers. As a consequence of these factors, a significant percentage of asylum seekers appear in immigration court without legal representation. A nationwide study of representation in immigration court reported that only 37 percent of immigrants obtained representation; the number went down to 14 percent for detained immigrants.[49]

Asylum seekers who have legal representation are far more likely to succeed in their claims than those who do not. Recent statistics show a success rate in immigration court proceedings that is five times higher for represented than unrepresented asylum seekers.[50] It is not difficult to understand why this is so. The law of asylum and withholding is extremely complex. Many experienced attorneys struggle to understand the evolving and sometimes counterintuitive interpretations of key elements of the refugee definition.

The evidentiary requirements are also rigorous; asylum seekers are expected to provide actual physical proof of facts relevant to their claims when that proof is deemed to be "reasonably available." For example, a woman who was beaten by her husband and seen at a hospital may be expected to have requested and brought with her the medical records showing her visit and treatment. In addition, the conditions in the home country that are pertinent to the asylum seeker's case must be established—requiring either the submission of reports and other written materials or the testimony of country conditions experts. An unrepresented asylum seeker would likely not know of these requirements, much less be able to comply with them.

The law that precludes government-appointed counsel makes no exceptions for children, who are also expected to represent themselves if they are unable to secure counsel. The image of small children in immigration court, sitting before robed judges, and subject to cross-examination by government attorneys, has justifiably evoked outrage and advocacy for appointed counsel for minors. The outrage was stoked when an official of the DOJ testified in a court deposition that he could teach immigration law well enough to toddlers that they did not need representation.[51] There have been legislative efforts as well as litigation in an attempt to secure the right to representation for children in immigration proceedings, but there has yet to be a change in the law.

U.S. Refugee Law and Policy—January 2017 to the Present—the Trump Administration's Executive Orders

The Trump administration issued three Executive Orders dealing with immigration and refugee issues. Their formal names and date of issuance are as follows:

- Protecting the Nation from Foreign Terrorist Entry into the United States, January 27, 2017 (referred to as the "Muslim Ban" or "Travel Ban");[52] a revised version was issued on March 6, 2017.[53]
- Border Security and Immigration Enforcement Improvements, January 25, 2017.[54]
- Enhancing Public Safety in the Interior of the United States, January 25, 2017.[55]

Although people are more familiar with the Muslim or Travel Ban, all three Orders dramatically impact the U.S. refugee and asylum regime. The following sections will detail the contents of the three Executive Orders and discuss the changes they would effectuate to the existing systems.

Protecting the Nation from Foreign Terrorist Entry into the United States

This Executive Order, first issued on January 27, 2017, is known as the "Muslim Ban" or "Travel Ban" because it prohibits the entry of immigrant and nonimmigrant entries of individuals from seven Muslim majority countries.[56] There have been two subsequent iterations of it. We will refer to the January 27, 2017, version as EO1, and the two subsequent ones as EO2 and EO3. EO1 suspended the USRAP for six months, indefinitely banned the admission of Syrian refugees, and reduced the number of annual fiscal year refugee admission slots from 110,000 to 50,000. The Executive Order provided a "national interest" exception to the suspension of refugee admissions, "including when the person is a religious minority in his country of nationality facing religious persecution[.]"[57] This was interpreted as providing a preference for Christian refugees.

The Muslim Ban EO1 sparked outrage and activism; there were demonstrations and protests across the country, with attorneys and supporters of immigrants and refugees flocking to airports to offer assistance to those caught up in the ban. Numerous legal challenges were immediately filed, and a nationwide court order was issued, putting the implementation of the ban on hold.

In response to court decisions blocking the ban, the administration issued a revised version of this Executive Order, EO2, on March 6, 2017.[58] It removed

Iraq from the list of banned countries, eliminated the indefinite suspension on the entry of Syrian refugees, and deleted the specific language favoring the admission of religious minorities. The revised Muslim Ban was also challenged in court, and its implementation was once again largely blocked by court orders.

The Trump administration brought a challenge to the U.S. Supreme Court, asking it to lift the court orders that had prevented the ban from going into effect. The Supreme Court gave the administration a partial victory by allowing specific provisions of EO2 to go into effect. On September 24, 2017, the Trump administration issued a third iteration of the Muslim Ban, EO3. It indefinitely blocked the entry of individuals from eight countries; five of them were included in the original ban—Iran, Libya, Syria, Somalia, and Yemen. EO3 dropped Sudan from the list, but added Chad, North Korea, and certain high-level officials from Venezuela. To many people's surprise, EO3 did not address refugee admissions.

On October 17, 2017, district court judges in Hawaii and Maryland prevented most of the provisions of EO3 from going into effect. Litigation over EO3 is currently ongoing, with the Fourth and Ninth Circuit Courts of Appeal ruling that the majority of EO3 should be stayed from going into effect. The case is headed to the Supreme Court, with oral arguments most likely to take place by April 2018.

As noted earlier, EO3 did not include any provisions on refugees. However, on October 24, 2017, the Trump administration issued another Executive Order entitled Resuming the USRAP with Enhanced Vetting Capabilities.[59] This order allows refugee admissions to resume, but with "enhanced vetting" for individuals from nine Muslim-majority countries. This EO is also being challenged in the courts.

Impact of the Ban on USRAP

With UNHCR reporting over 65.6 million forcibly displaced individuals at the end of 2016, the need for refugee resettlement is at an all-time high. The United States, with its relative wealth and resources, should be doing more to resettle refugees—including Syrian refugees—rather than less. Canada, our neighbor to the north, resettled more than 25,000 Syrian refugees between November 2015 and February 2016 and has stated its intention to continue accepting refugees.[60] Many other countries in close proximity to Syria have hosted tens of thousands of Syrian refugees.[61] A primary justification for limiting refugee admissions has been national security, with the stated concern that terrorists would enter as refugees. However, as noted earlier, refugees go through an extensive security check, and as many have pointed out, would-be terrorists are highly unlikely to favor the refugee admission process as a way to enter the U.S. In fact, according to the Migration Policy Institute, data shows that refugees are not a threat; between September 11, 2001, and October 2015, the United States resettled 784,000 refugees and "[in] those 14 years, exactly three resettled refugees have been arrested for planning terrorist activities—and it is worth noting two were not planning an attack in the United States, and the plans of the third were barely credible." [62] There are simply no credible justifications for the suspension or reduction of refugee admissions, or the attempted ban on Syrian refugees.

The United States should be setting an example that encourages other countries to participate in a "burden-sharing" of desperate refugees, rather than cutting back as it has attempted to do through this Executive Order. It remains to be seen what the decision of the Supreme Court will be when it actually rules on the merits of the case; to date, it has only ruled on the lower courts' stays of the Executive Order. Hopefully, the legal bases relied upon by the lower courts that found the ban in violation of constitutional and statutory norms will be persuasive.

Two Executive Orders: Border Security and Immigration Enforcement Improvements and Enhancing Public Safety in the Interior of the United States

These two Executive Orders—the Border Security and Immigration Enforcement Improvements ("Border Enforcement") and the Enhancing Public Safety in the Interior of the United States ("U.S. Interior")—when fully implemented, will have a tremendously adverse effect on individuals seeking asylum at the border or from within the United States. They will make it more difficult for asylum seekers to access the United States, and to enter the asylum system, and will impose penalties and hardships on a vulnerable and traumatized population.

Access to Asylum

Requirement to Remain in Mexico

During the "surge" of Central American migrants, discussed earlier, the United States put pressure on Mexico to stem the flow of asylum seekers to the U.S. border.[63] The Border Security Executive Order goes a step further, requiring that individuals who arrive by land from Mexico[64] be returned there to await their removal hearings. Mexico does not have a good record of protecting asylum seekers or providing them with due process of law. In addition, migrants, including asylum seekers, have been the victims of violence and crime, in Mexico, which is committed with impunity. Requiring them to wait in Mexico will deprive them of the support and assistance of nonprofit agencies that they would be more likely to receive in the United States. Many have observed that the provision is without precedent and will not be able to be done without the cooperation of the Mexican government. It is unclear whether or how it will be implemented.

The Border Wall

The Border Security Executive Order includes Trump's wall on the southern border. The estimated cost of the border wall ranges from $15 to $25 billion. Experts have observed that members of sophisticated criminal enterprises will find ways to enter notwithstanding the construction of a continuous wall, and those who will be most adversely affected will be migrants fleeing persecution. Historical data demonstrates a correlation between U.S. measures that militarize or harden the border and the deaths of migrants who are forced to take increasingly risky routes. Steps that make it near impossible for asylum seekers to access the United States violate the spirit and letter of the 1980 Refugee Act, as well as the international Refugee Convention and Refugee Protocol.

Expanded Expedited Removal and Higher Credible Fear Screening Standard

As discussed earlier, in 1996 Congress enacted expedited removal, the process that requires undocumented individuals to express fear immediately upon arriving and then to establish a strong enough claim—a "credible fear of persecution" in order to be permitted to apply for asylum. When expedited removal was first enacted, the attorney general chose to apply it only at air, land, and sea ports of entry. In 2002 it was expanded to individuals who arrived by sea, were not legally admitted, and could not prove they had been physically present in the United States for two years. In 2004 it was expanded to individuals without valid documents who were apprehended within 14 days of entry to the United States and 100 miles of the Mexican or Canadian border.

The Border Security Executive Order calls for expedited removal to be expanded throughout the entire country and to apply to any individual who cannot prove she has been continuously present for the previous two years. Because of flaws in the expedited removal process as designed—with its expectation that asylum seekers will divulge painful facts about persecution immediately—and because of CBP officer misconduct and/or failure to apply the law properly, this expansion increases the risk of asylum seekers being returned without a chance to express their fear. They can be returned to persecution without ever appearing before a judge.

The Border Security Executive Order also implies that the credible fear standard should be applied more stringently (stating that it should be applied in a way so that protection is not "exploited"). Unfortunately, it appears that this "suggestion" is having an impact; recent statistics show a decrease in the number of asylum seekers found to have a credible fear.[65]

Prioritizing Prosecution for "Illegal" Entry

The Border Security Executive Order calls for prioritizing the prosecution of any offense related to the southern border, including nonviolent offenses, such as unlawful entry or unlawful reentry. Bona fide asylum seekers cannot be expected to have valid documents permitting them to enter the United States—that is why the asylum statute indicates that individuals "irrespective of status" are entitled to apply. The call for stepped-up prosecution ignores their plight and punishes them for exercising the right under domestic and international law to seek asylum. A conviction for unlawful entry can hurt their chances of being granted protection.

Expanded Detention

The Border Security Executive Order contemplates a massive expansion in detention. It calls on DHS to construct additional facilities near the southern border and to detain on the "mere suspicion" of violation of the law—including such violations as unlawful entry by asylum seekers. It also urges a curtailment of "humanitarian parole," which is the release from detention for humanitarian reasons or significant public benefit. Family detention has already been greatly expanded under the Obama administration, and this Executive Order—which applies to families as well as all other asylum seekers—builds on an already-misguided policy.

Making all Migrants an Enforcement Priority, Increasing Funding, Punishing Sanctuary Jurisdictions

There are a number of provisions in the U.S. Interior Executive Order calling for overall harsher enforcement policies, which will have an adverse impact on asylum seekers, among others. For example, under Obama administration policy, not all undocumented individuals were considered "priorities" for arrest and removal. The U.S. Interior Executive Order makes *every* undocumented individual a priority for removal. As a consequence, numerous undocumented individuals who have unblemished records, are contributing in meaningful ways to their communities, and have U.S. citizen children have been targeted for arrest and deported.

Aside from the human tragedy that this constitutes, it also implicates refugee protection. Many of these individuals originally come to the United States fleeing persecution and are still at risk. The U.S. Interior Executive Order asks for increased funding for enforcement and removal, directing DHS to hire 10,000 additional ICE officers, and it will be using these officers to even more aggressively pursue individuals who should not be enforcement priorities.

The U.S. Interior Executive Order also directs the DOJ and DHS to limit or terminate federal grants for the so-called sanctuary jurisdictions. Although there is no clear legal definition for "sanctuary jurisdiction," the term is generally understood to apply to localities that do not engage in immigration enforcement or cooperation with federal immigration authorities beyond what is legally required. The concept of sanctuary cities has its origin in the 1980s when faith-based communities came together to provide protection for Central American refugees, whose strong claims for a safe haven were being denied. Under what conditions the DOJ and DHS could cut off funding involves complicated legal issues beyond the scope of this chapter. It should be noted, however, that there have been legal challenges to the sanctuary jurisdiction provision, and a federal district judge in California partially blocked it, finding that its application was likely unconstitutional.[66]

Targeting the Parents and Family Members of Child Migrants

On February 20, 2017, DHS issued a memorandum regarding the Border Enforcement and U.S. Interior Executive Orders.[67] This memo expressed the intent to prioritize the prosecution of parents and family members who paid smugglers to assist their children's arrival to the United States. Although the memo frames the targeted enforcement as addressing the children's best interests (the heading for this section is "Accountability Measures to Protect Alien Children from Exploitation and Prevent Abuses of Our Immigration Laws"), it does anything but that.

Parents and family members who are aware that their children are at great risk in their home countries often have no alternative but to resort to smugglers to facilitate their journey to the United States. To punish the parents for trying to protect their children is cruel, and when the prosecution concludes with imprisonment or deportation, it results in the child being deprived of a parent or family member with whom she may have just reunited after a long separation. This policy is hardly in anyone's best interest.

Conclusion

The failure of the international community to protect those fleeing Nazi persecution was the catalyst for the 1951 Refugee Convention. While the 1951 Convention was retrospective—addressing the refugee crisis caused by World War II—its 1967 Protocol was forward-looking and constituted an ongoing commitment to protect those fleeing persecution.

The United States, along with the majority of nations, has bound itself to comply with the obligations of these international agreements, and it did so explicitly with congressional passage of the 1980 Refugee Act. However, U.S. adherence to international norms has been uneven from its onset, with measures that severely undercut the nation's lofty commitments. These included interdiction and return of bona fide refugees at sea (Haitians)—a policy upheld by the U.S. Supreme Court—as well as a discriminatory application of the refugee definition, animated by foreign policy goals rather than international understandings and obligations to protect.

Although there is much to criticize about U.S. refugee protection prior to January 2017, the Trump administration's Executive Orders represent a retrenchment and threat to international obligations of an exponentially different magnitude. The Executive Orders impact refugees who would be admitted through the USRAP as well as those who arrive at the U.S. border seeking protection. Measures to eviscerate USRAP include attempts to indefinitely ban Syrian refugees—who unquestionably are in desperate need of protection—to suspend USRAP, and to dramatically reduce refugee numbers. Individuals seeking to access protection at the U.S. border would be pushed back to Mexico, or if allowed to enter, would be subject to even harsher and more punitive policies, including expanded use of detention.

At a point in history where there are more refugees and displaced persons than at any time since World War II, the need for countries to step up and comply with their international obligations could not be greater. Almost every school child recalls the story of the *St. Louis*, a ship carrying Jews escaping the Holocaust, who were denied landing rights in the United States. They returned to Europe, where the majority of them perished. The refrain of "never again" refers to this, and other acts of callous disregard for the plight of the vulnerable. Perhaps it is too much to hope that the memory of the *St. Louis* can serve as a clarion call to resist the forces pulling the United States back to policies that should remain in the dust bin of history. But given the stakes, it is worth hoping—as well as advocating—for just, humane, and enlightened policies.

Notes

1. *The Chinese Exclusion Case*, 130 U.S. 581 (1889).

2. Protecting the Nation from Foreign Terrorist Entry into the United States, Exec. Order No. 13,769, 82 Fed. Reg. 8,977 (January 27, 2017). This executive order went through three iterations—the first was issued on January 27, 2017; the second on March 3, 2017; and the third on September 24, 2017. As discussed in this chapter, there have been various legal challenges, and the Supreme Court has yet to reach a final decision on legitimacy.

3. Karen Musalo, Jennifer Moore, and Richard A. Boswell, *Refugee Law and Policy: A Comparative and International Approach*, 5–10 (Carolina Academic Press, 4th ed., 2011).

4. United Nations Convention Relating to the Status of Refugees, *opened for signature* July 28, 1951, 189 U.N.T.S. 150 (entered into force April 22, 1954) (hereinafter Refugee Convention).

5. Ibid., Art. 1.A(2).

6. Ibid., Art. 34.

7. Article 31.1 provides:

The Contracting States shall not impose penalties, on account of their illegal entry or presence, on refugees who, coming directly from a territory where their life or freedom was threatened . . . enter or are present in their territory without authorization, provided they present themselves without delay to the authorities and show good cause for their illegal entry or presence.

8. Refugee Convention, *supra* note 4, at art. 1.A(2).

9. Refugee Convention, *supra* note 4, at Art. 1.B(1)(a).

10. United Nations Protocol Relating to the Status of Refugees, *opened for signature* January 31, 1967, 606 U.N.T.S. 1267 (entered into force October 4, 1967) (hereinafter Refugee Protocol).

11. UNHCR, *State Parties to the 1951 Convention Relating to the Status of Refugees, and the 1967 Protocol*, http://www.unhcr.org/en-us/protection/basic/ 3b73b0d63/states-parties-1951-convention-its-1967-protocol.html.

12. Ibid., 4.

13. The 1980 Refugee Act amended the Immigration and Nationality Act and is incorporated into various sections of the U.S. Code.

14. 8 U.S.C. § 1157 (2005).

15. 8 U.S.C. §§ 1158 & 1251(b)(3) (2005).

16. Department of Homeland Security, The United States Refugee Admissions Program (USRAP) Consultation and Worldwide Processing Priorities, https:// www.uscis.gov/humanitarian/refugees-asylum/refugees/united-states-refugee-admissions-program-usrap-consultation-worldwide-processing-priorities (https://perma.cc/2YC5-H8GJ).

17. See Linda Qui, "Wrong: Donald Trump Says There's 'no system to vet' Refugees," *Politifact* (June 13, 2016), http://www.politifact.com/truth-o-meter/ statements/2016/jun/13/donald-trump/wrong-donald-trump-says-theres-no-system-vet-refug/ (https://perma.cc/2P2P-GVTR).

18. The White House, under President Barack Obama, set forth a graph and detailed information regarding the multilayered security process. The White House, Infographic: The Screening Process for Refugee Entry into the United States (November 20, 2015), https://obamawhitehouse.archives.gov/blog/2015/ 11/20/infographic-screening-process-refugee-entry-united-states (https://perma .cc/2A8S-Y4F9).

19. Adrian Edwards, *Global forced displacement hits record high*, UNHCR (June 20, 2016), http://www.unhcr.org/en-us/news/latest/2016/6/5763b65a4/ global-forced-displacement-hits-record-high.html (https://perma.cc/9R98-54FR).

20. Ibid.

21. Ibid.

22. Jie Zong and Jeanne Batalova, "Refugees and Asylees in the United States," Migration Policy Institute 2 (June 7, 2017), http://www.migrationpolicy.org/ article/refugees-and-asylees-united-states#Admission_Ceiling (https://perma. cc/XW8U-J9C4).

23. The asylum offices are located in Arlington, Chicago, Houston, Miami, Newark, New York City, Los Angeles, and San Francisco.

24. The "granting of certiorari" is the term used when the U.S. Supreme Court exercises its discretion to hear a case.

25. Some of the most significant cases and holdings are as follows: *INS v. Stevic*, 467 U.S. 307 (1984) (stating that in order to qualify for withholding, an individual is required to show that a threat to life or freedom is more likely than not; this decision rejected the argument that all refugees are entitled to nonrefoulement); *INS v. Cardoza-Fonseca*, 480 U.S. 421 (1987) (affirming that the standard of proof for asylum is "well-founded fear"), *Sale v. Haitian Centers Council*, 509 U.S. 155 (1993) discussed *infra*, (upholding the U.S. practice of interdiction and forcible return of Haitian asylum seekers) and *Aguirre-Aguirre v. INS*, 526 U.S. 415 (1999) (addressing the definition of "serious non-political crime," which is a statutory bar to asylum and withholding).

26. Jaya Ramji-Nogales, Andrew I. Schoenholtz, and Philip G. Schrag, *Refugee Roulette: Disparities in Asylum Adjudication and Proposals for Reform* 89 (New York University Press, 2009).

27. For example, an analysis of 5,800 asylum decisions rendered from May 2014 through January 2016 in the cases of Central American minors showed a high grant rate of 86 percent at the San Francisco Asylum Office and a low grant rate of 15 percent at the Chicago Asylum Office. Lorelei Laird, "Asylum Decisions for Central American Children May Depend on Where They Live," *American Bar Association Journal* (June 2, 2016), http://www.abajournal.com/news/article/asylum_decisions_for_central_american_children_may_depend_on_where_they_liv (https://perma.cc/ZEA4-QQA4).

A recent analysis by the Transactional Records Access Clearinghouse (TRAC) at Syracuse University notes that "while judge-to-judge decision disparities have long existed, a detailed comparison . . . showed by differences in judge denial rates have significantly increased during the last six years." Transactional Records Access Clearinghouse, Asylum Outcome Increasingly Depends on Judge Assigned (December 2, 2016), http://trac.syr.edu/immigration/reports/447/ (https://perma.cc/QP2V-YG35).

28. Ramji-Nogales, Schoenholtz & Schrag, *supra* note 24, at xvi.

29. Cheryl Little, *United States Haitian Policy: A History of Discrimination*, 10 N.Y.L. Sch. J. Hum. Rts. 269 (1993).

30. *Sale v. Haitian Centers Council*, 509 U.S. 155, 162 (1993).

31. The Guantanamo Naval Base was selected in order to keep Haitians out of the mainland United States, where they would benefit from protections of the U.S. Constitution.

32. See Joan Fitzpatrick, "The International Dimension of U.S. Refugee Law," 15 *Berkeley Journal of International Law* 1, 9–10 (1997).

33. *Sale v. Haitian Centers Council*, *supra* note 28.

34. 8 U.S.C. § 1235.3.

35. These questions appear on Form I-867, Record of Sworn Statement in Proceedings.

36. See, e.g., James Silk, Despite a Generous Spirit: Denying Asylum in the United States (U.S. Committee for Refugees 1986); GAO, Uniform Application of Standards Uncertain—Few Denied Applicants Deported (1987), https://www.gao.gov/assets/80/76210.pdf (https://perma.cc/BC8G-DBKT).

37. James Silk, *supra* note 34, at 7–10.

38. 760 F. Supp. 796 (N.D. Cal. 1991).

39. Ibid., 799.

40. See Karen Musalo, *A Short History of Gender Asylum in the United States: Resistance and Ambivalence May Very Slowly Be Inching towards Recognition of Women's Claims*, 29 Ref. Surv. Q. (Special Issue) 46 (2010); Karen Musalo, Personal Violence, Public Matter: Evolving Standards in Gender-Based Asylum Law, *Harvard International Review* 45 (Fall 2014/Winter 2015).

41. The fear of floodgates is misplaced; Canada recognized gender persecution, including claims based on domestic violence, beginning in the early 1990s and never experienced a skyrocketing number of claims. Karen Musalo, Protecting Victims of Gendered Persecution: Fear of Floodgates or Call to (Principled) Action?, 14 *Virginia Journal of Social Policy & the Law* 119, 132–33 (2007).

42. As discussed earlier, in order to qualify for refugee status, an individual must establish a well-founded fear of persecution "on account of" race, religion, nationality, political opinion, or membership in a particular social group. The majority of claims are argued under the "social group" ground. The BIA has diverged from international guidance and has made it more difficult to prove social group membership. It did this by adding two new criteria that had to be met in order to establish a "particular social group."

43. UNHCR, Guidelines on the Applicable Criteria and Standards Relating to the Detention of Asylum-Seekers and Alternatives to Detention (2012), http://www.unhcr.org/en-us/505b10ee9.pdf (https://perma.cc/8NLR-VRZ9).

44. "Surge" is the term used to describe the 2014 jump in the number of Central American children from the northern triangle countries. They numbered 38,833 in fiscal year 2013 and then almost doubled to 68,631 in fiscal year 2014. Karen Musalo and Eunice Lee, "Seeking a Rational Approach to a Regional Refugee Crisis: Lessons from the Summer 2014 'Surge' of Central American Women and Children at the US-Mexico Border," 5 *Journal on Migration and Human Security* 5, (No. I) 137 (2017), http://jmhs.cmsny.org/index.php/jmhs/article/view/78 (https://perma.cc/QW7V-7B5V). Although this was a significant increase, it was relatively small in terms of the United States' capacity to absorb, and certainly palls in light of the millions of Syrian refugees who sought protection in adjacent countries, as well as within the European Union.

45. The Obama administration admitted it was using detention as a deterrent: "In testimony before the Senate Committee on Appropriations in June 2014, DHS Secretary Jeh Johnson asserted, '[T]here are adults who brought their children with them. Again our message to this group is simple: We will send you back . . . Last week we opened a detention facility in Artesia, New Mexico for this purpose.'" Musalo & Lee, *supra* note 42 at 142.

46. *R.I.L.R. v. Johnson*, 80 F. Supp. 3d 164 (D.D.C. 2015).

47. Physicians for Human Rights and the Bellevue/NYU Program for Survivors of Torture (2003, June). *From persecution to prison: The health consequences of detention for asylum seekers*. Boston and New York City: Authors. Retrieved from: http://physiciansforhumanrights.org/library/reports/from-persecution-to-prison.html.

48. 8 USC § 1362.

49. Ingrid Eagly & Steven Shafer, *Access to Counsel in Immigration Court*, American Immigration Council (September 28, 2016), https://www.americanimmigration council.org/research/access-counsel-immigration-court (https://perma.cc/X8JD-N8KZ).

50. Transactional Records Access Clearinghouse, "Continued Rise in Asylum Denial Rates: Impact of Representation and Nationality" (December 13, 2016), http://trac.syr.edu/immigration/reports/448/ (https://perma.cc/8NMV-T8D3).

51. The official testified: "I've taught immigration law literally to 3-year-olds and 4-year-olds. . . . It takes a lot of time. It takes a lot of patience. They get it. It's not the most efficient, but it can be done." Jerry Markon, "Can a Three Year Old Represent Herself in Immigration Court? This Judge Thinks So," *Washington Post* (March 5, 2016), https://www.washingtonpost.com/world/national-security/can-a-3-year-old-represent-herself-in-immigration-court-this-judge-thinks-so/2016/03/03/5be59a32-db25-11e5-925f-1d10062cc82d_story.html?utm_term=.59469ba59e18 (https://perma.cc/AK9J-K7BD).

52. Exec. Order No. 13,769, *supra* note 2.

53. Protecting the Nation from Foreign Terrorist Entry into the United States, Exec. Order 13,780, 82 Fed. Reg. 13,209 (March 6, 2017).

54. Border Security and Immigration Enforcement Improvements, Exec. Order 13,767, 82 Fed. Reg. 8,793 (January 25, 2017).

55. Enhancing Public Safety in the Interior of the United States, Exec. Order 13,768 number, 82 Fed. Reg. 8,799 (January 25, 2017).

56. The countries are Iraq, Iran, Libya, Somalis, Sudan, Syria, and Yemen.

57. Exec. Order No. 13,769, *supra* note 2, section 5(e).

58. Exec. Order No. 13780, *supra* note 50.

59. Exec. Order No. 13, 815, 82 Fed. Reg. 50055 (October 24, 2017).

60. Government of Canada, #WelcomeRefugees: Key figures, http://www.cic.gc.ca/english/refugees/welcome/milestones.asp (https://perma.cc/S2WS-TNVR).

61. 2.9 million Syrians are in Turkey, 660,000 are in Jordan, 241,000 are in Iraq, and 122,000 are in Egypt. UNHCR, Syria Emergency, http://www.unhcr.org/en-us/syria-emergency.html (https://perma.cc/2K3R-GSW2).

62. Kathleen Newland, *The U.S. Record Shows Refugees Are not a Threat*, Migration Policy Institute (October 7, 2015), https://www.migrationpolicy.org/news/us-record-shows-refugees-are-not-threat (https://perma.cc/S4TJ-RYS8).

63. Musalo and Lee, *supra* note 42, at 149–50.

64. This provision of the Border Security Executive Order also applies to immigrants entering the United States from Canada. However, it is clear that it will apply primarily to Mexico, since there is little to no evidence of asylum seekers traveling from Canada to the United States. In fact, the xenophobic policies

and rhetoric in the United States, and the fear they have evoked, have caused thousands of immigrants to stream over our northern border into Canada. See, e.g., Anna Nicoleau, "Refugees Evade Trump by Fleeing to Canada," *Financial Times* (April 23, 2017), https://www.ft.com/content/4b54189c-1940-11e7-a53d-df09f373be87.

65. USCIS, Federal Government Workload Report Summary, https://www. uscis.gov/sites/default/files/USCIS/Outreach/Upcoming%20National%20 Engagements/PED_CredibleFearandReasonableFearStatisticsandNationality Report.pdf (https://perma.cc/TH7J-U9ET).

66. See *Cty. of Santa Clara v. Trump*, No. 17-CV-00485-WHO, 2017 WL 1459081, at *21 (N.D. Cal. April 25, 2017), *reconsideration denied*, No. 17-CV-00485-WHO, 2017 WL 3086064 (N.D. Cal. July 20, 2017).

67. Department of Homeland Security, *Implementing the President's Border Security and Immigration Enforcement Improvement Policies* (February 20, 2017), https://www.dhs.gov/publication/implementing-presidents-border-security-and-immigration-enforcement-improvement-policies (https://perma.cc/TV2V-M4RK).

CHAPTER THREE

Locked Up and Kicked Out

Detention and Deportation in the United States and the United Kingdom

Carol Bohmer and Amy Shuman

I came to the UK to escape persecution. Because I am stateless I had to use false documents to get here. When I arrived I was put in prison for a short time because of this. I thought when I left prison I would be a free man. I did not think I would be taken somewhere worse. Detention is worse than prison because in prison you count your days down and in detention you count your days up . . . and up . . . and up . . . and up. (Lindley 2017)

The men shuffle in a line across a lonely tarmac, one by one. Chains around their ankles clank with each step, a steady beat punctuating the engines' roar. Some men walk in sneakers without laces. Some sport navy blue prison-issue shoes. One wears work boots, still stained with paint. This may be the last time they touch US soil. The Boeing 737 beside them is bound for Guatemala City. And these men, like all passengers on Ice Air have one-way tickets. (Shoichet 2017)

Introduction

Detention and deportation have increased enormously in the last 30 years throughout the developed world. They are visible symbols of the changes that have taken place in national attitudes toward immigrants in general and asylum seekers in particular. They mirror the hardening of attitudes toward immigrants and point to the categorization of immigrants as either illegal or criminals.

In the United States, deportation historically has been used for a variety of purposes, since the late 19th century, when it was used to eliminate those considered undesirable at the border, including those seen as political troublemakers or convicted of crimes (Hernandez 2014). Thus, it became both a political and an immigration issue, and this dual focus continues today in the ways in which the government deals with both those who entered illegally and those suspected of terrorism. In the United States, immigration detention has also recently been used as a means of dealing with unauthorized immigrants, the so-called illegals, who are currently the subject of so much public attention (DeGenova 2012; Silverman 2018). Individuals fleeing persecution to seek asylum in the United States also have been subjected to detention. Because of enhanced border control, many people claiming asylum at the border are detained on arrival, though some of them are sent back without any hearing on their asylum claim (Silverman 2018; Stillman 2018). The law requires that someone be asked questions at the border to determine whether they have a "credible" fear of returning. A study of the practices at the border illustrates that those detained are in fact the lucky ones; the others are immediately deported without any hearing to determine whether they are legitimate asylum claimants (Silverman 2018). Thus, since the 1980s, detention has gone from being one means of controlling immigration to the "central feature of immigration policing" (Hernandez 2014, 1372). Part of the reason for this is the connection between the control of drug trafficking and drug traffickers and immigration control more generally. Vast sums of money have been spent on detention, despite arguments by nongovernmental organizations (NGOs) that similar results could be achieved at far less expense if alternatives to detention were utilized (Global Detention Project 2016, 2).

What Is Detention and How Does It Work?

The classification of illegal entry as a civil or criminal act is an important one both in the United States and the United Kingdom (UK). Both countries have criminal penalties for illegal entry. Under Title 8, Section 1325 of the U.S. Code (U.S.C.), or Section 275 of the Immigration and Nationality Act (INA), it is a misdemeanor for an alien (i.e., a noncitizen) to "enter or attempt to enter the United States at any time or place other than designated by immigration officers." In the United Kingdom, it is a summary offence, under the Immigration Act of 1971, section 24 1(a) to "knowingly enter the United Kingdom in breach of a deportation order or without leave."

Complicating this civil-criminal divide, people caught having entered illegally or having overstayed their visas are detained, in the United States, not because they are criminals but rather as an administrative procedure for the authorities to decide what to do with them (Silverman and Massa 2012). This waiting can take a long time. The government must "resolve a perceived irregularity in their immigration proceedings. Because these irregularities range from disputed identities to failed asylum claims, however, people may 'wait' in immigration detention for weeks, months, and even years" (Silverman and Massa 2012, 677). So those in detention can find themselves "incarcerated" for indefinite periods of time, because detention in the United States is also legally considered an administrative procedure rather than what it in fact is: a punishment (Hernandez 2014). Those incarcerated for criminal offenses, by contrast, are protected by a variety of legal rights that are not available to those detained under administrative rules; for example, people cannot be imprisoned indefinitely for criminal offenses. Detention can be indefinite for people accused of entering the country illegally, and the conditions are like those in prisons, even though it is not called imprisonment.

Indefinite detention also exists in the United Kingdom even though the European Union (EU) Returns Directive limits detention to a maximum period of 18 months; many countries have much shorter maximum periods (in France it is 45 days) (The State of Detention 2014, 5). However, the United Kingdom does not adhere to EU immigration law and routinely violates these limitations.

While most of those detained in the United Kingdom remain in detention for short periods, some of them do not. The most recent figures from the year ending June 2017 indicate that "27,862 people left detention. Of these, 64% had been in detention for less than 29 days, 17% for between 29 days and 2 months, and 11% for between 2 and 4 months. Of the 1,943 (7%) remaining, 172 had been in detention for between 1 and 2 years, and 28 for 2 years or longer" (UK National Government Statistics 2017). Some of this detention has been the subject of lawsuits on the grounds that it is unlawful. Recent reports indicate that the UK government has paid out £21.2 million for unlawful detention claims in the last few years (Cante 2018a).

The United States also detains people both administratively and for criminal immigration violations for indefinite periods. As the law has made immigration violations increasingly criminal, the number of those detained in criminal contexts has accordingly increased. The Trump "zero tolerance" policy provides major implementation of this, though this aspect of the "zero tolerance" policy required no legal change. As a recent report put it:

> The United States operates the world's largest immigration detention system. On any given day, the country has some 30,000 people in administrative immigration detention at an estimated cost of nearly $150 a day. In 2016, the combined budget of enforcement agencies was $19 billion. The country's sprawling detention estate counts on some 200 facilities, including privately

operated detention facilities, local jails, juvenile detention centres, field offices, and euphemistically named "family residential centres." (Global Detention Project 2016)

Though not many statistics are available yet, detention will most likely have increased under the Trump administration. Detainees are held on average longer than previously; in 2017 the average length of stay at any one immigrant prison or jail was 34 days compared to 22 days in 2016 and 21 days in 2015 (Freedom for Immigrants, n.d.).

With the merging of civil and criminal approaches toward those apprehended for illegal entry, immigration detainees are increasingly also treated like criminals in other ways. They "are represented as a threat to public safety, locked behind barbed wire, often in remote facilities, and subjected to the detailed control emblematic of all secure environments. Often they are held alongside their criminal counterparts. People serving time as a sanction for engaging in criminal activity are housed in the same facilities as people waiting to receive an immigration court's decision about which country will become their next residence" (Hernandez 2014, 1349). Like the United States, but unlike the rest of Europe, the United Kingdom also routinely detains "migrants in prisons, a practice that is unlawful in the rest of the European Union. It is alone in detaining large numbers of asylum seekers, simply for administrative convenience in processing their cases" (The State of Detention 2014, 3). The use of prisons continues, though the Home Office does not publicize the number of those detained in prison, but "a recent snapshot survey found 360 people held in prison solely under immigration powers" (Amnesty International United Kingdom Section 2017, 16). Another study indicates that 14 percent of detainees are kept in prisons (Lindley 2017, 4).

Under the Trump administration, the practice of family detention and the separation of children from their families have vastly increased (Eagly 2018; Silverman 2018). Recent figures indicate that a total of 12,800 children were detained in federally contracted shelters in September 2018, up from 2,400 such children in custody in May 2017 (Dickerson 2018b). In the United Kingdom, by contrast, there has been pressure on the government not to detain children, and the practice has been significantly reduced. In 2009, more than 1,100 children entered immigration detention; by 2017, only 42 children were detained (Silverman and Griffiths 2018).

The Purpose of Detention

The ostensible purpose of detention is to prevent people from absconding and remaining in the country while living under the radar. It is supposed to isolate those who are considered to be a risk to the community (the fear of terrorism). It is used to punish those who have violated immigration laws and is intended to act as a deterrent. This last purpose has become more important recently both in the United States and the United Kingdom. The use of detention as a possible deterrent is especially prominent in the United States, where there has been a vast increase in the number of people seeking asylum from violence in Central America (Martinez 2018). As is so often the case, desperate people are not deterred by such measures (Bohmer and Lebow 2015; Martinez 2018).

Detention is also supposed to facilitate the deportation of those illegally in the country. But one of its major purposes is directed toward reassuring citizens that efforts are being made by the authorities to control immigration. It may be for this reason that, as we shall see, both the U.S. and UK governments are so reluctant to use the available alternatives, such as bail and conditional release. Such alternatives are both much less costly and extremely effective, not to mention far more humane and less intrusive (Global Detention Project 2016, 11).

The Effects of Detention

Among the multiple effects of detention on those who are detained, many detainees describe the difficulties of never knowing when they will be released or what will happen to them when they are released. As one detainee put it: "You are not given any information about how long you will have to stay. It feels like you will be there forever. It feels like prison. I was worried about being taken to a plane" (The APPG Inquiry into the Use of Immigration Detention in the United Kingdom 2015, 20). In the United Kingdom, over half of those in detention are eventually released on bail into the community, which defeats the stated purpose of detention as a gateway to deportation (BID 2017).

A number of reports describe detainees being mistreated while in detention in the United States and the United Kingdom (Gumbel 2018; Juarez, Gomez-Aguinaga, and Bettez 2018; Pennington 2014; The State of Detention 2014). In the United Kingdom, there have been six cases in Administrative Court in three years in which the Home Office has been determined to have provided inhuman and degrading treatment under Article 3 of the European Convention of Human Rights (The State of Detention 2014, 17; Pennington 2014). In the most recent one, the Court reported that "detention caused the onset of a mental disorder sufficiently serious to lead to an Article 3 breach. For MD [the plaintiff in the case], detention did not exacerbate a pre-existing mental disorder—it caused the disintegration of her mental health" (The State of Detention 2014, 17). These cases illustrate what is widely known by NGOs that work in the detention system: that detention causes or exacerbates psychiatric disorders and contributes to psychological distress among those detained. A report by the Jesuit Refugee Service concludes, "The vast majority of detainees describe a scenario in which the environment of detention weakens their personal condition. The prison-like environments existing in many detention centres, the isolation from the 'outside world', the unreliable flow of information and the disruption of a life plan lead to mental health impacts such as depression, self-uncertainty and psychological stress" (Jesuit Refugee Service-Europe 2010, 13). One detainee described it this way: "All these people here, and no one knows how long they will be there. Some lose hope, and they try to kill themselves. Some try burning themselves with whatever they can get. Some try hanging themselves in the shower. They think it's the only way out. I've seen this with my own eyes. Detention is a way to destroy people: they do not kill you directly, but instead you kill yourself" (The APPG Inquiry into the Use of Immigration Detention in the United Kingdom 2015, 20).

The recent "zero tolerance" policy in the United States has produced extensive evidence of appalling conditions in the detention centers to which migrants are being sent. An expose by *The Guardian* describes detainees being kept in freezing, filthy conditions with insufficient food, water, or medical care, and undergoing verbal and physical abuse by some staff (Gumbrel 2018). This is denied by the Customs and Border Protection Agency but has been corroborated by a number of doctors, lawyers, and NGO workers who have been working with the detainees (Gumbrel 2018).

Recent evidence has also come to light that psychotropic medication is being administered to children who are detained on a regular basis as a means of control (Baey et al. 2018). The government claims that this is to treat mental illness and is used when the child is considered a danger or an escape risk. Children have reported being told they have to take the medication if they ever hope to leave detention and that they have been forcibly injected (Gonzales 2018). The Los Angeles–based Center for Human Rights & Constitutional Law and a number of other groups have filed a lawsuit challenging the government, alleging in federal court that the government is giving powerful psychiatric medications to immigrant minors without the permission of parents, guardians, or a court (Laird 2018).

Sexual abuse in detention centers in the United States is so widespread that it has been described as endemic (Speri 2018). A recent report revealed 1,224 complaints of sexual and physical abuse in immigration detention between 2010 and 2017 based on a public records request with the Department of Homeland Security's Office of Inspector General (Speri 2018). Research based on police reports indicates that sexual abuse is widespread among children as well (Grabell and Sanders 2018). The American Civil Liberties Union also found widespread abuse of immigrant children in custody, based on an examination of thousands of government documents (ACLU 2018).

The UK Home Office has a policy under which vulnerable people are not to be detained except in exceptional circumstances. Rule 35 of the Detention

Centre Rules, 2001, requires doctors treating detainees to bring to the Home Office's attention anyone whose health is likely to be "injuriously affected" by detention, with the assumption that such people would not be detained. However, reports indicate that this policy is routinely ignored, and people with mental health problems are nevertheless detained:

> An analysis of cases of vulnerable detainees shows that 80 per cent have been defined by medical practitioners as being "at risk," but all have remained in detention despite a Home Office policy designed to ensure vulnerable people are not detained. The Home Office is systematically ignoring independent medical advice not to detain people who are mentally ill as part of their bid to crackdown on immigration. (Bulman 2017)

A recent case illustrates this Home Office behavior (*Ilori v SSHD* 2017). The court ruled that the Home Office was not entitled to continue to detain someone who had been shown to have been tortured and who was considered to be "vulnerable" under Rule 35. Despite that determination the Home Office continued to detain the Nigerian for over nine months, using the claim that there were "very exceptional circumstances." The government now has to pay compensation for wrongful detention. A recent official inspection report into Harmondsworth, the immigration removal center, near Heathrow airport, reported that despite accepting evidence of torture in 9 out of 10 sample cases, the Home Office continued to detain all but one of the people involved (Travis 2018).

Michael, one of the people represented by Bail for Immigration Detainees (BID), a UK NGO that helps detainees obtain bail, was tortured in his home country before fleeing and ultimately arriving in the United Kingdom. He describes detention in these words: "Detention is by far the worst place and experience I have gone through in my life. For someone like me who endured torture, harm, torment and abuse in my home country. The endless trauma and flashbacks which followed me across the oceans was relived in detention and made my conditions rather worse. . . . Detention made me suicidal and also made me physically attempt to end my life four times because I couldn't see past those four walls. There is nothing to stimulate your brain positively and there isn't any form of Nirvana for those of us who were there" (Bail for Immigration Detainees 2017).

The story is the same in the United States. Research conducted by Physicians for Human Rights shows "extremely high symptom levels of anxiety, depression and post-traumatic stress disorder (PTSD) among detained asylum seekers. Significant symptoms of depression were present in 86% of the 70 detained asylum seekers, anxiety was present in 77% and PTSD in 50%" (Physicians for Human Rights and the Bellevue/NYU Program for Survivors of Torture 2003, 1–2). As in the UK, and elsewhere, they found that it is the detention itself that either causes or exacerbates the problem.

Medical care is also notoriously poor in detention centers both in both countries. In the United States, even something as simple as providing eyeglasses to someone who was exposed to tear gas in her home country took two years in detention (Physicians for Human Rights and the Bellevue/NYU Program for Survivors of Torture 2003, 9). The report indicated that dissatisfaction with the level of medical care was widespread (Gallagher 2017; Human Rights Watch 2017; Physicians for Human Rights and the Bellevue/NYU Program for Survivors of Torture 2003). The situation remains dire; poor medical care was documented recently by medical staff who have been working at the central processing center in MacAllen, Texas (Gumbrel 2018). These included "outbreaks of vomiting, diarrhea, respiratory infections and other communicable diseases" (Gumbrel 2018). While conditions in some detention centers do not appear to be so bad, corroboration of poor medical conditions and medical negligence was widespread enough to support the view that such treatment is routine. The British Medical Association recently published a scathing report about detention in the United Kingdom. They concluded, "Problems with the accuracy and timeliness of health assessments, availability of services, staff shortages, and ensuring continuity of care have all been identified as adversely impacting on the standard of care provided in detention" (Campbell 2017). Flaws in the medical care of those in US detention centers are equally bad, with staff consistently overworked and underqualified (Global Detention Project 2016, 12; Juarez, Gomez-Aguinaga, and Bettez 2018).

Deaths in detention are not uncommon. In the United Kingdom, 10 deaths were reported in detention centers in 12 months (Taylor 2017). Some of the deaths are caused by bad medical care, while others are the result of suicide. Of the most recent reported deaths in UK detention, two were self-inflicted, one was a suspected homicide, three were drug related, and two followed sudden illness (Campbell 2017, 21). In 2017, the highest recorded number of attempted suicides in detention in the United Kingdom occurred, with 446 attempts being recorded (Cante 2018b). In the United States, there were 107 deaths in detention counted by Immigration and Customs Enforcement (ICE) between October 2003 and 2010 (Bernstein 2010). The American Immigration Lawyers Association (AILA) listed all ICE reports of deaths in adult immigration detention facilities and found a total of 30 deaths between December 24, 2015, and July 26, 2018 (Deaths in Adult Detention Centers 2018). This may be an underestimate, as one of the news reports described a death in September 2017 as the eleventh, though it was only the seventh reported in the AILA list (Deaths in Adult Detention Centers 2018). The Physicians for Human Rights report indicates that about a quarter of the asylum seekers interviewed said that they had suicidal thoughts while in detention, and two had attempted suicide (Physicians for Human Rights and the Bellevue/NYU Program for Survivors of Torture 2003, 5).

Governments are, not surprisingly, unenthusiastic about reporting such problems in detention centers. A 2010 report by *The New York Times* found a "culture of secrecy" in the way the U.S. government handled deaths in detention facilities (Bernstein 2010). Details of how the deaths had occurred were hidden from the public and the families of those who died. Despite the statement of a spokesperson from ICE after one particularly egregious cover-up that there would be transparency, the secrecy continues (Bernstein 2010). More recently, a case has been filed by the family of a long-time U.S. resident who killed himself while in solitary confinement in a for-profit detention center. He had been identified on arrival as a suicide risk, and the staff knew of his documented history of schizophrenia and numerous previous confinements. Nevertheless, they repeatedly placed him in solitary confinement and denied him access to mental health treatment. Despite the family's ongoing efforts to get answers about his death using the nation's open records laws, ICE has repeatedly refused to hand over a single document in response to their requests (*Chaverra v. ICE et al.* 2018). The situation is similar in the United Kingdom. The former prison ombudsman reported to Parliament that self-inflicted deaths in immigration removal centers were being kept a "state secret" by the Home Office, a situation he described as "odd, and frankly self-defeating" (Bulman 2018).

Among those who benefit from the current extensive use of detention in both the United States and the United Kingdom are the private contractors who increasingly run the detention facilities (Corporate Watch 2018; Fernandez and Benner 2018; Luan 2018). Part of the explanation for the increase in the numbers of those detained as well as the increasingly prison-like conditions of detention stems from the involvement of private contractors in running most detention facilities. Clearly, these corporate institutions have particular interests in how these facilities are managed. They have an interest in keeping the facilities full, as they may be reimbursed by a fee per detainee per day (Bacon 2005, 3; Planas 2018). They also have an interest in keeping the costs as low as possible to enhance their profits. As one report puts it:

> Detained individuals are often exposed to physical and mental abuse through isolation, solitary confinement, or the opposite—overcrowded facilities. Limited or no access to basic necessities such as clean clothing, bedding, hygiene, or healthcare is rampant. Detainees have reported having to wait over 15 hours between meals, which are often of poor quality and past its expiration date. (Juarez, Gomez-Aguinaga, and Bettez 2018, 80)

The CEO of one private prison corporation, GEO Group, George Zoley, said they were "very pleased" by the improved occupancy rates at their detention centers. He expressed optimism about future profits, largely driven by current contracts with their largest client, the U.S. ICE agency (Lee 2017).

Private sector providers also have an interest in saving money when providing the services detainees are supposed to receive, such as medical services. As we saw earlier, the medical services are limited, and those providing them are underpaid and insufficiently qualified (Gumbrell 2018; Human Rights Watch 2017). These contractors also run private prisons, and they appear to see the two kinds of institutions as basically similar, even when those detained are children, who clearly have very different needs. For example, one company lists its immigration contracts under the heading "Justice Sector" and sees the running of detention facilities as a natural extension of running prisons (Bacon 2005, 2–3).

In the United States, private contractors have been involved in running detention facilities since the 1980s under the Reagan presidency, soon after the movement toward the privatization of prison administration began (Bacon 2005, 10). The Corrections Corporation of America (CCA) opened its first privately run detention center in 1984 in a former hotel. Repeated criticisms of this multi-million-dollar corporation have been made since then, with ongoing claims about inadequate staffing, poor conditions, high turnover of staff, and the falsification of business records (Global Detention Project 2016, 14; Juarez, Gomez-Aguinaga, and Bettez 2018, 80). Nevertheless, the renamed CoreCivic (formerly CCA) is thriving; its stock went up 58 percent after Trump's election (Juarez, Gomez-Aguinaga, and Bettez 2018). They and other equally lax companies continue to receive contracts to run detention centers and to make huge profits from these activities (Juarez, Gomez-Aguinaga, and Bettez 2018, 79). The government appears to accept the lowest bid in contracts for these facilities (Loewenstein 2014). A recent report indicates that the Trump administration has provided a huge boost to the fortunes of the private prison industry (Dayen 2018; Eisen 2018; Planas 2018). The first year of his administration was the most profitable ever, and profits are destined to rise even further as the administration implements its plans to increase the number of undocumented immigrants held in detention centers (and prisons) (Salon 2018). Private detention facilities have an increased share of the market compared to other detention facilities. A recent report stated thus: "As of August 2016, nearly three-quarters of the average daily immigration detainee population was held in facilities operated by private prison companies—a sharp contrast from a decade ago, when the majority were held in ICE-contracted bedspace in local jails and state prisons" (Luan 2018, 1).

It isn't just the private prison corporations that benefit from the detention of migrants. A vast array of services are outsourced to many other private entities, from food service to security to medical care and social work (Luan

2018, 15). Another way private firms benefit is by relying on the labor of the detained, who, in one case in the United Kingdom, were reported to be paid as little as £1 per day (Lindley 2017, 4). This is another issue that has come to the attention of the UK government, without anything being done about it (Ford and Miller 2018). Not surprisingly, the situation is similar in the United States, though with a U.S. twist, it is now the subject of legal challenges. The Washington State attorney general is suing GEO Group, mentioned earlier, for paying their immigration detainees less than a dollar a day (Wattles 2017). The ongoing lawsuit alleges that virtually all nonsecurity functions, from cooking to cleaning to painting, are undertaken by the detainees at wages well below minimum wage (Wattles 2017). Another lawsuit, filed as a class action against CoreCivic forcing detained immigrants at Stewart Detention Center in Lumpkin, Georgia, to work for as little as $1 a day to "clean, cook, and maintain the detention center in a scheme to maximize profits" (Project South 2018). Other reports describe widespread exploitation of detainee labor, including accounts of detainees taking on kitchen duties in order to have access to food, despite being either not paid at all or being paid between $1 and $3 per day (Juarez, Gomez-Aguinaga, and Bettez 2018, 81). Children in detention are also expected to work while in detention (Barry et al 2018).

There is relatively little accountability for those running these institutions under contract from the government, and even when inspections are undertaken or government concern expressed, not much seems to change (Global Detention Project 2016, 14; Ward 2017). Even when the private corporations are fined for not meeting their contractual obligations, the fines are so low that it is cheaper for them to pay the fine than to meet their obligations (Global Detention Project 2016, 12).

A recent television show by the *BBC Panorama* program caused an outcry when it exposed an "alarming culture of abuse and neglect" at Brook House, an immigration detention center, during the time it was run by G4S, a private contractor operating private detention centers in the United Kingdom (Ward 2017). Previous exposes by the team from *Panorama* of other privately run institutions had uncovered similar mistreatment, abuse, and neglect, after which the government made the usual pronouncements that lessons have been learned, but nothing happened and private contractors continue to manage these institutions. There is a move to set up an inquiry about the conditions at Brook House, as well as a legal challenge to designate G4S as a "high risk supplier." This would make it harder for the government to award them contracts in the future and mean that G4S is subject to closer monitoring (Crowdjustice 2018). Whether it will finally make a difference in the business-as-usual approach of the government to the running of immigration detention centers is still an open question.

Alternatives to Detention

As mentioned earlier, detaining people in detention facilities for extended periods is a vastly expensive undertaking. Alternative methods are both more efficient and less costly. Further, the supposed justification of punishing those who have violated immigration law is complicated by the fact that, for the most part, detainees have not committed a crime, and it is a violation of the law to incarcerate someone without a criminal conviction. The ostensible justifications for detention to prevent detainees from absconding and to facilitate their ultimate deportation can as easily be served by less restrictive measures at much lower cost, as we discuss below (The APPG Inquiry into the Use of Immigration Detention in the United Kingdom 2015, 25). There has been much talk on the part of the U.S. and UK governments about minimizing detention and using it only as a last resort, but, given the statistics on the ever-increasing numbers of those detained in both countries, that does not seem to have happened, perhaps in part because of the extensive lobbying power of private corporate interests. This is despite evidence that alternatives to detention from a range of studies have very high success rates, especially when they are well managed; the figures usually cited are that approximately 95 percent of those in the schemes attend their hearings, though the Home Office is unable to provide data on this question.

The United Kingdom currently uses two alternatives to detention: reporting and electronic monitoring. In the first case, the person is required to report to an immigration office or to the police, usually weekly. Currently, 60,000 people report in this way, at a cost to the government of £8.6 million a year, with a reporting rate of 95 percent. The second alternative, a radio frequency bracelet, is used in the case of just over 500 people a year, at a cost of £515 per month. This cost might seem high until it is noted that it represents about one sixth of the cost of incarcerating someone (The APPG Inquiry into the Use of Immigration Detention in the United Kingdom 2015, 25). An alternative that could be considered is bail, which is only an alternative for those who have already been detained. Detainees report that it is quite difficult to access bail in UK detention facilities because of lack of information and help obtaining it (The APPG Inquiry into the Use of Immigration Detention in the United Kingdom 2015). Bail is available for detainees after they have been in detention for seven days. An application is made and then heard in an immigration court by a judge. Applicants have to be able to provide an address where they plan to live, which is sometimes a barrier to a successful application. The more resources applicants have, including a lawyer representing them and a person willing to act as a surety to guarantee that they will not abscond, the higher the chances of a successful application.

All these alternative methods are individually based and are used only at the end of the process, once the person has been identified as someone to be detained or already detained (The APPG Inquiry into the Use of Immigration Detention in the United Kingdom 2015). Countries such as Sweden, which use a community-based model, have lower costs, higher levels of compliance, and higher rates of voluntary returns (The APPG Inquiry into the Use of Immigration Detention in the United Kingdom 2015, 26).

The United States has a wider array of alternatives to detention. They include parole/release on own recognizance, bond check-ins at ICE offices, home visits and check-ins, telephonic monitoring, and GPS monitoring through an electronic ankle bracelet (Detention Watch Network n.d.). Under the Obama administration, efforts were made to minimize the length of detention stays. As part of this effort, the Department of Homeland Security developed a risk assessment tool "to balance vulnerabilities with [other] factors, such as risk of flight and danger to the community, enabling decisions to be taken in respect of release and the types of conditions, if any, to be imposed" (Detention Watch Network n.d., 30). NGOs work with the government on various projects designed to identify those who can be released from detention and ensure their compliance with conditions of release. However, despite the efforts to reduce the numbers of those in detention by the use of alternatives, advocates argue that this has not translated into lower use of detention. Not surprisingly, these efforts have diminished in the Trump administration.

Nor have the costs of detention diminished with efforts to provide alternatives to detention. In fact, funds appropriated for alternatives have steadily increased over the last decade or so (Global Detention Project 2016, 11). It appears that this is because the emphasis is on the use of high-tech methods, including electronic-monitoring devices and other surveillance methods that, like the management of detention generally, is outsourced to the same private contractors who are its beneficiaries. According to Detention Watch Network, all but the bond and parole hearings that are already part of the legal system are outsourced to GEO Group Inc. mentioned earlier as one of the private contractors profiting from the detention system. Given such corporate interest in profits, it is hardly surprising that the use of such high-tech methods of control has increased, and that concerns about due process and the rule of law take second place.

Obtaining bail in the United States (called a bond or parole hearing) from immigration detention also appears to be difficult. This is part of the "zero tolerance" policy of the Trump administration, which has made claiming asylum more difficult in every way, though analysis of this process is beyond the scope of this chapter. Again, it is a matter of lack of information provided by the detention centers and a lack of available legal assistance. In the United States there is no mandatory legal aid available for those administratively detained, added to which is the fact that many detention centers are located in isolated places, far from legal centers. One positive effect of the Trump administration efforts to deter asylum seekers from coming to the United States and detaining when they seek asylum has been the outpouring of pro bono legal support by lawyers, legal clinics, and law students. Asylum seekers who are detained while awaiting the hearing of their claims are entitled to be considered for release on parole. In a recent case, a federal court ordered the Buffalo Federal Detention Facility in Batavia, New York, to stop detaining asylum seekers without a fair opportunity for release on parole or bond while awaiting asylum hearings. After the election of Donald Trump, federal officials stopped granting parole. The court order requires the authorities provide "in a language they understand . . . a parole interview with an immigration officer, be provided an explanation for their parole decision and be informed they can seek reconsideration if parole is initially denied" (NYCLU 2017).

Vulnerable People in Detention

There has been some public and governmental concern in both the United States and the United Kingdom about detaining those who are particularly vulnerable. Children, pregnant women, those with mental health problems, those who have been trafficked or tortured, and unaccompanied minors have all been considered to be vulnerable. The NGOs that work with these groups of migrants believe that they should not be detained at all, or if so, only for the minimum possible time with careful monitoring. The UNHCR has published guidelines about detention, which includes an extensive section about the appropriate ways of taking into account the special needs of some detainees (UNHCR Detention Guidelines 2012).

In the United States, ICE policy is that pregnant women should not be detained "absent extraordinary circumstances or the requirements of mandatory detention" (Garcia 2015). In November 2014, along with announcing expanded protections for some immigrants, the Department of Homeland Security reiterated the directive not to detain pregnant women and other vulnerable populations (Garcia 2015). Statistics are hard to come by, but for six detention centers, 559 of the women detained between 2012 and 2014 were pregnant (Garcia 2015). Ironically, in a recent case of a pregnant minor in custody, the Trump administration wanted to force her not to have a legal abortion (NBC News 2018). When the case went to federal court in Washington, the Trump administration was told that they cannot interfere with the ability of pregnant immigrant teens to obtain an abortion (NBC News 2018).

The United States has detained families, including children as well as unaccompanied minors, though until recently, women and children were rarely detained (Morales 2016). Under the Trump administration, this has increased exponentially, as the public has been made aware (see, e.g., Barry et al. 2018; Silverman 2018). The public concern about detaining families was precipitated by the huge influx in 2014, and subsequently, of migrants fleeing violence in the Northern Triangle States of Central America. New family detention centers (politely called "family residential centers") were constructed to house the families from Central America in Texas and Pennsylvania (Global Detention Project 2016, 8). This building boom has continued at a rapid rate under the Trump administration (Dayen 2018; Silverman 2018).

The medical treatment for pregnant women in detention is no better than the medical care in general, described earlier. A complaint has recently been filed against the U.S. Department of Homeland Security by seven rights groups, which accuses immigration officials of not only improperly detaining pregnant women but also failing to provide them with adequate medical care (Etehad 2017). In one case, a pregnant asylum seeker at the border showed officials her scan and said she was bleeding and needed immediate medical attention. The officials ignored her request and detained her; it took two days before she had a medical exam, and she was told four days later that she had had a miscarriage (Etehad 2017).

In the United Kingdom, the government has pledged to stop detaining both children and pregnant women. Under section 60 of the Immigration Act 2016, the detention of pregnant women is limited to 72 hours (with a limited possibility of an extension to 7 days). This change in the law came as a result of the outcry caused by the revelation in 2015 that 99 pregnant women were being held at Yarl's Wood, a major detention center in the United Kingdom (Boffey 2016). The UK Minister for Justice told the Parliamentary investigation that pregnant women were only detained for very short periods prior to removal, or as part of the fast-track removal process designed to deal quickly with people the government believes have little chance of success in their asylum claims (The APPG Inquiry into the Use of Immigration Detention in the United Kingdom 2015, 76). However, a team inspector at HM Prison Inspectorate said there was no evidence that pregnant women were only being detained in exceptional circumstances (The APPG Inquiry into the Use of Immigration Detention in the United Kingdom 2015).

Children are clearly vulnerable, and governments and researchers alike agree that they should not be put into detention. Under international law, they should only be detained as a last resort. In the United Kingdom, the coalition government of 2010–2015 made a pledge to end child detention entirely. However, despite this pledge, 71 children were detained in 2016 (Lindley 2017, 2). This problem is exacerbated in those cases where the children are incorrectly assessed as being adults, a practice that happens quite often in the United Kingdom (The APPG Inquiry into the Use of Immigration

Detention in the United Kingdom 2015, 32; Bohmer and Shuman 2018, 62–66). Some of these children were unaccompanied, which strengthens the argument that they should not be detained, especially in adult facilities.

In the United States, the policy on unaccompanied minors is as follows:

> When a child who is not accompanied by a parent or legal guardian is apprehended by immigration authorities, the child is transferred to the care and custody of the Office of Refugee Resettlement (ORR). Federal law requires that ORR feed, shelter, and provide medical care for unaccompanied alien children until it is able to release them to safe settings with sponsors (usually family members), while they await immigration proceedings. (Office of Refugee Resettlement 2017)

Despite this positive-sounding concern, the figures tell a very different story, especially recently. The latest figures available from the Department of Health and Human Services indicate that 10,773 unaccompanied immigrant children were in detention facilities as of May 2018, up from 8,886 on April 29, 2018 (Miroff 2018) This increase in just a month has been attributed to the Trump "zero tolerance" policy (Miroff 2018).

Given the U.S. and international law and policy toward unaccompanied minors, all detention is inappropriate. The Trump administration not only has been more willing to detain children but also has initiated policies to separate children. This practice of separating children from their parents has caused a huge public outcry, not to mention a statement by the United Nations that the practice is in violation of international law (Cumming-Bruce 2018). Children are now often detained for long periods, in violation of what is known as the *Flores Settlement*, a 1997 Federal Court agreement that sets down rules about how children should be treated in the immigration system (*Flores v. Reno* 1997). Under that agreement, the government agreed to release children without unnecessary delay, and when they have to detain them, to do so in the least restrictive setting possible. In early September 2018, the Trump administration moved to remove the time limits on the detention of migrant children by withdrawing from the consent decree of the *Flores Settlement*. This would make it possible for families to be held indefinitely in secure facilities as their cases wend through the immigration courts (Dickerson 2018a).

Victims of trafficking represent a clear example of a group that is clearly vulnerable and in need of special protection. In the United Kingdom, there has been much attention to the plight of those who have been trafficked into slave-like conditions, with the government expressing great concern both about prosecuting traffickers and protecting those who are trafficked. In April 2017, the Home Secretary, Amber Rudd, expressed concern about "thousands of poor souls being exploited and abused in brothels, nail bars and car washes across the country" (Trafficked into Detention 2017, 3). She gave the commitment that the government would get "immediate support to victims when they are their most vulnerable" (Trafficked into Detention 2017, 3). Unfortunately, as is so often the case, there is a conflict of interest between the government's concern to protect trafficking victims and their need to be tough on those in the country without legal status. Given the political priority of enforcing the laws that lead to deportation, it is not surprising that the government's claim to provide help to trafficking victims is honored more in the breach than the observance. A recent report by Detention Action claims that a significant minority of those in detention are trafficking victims (Trafficked into Detention 2017). Once in detention, it is much harder for trafficking victims to access the specialist help the government provides through its trafficking decision-making process, the National Referral Mechanism (NRM). Under the rules of that two-stage process, which are designed to comply with international law, a person is first determined to have reasonable grounds for being a trafficking victim, and then, in the second stage, a determination is made that there are conclusive grounds for this outcome. The Detention Action report describes a sample group of 16 Vietnamese men in detention who had indications of having been trafficked. Only nine had been referred into the NRM, and only two had received a positive reasonable grounds decision, which is a much lower rate than the national average of those referred to the NRM who are not in detention. The national average of those not in detention is between 74 and 90 percent (Trafficked into Detention 2017, 3–4). Many of the men referred to the NRM whose claims were rejected continued to be detained, in one case for 15 months (Trafficked into Detention 2017, 1).

The United States is also concerned about protecting those who are trafficked into the country. In fact, the United States has been a leader in identifying, and working to reduce, the problem of trafficking worldwide. In its annual reports on trafficking in persons, the United States ranks those countries that are working to reduce trafficking as well as those where the problem is rife (U.S. Trafficking in Persons Report 2017). The criterion for this ranking includes assessments of available services and protections as an alternative to detention and more particularly legal alternatives for victims who "would face retribution or hardship" if returned to their home countries (U.S. Trafficking in Persons Report 2017, 26). However, despite this concern, the United States also seems to follow the UK pattern of detaining those who have been the subject of such concern in the work to reduce trafficking. In a letter to an official in the Trafficking in Persons Unit, a representative of Human Rights Watch describes a number of trafficking victims they have discovered during their research who have been detained in the United States despite having been trafficked (Human Rights Watch 2010).

The Unreturnables

According to a fundamental principle of international law (known as *nonre-foulement*), a state cannot return someone to his or her country of origin when the person is at risk of persecution based on one of the asylum grounds (race, religion, nationality, membership in a particular social group, or political opinion) (UN High Commissioner for Refugees 1997). Under this principle, people cannot be repatriated to war zones or other disaster areas. What this means, for our purposes, is that some people, whose asylum claims have been denied, cannot be returned to their countries of origin without violating international law. The problem is that, from the point of view of dealing with migrants who have no legal status, the assumption is that if they are not permitted to stay in the host country, they are to be returned to their home country.

There are also other reasons why migrants without legal status cannot be returned; they may be stateless (i.e., have no state that recognizes them as citizens), or they may be from a particular country but that country refuses to acknowledge it or give them a passport or accept them back (for whatever reason). In the United Kingdom, the Home Office makes a great effort to persuade such recalcitrant countries to accept "their" nationals, with mixed success. Meanwhile, the person is likely to be in detention for an indefinite period. As the Detention Action report puts it: "If you visit any detention centre, you will quickly meet unreturnable migrants. They will usually be the people who have been there longest. They will show you monthly reports from the Home Office: updates on the progress of attempts to remove them. Sometimes they chart the third, fourth, fifth futile meeting with the embassy. Sometimes the chronology simply stops: nothing has happened for months" (The State of Detention 2014, 8). The United Kingdom, as mentioned earlier, stands out in Europe in having indefinite detention in which unreturnable people are left in limbo in detention centers. In other countries, Germany, for example, such migrants are given some sort of temporary status, which, while remaining a kind of limbo, at least enables them to live outside a detention center (The State of Detention 2014, 9).

In the United States, Supreme Court decisions have ruled that stateless persons cannot be detained indefinitely if they cannot be deported (*Clark v. Martinez* 2005; *Zadvydas v. Davis* 2001). After someone has been in detention for six months, the burden shifts to the U.S. government to prove that the removal of a noncitizen in deportation proceedings is possible in the reasonably foreseeable future, thereby limiting the possibility that someone will languish in detention indefinitely. Nonetheless, a Migration Policy Institute report in 2009 found that 950 people were detained for more than six months after receiving a final deportation order (Kerwin and Yi-Ying Lin 2009, 4). Clearly, the U.S. government is reluctant to admit that there are people who cannot be returned but do not have legal status to stay.

Deportation

As we saw earlier, the major reason to detain someone in immigration detention is to facilitate their deportation. Both the United States and the United Kingdom officially use the term "removal" (voluntary or forced) rather than deportation. Other terms used are "repatriation" (the general term) and "return" as a synonym for voluntary removal. This illustrates the common practice of using terms that seem more neutral as the old ones collect negative baggage.[1] In the United States, it is deportation that is currently in the news; the Trump administration is focusing on removing as many people as possible, including those who have been in the United States for many years and are model migrants except for their undocumented status. Among those who are horrified by what they view as callous and inappropriate governmental action, the term "deportation nation" has now become widespread; the term seems to have been originally used by Daniel Kanstroom (2007).

In his first week in office, Trump implemented his campaign promise to deport "bad hombres." The definition of "criminal alien" at high risk of deportation now includes "any undocumented immigrant convicted of a crime or believed to have committed 'acts that constitute a chargeable criminal offense'—essentially, anyone who is suspected of a crime, but has not yet been charged" (Santos 2017). How that translated into numbers is a more complicated issue; under both the Bush and Obama administrations, large numbers of people were also deported. The numbers are dependent on a variety of factors, including how many people try to cross the border and how often, and what the "push" factors are, such as economic conditions and the amount of violence in the home country. In 2016, a total of 240,255 persons were deported from the United States, and 226,119 in 2017. While the figure for 2017 was less than that for 2016, this can be accounted for by a significant reduction in the numbers of those trying to cross the border and a significant increase in those apprehended and deported from within the country (U.S. Immigration and Enforcement 2017, 12). These figures might change in the future as a result of the recent Supreme Court decision of *Pereira v. Sessions* (2018). As one commentator pointed out: "For years, immigration authorities have been skipping one simple step in the process: When they served notices to appear in court, they routinely left the court date blank. Now, because of that omission and a recent Supreme Court decision, tens of thousands of deportation cases could be delayed, or tossed out altogether" (Rose 2018).

In the United Kingdom, little public attention was paid to deportation until the recent Windrush scandal, which surfaced in 2017 and became front-page news in 2018 (Rawlinson 2018). It was revealed that the government had refused citizenship to hundreds of people from the Caribbean, despite the fact that they had been living legally in the United Kingdom for many decades. Many of those people have been detained, and some of them deported; in the year before the matter came to public attention, the government had deported 996 people to the Caribbean (Grierson 2018).

Before the publicity of the treatment of those included in the Windrush scandal, as we saw earlier, attention was on the conditions and duration of detention. Out of the public eye, however, the government has actually had targets of numbers for removal, information that has only become public recently. Information leaked to *The Guardian* newspaper revealed that the target for 2017–2018 was 12,800 and that the government was on the "path towards the 10% increased performance on enforced returns, which we promised the home secretary earlier this year" (Hopkins and Stewart 2018).

The UK government also puts efforts into persuading undocumented migrants to return "voluntarily." The total number of those deported in fiscal year 2017 was 12,542 (National Statistics 2017). Of those, 1970 were failed asylum seekers (National Statistics 2017).

Forced returns are costly for governments, though, of course, much cheaper than detention. Figures are hard to come by, but the costs are considerable. As a result of the attention drawn to this issue by the Windrush case, some light has been shed on how much it costs the UK government to deport migrants. "The data provided reveals that in a two-year period from 2015 to 2017, the government spent £52m on all deportation flights" (National Statistics 2017). Many forced returns are on chartered flights, which require hiring the planes and staffing them with security staff to manage the returns. Between March 2015 and March 2018, there were 114 charter flights, including 40 in the most recent 12-month period; the cost for the last two years was £17.7 million (National Statistics 2017). Even if someone is deported on an ordinary flight, in the United States that person is accompanied by an ICE agent, who will need a round-trip ticket. The UK government has a program that assists those willing to return voluntarily; they offer up to £2,000 to eligible people who are willing to return home voluntarily (UK Government, n.d.). According to an EU research report, the program assisted 10,000 people to return home between 2008 and 2011 (Assisted Voluntary Return n.d.). These voluntary return programs are a worldwide phenomenon: the International Organization of Migration (IOM) provided Assisted Voluntary Return (AVR) support to 69,000 migrants in 2015 and 98,000 in 2016; the number was expected to rise further in 2017 (Newland and Salant 2017). Research shows, however, that these programs have little effect on the numbers returning; the benefits are used by those who were planning to return anyway, leaving unresolved the larger problem of forced return (Newland and Salant 2017). In the United States, voluntary departure is the equivalent to voluntary return in the United Kingdom and elsewhere, though there is no money involved; its only benefit is in the circumstances under which someone can legally return to the United States.

Several scholars question the "voluntary" nature of AVR schemes, also called "pay-to-go programmes" (Collyer 2017, 105). The goal is to incentivize migrants to leave, not necessarily to return to their home countries. Michael Collyer observes that some immigrants agree to leave only because the alternative is to remain in detention (2017, 106).

The problem of nonrefoulement, discussed earlier, is relevant here. Both the United States and the United Kingdom have been accused of sending people back to dangerous places in violation of that international legal principle. In the United Kingdom, the Home Office has been stripping refugees of their status if they have a criminal record, opening the possibility of their being sent back to places like Somalia, Afghanistan, and the Democratic Republic of the Congo (McKinney 2018). The United Kingdom is not alone in returning many people to Afghanistan, at a time when there is ample evidence that the security situation is dangerous and worsening (Boffey 2017). The number returned by the European Union has tripled between 2015 and 2016, including Christian converts and unaccompanied children who are at particular risk on return. Even countries that have traditionally welcomed migrants, like Sweden and Norway, have been involved in sending back young people (Girouard 2017). It seems that the European Union is tired of the influx of asylum seekers from Afghanistan and is responding by denying asylum to an increased number, as well as returning them in likely violation of the principle of nonrefoulement. The situation has so horrified pilots in Germany assigned to fly the asylum seekers back that they refused to fly the planes (Sharman 2017).

In the United States, many individuals determined to have entered illegally are returned to dangerous places in Central America. Since Trump came to power, the efforts to deport those who fled the violence of Central America, especially since 2014, have increased dramatically. Just as in Europe, the numbers of those granted asylum in the United States (or even been permitted to stay in the United States and claim asylum instead of being summarily returned at the border) have diminished significantly (Silverman 2018). Also, as discussed earlier, many of those who have lived in the United States for decades are being deported, often to places they barely know. For some, the return is simply to a miserable life with no future (Lakhani 2017). To others, it can be a death sentence. An in-depth study followed a number of those deported back to the countries from which they fled, resulting in some cases in their deaths, which was exactly what they or their families had predicted would happen (Stillman 2018). Despite this clear evidence that international law has been violated, sadly it is too late for those who have already died, and the current administration does not seem to be troubled by the fate of those who are deported from the United States. The efforts to deport a planeload of undocumented Somalis (one of five flights carrying those who were deported in 2017) who had lived in the United States for decades illustrates the length the U.S. government will go to deport people, however unsafe their country of origin is (Ibrahim 2018). The flight, in December 2017, never made it to Somalia. "Logistical problems forced the flight back to the U.S. after it reached Senegal in West Africa, according to immigration officials" (Ibrahim 2018). The flight is now the subject of a class-action lawsuit that claims that it is unsafe to send the migrants to Somalia, where they will be targeted as coming from the West by Al Shabab (Ibrahim 2018). A judge has placed a temporary stay on the deportation of Somalis while the case is being argued.

Conclusion

This chapter has outlined some of the effects of the current migrant crisis on the detention and deportation of those deemed not to be entitled to live in the United Kingdom and the United States. Both countries follow similar patterns: a significant increase in the number of those detained and an increased emphasis on deportation, sometimes with little regard for their fate on return and the legal requirements underpinning their return. It paints a harsh picture, when the fear of the "unwelcome other" overrides the concern for protection of those fleeing danger and harm in their home countries. There are some small positive efforts to fight back against these policies. There has been a huge effort by lawyers, law students, and social workers dealing on the ground with the recent "zero tolerance" policy, which has been mentioned earlier. There has also been a major effort on the part of legal NGOs to take test cases to court, in both the United States and the United Kingdom, which have had some positive results, which were also mentioned earlier. However, these efforts are individual and relatively small, compared to the widespread impact of the policies in both countries. While many people were appalled by the most egregious of the new policies by the Trump administration, notably the separation of children from their parents, there are many in both countries who are concerned about the perceived or real increase in unauthorized immigrants. They support tight measures to control immigration, and detention and deportation are obvious ways of doing this. The problem is global, even though the solutions we describe are local. As long as migrants keep coming, fleeing violence and poverty, host countries are likely to continue to push them back, by the various means available.

Note

1. "Removals (deportations) are the compulsory and confirmed movement of an inadmissible or deportable unauthorized immigrant out of the United States based on an order of removal. An unauthorized immigrant who is removed has

administrative or criminal consequences placed on subsequent reentry owing to the fact of the removal. Returns are the confirmed movement of an inadmissible or deportable unauthorized immigrant out of the United States not based on an order of removal. Most voluntary departures (returns) are of Mexican nationals who have been apprehended by the Border Patrol and are returned to Mexico" (Zong, Batalova, and Hallock 2018).

References

ACLU. 2018. "ACLU Obtains Documents Showing Widespread Abuse of Child Immigrants in U.S. Custody." May 22, 2018. https://www.aclu.org/news/aclu-obtains-documents-showing-widespread-abuse-child-immigrants-us-custody.

Amnesty International United Kingdom Section. 2017. *A Matter of Routine: Immigration Detention in the UK.* https://www.amnesty.org.uk/files/2017-12/A%20Matter%20Of%20Routine%20ADVANCE%20COPY.PDF?ya06n1Z2uH6J0bP8HmO7R2Pn7nabDymO=.

"The APPG Inquiry into the Use of Immigration Detention in the United Kingdom." 2015. A Joint Inquiry by the All Party Parliamentary Group on Refugees & the All Party Parliamentary Group on Migration. March 3, 2015. https://detentioninquiry.files.wordpress.com/2015/03/immigration-detention-inquiry-report.pdf.

Bacon, Christine. 2005. "The Evolution of Immigration Detention in the UK: The Involvement of Private Prison Companies." Refugee Studies Centre, RSC, Working Paper No. 27, September 2005.

Baey, Dan, Miriam Jordan, Annie Correal, and Manny Fernandez. 2018. "Cleaning Toilets, Following Rules: A Migrant Child's Days in Detention: A Portrait of Life in the Shelters for the Children Detained after Crossing the U.S.-Mexico Border." *The New York Times*, July 14, 2018. https://www.nytimes.com/2018/07/14/us/migrant-children-shelters.html.

Bernstein, Nina. 2010. "Officials Hid Truth of Immigrant Deaths in Jail." *The New York Times*, January 9, 2010. https://www.nytimes.com/2010/01/10/us/10detain.html.

Bail for Immigration Detainees. 2017. "Michael's Experience of Detention." November 28, 2017. http://www.biduk.org/posts/325.

Boffey, Daniel. 2016. "Theresa May to Put 72-Hour Limit on Detention of Pregnant Asylum Seekers." *The Observer*, April 17, 2016.

Boffey, Daniel. 2017. "Britain Accused of Unlawfully Deporting Afghan Asylum Seekers." *The Guardian*, October 5, 2017. https://www.theguardian.com/world/2017/oct/05/britain-accused-of-unlawfully-deporting-afghan-asylum-seekers-amnesty.

Bohmer, Carol, and Amy Shuman. 2018. *Political Asylum Deceptions: The Culture of Suspicion.* London: Palgrave Macmillan.

Bohmer, Carol, and Richard Ned Lebow. 2015. "Why Deterrence Won't Solve the Mediterranean Migrant Crisis." *The Telegraph*. April 21, 2015.

Bulman, May. 2017. "Home Office Systematically Ignores Medical Advice to Keep Mentally Ill Immigrants in Detention." *The Independent Online*. November 25, 2017. https://www.independent.co.uk/news/uk/home-news/home-office-mentally-ill-detention-centre-immigration-a8062446.html.

Bulman, May. 2018. "Suicides in Immigration Detention Centres Being Kept a 'State Secret', MPs Told." *The Independent*. September 12, 2018. https://www.independent.co.uk/news/uk/home-news/immigration-detention-centres-uk-suicides-prison-deaths-home-office-a8533366.html.

Campbell, Ruth. 2017. "Locked Up, Locked Out: Health and Human Rights in Immigration Detention." *British Medical Association*. https://www.bma.org.uk/-/media/files/pdfs/collective%20voice/policy%20research/ethics/locked-up-locked-out-immigration-detention-report-bma-2017.pdf.

Cante, Fabien. 2018a. "Unlawful Detention Cost the UK Government £21 Million." *Migrants Rights Network*. January 23, 2018. https://migrantsrights.org.uk/blog/2018/01/23/unlawful-detention-cost-uk-government-21-million/?mc_cid=a081e9e6c2&mc_eid=83c32043ad.

Cante, Fabien. 2018b. "Highest Recorded Number of Suicides in Detention Last Year." *Migrants Rights Network*. May 15, 2018. https://migrantsrights.org.uk/blog/2018/05/15/highest-recorded-number-of-suicides-in-detention-last-year/.

Chaverra v. ICE et al. 2018. Civil Action No.: 1:18-cv-289.

Clark v. Martinez. 543 US 371 (2005).

Collyer, Michael. 2017. "Paying to Go: Deportability as Development" In *After Deportation: Ethnographic Perspectives*. Edited by Shahram Khosravi, 105–125. New York: Palgrave Macmillan.

Corporate Watch. 2018. "Detention Centre Profits: 20% and Up for the Migration Prison Bosses." *Corporatewatch2*, July 18, 2018. https://corporatewatch.org/detention-centre-profits-20-and-up-for-the-migration-prison-bosses/.

Crowdjustice. 2018. "It's Like Hell"—It's Time to Stop G4S." https://mail.google.com/mail/u/0/?shva=1#inbox/1619f4a4b6538363.

Cumming-Bruce, Nick. 2018. "Taking Migrant Children from Parents Is Illegal, U.N. Tells U.S." *The New York Times*, June 5, 2018. https://www.nytimes.com/2018/06/05/world/americas/us-un-migrant-children-families.html.

Dayen, David. 2018. "How Private Contractors Enable Trump's Cruelties at the Border." *The Nation*, June 20. https://www.thenation.com/article/private-contractors-enable-trumps-cruelties-border/.

Deaths in Adult Detention Centers. 2018. *American Immigration Lawyers Association*. AILA Doc. No. 16050900. July 26, 2018. https://www.aila.org/infonet/deaths-at-adult-detention-centers.

DeGenova, Nicholas P. 2012. "Migrant 'Illegality' and Deportability in Everyday Life." *Annual Review of Anthropology*, 31, 419–447.

Detention Watch Network. n.d. "Alternatives to Detention." https://www.detentionwatchnetwork.org/issues/alternatives.

Dickerson, Caitlin. 2018a. "Trump Administration Moves to Sidestep Restrictions on Detaining Migrant Children." *The New York Times*, September 6, 2018. https://www.nytimes.com/2018/09/06/us/trump-flores-settlement-regulations.html.

Dickerson, Caitlin. 2018b. "Detention of Migrant Children Has Skyrocketed to Highest Levels Ever." *The New York Times*, September 12, 2018. https://www.nytimes.com/2018/09/12/us/migrant-children-detention.html?action=click&module=Top%20Stories&pgtype=Homepage.

Eagly, Ingrid, Steven Shafer, and Jana Whalley. 2018. "Detaining Families: A Study of Asylum Adjudication in Family Detention." *American Immigration Council*. Special Report, August 2018. https://www.americanimmigrationcouncil.org/research/detaining-families-a-study-of-asylum-adjudication-in-family-detention.

Eisen, Lauren-Brooke. 2018. "Trump's First Year Has Been the Private Prison Industry's Best." *Salon*, January 14, 2018. https://www.salon.com/2018/01/14/trumps-first-year-has-been-the-private-prison-industrys-best/.

Etehad, Melissa. 2017. "Complaint Alleges Harm to Pregnant Women in Immigration Detention Centers." *Los Angeles Times*, September 28, 2017. http://www.latimes.com/nation/la-na-pregnant-women-ice-20170928-story.html.

European Commission Migration and Home Affairs. n.d. Assisted Voluntary Return (AVR). https://ec.europa.eu/home-affairs/financing/fundings/projects/project_example_071_en.

Flores v. Reno. 1997. USDC Central District of California. Case Number 85–4544-RJK(Px). https://www.aclu.org/legal-document/flores-v-meese-stipulated-settlement-agreement-plus-extension-settlement.

Ford, Richard, and Phil Miller. 2018. "Immigration Centres Accused of Slavery Over £1-an-Hour Pay." *The Times*, January 28, 2018. https://www.thetimes.co.uk/article/immigration-centres-accused-of-slavery-over-1-an-hour-pay-n8qf2lc7t.

Freedom for Immigrants. n.d. Detention by the Numbers: Where Are People Detained in the United States? https://www.freedomforimmigrants.org/detention-statistics/.

Gallagher, Alanna. 2017. *The Impact of Immigration Detention on the Mental Health of Adults*. D.Clin.Psychol. thesis, Canterbury Christ Church University. http://create.canterbury.ac.uk/16429/#ZY0mzpVtG6l64wxB.99.

Garcia, Yamileth. 2015. "Immigration Detention Is Inhumane, but for Pregnant Women, It's Trauma." *The Guardian*, July 27, 2015.

Girouard, Catherine. 2017. "'Sweden Sends Us to Be Killed': Young Afghans Face Perilous Deportation." *The Guardian*, December 21, 2017.

Global Detention Project. 2016. *United States Immigration Detention Profile* https://www.globaldetentionproject.org/immigration-detention-in-the-united-states.

Gonzales, Richard. 2018. "Trump Administration and Advocates Clash over What's Next for Migrant Children." *National Public Radio*, June 11, 2018.

https://www.npr.org/2018/06/11/618831715/more-than-10-000-migrant-children-are-in-u-s-government-custody.

Grabell, Michael, and Topher Sanders. 2018. "Immigrant Youth Shelters: 'If You're a Predator, It's a Gold Mine.'" *ProPublica*, July 27, 2018. https://www.propublica.org/article/immigrant-youth-shelters-sexual-abuse-fights-missing-children?token=d0bN47zStvHcmbER7GvkvKAYTIy9JN7t.

Grierson, Jamie. 2018. "991 People Deported to Caribbean in Year before Windrush Row." *The Guardian*, June 5, 2018.

Gumbel, Andrew. 2018. "'They Were Laughing at Us': Immigrants Tell of Cruelty, Illness and Filth in US Detention." *The Guardian*, September 12, 2018. https://www.theguardian.com/us-news/2018/sep/12/us-immigration-detention-facilities?utm_source=esp&utm_medium=Email&utm_campaign=GU+Today+USA+-+Collections+2017&utm_term=285449&subid=19012606&CMP=GT_US_collection.

Hernandez, César Cuauhtémoc García. 2014. "Immigration Detention as Punishment." *UCLA Law Review* 61: 1346–1414.

Hopkins, Nick, and Heather Stewart. 2018. "Amber Rudd Was Sent Targets for Migrant Removal, Leak Reveals." *The Guardian*, April 28, 2018. https://www.theguardian.com/politics/2018/apr/27/amber-rudd-was-told-about-migrant-removal-targets-leak-reveals.

Human Rights Watch. 2010. "US: Victims of Trafficking Held in ICE Detention: Letter to the US Department of State on 2010 Trafficking in Persons Report." April 19, 2010. https://www.hrw.org/news/2010/04/19/us-victims-trafficking-held-ice-detention.

Human Rights Watch. 2017. "Systemic Indifference: Dangerous and Substandard Medical Care in US Immigration Detention." May 8, 2017. https://www.hrw.org/news/2017/05/08/us-detention-hazardous-immigrants-health.

Ilori, R. (On the Application of) v SSHD [2017 EWHC (Admin). December 21, 2017.

Jesuit Refugee Service, Europe. 2010. *Becoming Vulnerable in Detention: Civil Society Report on the Detention of Vulnerable Asylum-Seekers and Irregular Migrants in the European Union.* Jesuit Refugee Service. https://idcoalition.org/news/jesuit-refugee-service-europe-becoming-vulnerable-in-detention/.

Juarez, Melina, Barbara Gomez-Aguinaga, and Sonia P. Bettez. 2018. "Twenty Years after IIRIRA: The Rise of Immigrant Detention and Its Effects on Latinx Communities across the Nation." *Journal on Migration and Human Security* 6, no. 1: 74–96.

Kanstroom, Daniel. 2007. *Deportation Nation: Outsiders in American History.* Cambridge, MA: Harvard University Press.

Kerwin, Donald M., and Serena Yi-Ying Lin. 2009. *Immigrant Detention: Can ICE Meet Its Legal Imperatives and Case Management Responsibilities?* Washington, DC: Migration Policy Institute. https://www.migrationpolicy.org/research/immigrant-detention-can-ice-meet-its-legal-imperatives-and-case-management-responsibilities.

Laird, Lorelei. 2018. "Lawsuit Alleges Government Unlawfully Drugs Unaccompanied Minor Immigrants." *ABA Journal*, May 8, 2018. http://www.abajournal.com/news/article/lawsuit_alleges_government_unlawfully_drugs_unaccompanied_minor_immigrants.

Lakhani, Nina. 2017. "This Is What the Hours after Being Deported Look Like." *The Guardian*, December 12, 2017. https://www.theguardian.com/inequality/2017/dec/12/mexico-deportation-tijuana-trump-border.

Lee, Esther Yu Hsi. 2017. "Private Prison CEO 'Very Pleased' by 'Improved Occupancy Rates' at Immigration Detention Centers." *Think Progress*. https://thinkprogress.org/geo-group-3q-earnings-ice-4201f399b46d/.

Lindley, Anna. 2017. "Injustice in Immigration Detention: Perspectives from Legal Professionals." Bar Council, November 2017. https://zapdoc.tips/injustice-in-immigration-detention-perspectives-from-legal-p.html.

Loewenstein, Antony. 2014. "Lowest Cost Matters Most in Britain's Immigration Detention Centres." *The Guardian*, July 25, 2014. https://www.theguardian.com/commentisfree/2014/jul/25/lowest-cost-matters-most-in-britains-immigration-detention-centres.

Luan, Livia. 2018. "Profiting from Enforcement: The Role of Private Prisons in U.S. Immigration Detention." Migration Policy Institute, May 2, 2018. https://www.migrationpolicy.org/article/profiting-enforcement-role-private-prisons-us-immigration-detention.

Martinez, Sofia. 2018. "Today's Migrant Flow Is Different." *The Atlantic*, June 26, 2018. https://www.theatlantic.com/international/archive/2018/06/central-america-border-immigration/563744/.

McKinney, Connor James. 2018. "Refugees with Criminal Records Are Being Told It's Safe to Go Home." *Free Movement*. https://www.freemovement.org.uk/watchdog-investigates-how-people-are-stripped-of-immigration-status/.

Miroff, Nick. 2018. "Trump's 'Zero Tolerance' at the Border Is Causing Child Shelters to Fill up Fast." *Washington Post*, May 29, 2018. https://www.washingtonpost.com/world/national-security/trumps-zero-tolerance-at-the-border-is-causing-child-shelters-to-fill-up-fast/2018/05/29/7aab0ae4–636b-11e8-a69c-b944de66d9e7_story.html?noredirect=on&utm_term=.37fd8e842737.

Morales, Claudia. 2016. "Families Crossing the Border: 'We Are Not Criminals.'" *CNN*, November 2, 2016. https://edition.cnn.com/2016/11/02/us/family-immigration-detention-centers/index.html.

National Statistics. 2017. *How Many People Are Detained or Returned?* August 24, 2017. https://www.gov.uk/government/publications/immigration-statistics-april-to-june-2017/how-many-people-are-detained-or-returned.

NBC News. 2018. "Federal Court Rules Government Can't Block Detained Immigrant Teens from Abortion." *NBC News*, March 30, 2018. https://www.nbcnews.com/news/us-news/federal-court-rules-government-can-t-block-detained-immigrant-teens-n861671.

Newland, Kathleen, and Brian Salant. 2017. "Increased Focus on Forced Return of Migrants and Asylum Seekers Puts Many in Peril." *Migration Information Source*, December 12, 2017.

NYCLU. 2017. "Court Orders Federal Immigration Jail in Buffalo to Offer Parole, Bond Hearings for Asylum-Seekers." November 20, 2017. https://www.nyclu.org/en/press-releases/court-orders-federal-immigration-jail-buffalo-offer-parole-bond-hearings-asylum.

Office of Refugee Resettlement. 2017. "Unaccompanied Alien Children Released to Sponsors by State." June 30, 2017. https://www.acf.hhs.gov/orr/resource/unaccompanied-alien-children-released-to-sponsors-by-state.

Pennington, Jed. 2014. "Immigration Detention—A Shameful, Inhumane System." *Socialist Lawyer*, June 2014, 20.

Pereira v. Sessions 138 S. Ct. 2105 (2018).

Physicians for Human Rights and the Bellevue/NYU Program for Survivors of Torture. 2003. *From Persecution to Prison: The Health Consequences of Detention for Asylum Seekers*. New York: Physicians for Human Rights.

Planas, Roque. 2018. "Trump's Family Detention Policy Will Cost Billions of Dollars That ICE Doesn't Have." *Huffington Post*, June 26, 2018. https://www.huffingtonpost.com/entry/trump-family-detention-policy-cost-billions-dollars-ice_us_5b3186eae4b0b5e692f0ba3f?guccounter=1.

Project South. 2018. "Detained Immigrants Paid Dollars for a Full Day's Work at Stewart Detention Center." April 17, 2018. https://projectsouth.org/private-prison-company-uses-forced-labor-of-detained-immigrants-in-georgia-to-boost-profits/.

Rawlinson, Kevin. 2018. "Windrush-Era Citizens Row: Timeline of Key Events." *The Guardian*, April 16, 2018. https://www.theguardian.com/uk-news/2018/apr/16/windrush-era-citizens-row-timeline-of-key-events.

Rose, Joel. 2018. "Supreme Court Ruling Means Thousands of Deportation Cases May Be Tossed Out." *NPR. All Things Considered*, September 17, 2018. https://www.npr.org/2018/09/17/648832694/supreme-court-ruling-means-thousands-of-deportation-cases-may-be-tossed-out.

Santos, Fernanda. 2017. "The Road, or Flight, from Detention to Deportation." *The New York Times*, February 20, 2017. https://www.nytimes.com/2017/02/20/us/the-road-or-flight-from-detention-to-deportation.html.

Sharman, Jon. 2017. "Pilots Stop 222 Asylum Seekers Being Deported from Germany by Refusing to Fly." *The Guardian*, December 5, 2017.

Shoichet, Catherine E. 2017. "They Have One-Way Tickets, Paid for by Washington: Behind the Scenes on an ICE Air Deportation Flight." *CNN*, October 13, 2017. https://www.cnn.com/2017/10/13/us/ice-air-deportation-flight/index.html.

Silverman, Stephanie. 2018. "The Disgrace of Detaining Asylum Seekers and Other Migrants." *The Conversation*, July 15, 2018. https://theconversation.com/the-disgrace-of-detaining-asylum-seekers-and-other-migrants-99673.

Silverman, Stephanie J., and E. Massa. 2012. "Why Immigration Detention Is Unique." *Population, Space and Place* 18: 677–686. doi:10.1002/psp.1720. https://onlinelibrary.wiley.com/doi/abs/10.1002/psp.1720.

Silverman, Stephanie J., and Melanie E. B. Griffiths. 2018. "Immigration Detention in the UK." Migration Observatory Briefing. *COMPAS*, University of Oxford, UK. May 2018. https://migrationobservatory.ox.ac.uk/resources/briefings/immigration-detention-in-the-uk/.

Speri, Alice. 2018. "Detained, Then Violated." *The Intercept*, April 11, 2018. https://theintercept.com/2018/04/11/immigration-detention-sexual-abuse-ice-dhs/.

"The State of Detention: Immigration Detention in the UK in 2014." 2014. *Detention Action*, October 2014. http://detentionaction.org.uk/campaigns/publications

Stillman, Sarah. 2018. "When Deportation Is a Death Sentence." *The New Yorker*, January 15, 2018.

Trafficked into Detention. 2017. *Detention Action*. November 2017. http://detentionaction.org.uk/trafficked-into-detention.

Travis, Alan. 2018. "Home Office Keeping Torture Victims in Detention, Inspectors Report." *The Guardian*, March 13, 2018.

UK Government. n.d. "Get Help to Return Home if You're a Migrant in the UK." https://www.gov.uk/return-home-voluntarily.

UK National Government Statistics. 2017. "How Many People Are Detained or Returned?" August 24, 2017. https://www.gov.uk/government/publications/immigration-statistics-april-to-june-2017/how-many-people-are-detained-or-returned.

UN High Commissioner for Refugees (UNHCR). 1997. *UNHCR Note on the Principle of Non-Refoulement*, November 1997. http://www.refworld.org/docid/438c6d972.html.

UNHCR Detention Guidelines. 2012. "Guidelines on the Applicable Criteria and Standards Relating to the Detention of Asylum-Seekers and Alternatives to Detention." http://vw/Nkunhcr.org/reivorld/docid/503489533b8.html.

US Immigration and Enforcement. 2017. Fiscal Year 2017 ICE Enforcement and Removal Operations Report 2017. https://www.ice.gov/removal-statistics/2017.

US Trafficking in Persons Report. 2017. *US Department of State*. June 2017. https://www.state.gov/j/tip/rls/tiprpt/2017/.

Ward, Nathan. 2017. "Panorama's Exposé of Immigration Centre Abuse Is No Surprise: I Saw It for Myself." *The Guardian*, September 7, 2017.

Wattles, Jackie. 2017. "Lawsuit: ICE Detention Center Paid Imprisoned Workers Less Than $1 Per Day." *CNN Money*, September 20, 2017. http://money.cnn.com/2017/09/20/news/companies/washington-immigration-detainees-wage-attorney-general/index.html.

Zadvydas v. Davis. 2001. 533 US 678.

Zong, Jie Jeanne Batalova, and Jeffrey Hallock. 2018. "Frequently Requested Statistics on Immigrants and Immigration in the United States." Migration Policy Institute, February 8, 2018. https://www.migrationpolicy.org/article/frequently-requested-statistics-immigrants-and-immigration-united-states.

CHAPTER FOUR

Refugee Resettlement in the United States

The Central Role of Voluntarism in a Time of Backlash

Kathryn R. Libal, Grace Felten, and Scott Harding

Introduction

In 1979, A. Whitney Ellsworth and Hurst Hannum of the U.S. chapter of Amnesty International submitted written testimony to Congress related to hearings on the Refugee Act of 1980 (U.S. Committee on the Judiciary 1979). They called attention to their hope that the proposed legislation would increase the "normal flow" of refugees to 50,000 annually and admit them as immigrants rather than parolees with limited rights and access to services once settled in the United States. In their comments, Ellsworth and Hannum expressed hope that "American policy will become more consistent with the non-political, humanitarian concerns that underlie its international obligations as set forth in the Convention [on Refugees] and Optional Protocol" (U.S. Committee on the Judiciary 1979, 168). Congressional hearings revealed a deep desire among advocates to support those forcibly displaced in Southeast Asia due to the U.S. war in Vietnam and neighboring countries; in Cuba and Central America; and in Eastern Europe in the wake of Soviet expansion into Poland, Hungary, and Czechoslovakia. They pressed Congress and the White House to "regularize" the process for setting annual admissions goals, to grant immigrant visa status to those resettled through the program, and to expand federal funding to support states and voluntary agencies (nonprofit organizations recognized by the government) to carry out the work of fostering the integration of refugees into local communities.

The Refugee Act of 1980 was passed by Congress and signed into law by President Jimmy Carter. The legislation aimed to "revise the procedures for the admission of refugees" and "to establish a more uniform basis for the provision of assistance to refugees" (U.S. Refugee Act 1980). Carter emphasized that the new policy was intended to "permit fair and equitable treatment of refugees in the United States, regardless of their country of origin." Importantly, Carter noted that a goal of the new law was cooperation between the State Department and Congress in setting refugee admissions targets: "It allows us to change annual admissions levels in response to conditions overseas, policy considerations, and resources available for resettlement" (Carter 1980). The president also stressed the value of having refugees become "self-sufficient and contributing members of society," even as he emphasized the role of the federal government in fostering the integration of refugees within U.S. society. "Until now, resettlement has been done primarily by private persons and organizations. They have done an admirable job," Carter noted, "but the large numbers of refugees arriving now create new strains and problems. Clearly, the Federal Government must play an expanded role in refugee programs" (Carter 1980).

The 1980 Refugee Act was one of the first U.S. laws passed in alignment with international humanitarian legal standards, adopting the definition for "refugee" used by the United Nations Office of the High Commissioner for Refugees (UNHCR) as a core principle to determine eligibility for resettlement to the United States (Haines 2010). The Refugee Act amended the 1965 Immigration and Nationality Act to define refugee as any individual who is "outside any country of such person's nationality" or "outside any country in which such person last habitually resided," and "is unable or unwilling to return to, and is unable or unwilling to avail himself or herself of the protection of, that country" due to "persecution or a well-founded fear of persecution on account of race, religion, nationality, membership in a particular social group, or political opinion" (1980 Refugee Act, Sec. 201).

Yet, while the Refugee Act expanded admissions and strengthened social supports for refugees once resettled, it has also reflected political interests of particular U.S. presidential administrations. Carter believed that determining admissions targets and policies related to which refugees gain admission to the United States (from what countries and in what numbers) would entail consultation between the White House and Congress (Carter 1980), but in practice, this consultation has been a formality and determinations are largely set by the White House. The president and his advisors also play key roles in shaping regulations and funding for resettlement programs. Indeed, concentration of power in the White House over the U.S. International

Refugee Assistance Program (IRAP) has not resulted in the "nonpolitical" attention to humanitarian concerns, as hoped for by Ellsworth and Hannum. Rather, for nearly 40 years, each presidential administration has shaped priorities about which refugees to resettle based on ideological and political considerations. To some extent, civil society actors, including faith-based organizations and ethnic interest groups, have influenced these processes through advocacy with the White House and Congress. But as recent history following the events of September 11, 2001, reveal, substantial activism is required to actually move presidential administrations to adopt inclusive and just refugee resettlement policies. One example of this was the successful lobbying of George W. Bush's administration to begin admitting Iraqi refugees late in his presidency (Harding and Libal 2012).

Since the 2016 election of President Donald Trump, the challenges posed by concentrating power in the White House to determine U.S. refugee policy have become clear (International Crisis Group 2018). Within months, the Trump administration became a global leader in introducing measures to restrict immigration, refugee admissions, and those seeking asylum (Darrow 2018). Indeed, the manifestation of "restrictionism" under Trump is the most radical shift in U.S. immigration policy in more than 40 years and represents a rebuke of U.S. global leadership on these issues. The Trump administration has attempted to effectively close U.S. borders, limiting immigration and refugee resettlement from several—mostly Muslim majority—countries[1]; failed to provide due process rights to those claiming asylum at U.S. borders; enforced a "zero tolerance" policy that systematically separated parents and guardians from children at the U.S.-Mexico border and later detained families together; increasingly criminalized undocumented migrants, subjecting them to inhumane treatment during detention; and deported migrants without observing laws protecting due process rights (e.g., Bohmer and Shuman, Chapter 3, and Pierce, Bolter, and Selee 2018). Former attorney general Jeffrey Sessions reversed the interpretation of established standards for seeking asylum in the United States, including recognizing gender-based violence and victimization from gang violence as grounds for claiming persecution in certain cases (Blitz 2017). Immigration and Customs Enforcement has increased its targeting of businesses and communities where undocumented migrants live and work, detaining and deporting record numbers of migrants who have not committed crimes. And a new interpretation of the "public charge doctrine" promises to punish immigrants without permanent residence for accessing public benefits they have a legal right to use (Shear and Baumgaertner 2018; University of Minnesota Immigration and Human Rights Clinic 2018).

Of note, the Trump administration has sought to fundamentally transform the nearly 40-year-old refugee resettlement program with little reaction from Congress. Since President Trump entered office, annual refugee admissions were reduced via Executive Order in fiscal year 2018 to 45,000 per year and substantively lowered again in fiscal year 2019 to 30,000 (U.S. Department of State, U.S. Department of Homeland Security, and U.S. Department of Health and Human Services 2018).[2] While these cuts have raised alarm among human rights groups and voluntary resettlement agencies (VOLAGs) who historically partnered with the federal government to administer the refugee admissions program, their concerns have largely been ignored (International Crisis Group 2018).

In this chapter, we outline the historical roots and key features of the current U.S. refugee resettlement program, highlighting the important and sometimes contradictory legacy of community-based private actors in supplementing government support for refugees. We then profile several methods of engaging voluntarism in resettlement in three different U.S. states: Kentucky, Utah, and Connecticut. We demonstrate the diversity of approaches to resettlement at the state level and the strengths and limits of relying upon voluntarism as a key component of the refugee resettlement program.

The History of the U.S. Refugee Resettlement Program

A core principle of American identity has been the idea that Americans value self-sufficiency and achieving *individual* success through hard work and personal responsibility (Bellah, Madsen, Sullivan, Swidler, and Tipton 1985; Rank, Hirschl, and Foster 2014). This idea has also been an integral part of the modern refugee resettlement program since its inception; indeed, job-training and English-language programs included in the policy were designed explicitly to foster "economic self-sufficiency" (Gonzalez Benson 2016). While scholars have pointed to a gap between the ideology of self-sufficiency and the reality of the struggle that newcomer refugees experience in the United States (Haffejee and East, Chapter 12; Darrow 2018), those providing community- and state-based services to refugees rarely highlight these limitations out of fear that Congress and the public will view the program as too costly. Thus, a key part of the successes of the refugee resettlement program—and simultaneously one of its limitations—is the reliance upon voluntarism, charitable giving, self-help initiatives, and "public-private partnerships" that help compensate for inadequate public supports for refugees.

Resettlement of Refugees: 1880–1975

Historian Aristide Zolberg (2006) asserts that while the United States is often touted as a "nation of immigrants," it has never been open to just "any immigrants" (1). "From the moment they managed their own affairs, well before political independence, Americans were determined to select who might join them, and they have remained so ever since" (Zolberg 2006, 1). Zolberg describes the growing sentiment among political elites to limit immigration beginning in the 1880s, including the passage of the Chinese Exclusion Act in 1882. This was the same decade in which the Statue of Liberty was installed in New York Harbor. Between 1900 and 1920, the United States accepted over 14.5 million immigrants, mostly from Europe (U.S. Citizenship and Immigration Service 2016). Concerns over the rising number of immigrants living in the United States led to the creation of more selective immigration policy. The Immigration Act of 1917 contained many restrictive parameters. One provision that would greatly affect refugees in the future was a rule related to whether or not an immigrant was likely to become a "public charge" (dependent on the state) in making a determination of their admissibility to the United States. Originally written into an 1882 law (Zolberg 2006), the intent of the public charge doctrine was to restrict entry of those who were deemed to lack the physical and/or mental skills to gain employment and support themselves financially. According to Hester and associates (2018), "In 1903, the law further stipulated that any foreigner who became a public charge within five years of entry from causes that did not originate in the U.S. was subject to deportation." The State Department used this provision to limit the number of Mexican immigrants into the United States by interpreting the public charge rule to apply to *anyone* who they determined would be unlikely to be able to support themselves (Breitman and Kraut 1987).

The vagueness of the public charge rule led to varying interpretations and, thus, different policies for immigrants or refugees during various periods of U.S. history. It directly reflected the core American value of self-sufficiency, but in practice, the notion of a public charge provided a powerful means to discriminate against certain immigrant and refugee populations. For example, in 1930 the Hoover administration expanded the rule to mean any immigrant not likely to find a job "under current market conditions," severely restricting immigration during the Great Depression (Breitman and Kraut 1987, 7). These guidelines were in effect while large numbers of Jewish refugees were applying for visas to enter the United States, seeking to escape Nazi-controlled regions of Europe (Breitman and Kraut 1987). From 1933 through the end of World War II, the U.S. government was well aware of the persecution of Jews by the Nazis and actually debated making special exceptions for this population. Government officials and agencies argued over whether the public charge rule should be suspended for those facing persecution in Europe. But in a reflection of both U.S. isolationism and tolerance of anti-Semitism, the State Department used the public charge clause to justify excluding Jewish populations displaced by genocide (Breitman and Kraut 1987).

Jewish refugees also confronted newly established immigration quotas in the United States. The Immigration Act of 1924 instituted an annual quota system for all immigrants. It allowed visas for just 2 percent of the total population of each nationality already in the United States. However, the legislation used 1890 census data, which favored entry to those of British descent and other Northern Europeans. The Act also banned entry to the United States of anyone not eligible for citizenship, which eliminated most immigrants from Asia because of already-existing nationality laws (U.S. Department of State's Office of the Historian n.d.).

World War II prompted the largest mass (forced) migration in European history (Cohen 2011). Millions of Germans fled or were expelled, hundreds of thousands of Jewish survivors were forced out of their home countries, and citizens from various European countries escaped newly emerging Communist regimes. In December 1945, President Truman issued a directive on expediting admissions of "displaced persons and refugees" from Europe, prioritizing orphan children for resettlement. Truman's order expanded sponsorship of individuals to include humanitarian agencies. The public charge rule was applicable, however, which meant that sponsoring individuals or voluntary agencies were responsible for assuring that refugees—whether adults or children—received adequate private material support. As Truman explained:

> Of the displaced persons and refugees whose entrance into the United States we will permit under this plan, it is hoped that the majority will be orphaned children. The provisions of law prohibiting the entry of persons likely to become public charges will be strictly observed. Responsible welfare organizations now at work in this field will guarantee that these children will not become public charges. Similar guarantees have or will be made on behalf of adult persons. The record of these welfare organizations throughout the past years has been excellent, and I am informed that no persons admitted under their sponsorship have ever become charges on their communities. Moreover, many of the immigrants will have close family ties in the United States and will receive the assistance of their relatives until they are in a position to provide for themselves. (Truman 1945)

This began a relationship between the U.S. government and voluntary agencies (VOLAG) for the responsibility of resettling refugees that exists today. One stipulation was that the VOLAG needed to cover refugees' travel expenses (Brown and Scribner 2014). This also echoes a policy that is still in place. When a refugee is accepted into the United States, the International Organization for Migration (IOM) pays their initial airfare. However, this is considered a temporary loan that the refugee must repay to the U.S. government (U.S. Committee for Refugees and Immigrants n.d.). Thus, refugees arrive in the United States already in financial debt.

Truman's executive order helped nearly 40,000 refugees (Brown and Scribner 2014), but more permanent legislation was needed to deal with the mass migration throughout Europe. Congress eventually passed the Displaced Persons Act of 1948, which allowed for the temporary resettlement of displaced persons and refugees. Although the Act admitted 200,000 displaced persons to the United States over two years, it was predicated on an immigration quota system that afforded fewer slots to those from Eastern and Central Europe (Truman 1948); most Jewish refugees and Catholic displaced persons would be prevented from resettling in the United States. In a statement on June 25, 1948, Truman expressed displeasure with the legislation, saying, "If the Congress were still in session, I would return this bill without my approval and urge that a fairer, more humane bill be passed. In its present form this bill is flagrantly discriminatory. It mocks the American tradition of fair play" (para 2).

The Displaced Persons Act of 1948 was the first U.S. immigration law that addressed refugees explicitly. Although it was designed as temporary legislation, meant to address the specific population of displaced persons in Europe, it set the course for future refugee policy (Churgin 1996). The 1952 Immigration and Nationality Act (McCarran-Walter Act) opened the door for admission of tens of thousands of the more than one million displaced persons in Europe as refugees. And, in 1962, Congress passed the Migration and Refugee Assistance Act, which authorized "the president to provide assistance to refugees whenever it was 'in the interest of the United States'" (Garcia 2017, 4). As Garcia notes, with the passing of the 1965 Immigration and Nationality Act (Hart-Celler Act), small regional quotas for refugees were incorporated into the legislation. Until the passage of the Refugee Act of 1980, however, U.S. policy toward refugees was made in an ad hoc fashion that privileged European refugees over those from other regions.

The Aftermath of the Vietnam War and the Refugee Act of 1980

The end of the Vietnam War created a mass exodus of refugees from Southeast Asia. Between 1970 and 1974, the United States only admitted 15,045 refugees (listed as immigrants), with more than 14,000 from Vietnam (Gordon 1985). In 1975, when the last U.S. troops withdrew from Vietnam, more than 130,000 Southeast Asian refugees were admitted to the United States through humanitarian parole (U.S. Department of State Office of Admissions—Refugee Processing Center 2018). The mass exodus from Indochina continued, and by 1979, President Carter decided to lift quota restrictions to allow 168,000 refugees per year. The Southeast Asian refugee crisis impelled Carter and Congress to act in the landmark 1980 Refugee Act. The new law standardized resettlement procedures, formed the basis of the Office of Refugee Resettlement (ORR), and created the U.S. Refugee

Resettlement Program "for the effective resettlement of refugees and to assist them to achieve economic self-sufficiency as quickly as possible after arrival in the United States" (U.S. Office of Refugee Resettlement 2012, para 1). The Act also aimed to standardize criteria for which groups of refugees would be prioritized for admission and clarified the roles of different federal agencies in refugee resettlement (Refugee Act 1980). The legislation included a stipulation that refugees were not required to seek employment for their first 60 days in the country, but this provision was eliminated 2 years later by Congress. This further made clear the emphasis on refugee "self-sufficiency" as soon as possible. At the same time provisions providing language classes and employment training for new refugees were deemphasized, making it less likely that many would easily gain the necessary skills to secure meaningful and well-paying employment.

Overview of the U.S. Refugee Resettlement

Since 1980, the United States has permanently resettled more than three million refugees through the U.S. Refugee Resettlement Program, via a variety of programs administered by ORR (Refugee Council USA 2017). The Department of Homeland Security's U.S. Citizen and Immigration Services (USCIS) has been responsible since 2002 for identifying and vetting security risks that may be associated with individual refugees slated for resettlement. The State Department's Bureau for Population, Refugees, and Migration works with the Office of Refugee Resettlement in the Department of Health and Human Services, and U.S. government recognized voluntary agencies to determine where refugees will initially be resettled (U.S. Office of Refugee Resettlement 2015). The president, in consultation with key advisors in the State Department, Homeland Security, and other staff, proposes admissions targets and priorities for which populations of refugees to accept in a given year.

Since passage of the Refugee Act of 1980, annual admissions to the United States peaked in fiscal year 1980 at 207,000 and were lowest in fiscal year 2018 at 22,491 refugees (U.S. Department of State Bureau of Population, Refugees, and Migration 2018a; U.S. Department of State, U.S. Department of Homeland Security, and U.S. Department of Health and Human Services 2018). Widely varying refugee admissions levels were due to political and ideological pressures within the White House and to a lesser degree from Congress and the U.S. public. Since the 1980 Refugee Act passed, more than one million refugees from Vietnam, Cambodia, and Laos were admitted to the United States (Packer 2015). Between fiscal years 1989 and 1994, more than 100,000 refugees were admitted each year (U.S. Department of State, U.S. Department of Homeland Security, and U.S. Department of Health and Human Services 2018). Reflecting the impact of the September 11 attacks, in fiscal years 2002 and 2003, admissions were restricted to just over 27,000 and 28,000 refugees, respectively (U.S. Department of State, U.S. Department of Homeland Security, and U.S. Department of Health and Human Services 2018). By fiscal year 2007, admission of Iraqi and Afghan refugees, through both the traditional resettlement program and a new Special Immigrant Visa Program, expanded considerably, reflecting political pressure by U.S. military veterans and human rights groups to address the humanitarian consequences of the U.S.-led war in Iraq (Harding and Libal 2012).[3]

While resettlement numbers under the Obama administration ranged from 56,000 to 70,000 in most years, by fiscal year 2016, its admissions goals rose to nearly 85,000 refugees and aimed to reach 110,000 in fiscal year 2017 (U.S. Department of State, U.S. Department of Homeland Security, and U.S. Department of Health and Human Services 2016). In September 2016, President Obama convened an international summit of leaders on refugees, demanding that the United States and the global community meet the test of "our common humanity" reflected in the mass migration stemming from the war in Syria:

> And finally, this crisis is a test of our common humanity—whether we give in to suspicion and fear and build walls, or whether we see ourselves in another. Those girls being trafficked and tortured, they could be our daughters. That little boy on the beach could be our son or our grandson. We cannot avert our eyes or turn our backs. To slam the door in the face of these families would betray our deepest values. It would deny our own heritage as nations, including the United States of America, that have been built by immigrants and refugees. And it would be to ignore a teaching at the heart of so many faiths that we do unto others as we would have them do unto us; that we welcome the stranger in our midst. And just as failure to act in the past—for example, by turning away Jews fleeing Nazi Germany—is a stain on our collective conscience, I believe history will judge us harshly if we do not rise to this moment. (Obama 2016)

By highlighting the consequences of failing to act on behalf of Jews seeking refuge from genocide in Europe, as well as religious underpinnings to support Syrian refugees, Obama aimed to build consensus at home and abroad for accepting refugees. Yet, a few months later, when Donald Trump became president, the White House moved to radically restrict refugee resettlement. In fiscal year 2017, fewer than 54,000 refugees were resettled to the United States, and 2018 marked the lowest admissions level in the history of the program, with fewer than 23,000 refugees admitted (U.S. Department of State Bureau of Population, Refugees, and Migration 2018a; U.S. Department of State, U.S. Department of Homeland Security, and U.S. Department of Health and Human Services 2018).

Table 4.1. Total Refugee Arrivals in Fiscal Year 2016–2018

Region	Total Refugee Arrivals		
	2016	2017	2018
Africa	31,624	20,232	10,459
East Asia	12,518	5,173	3,668
Europe	3,957	5,205	3,612
Latin America/Caribbean	1,340	1,688	955
Near East/South Asia	35,555	21,418	3,797
Total	84,994	53,716	22,491

What is also striking under President Trump is the shift in regional prioritization (see Table 4.1). Departing from established past practice, Trump largely closed off access to refugees from the Middle East (Near East/South Asia in ORR records), a stark shift from earlier administrations (U.S. Department of State Bureau of Population, Refugees, and Migration 2018a). In fiscal year 2016 (under Obama), more than 35,000 refugees were admitted from the Middle East, while in fiscal year 2018 (under Trump), fewer than 4,000 were admitted from the same region.

Resettlement Programs Implemented at the State and Local Levels

Since the refugee resettlement program's inception in 1980, California, New York, Texas, Michigan, Ohio, and Arizona are the top states for resettlement in most years. Connecticut, Kentucky, and Utah have all resettled a much smaller number of refugees since 1980, but they are also much smaller states in terms of population. Wyoming is currently the only state that does not participate in the refugee resettlement program, while Arkansas, Delaware, Hawaii, Mississippi, Montana, and West Virginia, have resettled fewer than 500 refugees since 2002 (U.S. Department of State Bureau of Population, Refugees, and Migration Office of Admissions 2018b).

Implementation of the resettlement program and financial and other supports for refugees are administered through national resettlement voluntary agencies, which subcontract with affiliated local providers, sometimes called refugee resettlement organizations (RROs) (Darrow 2015). This financial aid is more limited than in other countries that have historically resettled refugees. The Reception and Placement Program (R&P Program) provides "the initial building blocks for a refugee's successful transition" during the first 90 days after arrival, when the Department of State offers support to the refugee and resettlement organization (Darrow 2015, 92). Following the first 90 days,

RROs continue to administer financial and other resources to refugees, the most significant of which is a modest monthly cash benefit given through the first eight months of the initial resettlement period. As Darrow (2015) notes, "The intention of this support is to give the refugee a leg up on their journey to self-sufficiency, to stabilize the individual or family so that they can gain access to the labor market, and otherwise thrive" (92).

Nonetheless, the level of assistance that refugees receive from the federal government, states, and refugee resettlement agencies is almost uniformly inadequate to meet basic needs. Refugee Cash Assistance levels, for example, vary by state and are generally indexed to the levels of cash aid provided through the Temporary Assistance to Needy Families program—which does not provide enough by itself to lift a family out of poverty (U.S. Department of Health and Human Services, Administration for Children and Families, Office of Refugee Resettlement, n.d.). The resettlement program's success thus hinges on the efforts of service providers and large teams of volunteers to help refugees resettled to the United States transition to economic "self-sufficiency" within a short period of time (see Haffejee and East, Chapter 12; Eby, Iverson, Smyers, and Kekic 2011).

The Centrality of Volunteers in U.S. Refugee Resettlement

Historically, volunteers, community members, and others in the private sector have played a critical role providing support and services to refugees in the United States (Eby, Iverson, Smyers, and Kekic 2011; Haines 2010). This work has often been facilitated by members of faith communities, including Christian, Jewish, and Muslim groups, and the major voluntary agencies that have been authorized to administer resettlement nationwide primarily represent Christian and Jewish organizations. Next, we provide insights into the roles and motivations of volunteers working in Connecticut, Kentucky, and Utah based on 28 semi-structured interviews with volunteers and service providers that the authors conducted between 2016–2018. While admitting a relatively small number of refugees, these states have developed substantial programs incorporating volunteers.[4] In Connecticut, a local agency experiments with community cosponsorship, arguably the most robust model of engaging volunteers in the work of refugee resettlement. Kentucky represents a "Wilson/Fish" state, which devolves responsibility for resettlement to a nongovernmental organization, which, in turn, is responsible for overseeing the program and work of other resettlement organizations in this "alternative" privatized model of coordination and implementation. Finally, Utah demonstrates a hybrid (or more "traditional") approach that balances state coordination with robust private, nongovernmental organizational involvement in resettlement. Each model is predicated on substantial input from volunteers, though the extent to which volunteers exercise control over resettlement processes varies.

Connecticut: Experimenting with Community Cosponsorship

One of the smallest U.S. states geographically, Connecticut consistently ranks among the wealthiest states, though it is also one of the most "unequal" states and has one of the highest costs of living nationally. While resettlement organizations have been active in refugee resettlement in the state for decades, a relatively small number of refugees are resettled in Connecticut each year. The state's high housing costs, uneven public transportation, limited social welfare supports, and a low rate of job growth are among the challenges facing new immigrant arrivals.

Integrated Refugee and Immigrant Services (IRIS), one of three Connecticut-based RROs, resettles the largest number of refugees in the state. Until 2015, IRIS managed a caseload of approximately 300 newly resettled refugees per year, relying on volunteers to provide tutoring, transportation, and other critical support. The group took a lead role in the state in resettling Arabic-speaking refugees during both the Iraq and Syrian wars. Throughout its history, IRIS worked with volunteer-led community groups that resettled refugees, though this was usually done at a small scale; the majority of their efforts focused on "traditional" refugee resettlement.

By 2015, media attention about the Syrian migration "crisis," along with the outcry associated with the drowning of three-year-old Alan Kurdi, had made refugee issues highly visible (Mackey 2015). In the United States, the Obama administration pledged to resettle 15,000 Syrian refugees in 2016, a symbolic gesture in light of the more than five million Syrians displaced by civil war. In late 2015, citing a recent terrorist attack in Paris, a majority of U.S. governors (including then Indiana governor Mike Pence) publicly opposed resettling any Syrian refugees in their state. The election of Donald Trump, who used explicit anti-immigrant and anti-Muslim rhetoric in his presidential campaign, drew further public attention to U.S. refugee policy. The backlash against Trump's 2017 proposed travel ban and sharp cut in refugee admissions—announced on his eighth day in office—offered a new opportunity to revive and expand volunteer-led refugee resettlement in Connecticut.

As occurred in communities nationwide, in Connecticut, thousands of people spontaneously protested against Trump's policies, demanding that the United States admit Syrian refugees fleeing war and persecution. Chris George, executive director of IRIS, stated a willingness to have IRIS resettle Syrian refugees in Connecticut, a move that coincided with growing community interest in sponsoring refugee families (Griffin 2015). Soon, dozens of local groups and Christian, Jewish, and Muslim faith-based institutions across the state contacted IRIS to find out how they could "cosponsor" a (Syrian) refugee family in their community. Throughout 2016 and 2017, IRIS took the lead in reviving community cosponsorship of refugees and helped support the formation of dozens of local cosponsorship groups across the state. Unlike in the past, refugee resettlement led by volunteers became an integral aspect of IRIS's work in this period. Citing the high level of community interest, George proclaimed 2017 the "year . . . of the volunteers. . . . It's really taken off here, and we'd like to see it replicated across the country" (Stannard 2017).

Trained and directly supported by IRIS, dozens of cosponsorship groups assumed many key roles typically carried out by professional resettlement agencies. IRIS required local groups, most of which were new, to support a refugee family and take responsibility for costs associated with resettlement in their community for at least one year. Cosponsorship groups had to commit to help refugees locate housing, connect them to social services, help secure employment, provide connections to schools, access English-language courses, and find transportation. Consistent with U.S. refugee policy, these efforts also had to prioritize achieving "self-sufficiency" for refugees (typically within one year).

The cosponsorship model promoted by IRIS serves a number of significant goals, at both an organizational and a community level. In less than three years, a dramatic increase in cosponsorship occurred: IRIS supported 45 (mostly new) groups to resettle nearly 300 refugees in more than 30 communities (Integrated Refugee and Immigrant Services 2018). The cosponsorship program thus strengthened the overall capacity of IRIS, allowing it to maximize its resources and provide more refugees with more services than would normally occur. At its peak, in 2016–2017, IRIS more than doubled the number of refugees it resettled across Connecticut, with nearly 40 percent of this increase due to cosponsorship efforts.

Among other outcomes, interviews underscore how community cosponsorship provided greater visibility and support for refugees. In order to scale up resettlement in the state to admit nearly double the number of refugees that had been placed in recent years, IRIS staff had to train and mentor new community groups. In Connecticut, hundreds of people without prior experience became involved in refugee resettlement. Aside from connections to faith-based groups, participants came from diverse backgrounds, including local government, the business sector, local ethnic associations, health sector, and education sector.

Under the cosponsorship model, the social networks that refugees typically form in host countries, essential to their ability to thrive, were dependent on the support of volunteers rather than staff members in a local resettlement organization. Most volunteers had deep ties to their local community and could thus help connect refugees to important community institutions and relevant services. As Chris George observed, "It's better for the refugee family to have a community group working with them that knows the schools and knows where to shop and knows where the jobs are" (Stannard 2017).

In light of their history in a local community, volunteers also proved uniquely positioned to solve problems facing refugees and to advocate on their behalf. The cosponsorship model thus enabled volunteers to address stereotypes and potential hostility to newly relocated refugees. This has been significant in Connecticut, where many refugee families were placed in small communities lacking ethnic, racial, and religious diversity and without a history of refugee resettlement. One interviewee reflected:

> And if somebody is anti-immigration, or anti-Muslim immigration, then of course the best education is meeting somebody from that culture. . . . Just sharing something simple like good food makes people connect with each other. So that I think is the great advantage for the community. It connects people to a different part of the world, and different cultures, who might not otherwise have connected. And it opens up forums for debate and discussion. (Interview, August 29, 2018)

Interviews for also illustrate how these volunteer efforts concretely impacted refugees. Those who were resettled in Connecticut through cosponsorship in 2016–2017 were able to find employment, learn English, and adapt to their environment more quickly than those resettled directly by IRIS (Interview, November 22, 2017). By helping build diffuse nodes of community support, volunteers facilitated community integration among refugees, helping them generate vital social capital. This strongly suggests that community cosponsorship can help refugees quickly achieve "self-sufficiency," thereby supporting a fundamental principle of U.S. refugee policy.

Kentucky: Volunteers in a "Wilson Fish" State

Kentucky has a long history of receiving refugees, beginning more than 40 years ago, with the end of the Vietnam War (Catholic Charities of Louisville, Inc. 2018a). Kentucky is 1 of 13 states that opt for an alternative method of resettlement administration known as Wilson-Fish (U.S. Office of Refugee Resettlement 2018). Functioning as a "Wilson-Fish" state means that state-wide support for refugee resettlement occurs via a nonprofit organization rather than the state government (Welch 2017). In this case, the Kentucky Office for Refugees (KOR) is housed within Catholic Charities of Louisville. KOR receives funding from ORR, and KOR, in turn, awards this funding through grants to resettlement agencies and community groups within the state and provides grants management and program development resources (Catholic Charities of Louisville, Inc. 2018b). Several staff and volunteers interviewed for this study suggested that one strength of working within a

Wilson Fish state was having increased flexibility, with the ability to adapt quickly and create new programs based on community feedback (Interview, July 31, 2017, and Interview, August 22, 2017).

These interviews also underscored the welcoming nature of Kentucky's largest city, Louisville. Described by one participant as a "progressive city" in a "very red state" (Interview, July 31, 2017), the city's long-standing history of accepting refugees and its mayor, Greg Fischer, were frequently recognized (Interview, September 27, 2017). One volunteer described a speech the mayor delivered at a refugee community event, saying, "He stood up and said, 'We welcome you; we hope more come to the United States. We're thrilled to have you. This is a country built from immigrants. And you know we're here for you'" (Interview, November 15, 2017). In 2011, Mayor Fischer signed a resolution making Louisville an international compassionate city, joining a global campaign called the Charter for Compassion (Charter for Compassion 2017a). The charter challenges members to create spaces where "every man, woman and child treats others as they wish to be treated—with dignity, equity and respect" (Charter for Compassion 2017b, para 2). Part of the objective is to work toward achieving the UN Sustainable Development Goals. Currently, almost 50 countries have signed the charter, and an additional 70 cities (55 in the United States) have affirmed it, including Louisville (Charter for Compassion 2017b).

Louisville is not the only city where refugees resettle in Kentucky. KOR also works with resettlement agencies in Lexington, Owensboro, and Bowling Green. Initially, when Muslim refugees started to be resettled in Owensboro, some staff were concerned about how the refugees would be accepted in a mostly rural, Christian area. However, when refugees were asked by staff how they were faring, the majority responded by saying that they loved living in Owensboro because "it's safe, it's quiet," and the "people are nice" (Interview, July 31, 2017). In fact, in November 2016, when an Islamic center was defaced for the second time that year, the scheduled clean-up was cancelled, because, before it could happen, a local Christian church had already repaired the vandalism. The community then decided to gather and write positive messages in sidewalk chalk at the community center (WFIE 2016).

Support from volunteers is an integral component to successful resettlement in Kentucky, especially in light of financial strains on to organizations because of cuts in new refugee arrivals imposed by the Trump administration. Since funding for resettlement agencies depends on the number of refugee arrivals, some resettlement agencies have laid off staff (Cepla 2018). This caused one staff member of a resettlement organization to lament the loss of "years of skills and experience" (Interview, December 15, 2017). Even before these cuts, however, the agency worked hard to involve volunteers in all aspects of its work, creating opportunities for community members to participate in letter-writing campaigns, tutor in English, or buy groceries for a newly arrived refugee family (Interview, December 15, 2017).

One volunteer, who works fulltime, arranges her work schedule so that she can volunteer weekly. One of her activities is helping other volunteers provide daycare to a group of two- to five-year-old children while their parents attend an English-language class provided by the resettlement agency. Staff and volunteers cite English proficiency as one of the biggest challenges for refugees in finding a job that pays enough for them to support their families. One interviewee noted that "everything refugees do job-wise would be more successful with English" (Interview, December 15, 2017). Throughout Kentucky, resettlement agencies design and support programs, while volunteers meet with refugees weekly. This synergy between agencies and volunteers may provide refugees a better chance for successful integration. With cuts in staff, agencies will likely find it more difficult to provide adequate training for volunteers, which over time may create a more ad hoc nature of support for refugees.

In Kentucky, some people volunteer on their own, but, traditionally, volunteers do so as part of a larger group. It is common for churches, mosques, families, and even businesses to sponsor a newly arrived refugee family and provide mentorship to the family for at least three to six months (Interview, December 15, 2017, and Interview, September 27, 2017). Some community groups raise funds to help a refugee family for the first few months, and others help in nonmonetary ways; this depends on the approach of the resettlement agency that the volunteers work with. Some agencies require volunteers to raise funds, while others prohibit this type of fund-raising. In preparation for their arrival, volunteer groups are often responsible for furnishing a family's new apartment, meeting them at the airport, and helping to prepare a welcome meal. Members of the group then visit the family on a regular basis, helping them become familiar with their new community. Since everyday tasks may be different from in the refugee family's home country, volunteers assist with grocery shopping, banking, and teaching the family how to navigate public transportation (Interview, September 27, 2017, and Interview, December 15, 2017).

A volunteer described how people often begin volunteering on a one-time basis or for an event, but once they get to know a refugee family, they become more involved, including volunteering abroad. Based on experiences in Greece, the interviewee speaks to community groups in Kentucky about the condition refugees face in other countries in order to dispel common myths and raise public awareness about the hardships of forced migration. They noted that the public often assumes that "when things are good, we need to build a wall to keep people out . . . because everyone wants to live here" (Interview, September 26, 2017). In fact, according to the interviewee, most refugees want to return to their home country, but in cases such as

Syria when return is unlikely, it is important to welcome refugees. "We need the diversity, the richness of folks" (Interview, September 26, 2017).

Volunteers in Kentucky cited a range of reasons for getting involved. One common motivation was religious values, including the notion of "welcoming the stranger." One volunteer said that doing this work is putting their "faith into action" (Interview, September 26, 2017). Others became active for political reasons, as a way of challenging policy and negative rhetoric about refugees. One volunteer had been contemplating volunteer work, but when they heard then presidential candidate Donald Trump talk about "closing the borders for refugees" (Interview, November 15, 2017), they decided to act. Several resettlement agency staff noted a "record number" of volunteers after President Trump was elected and announced his travel ban (Interview, September 27, 2017). Although heartened by this development, some interviewees expressed concern about a drop in the number of volunteers when news coverage focused less on refugees (Interview, December 15, 2017).

Some of the motivations of volunteers seem to come from a practical sense of awareness that there is a need that exists, and someone must fill it. One volunteer, referring to how people in Kentucky help each other, said "this is just something people do here" (Interview, January 17, 2018). Another said, although inspired by faith, it really comes down to the straightforward idea that if "people need help, you need to just help them" (Interview, January 31, 2018). A resettlement agency staff member elaborated on this type of practical helping of neighbors, noting that there is an "authentic hospitality" and "general friendliness" in the state, which aids in successful resettlement for refugees (Interview, September 27, 2017). Those working for resettlement organizations and volunteers interviewed for this study underscored the importance of voluntary action in building community- and state-level support for refugees, even in the face of broader politics of exclusion.

Utah: Robust State and Private Partnership

Utah's history plays an important role in how the state addresses the needs of refugees today. Nineteenth-century settlers fleeing religious persecution are recognized as "refugee pioneers," who founded the state. An appreciation of refugees directly influences state policies and efforts to create a welcoming community. In 2015, when most Republican governors declared Syrian refugees unwelcome, Utah's Republican governor Gary Herbert dissented. He suggested that there should be a way to protect the state from "terrorists" without discriminating against refugees from predominantly Muslim countries. Instead of refusing Syrian refugees, he met with national security officials to understand the refugee-screening process (Jordan 2016).

Utah's commitment to refugees has led to some tensions between immigrant and refugee communities. According to an interview with a service provider, some in the immigrant community felt that they received fewer benefits and services than refugees (Interview, January 13, 2017). To address this, the Office for New Americans was created in Salt Lake City in 2016, with the goal of integrating all refugees and immigrants. Anyone born outside of the country is considered a *New American*. One of the first priorities of the office was to create a New Americans Taskforce Welcoming Plan, comprised of approximately 100 business leaders, legislators, providers, and community partners. After drafting the plan, the agency sought community feedback using town-hall-style meetings, focus groups, and one-on-one meetings of local community members (Interview, January 13, 2017). The result is a strategic plan to work toward the goals of making Utah the "most welcoming state," ensuring that "all Salt Lake residents live in safe, healthy, and connected communities" and are able to maximize "the economic potential of New Americans" (New Americans Taskforce Welcoming Plan n.d., 1).

The Office for New Americans works with the Utah Department of Workforce Services and two local voluntary refugee resettlement agencies, the International Rescue Committee (IRC) and Catholic Community Services (CCS). Additionally, Utah's Department of Workforce Services partners with Utah State University and Salt Lake Community College to provide services through the Refugee Education and Training Center. This partnership began when research showed that the average wage for resettled refugees in Utah is approximately $8.25 per hour, inadequate to meet the basic needs of refugee families (Utah Department of Workforce Services 2016). The Refugee Education and Training Center offers employment and training services to assist refugees in attaining more long-term, livable incomes. They also provide youth education and community-led events (Utah Department of Workforce Services 2016). Recently, they initiated a project to create a commercial kitchen that will also act as a "community education kitchen," a place where refugees receive training for food service and culinary skills as well as a space for the refugee community to use to prepare food for events (Interview, September 13, 2018).

Interviewees cite a uniquely collaborative quality to the resettlement community in Utah. The two resettlement agencies, CCS and IRC, work together along with the Asian Association of Utah (AAU). The AAU is a nonprofit focused on helping refugees from all countries, providing services such as mental health counseling, extended case management, assistance with secondary migration, and substance abuse programs (Interview, January 13, 2017). Each of the organizations has its own programming and services, yet the groups avoid competing for funding by communicating clearly among themselves, offering different services, and then actively referring clients to each other depending on refugee needs. Every month, they participate in a refugee provider roundtable discussion to facilitate such cooperation (Interview, January 25, 2017).

Agencies involved in resettlement in Utah also work with business leaders to assist in securing employment for refugees. The Refugee Services Office, within the Utah Department of Workforce Services, receives federal funding for refugee resettlement and contracts with the resettlement agencies to provide needed services. Additionally, the state sets aside an annual budget of approximately $200,000 for capacity building within refugee communities. These funds support trainings and mini-grants for various community organizations (Interview, January 13, 2017). The state also allows some of their Temporary Aid for Needy Family (TANF) funds to go toward refugee case management. And in special cases, for single parents with children, some of these funds are used to subsidize housing temporarily (Interview, January 25, 2017). The resettlement agencies work alongside the Office for New Americans to coordinate with local area churches and community members, mobilizing community members to do political advocacy with Utah legislators.

The final and critical element of the resettlement community is volunteers. While Utah does not promote a community cosponsorship model, they do rely on local volunteers to help refugees integrate into their new communities. Utah was ranked the top state of all 50 U.S. states in the percentage of residents volunteering, according to Volunteering and Civic Life in America's 2015 report (CNCS n.d.). Nationally, the volunteer rate is 29.4 percent; in Utah, it is 43.2 percent (CNCS n.d.).

Volunteers primarily assist resettlement agencies with tasks such as accessing public transportation, utilizing local resources such as libraries or community centers, or practicing English. Unlike some community cosponsorship models, volunteers do not provide services for refugees like financial support for housing or assistance with attaining social service benefits (Interview, January 13, 2017). One volunteer, who has been actively mentoring new refugee families for seven years, said the main goal of volunteering is to befriend refugees who are attempting to rebuild their lives in Utah. Although helping them learn how to navigate their new communities is necessary, "the most important job is to be a friend" (Interview, September 13, 2018). Particularly, in the face of the current political climate, in which refugee families in some states may be afraid of heightened discrimination and anti-immigrant policies, such "be-friending" is crucial to integration and refugee well-being.

While the Church of Jesus Christ of Latter-Day Saints has been involved in international humanitarian programs to support refugees since the mid-1980s, they have taken a more prominent role in Utah in recent years. Mormon leadership sent out "A First Presidency Letter" in 2015, urging parishioners to respond to the refugee crisis. Since then, there has been a powerful response;

the church has partnered with other churches and donated to refugee resettlement agencies across the country. The church also started a campaign, "I Was a Stranger," which urges women and girls to assist refugees in their communities however they can, asking them to contemplate "what if *their* story were *my* story?" and then respond to the call within themselves (Burton 2016, para 11).

Eby, Iverson, Smyers, and Kekic (2011) argue that the involvement of faith-based communities has led to the United States being the leading refugee resettlement country in the world, though this distinction is now in question at least in the short term, under the Trump administration. They note the role of faith communities in helping refugees in areas such as employment, housing, and social connection, providing them with cultural knowledge, and facilitating their integration into local communities. This is certainly the case in Utah. One volunteer cited her fortune to live in the state: "There's really good organizations. And we're trying to work together and collaborate to focus on what's best for our state, and that includes what's best for refugees" (Interview, September 13, 2018).

Conclusion

Refugee admissions have been a key part of U.S. humanitarian and foreign policy for more than 70 years (García 2017; Loescher 2017). Civil society actors, including faith-based voluntary agencies and resettlement organizations, have advocated for increasing admissions and for particular groups of refugees to be admitted to the United States. Yet, the groups have played a more profound role in carrying out support for refugees once they arrive in the United States. Resettlement has always been predicated on the involvement of volunteers, faith-based institutions, and community groups. While voluntary agencies and refugee resettlement organizations have generally avoided politicizing admissions and resettlement, they face a crossroads today when the Trump administration seeks to transform the refugee program as part of an effort to restrict immigration to the United States in general. As García (2017) notes, "the major challenge will be to raise public consciousness about refugees—and the conditions that produce them—so that fears and cultural biases do not negatively influence assessments of who is 'worthy' of admissions to the United States" (203).

In this context we underscore the importance of community-based voluntarism and state-level advocacy in support of refugees. Given shifting political dynamics, it is imperative to build public support for the refugee resettlement program. As recent polls by the Pew Research Center indicate, the Trump administration's policy decisions and rhetoric have had an impact on the public. In 2018, among Republican and Republican-leaning independents, only 26 percent agreed that the United States has a responsibility to accept refugees (Hartig 2018). Overall, a slim majority (51%) of Americans agreed that the country had such a responsibility, though whites are less likely to support refugee admission than African Americans and Latinos. In light of the polarization of refugee and immigration policies, one theme underscored by those we interviewed is the importance of building broad-based community involvement in refugee resettlement, precisely to create public support for the refugee resettlement program. Engaging at the grassroots, community level, through voluntarism and community cosponsorship, is one means to build such support for refugees—one community, one state at a time.

Notes

1. As of April 2019 this includes North Korea, Venezuela, Syria, Iran, Libya, Somalia, and Yemen.

2. In FY 2019, the Trump administration has recommended admissions ceilings by region as follows: Africa, 11,000; East Asia, 4,000; Europe and Central Asia, 3,000; Latin America and the Caribbean, 3,000; and the Near East and South Asia, 9000 (U.S. Department of State, U.S. Department of Homeland Security, & U.S. Department of Health and Human Services 2017 2018). This differs markedly from the last year of the Obama administration, which, for FY 2018, had recommended admissions of 40,000 from the Near East and South Asia; 35,000 from Africa; 12,000 from Asia; and 9,000 combined for Europe and Latin America/Caribbean (U.S. Department of State, U.S. Department of Homeland Security, and U.S. Department of Health and Human Services 2016).

3. Toward the end of the Obama administration, refugee arrivals reflected only part of a much larger number of individuals who were served by the Department of Health and Human Services under the broader refugee program. In FY 2016, for example, nearly 85,000 refugees were resettled, while approximately 25,000 were recognized as asylees, and 87,111 Haitian and Cuban entrants were also part of the ORR program. In addition, more than 14,000 Special Immigrant Visa holders (Iraqis and Afghans) and 797 victims of trafficking were admitted. (U.S. Department of Health and Human Services, Administration of Children and Families 2018).

4. Between 2002 and 2018, Utah (population 3.1 million in 2017) admitted 14,146 refugees; Connecticut (population 3.5 million in 2017) admitted 7,407 refugees; and Kentucky (population 4.4 million in 2017) admitted 21,020 refugees (U.S. Department of State Bureau of Population, Refugees, and Migration Office of Admissions 2018b).

References

Bellah, Robert N., Richard Madsen, William M. Sullivan, Ann Swidler, and Steven M. Tipton. 1985. *Habits of the Heart: Individualism and Commitment in Daily Life*. Berkeley, CA: California University Press.

Blitz, Brad. 2017. "Persecution and the Threat to the Refugee System." *OpenGlobalRights*, January 27, 2017. https://www.opendemocracy.net/can-europe-make-it/brad-k-blitz/persecution-and-threat-to-refugee-system.

Breitman, Richard, and Alan Kraut. 1987. *American Refugee Policy and European Jewry, 1933–1945*. Bloomington: Indiana University Press.

Brown, Anastasia, and Todd Scribner. 2014. "Unfulfilled Promises, Future Possibilities: The Refugee Resettlement System in the United States." *Journal of Migration and Human Security* 2, no. 1: 101–120.

Burton, Linda K. 2016. "The Church of Jesus Christ of Latter-Day Saints: I Was a Stranger." https://www.lds.org/general-conference/2016/04/i-was-a-stranger?lang=eng.

Carter, Jimmy. 1980. "Refugee Act of 1980 Statement on Signing into Law." http://www.presidency.ucsb.edu/ws/?pid=33154.

Catholic Charities of Louisville, Inc. 2018a. "Refugee Resettlement in Kentucky." https://www.kentuckyrefugees.org/.

Catholic Charities of Louisville, Inc. 2018b. "Our Role." https://www.kentuckyrefugees.org/about-kor/.

Cepla, Zuzana. 2018. "Fact Sheet: US Refugee Resettlement." May 14, 2018. https://immigrationforum.org/article/fact-sheet-u-s-refugee-resettlement/.

Charter for Compassion. 2017a. "Louisville: A Model Compassionate City." https://charterforcompassion.org/louisville-a-model-compassionate-city.

Charter for Compassion. 2017b. "Our Vision, Our Work." https://charterforcompassion.org/communities/participating-communities#affirmed-the-charter.

Churgin, Michael J. 1996. "Mass Exoduses: The Response of the United States." *International Migration Review* 30, no. 1 (Spring): 310–324.

Cohen, Gerard Daniel. 2011. *In War's Wake: Europe's Displaced Persons in the Postwar Order*. New York: Oxford University Press.

Corporation for National and Community Service (CNCS). n.d. "State Rankings by Volunteer Rate." https://www.nationalservice.gov/vcla/state-rankings-volunteer-rate.

Darrow, Jessica H. 2015. "The (Re)Construction of the U.S. Department of State's Reception and Placement Program by Refugee Resettlement Agencies." *Journal of the Society for Social Work and Research* 6, no. 1: 91–119.

Darrow, Jessica H. 2018. "Working It Out in Practice: Tensions Embedded in the U.S. Refugee Resettlement Program Resolved through Implementation." In *Refugee Resettlement: Power, Politics, and Humanitarian Governance*, edited by Adele Garnier, Liliana Lyra Jubilut, and Kristin Bergtora Sandvik, 96–117. New York: Berghahn Books.

Eby, Jessica, Erika Iverson, Jenifer Smyers, and Erol Kekic. 2011. "The Faith Community's Role in Refugee Resettlement in the United States." *Journal of Refugee Studies* 24, no. 3: 586–605.

García, María Cristina. 2017. *The Refugee Challenge in Post-Cold War America*. New York: Oxford University Press.

Gonzalez Benson, Odessa. 2016. "Refugee Resettlement Policy in an Era of Neoliberalization: A Policy Discourse Analysis of the Refugee Act of 1980." *Social Service Review* 90, no. 3: 515–549.

Gordon, Linda W. 1985. "Southeast Asian Refugee Migration to the United States." In *Pacific Bridges: The New Immigration from Asia and the Pacific Islands*, edited by James T. Fawcett and Benjamin V. Carino, 153–173. Staten Island, NY: Center for Migration Studies.

Griffin, Elaine. 2015. "Resettlement Expert: Welcoming of Refugees, Screening Is Strong." *The Courant*, November 25, 2015. https://www.courant.com/news/connecticut/hc-ct-syrian-refugees-crisis-in-connecticut-1126-20151125-story.html.

Haines, David W. 2010. *Safe Haven? A History of Refugees in America*. Boulder, CO: Kumarian Press.

Harding, Scott, and Kathryn Libal. 2012. "Iraqi Refugees and the Humanitarian Costs of the Iraq War: What Role for Social Work?" *International Journal of Social Welfare* 21, no. 1: 94–104.

Hartig, Hannah. 2018. "Republicans Turn More Negative towards Refugees as Number Admitted to the U.S. Plummets." May 24, 2018. http://www.pewresearch.org/fact-tank/2018/05/24/republicans-turn-more-negative-toward-refugees-as-number-admitted-to-u-s-plummets/.

Hester, Torrie, Hidetaka Hirota, Mary E. Mendoza, Deirdre Moloney, Mae Ngai, Lucy Salyer, and Elliott Young. 2018. "Historians' Comment: DHS Notice of Proposed Rule 'Inadmissibility on Public Charge Grounds,' FR 2018–21106." October 5, 2018.

Integrated Refugee and Immigrant Services. 2018. "Community Co-Sponsorship: An Essential Complementary Model for Refugee Resettlement Agencies." Unpublished report.

International Crisis Group. 2018. *How to Save the U.S. Admissions Program*. September 12, 2018. https://www.crisisgroup.org/united-states/002-how-save-us-refugee-admissions-program.

Jordan, Miriam. 2016. "With Welcoming Stance, Conservative Utah Charts Its Own Course on Refugees." *The Wall Street Journal*, March 27, 2016. http://www.wsj.com/articles/with-welcoming-stance-conservative-utah-charts-its-own-course-on-refugees-1459125392.

Loescher, Gil. 2017. "UNCHR's Origins and Early History: Agency, Influence, and Power in Global Refugee Policy." *Refuge* 33, no. 1: 77–86.

Mackey, Robert. 2015. "Brutal Images of Syrian Boy Drowned Off Turkey Must Be Seen, Activists Say." *The New York Times*, September 2, 2015. https://www.nytimes.com/2015/09/03/world/middleeast/brutal-images-of-syrian-boy-drowned-off-turkey-must-be-seen-activists-say.html.

New Americans Taskforce. n.d. "New Americans Taskforce Welcoming Plan." http://slco.org/welcoming-salt-lake/reports-and-plans/.

Obama, Barack. 2016. "Remarks by President Obama at the Leaders Summit on Refugees." September 20, 2016. https://obamawhitehouse.archives.gov/the-press-office/2016/09/20/remarks-president-obama-leaders-summit-refugees.

Packer, George. 2015. "Powerful Gestures." *The New Yorker*, November 9, 2015. https://www.newyorker.com/magazine/2015/11/09/powerful-gestures.

Pierce, Sarah, Jessica Bolter, and Andrew Selee. 2018. "U.S. Immigration Policy under Trump: Deep Changes and Lasting Impacts." Migration Policy Institute. https://www.migrationpolicy.org/research/us-immigration-policy-trump-deep-changes-impactshttps://www.migrationpolicy.org/research/us-immigration-policy-trump-deep-changes-impacts.

Rank, Mark Robert, Thomas A. Hirschl, and Kirk A. Foster. 2014. *Chasing the American Dream: Understanding What Shapes Our Fortunes.* New York: Oxford University Press.

Refugee Council USA. 2017. "Refugee Resettlement in the United States." April 2017. https://static1.squarespace.com/static/577d437bf5e231586a7055a9/t/58f79a3a59cc6842015ce50f/1492621883823/Refugee+101+Document+-+April+2017.pdf.

Shear, Michael D., and Emily Baumgaertner. 2018. "President Trump Aims to Sharply Restrict New Green Cards for Those on Public Aid." *The New York Times,* September 22, 2018. https://www.nytimes.com/2018/09/22/us/politics/immigrants-green-card-public-aid.html.

Stannard, Ed. 2017. "Register Person of the Year: Chris George, Leader in Refugee Resettlement." *New Haven Register,* December 24, 2017. https://www.nhregister.com/news/article/Register-Person-of-the-Year-Chris-George-leader-12453322.php.

Truman, Harry, S. 1945. "Statement and Directive by the President on Immigration to the United States of Certain Displaced Persons and Refugees in Europe." December 22, 1945. https://www.trumanlibrary.org/publicpapers/index.php?pid=515&st=&st1=.

University of Minnesota Immigration and Human Rights Clinic. 2018. "Analysis of DHS Proposed Rule on Public Charges Prepared for the International Refugee Assistance Program." Unpublished manuscript, last modified October 29, 2018.

U.S. Citizenship and Immigration Service (USCIS). 2016. "Mass Immigration and WWII." https://www.uscis.gov/history-and-genealogy/our-history/agency-history/mass-immigration-and-wwi.

U.S. Committee for Refugees and Immigrants (USCRI). n.d. "Travel Loan Services." http://www.uscripayments.org/.

U.S. Committee on the Judiciary, House of Representatives. 1979. *Refugee Act of 1979: Hearings before the Subcommittee on Immigration, Refugees, and International Law of the Committee of the Judiciary, House of Representatives, Ninety-sixth Congress, First Session on H.R. 2816, Refugee Act of 1979.* Washington, DC: U.S. Government Printing Office.

U.S. Department of Health and Human Services, Administration for Children and Families, Office of Refugee Resettlement, n.d. "ORR Benefits at a Glance." https://www.acf.hhs.gov/sites/default/files/orr/orr_fact_sheet_benefits_at_a_glance.pdf.

U.S. Department of Health and Human Services, Administration for Children and Families. 2018. *Annual Report to Congress: Office of Refugee Resettlement Fiscal Year 2016,* June 14, 2018. Retrieved from https://www.acf.hhs.gov/sites/default/files/orr/arc_16_508.pdf.

U.S. Department of State Bureau of Population, Refugees, and Migration. 2018a. "Refugee Arrivals by Region (Based on Nationality of PA), All Nationalities, October 01, 2017 through September 30, 2018." http://www.wrapsnet.org/archives/.

U.S. Department of State Bureau of Population, Refugees, and Migration. 2018b. "Refugee Processing Center Refugee Arrivals from January 1, 2002, through January 1, 2018." http://ireports.wrapsnet.org/Interactive-Reporting/EnumType/Report?ItemPath=/rpt_WebArrivalsReports/Map%20-%20Arrivals%20by%20State%20and%20Nationality.

U.S. Department of State Office of Admissions—Refugee Processing Center. 2018. *Refugee Admissions by Region, Fiscal Year 1975 through 31-Oct-2018, Cumulative Summary of Admissions.* Data extracted from the Worldwide Refugee Admissions Processing System (WRAPS), November 5, 2018.

U.S. Department of State Office of the Historian. n.d. "The Immigration Act of 1924 (The Johnson Reed Act)." https://history.state.gov/milestones/1921-1936/immigration-act.

U.S. Department of State, U.S. Department of Homeland Security, and U.S. Department of Health and Human Services. 2016. *Proposed Refugee Admissions for Fiscal Year 2017: Report to Congress*, September 15, 2016. https://www.state.gov/documents/organization/262168.pdf.

U.S. Department of State, U.S. Department of Homeland Security, and U.S. Department of Health and Human Services. 2017. *Proposed Refugee Admissions for Fiscal Year 2018: Report to Congress*, October 4, 2017. https://www.state.gov/documents/organization/274857.pdf.

U.S. Department of State, U.S. Department of Homeland Security, and U.S. Department of Health and Human Services. 2018. *Proposed Refugee Admissions for Fiscal Year 2019: Report to Congress*, September 24, 2018. https://www.state.gov/documents/organization/286401.pdf.

U.S. Office of Refugee Resettlement. 2012. "The Refugee Act." http://www.acf.hhs.gov/orr/resource/the-refugee-act.

U.S. Office of Refugee Resettlement. 2015. "The U.S. Refugee Resettlement Program—An Overview." https://www.acf.hhs.gov/orr/resource/the-us-refugee-resettlement-program-an-overview.

U.S. Office of Refugee Resettlement. 2018. "About Wilson/Fish." www.acf.hhs.gov/orr/programs/wilson-fish/about.

U.S. Refugee Act of 1980, Pub. L. No. 96-212, 94 Stat. 102.

Utah Department of Workforce Services. 2016. "Programming." http://jobs.utah.gov/refugee/center/program.html.

Welch, Keith. 2017. *A Pivotal Moment for the US Refugee Resettlement Program.* Berkeley, CA: Haas Institute for a Fair and Inclusive Society. http://haasinstitute.berkeley.edu/sites/default/files/haasinstitute_usrefugeeresettlement_june2017_publish.pdf.

WFIE. 2016. "Vandalism Clean-Up Event at Islamic Center Canceled." *WFIE*, November 19. http://www.14news.com/story/33749451/vandalism-clean-up-event-at-islamic-center-canceled/.

Zolberg, Aristide R. 2006. *A Nation by Design: Immigration Policy and the Fashioning of America*. Cambridge, MA: Harvard University Press.

CHAPTER FIVE

Migration Policies in Europe and the United States

Securitization, Safety, and the Paradox of Human Rights

Marciana Popescu

On April 21, 2017, 12 migrants trapped at Moria, considered by many as the worst refugee camp in Lesbos, Greece, started a hunger strike (Legal Centre Lesvos 2017). Their protest conveyed that mere existence (rather than life) is worse than death. This incident followed a series of desperate actions, including several other hunger strikes, refugees setting themselves on fire, violence, and suicide attempts, all signaling a crisis. This is not a "refugee crisis," as labeled by media and politicians, but rather a crisis of the states and governments throughout the world, unable, unwilling, or unprepared to provide an effective response to the increased human mobility and the widespread mass displacement.

The magnitude of displacement today is unprecedented: 68.5 million people forcibly displaced worldwide, of which 25.4 million are refugees and at least 3.1 million are asylum seekers (UNHCR 2018a). Vulnerability and lethality are on the rise, with over 300,000 unaccompanied migrant children (UNICEF 2018) at increased risks. Human trafficking is escalating among migrants (International Organization for Migration 2016), and sexual victimization is removing any illusion of safety from refugee camps or asylum facilities (Women's Refugee Commission 2016). The scale of suffering and deaths happening during migration ultimately challenges the notion that state and international actors are earnest about fostering safe migration.

In Europe, the number of incoming forced migrants includes over 600,000 stateless people (Institute on Statelessness and Inclusion 2017); 1,875,947 refugees and asylums seekers who arrived by sea since 2014 (UNHCR 2018b); and 538,000 children migrants, of which about a third were registered as unaccompanied (by the end of 2017). There are also 28,627 missing or dead migrants, since 2014, with 2,160 deaths recorded in 2018 alone (IOM 2018). These numbers do not take into account the number of refugees and asylum seekers in Turkey, which in 2018 rose to close to 4 million refugees (of which 3.54 million were Syrian refugees) (UNHCR 2018c). Most of the forced migrants in Europe come from three countries: Syria, Iraq, and Afghanistan. Between 2014 and 2017 forced migrants from these three countries accounted for 1,678,005 people or 45.6 percent of all first-time asylum applications (Eurostat 2018). Of the 28 EU member countries, Germany, France, and Italy are overwhelmingly bearing the burden of care for asylum seekers and refugees. In 2017, these three countries accounted for 75 percent of all positive decisions on asylum applications within the EU. In terms of resettlements, the numbers are much lower at 23,925 (Eurostat 2018). Five EU member countries, the United Kingdom, Germany, Sweden, Norway, and France, resettled over 75 percent of the total resettled population in 2017.

In the United States, current rhetoric on migration favors major restrictions. Policies include curtailing refugee resettlements to the lowest limits ever, with a cap of 30,000 resettled people for 2019 (Rush 2018) and implementing a "zero tolerance" policy that separates asylum seeker families at the U.S.-Mexico border. This policy undermines the principles and practices of U.S. and international law that have been in place for many decades (Davis 2018).

Such trends shift global and regional migration policies toward claiming or maintaining security and ignore mandates to provide global protection measures for populations that should be the primary beneficiaries of such measures. This chapter examines key policies addressing forced migrants in Europe and the United States. After outlining the current international and regional legal frameworks on forced migration, the chapter examines the effects of a heightened securitization regime. It underscores how regional and national securitization regimes pose challenges for forced migrants, undermining emerging processes for safe migration, protection, and realization of rights for asylum seekers and refugees. Finally, it explores steps that need to be taken to shift the paradigm from securitization to safe migration using case exemplars from Germany and Austria.

International Legal Framework and Emergent Trends in Migration Policies

Over the last four years, migration discourses have been dominated by an emphasis on restrictive policies in order to keep countries safe. They have focused on securing borders, establishing stricter immigration criteria, reducing existing resettlement quotas, and expediting and limiting asylum requests (Carrera, Blockmans, Gros, and Guild 2015). In Europe, FRONTEX, an intergovernmental agency charged with improving border protection within the EU space, resorted to the externalization of borders, to prevent migrants from reaching EU countries at all costs (Moreno-Lax 2018). Individual countries within the EU called for a restoration of the *Schengen space*,[1] while several national governments closed their borders to refugees and asylum seekers (Ciobanu 2017; Lendaro 2016). Although far-right movements were slowed by the loss of national elections in 2016, they have regained momentum and continued to push a xenophobic, nationalist platform throughout Europe. Austria seeks to restrict immigration, by reducing access to basic rights for asylum seekers, while working with Germany and Italy on "protecting" the borders.

In the United States, the externalization of borders was accompanied by a "zero tolerance" policy, preventing migrants predominantly from Central America to access the existing legal venues for asylum requests (Romero and Jordan 2018). The Trump administration has implemented restrictionist immigration policies, including refugee resettlement, asylum procedures, and policies for the undocumented migrants, under the promise of "keeping America safe." Even existing paths to citizenship have been challenged while social benefits for authorized immigrants are being insidiously curtailed (Blitzer 2018; Migration Policy Institute 2018).

Although alarming, this approach is not new: in the United States, immigration laws have gone through alternating cycles of restrictionism and securitization and open immigration, as well as shifting focus between different target population groups (Abramitzki and Boustan 2017). Australia established externalized territories for migrants: Nauru Island has become infamous for its migrant camps, with a rise in suicidality among migrants prevented from ever reaching a true safe haven (Refugee Council of Australia 2018). The exodus of Rohingya from Myanmar reveals the reemergence of ethnic cleansing as a cause for forced migration (Patel 2017). More recently, Denmark has begun considering the isolationist Australian model as an option for the containment of "unwanted immigrants" (Loewenstein 2016).

In part, the rhetoric was described as a normal response to unprecedented numbers of displaced people (European Commission 2017). The complex causality of such displacement guarantees an extended crisis: besides ongoing conflicts in Syria, South Sudan, Afghanistan, Yemen, and Venezuela, natural disasters and protracted emergencies continue to contribute to the intensified displacement and movement of populations within and between countries. While most of the forcefully displaced people are hosted by neighboring countries, with the burden of care for migrants being highest in low- and middle-income economies, strong voices from the European Union and the United States framed the current wave of forced migration as a crisis for the old and new world, to which their respective governments were neither prepared nor willing to respond.

Within this context, a few relevant challenges need to be addressed: (1) The definition challenge and the need to reframe definitions and policies that were developed in the 20th century to address 21st century realities; (2) the legal challenge, including the complexity of migration policies, laws, and regulating frameworks; and (3) the paradox of human rights within a humanitarian framing of the migration response.

Forced Migration: The Definition Challenge

Migration was historically linked to the concept of human mobility and the movement of populations within and across national borders. Theorists have analyzed migration as adaptation (Ober and Sakdapolrak 2017); as a development strategy; and as a major force in defining/refining regimes, territories, and jurisdictions (Horvath, Amelina, and Peters 2017). Even if not fully constructed as a human right, migration was also framed as a fundamental freedom (UDHR 1948, Article 13). However, the legal parameters for such free movement were developed within the context of national sovereignty, and the implicit rights of nation-states to establish their own needs and priorities related to free flows of migrants to and from their respective territories, and to contribute to the clear differentiation between citizens and noncitizens (Benhabib 1999). And while migration in general refers to individual or collective choices people make based on a risk and opportunity assessment (Klabunde and Willekens 2016), forced migration refers to the movement of people determined and controlled by external factors, pushing them out of their own communities into new and unknown territories, and often under extreme, unsafe conditions. When Arendt first discussed the plight of refugees in the aftermath of the Holocaust, she reflected on the central element of the refugees' identity—as people who lost their fundamental right to have rights (Arendt 1949). And that compounded loss is determined by the actual concepts we are operating with—to understand, assess, and respond to forced migration.

Within a human rights paradigm, migration must be redefined as one of the fundamental human rights and anchored accordingly in human rights principles (Oberman 2016; Zard 2005). Yet, while human rights are universal and nondiscriminatory, when it comes to migrants as right holders, citizenship and national sovereignty are still the basic dimensions used in the politics of migration, in framing migration policies, and in contributing to developing instruments for migration management and for the protection of forced migrants (Gregg 2017). The role of state governments in managing both the definitions and the rights appears to be increasingly blurred by international agreements that slightly changed the rights-based understanding of migration. And while new global instruments aim to establish some consistency in the definitions used by state actors, contradictions inherent in past and current migration laws continue to challenge protection claims for so-called "irregular" migrants, the internally displaced, or the *persons of concern* who fall outside the realm of agreed-upon legal categories (Bloch and Chimienti 2011).

Migration theories propose different conceptual frameworks for understanding, analyzing, and managing migration. Current trends suggest a prevalence of the securitization framework (Horvath 2014; Huysmans 2000). This framework prioritizes border control and the protections provided based on citizenship, nationality, or legal migration status (Léonard 2011). Such protections are limited to the most vulnerable, as per varying, and often discretionary, definitions and categorization of the migrants.

Different international instruments operationalize current definitions to differentiate between migration protection categories and to establish the range of rights provided for each category and the jurisdiction for these rights under international, regional, and national laws. Within the European Union, forced migrants can have the status of *refugees* and arrive to Europe either through resettlement or as *asylum seekers*. The *asylum seeker* designation is used for people seeking asylum in the host countries. Asylum applications can lead to two other *lesser* migrant designations: *subsidiary protection status* (people who do not qualify as refugees but for whom, based on substantial grounds, the return to their country of origin would present the risk of serious harm) and *humanitarian protection* (for persons covered by a decision granting authorization to stay for humanitarian reasons under national laws concerning international protection).

Historically, legal definitions for refugees were strictly connected to war, civil conflicts, or state-level persecution targeting specific populations (as framed by the 1951 Convention Relating to the Status of Refugee). Yet, such narrow definitions exclude migrants who do not fit the historic characteristics, including irregular migrants, who enter and "stay or work in a country without necessary authorization or documents required under immigration regulations" (Perruchoud and Redpath-Cross 2011, 54); *internally displaced populations (IDPs)*, for which the protection responsibilities rest with their own governments; and those who are *stateless*. While statelessness has been granted more attention under the UN Convention related to the Status of the Stateless Persons (1954), current protections do not extend to all stateless groups. Some examples include the Rohingya of Myanmar and the Haitian population in the Dominican Republic. One other group to consider is *environmental refugees*, defined by El-Hinnawi (1985) as "people who have been forced to leave their traditional habitat, temporarily or permanently, because of a marked environmental disruption . . . that jeopardizes their existence and/or seriously affects the quality of their life" (4). No specific international protections are accorded to environmental refugees to date.

The Legal Challenge: Complexity and Lack of Coordination on Migration Laws between Varied Levels of Governments

The conceptual challenges discussed in the previous section are caused by contradictions and varied standards of current migration laws, as well as the disconnect between policy provisions and implementation. The legal framework of migration at the global level consists of three sets of laws: international human rights laws, refugee laws, and international humanitarian laws.

International Human Rights Laws

The international human rights laws contribute to framing migration as a human right. According to the Universal Declaration of Human Rights (UDHR 1948), "Everybody has the right to seek and to enjoy in other countries asylum from persecution" (Article 14.1). No limitations based on migration status should affect the fundamental human rights of the forced migrants. Such rights apply to the entire migration context, from the point of origin (civil and political rights in the countries of origin; as well as social and economic rights as grounds for protection by the states), through the migration journey, to the point of destination. Although neither the UDHR nor the related legal instruments establish an obligation for the states as duty bearers to admit refugees or asylum seekers into their countries, the freedom of movement and the right to seek and secure asylum are clearly stated in various human rights documents.

The most relevant international human rights instruments used to establish a framework for migration governance, with implications for all signatories of these instruments, include: the International Covenant for Civil and Political Rights (ICCPR 1966); the International Covenant for Economic, Social, and Cultural Rights (ICESCR 1966); the Convention for the Elimination of all forms of Racial Discrimination (CERD 1969); the Convention for the Rights of the Child (CRC 1989); the Convention for the Elimination of all forms of Discrimination against Women (CEDAW 1979); the Convention against Torture and Cruelty (CTC 1984); the International Convention for the Protection of the Rights of Migrant Workers and Families (ICPRMW 1990), and the Convention for the Protection of All Persons against Enforced Disappearance (ICPED 2006). These rights are elaborations of those articulated in the Universal Declaration of Human Rights (1948) and have either general applications to migrant rights or specific/population-based protections (see Tables 5.1 and 5.2).

These instruments were created to address the complexities and fluidity of migration processes. While the UDHR was developed in response to World War II and the Holocaust, as the guiding principles for all nations in

Table 5.1. International Human Rights Framework for Migration Governance: Civil and Political Rights

	ICCPR	CERD	CRC	CEDAW	CTC	ICPRMW	ICPED
Right to free movement	Article 12	Article 5	Article 15			Articles 8, 39	
Right to asylum	**		**	**	Article 3*		
Right to fair representation	Article 26	Article 5	Article 3	Articles 8, 9	Article 14	Article 7	Articles 13, 14, 17
Right to due process	Article 14	Article 5	Articles 4, 9	Article 15	Articles 4, 5	Article 18	Articles 23, 24, 25
Right to be protected from torture or cruel treatment	Article 7	Article 5	Articles 19 34, 36	Article 6	Articles 11, 13, 16	Article 10	Articles 17, 18
Right to not be subjected to slavery	Article 8		Article 35	Article 5		Article 11	
Right to nationality	Article 24	Article 5	Article 7	Article 9		Article 29	
Right to vote	Article 25	Article 5	N/A	Article 7		Article 41	
Right to family	Article 23	Article 5	Article 20	Article 16		Article 44	Article 17

* While not specifically addressing the right to request asylum, the CTC/Article 3 frames the obligations of state to abide by the principle of nonrefoulement.

** The right to asylum, as framed by the UDHR (Article 14), was not transferred/further supported by either the ICCPR/ICESCR or the more specialized human rights instruments, such as the CRC or CEDAW. The principle of nonrefoulement found its place in international human rights laws—specifically mentioned by the CTC/ Article 3.

Table 5.2. International Human Rights Framework for Migration Governance: Social, Economic, and Cultural Rights

	ICESCR	CERD	CRC	CEDAW	ICPRMW	ICPED
Right to education	Article 13	Article 5	Articles 28, 29	Article 10	Articles 30, 43	
Right to health care	Article 12	Article 5	Article 24	Article 12	Article 28	
Right to employment	Article 6	Article 5	N/A	Articles 11, 13	Articles 43, 45	
Right to social services	Articles 9, 10	Article 5	Article 26	Article 11	Article 27	Article 24
Right to housing	Article 11	Article 5	Article 27		Article 43	

safeguarding humanity, the later covenants and conventions created more specific and legally binding parameters, establishing categories of right holders and responsibilities for the states. Yet one common critique is the lack of enforceability of human rights laws, due to the lack of UN power, fragmentation in the protections conferred by these laws at state levels, or the lack of commitment of UN member countries to provide resources needed to support implementing and monitoring through national immigration policies.

In part because of the failures of the international human rights and humanitarian law regimes to protect the rights of forced migrants, the global community has pursued a new initiative at the United Nations to create a pair of global compacts on migration and refugees. On September 19, 2016, following growing concerns related to ineffective global responses to unprecedented numbers of asylum seekers and refugees on the move, the New York Declaration for Refugees and Migrants was adopted and signed by the 193 participating member states. At the UN Leaders' Summit, a total of 47 countries pledged their commitment to work on legal and policy changes to enhance refugees' access to education, employment, health care, and social services; to increase humanitarian aid; and to expand access to third-country solutions, through resettlement and improved family reunification policies (UN New York Declaration 2016).

The New York Declaration set the groundwork for two global compacts: the Global Compact on Safe and Orderly Migration (GCM), aiming to establish a framework for addressing mass migration and improving states' responses/protection of migrants; and the Global Compact on Refugees (GCR), building on the Global Framework for the Comprehensive Refugee Response Framework (CRRF) included in the New York Declaration and on the existing legal framework for the protection of refugees. Yet, from this early historical vantage point, having *two* compacts may further divide protections, rights, and responsibilities toward migrants based on their assigned status and maintains the dichotomy of regular versus irregular migration, with irregular migrants falling outside the immediate scope of both proposed frameworks.

The two compacts' nonbinding nature also raises questions regarding the capacity to consistently implement the principles set out in the two compacts at global, regional, and national levels. In addition, the recent withdrawal of five countries (United States, Hungary, Poland, Czech Republic, and Israel) and the abstention of twelve others (including six European nations) from signing the Global Compact on Safe Migration on December 19, 2018 (United Nations General Assembly 2018), threaten to render the accord much weaker. This is reminiscent of the legacy of the UN Convention on the Protection of the Rights of All Migrant Workers and Members of Their Families (1990), which has failed to gain parties from the Global North despite being in force for nearly 30 years.

Nevertheless, the global compacts introduce, for the first time, a global platform for rethinking and reframing migration policies proposing a different narrative of protecting human rights and creating safe spaces for refugees and asylum seekers. Effective implementation of the compacts' guidelines and principles rests on states and the United Nations recognizing the indivisibility of the two compacts and other international human rights laws and mechanisms.

International Refugee Laws

The main international legal instrument providing a framework for the protection of refugees is the UN Convention Relating to the Status of Refugees (1951). The additional UN Protocol Relating to the Status of Refugees (1967) removes the geographical limitations from the initial convention that were constrained to Europe, thus expanding the definition to all people who otherwise fulfill the criteria as listed in the convention.

Described as "both a status and a rights-based instrument" by the High Commissioner for Refugees (UNHCR 2010), the Convention is grounded in Article 14 of the UDHR, and defined by several fundamental principles: the principle of nondiscrimination (1951 Convention, Article 3) that prohibited discriminatory treatment of refugees; the principle of nonpenalization (1951 Convention, Article 31) that prohibited states from assigning penalties to refugees or asylum seekers for unlawful entry; and the principle of nonrefoulement (1951 Convention, Article 33) that stated "no one shall expel or return a refugee against his or her will, in any manner whatsoever, to a territory where he or she fears threats to life or freedom" (UNHCR 2010, 30).

In light of these principles and of the recent questions raised on the effectiveness of the convention in providing the needed framework for the protection of refugees, there are a few challenges that need to be addressed: (1) the nature of the convention as a human rights instrument; (2) the conditionality of rights and protections on the "burden of proof"; and (3) the unequivocal principle of nonrefoulement.

1. *Convention as a human rights instrument:* The emphasis placed on the definition and legal categorization of refugees as central to the convention diminishes its role as a human rights instrument, refugees' rights being secondary to the states' powers in determining who could claim such rights. According to the Refugee Convention, a refugee is a person who

> owing to *well-founded fear* of being persecuted for reasons of race, religion, nationality, membership of a particular social group or political opinion, is outside the country of his nationality and is unable or, owing to such fear, is unwilling to avail himself of the protection of that country; or who, not having a nationality and being outside the country of his former habitual residence as a result of such events, is unable or, *owing to such fear,* is unwilling to return to it. (Article 1)

This part of the convention is the most often cited; other parts of the treaty that address obligations for the protection of refugees' rights no matter where they reside receive less attention (Hathaway 2007). Rather than focusing only on the definition of refugee and conditions of flight, we must attend more carefully to the root causes and violation of rights in the country of origin and the deprivation they suffer in the host countries (Edwards 2005).

Another factor is the overwhelming predominance of a *national sovereignty* discourse in migration politics. Considering the nonpenalization principle, the UNHCR high commissioner stated that the understanding of this principle is based on the fact that seeking asylum "can require refugees to breach immigration rules." States are prohibited to use penalties such as "being charged with immigration or criminal offences relating to the seeking of asylum, or being arbitrarily detained purely on the basis of seeking asylum" (UNHCR 2010, 3).

2. *The burden of proof and conditionality of refugee rights:* The "well-founded" aspect of the refugee definition needs to be thoroughly proven by those seeking asylum. This can be a daunting task, given that often asylum seekers have limited to no access to documents to support their claims. Moreover, many countries do not have a coordinated approach to identify and process such claims. The power of interpretation of how "well-founded" the fear of the person requesting asylum is resides with state actors who have multiple and often conflicted responsibilities and limited understanding or knowledge of the context of forced migration.

3. *Principle of nonrefoulement—unequivocal:* The 1951 Convention Relating to the Status of Refugees does not establish an obligation to grant asylum. State parties are required, however, to *not return* people who request asylum without proper review of their case. Yet states frequently violate this principle, using national sovereignty or security concerns as the main justification.

There are also three regional documents adding to the refugee laws: The Organization for the African Unity (OAU) Convention on Refugee Problems (UNHCR 1969); the Cartagena Declaration, providing a framework for international protections for refugees in Latin-American countries (UNHCR 1984); and the 1999 Common European Asylum System (CEAS) (European Asylum Support Office 2016; European Commission 1999).

International Humanitarian Laws

International Humanitarian Laws (IHL) provide a legal framework for the protection of victims of armed conflict, whether or not they have been displaced or are inside or outside their country of origin. These protections needed by people escaping armed conflict are the third pillar of the overall international legal framework regulating forced migration, including the Fourth Geneva Convention (ICRC 1949) and the Additional Protocol I (ICRC 1977).

The IHL act to prevent displacement inasmuch as possible and to provide additional protection for refugees when displacement occurs. In case of displacement, specific rules are established in regard to shelter, health care, and access to basic goods and services for the displaced populations. It is the IHL that govern the management of refugee camps, aiming to increase protection and create a safe space that allows asylum seekers and refugees the protection their own countries of origin cannot or will not provide.

The EU Migration Framework: Burden Sharing, Shared Inequality, and the Limits of Universal Freedoms

At the EU level, the international laws governing migration are further classified into (1) EU human rights laws, (2) EU Refugee Laws, and (3) bilateral agreements/national laws.

EU Human Right Laws

This includes the European Convention on Human Rights (1953), which was last amended in 2018 (Protocol 16). It establishes a framework for the protection of civil and political rights of people within Europe, and it aligns with the international human rights laws in providing protection for asylum seekers and refugees. Several of its articles have direct application to forced migration. The responsibility of EU member states to protect the right to asylum in accordance with international refugee laws is specified in the European Union Charter/Article 18 (*Official Journal of the European Union* 2010). The European Social Charter (ESC revised/1996) focuses on social and economic rights for all people in Europe (Council of Europe 1996).

EU Refugee Laws

The Common European Asylum System (CEAS) is the cornerstone of the EU refugee/asylum laws, which emerged following the 1990s displacement and migration waves determined by the fall of the Communist block and the Balkan conflicts. Currently, the CEAS includes primary laws, establishing the EU policy framework; and secondary laws, respectively all directives, regulations, and mechanisms dealing with asylum procedures and protections, within the EU (European Asylum Support Office 2016). Coexisting secondary laws relevant for asylum within the EU, but not part of the CEAS, include the Family Reunification Directive (2003), the Long-Term Residents Directive (2003), and the Returns Directive (2008).

One of the most problematic aspects of the EU refugee laws is related to the nature and implementation of the Dublin III Agreement (European Union Law 2013) and its implications for migration policies, in general, and the rights of the asylum seekers, in particular. The Dublin Agreement aims to manage migrants' access to the European space, and it follows three main principles: *one* opportunity to apply, *one* designated EU country in charge of reviewing the application, and a possible transfer of migrants to the assigned country for their asylum application (Garcés-Mascareñas 2015).

The EU country in charge with the asylum application is determined based on either family ties or first EU country of arrival by the asylum seeker. This, since 2015, posed a significant burden on both Greece and Italy—first countries to be reached on the Balkan or Italian migration routes. This poses a *question of fairness* in regard to the distribution of responsibilities for asylum requests and decisions, among EU countries.

Although it was created to prevent "asylum-shopping"—or multiple applications for asylum in different EU countries—the Dublin regulation does not fulfill that goal. This raises the *question of effectiveness*: The assumption was that once safety is ensured, it shouldn't matter what country would fulfill the applicant's right to asylum and where people will be relocated. In reality, personal preferences do matter, as migration decisions are based on networks of support (through presence of either family or friends), perception of countries based on the (assumed) welcome, and generosity of local policies toward migrants.

Finally, the Dublin Agreement appears to have further contributed to the *violation of the rights of refugees*, including violations of due process, fair representation and a just relocation system. The burden-sharing policy was created to start addressing some of these questions, and it led to several adjustments/revisions of the Agreement and suggestions of alternative strategies to increase choice. One proposed change is to allow asylum seekers to decide the country they will apply for asylum, with potential compensatory funding for countries that would incur a higher number of applications to facilitate free movement within the EU space.

Bilateral Agreements and National Migration Platforms

There are several bilateral agreements that further contribute to the complexity of the migration legal framework in Europe. Most relevant for our understanding of the current EU migration context are the EU-Turkey Agreement and the EU-Afghanistan Agreement.

The EU-Turkey Agreement (March 18, 2016) was designed to deter refugees from coming to Europe and limit migrants' deaths at sea. For every Syrian refugee returned to Turkey, another vulnerable migrant was supposed to be resettled within the European Union—aiming to provide protections to most vulnerable migrants. Instead, the deal established several securitization mechanisms: additional funding was allocated to keep people out of Europe and Turkey was declared, de facto, a safe third country, allowing migrants' returns. While the Agreement achieved its goal to limit the number of refugees arriving in Greece and significantly lowered migrant deaths rates (European Commission 2018), it incurred several problems regarding the treatment of migrants both in Turkey and Greece. Médicins Sans Frontières (MSF) indicated that the conditions on the Greek islands created a mental health emergency that cannot be easily contained (MSF 2017). With an insufficiently developed asylum system (Asylum in Europe 2018a), Turkey faces the challenge of housing almost four million refugees (Kirişci, Brandt, and Erdoğan 2018). The humanitarian crisis brewing on the Greek islands cumulated with the increasing burden on all services in Turkey, posing serious questions regarding the effectiveness of the deal.

The EU-Afghanistan Agreement of 2016 represents another plank of the securitization framework for migration within the European Union. This policy created a path for returns/repatriations of Afghan asylum seekers, lowering their chances to be granted asylum in Europe (Ruttig 2017). Since the agreement was reached, the rates of recognition for Afghan asylum seekers within the European Union changed dramatically. According to a 2018 report from the European Council on Refugees and Exiles, nine EU countries actively use the agreement to return people to Afghanistan. Germany has deported over 150 people to Afghanistan since the signing of the agreement, and the recognition rate for Afghan asylum seekers dropped from 55.8 percent to 47.4 percent by the end of 2017 (European Council on Refugees and

Exiles 2018). The Norwegian Refugee Council and the International Displacement Monitoring Center (IDMC) indicate that 72 percent of the Afghan returnees are forced to leave again shortly after their return, due to the violence in the region (Internal Displacement Monitoring Center 2018).

Individual EU member countries took an increasingly hard stand on forced migration, citing national sovereignty to justify countries' resistance to the quota system. Hungary closed its borders on October 17, 2015, building fences to keep people out, deploying harsh anti-immigrant discourse that has become increasingly popular in the region, and introducing laws to criminalize support for those who, by law, are categorized as asylum seekers (Gardos 2018). Poland followed suit, refusing migrants due to national security concerns (Human Rights Watch 2017). Austria hardened its immigration policies, focusing on strengthening its external borders and curtailing services for asylum seekers within the country (*The Economist* 2018). Italy, under its populist government, created new restrictions to migration that further threatens the well-being of migrants within the EU block (Scherer 2018).

Forced Migration and the EU Response: Best Practices and Lessons Learned

Migration to Europe in general, and EU member countries in particular, is not a new phenomenon. It can be validly identified as "a crisis" today, however, not only because of the inability of EU governmental institutions and individual state governments to respond to mass movements but also due to two notable differences in migration patterns experienced since 2015. These include (1) the scale of migration, particularly on the Eastern Mediterranean route with unprecedented numbers peaking in 2015; and (2) the proportion of asylum seekers from countries experiencing high levels of conflict and instability, with over 90 percent of all forced migrants in 2015 coming from Syria, Afghanistan, and Iraq (Collett and Le Coz 2018). In light of the relatively weak or underenforced international and EU policies related to migration, it is important to highlight a few notable good policies and practices. Doing so provides a lens into lessons learned that could contribute to improving regional responses to migration and human mobility, and eventually shifting from a securitization to a rights-based approach, emphasizing safety and well-being as the most desirable outcomes.

This section will highlight best practices and lessons learned in two areas: (1) integration through education and employment in Germany; and (2) asylum processes, including access to due process and the role of nongovernmental organizations (NGOs), in Austria. These examples identify innovative practices and highlight the turning points in shifting paradigms toward a rights-based approach in migration policies and practice in the context of current challenges.

Germany: Education and Employment for Effective Integration of Migrants

Germany's relatively open position on forced migration reflected a rights-based approach in 2015. Chancellor Angela Merkel, despite strong political opposition and a heavy toll on her political career, pushed for an open-border approach and admission of up to one million asylum seekers and refugees. She emphasized the collective responsibility of Europe, and Germany's responsibility, in particular.

Between 2014 and 2016, the number of asylum applications saw a sharp increase, followed by a decrease in 2017. Using its own quota system, Germany mobilized government actors, local and international NGOs in the country, as well as UN agencies, to develop innovative best practices, measure the effectiveness of current policies, and protect the rights of the migrants, while also benefiting local communities. The German quota system, *Konigsteiner Key* (Federal Office for Migration and Refugees 2018), uses a formula based on tax revenue and population size, aiming to ensure a reasonable burden for each federal state ("land").

Historically, asylum seekers in Germany (and throughout the EU) did not have access to employment until their migration status has been clarified. And while recognition rates for some asylum seekers remained high throughout the past five years (particularly for Syrian and Iraqi refugees), the slow processes as well as the increase in rejection rates (Table 5.3) suggest the need for reformed approaches.

The German government promoted a pro-immigration discourse, focusing on the economic benefits of a rapid integration of migrants, and the added sociocultural benefits associated with highly cohesive communities. Rietig (2016) identifies five challenges that Germany needs to address to enhance integration: language, training/skills, qualifications recognition, employers, and governance. In light of these identified challenges, a multi-stakeholder/multilevel approach was employed, that engaged state actors across sectors, interdisciplinary scholars, businesses, and civil society, and ultimately changed policies to facilitate education and employment.

Language can act either as a core barrier to employment, education, and integration in the German society or as a facilitator, which increases access to all existing opportunities. While policies establish clear guidelines for language programs, implementation is often affected at an individual level, by migrants' perception of language difficulty, ability to participate fully in the training program, and ability to use training to secure jobs. At a structural level, further challenges are created by the lack of specialized training, delayed access (language training is linked to the recognition rates and expected protection quotas), and lack of diversified levels of training for higher language competency (Rietig 2016).

Table 5.3. Asylum Application Status—Germany (2015–2017)—From Select Countries of Origin

Country of Origin	Year	Total Applicants	Refugee Status	Subsidiary Protection	Humanitarian Protection	Positive Decision Rate (%)	Rejection	Rejection Rate (%)
Syria	2015	103,708	57,036	55	164	99.9	11	0.02
	2016	268,866	166,520	121,562	910	99.9	167	0.1
	2017	50,422	34,880	55,697	534	98.8	133	0.2
Iraq	2015	21,303	10,676	185	60	99.5	50	0.46
	2016	97,162	36,801	10,912	439	77.2	14,248	22.8
	2017	21,930	24,320	14,300	1,637	64.5	22,170	35.5
Afghanistan	2015	20,830	1,361	254	599	79.4	574	20.6
	2016	127,892	13,813	5,836	18,441	60.6	24,817	39.4
	2017	16,423	17,932	6,892	26,345	47.4	56,722	52.6

Source: Adapted from AIDA 2018.

To improve employment prospects and outcomes, Germany developed a Vocational Education and Training System (VET) to enable refugees to match their skills with the needs of local economic markets. However, difficulties in accessing the system by asylum seekers and refugees and economic and social costs involved lower the functionality of this system. High levels of dropout are justified economically, as asylum seekers and refugees tend to either drop out or opt out of VET programs and choose lower-qualification jobs, simply to make ends meet.

Capacity building is also affected by the ability of current systems to identify and recognize skills asylum seekers and refugees already have. The current systems include multiple options: One is the effective implementation of the legal framework (Recognition Act of 2012) that establishes parameters for the identification and evaluation of such qualifications earned outside the country. Another is the use and development of platforms/networks aiming to facilitate recognition—such as the IQ network (integration through qualification). And another is calling for industry to create paths to faster qualification recognition within sectors (Rietig 2016). Challenges include inconsistencies of the standards used for the evaluation of skills/qualifications; lack of coordination between different actors responsible for such evaluations and their criteria; and high complexity of processes, particularly as they relate to navigating the overlapping migration systems.

Employers' attitudes toward migrants vary, and the lack of consistent government support or incentives for hiring asylum seekers or refugees adds to employers' reluctance to integrate this population in the workforce. While some German states are working closely with employers to match refugees' skills with the demands at the state level, others are more politically motivated to lower the number of refugees under their jurisdiction.

Ultimately, how the government chooses to engage in creating paths to integration and a safer migration system matters. Integration policy is built on two axes as part of a safe migration approach in Germany: (1) governance at federal versus local levels, with directives and guidelines from the EU often framing federal and local governance; and (2) integration policy involving multiple areas/sectors and stakeholders (labor market, education, general integration). With federal, state, local governments, and civil society actors involved in interventions, the success of any integration effort will rely on the good coordination and collaboration of all these actors (Rietig 2016).

One promising example comes from Saarland, one of the smallest German states in size and economy. Thus, Saarland has one of the lowest quotas of refugees/asylum seekers (1.2%—EASY 2018) and a high proportion of the refugees are Syrian refugees. The director of the Asylum Reception Center of the state noted this as an advantage for the local government to promote and support innovative integration strategies (Popescu n.d.). In 2016, the University of Saarland decided to create a path to higher education for the refugees relocated in the neighboring communities and developed an admission system, integrating existing qualification recognition tools, and curriculum options for the refugees who would be admitted in the program. All entry exams/tests were translated in Arabic to make this program as inclusive as possible, and more than 100 students were admitted. However, it became quickly evident that the program had a high rate of attrition. The challenge was primarily caused by the change in status from refugees to students, which in turn drastically affected their benefits. While the policy was established at a federal level and implemented by state actors, it was the university that challenged this policy, advocating for rapid changes to support integration. Within weeks, the policy was revisited by the state and local governance, and migrant status was adjusted to allow students to receive the same level of social benefits and continue to study. Two years later, participants in the program shared their gratitude for the opportunity created. The program administrators spoke about the importance of coordination between stakeholders, and the significant role of the university in reviewing and challenging existing policies, to foster refugee integration and well-being. Access to education and employment contributed to a paradigm shift, allowing asylum seekers and refugees to reclaim their human dignity and be recognized as active participants in the society.

While EU policies still limit access to education and employment for irregular migrants, such best practices provide models that could be used to shift the narrative on migration, particularly regarding the role of migrants in their host communities. In the words of one young Syrian refugee, housed at Cosmopolis Grand Hotel in Augsburg: "Yes, we are grateful, we have a nice place to stay, food to eat, and clothes to wear. Yet we are humans not cattle: We need to be able to work and support ourselves, to feel that we really belong" (written note, guest book, Cosmopolis). Participation in higher education or vocational trainings is an important element in accessing employment and increasing the sense of belonging.

Austria: Asylum Seeking—Regional Responses and National Constraints

Austria is regarded as one of the gateways to Germany and Northern Europe and a life of safety and security. Although the number of forced migrants in Austria has historically not been as high as neighboring countries like Germany, Austria experienced sharp increases at the height of the mass migrant mobility into Europe. Figure 5.1 shows asylum application trends in Austria, from Syria, Iraq, Afghanistan, Pakistan, and Nigeria, which peaked in 2015.

ASYLUM APPLICATIONS

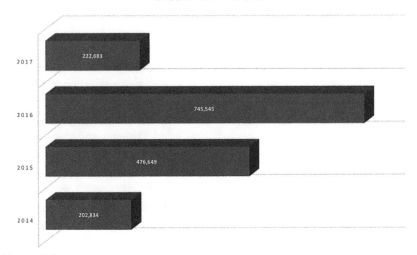

Figure 5.1.
Source: Data retrieved from AIDA, 2018

Asylum processes are complex in Austria, marked by different jurisdictions over decisions. In the legal system, the asylum applications fall under three separate jurisdictions: (1) EU immigration laws and respective regulations and directives (the Common European Asylum System components, discussed earlier), which establish the role of EU countries in addressing asylum applications and the specific responsibilities for each stakeholder involved in reviewing and channeling these applications; (2) Austrian immigration laws (Asylum in Europe 2018b); and (3) laws governing matters such as housing, employment, and welfare, and establishing the level of support and institutions responsible in providing access to basic goods and services, and, depending on the final decision, in facilitating integration of migrants in the local communities or deportation procedures (Asylum in Europe 2018c).

The primary federal authority for forced migration in Austria is the Department for Foreign Citizens and Asylum Seekers (BFA), which overviews the asylum processes. First-level decisions are made by BFA's employees, who currently number over 1,800 in the country. They are trained in short, intensive on-the-job training, and there are no prior qualification requirements except for having a high-school diploma. The process of asylum adjudication involves power dynamics between BFA employees and the asylum seeker. These can be exacerbated by asylum seekers' experiences of trauma, language difficulties, and fear of dismissal as well as a lack of an in-depth understanding of migration processes, national contexts in the country of origin, and proper risk assessment skills on the part of BFA staff (as per interviews with NGO representatives working with the BFA and with asylum seekers, 2016–2017). The initial decision can be appealed. This administrative procedure does not require representation by lawyers. Moreover, most of the legal counseling services at this stage are provided by NGO staff, who are usually highly committed and professional, yet with no power of representation in courts. According to an interview with one of the program directors at an NGO providing legal counseling and services to refugees:

> There is the law, and then there is the immigration law, under which one starts with the presumption of guilt. And in Austria, the immigration courts are operating differently from the start. Our staff, although working hard to prepare and document each appeal well, faces discretionary powers in the court system, while having no voice at all in the legal process. (Interview, January 2017)

Only during the second appeal can asylum seekers request legal representation by lawyers. Yet the percentage of cases that make it to a second appeal is low, due to extensive waiting periods, lack of understanding or proper information provided to applicants on the appeal process (e.g., time periods, rights as per Austrian laws, rights as per EU laws, and possibility of free legal representation), and desperation. This desperation can lead people to resorting to other options, such as smuggling, often linked to human trafficking (Aloyo and Cusumano 2018). Time limits for appeals are very strict and rather short, ranging between seven days, in case of inadmissibility, to four weeks for other appeals. Yet, processing time for each stage can range anywhere between six months to six years. The official average time of the entire process should not exceed 15 months; however, factors such as the country of origin, governmental jurisdiction (federal authority) processing the case, judge/courts that appeals are assigned to, and other contingencies contribute to extended processing times.

The Austrian asylum laws, aligned with the EU immigration laws, establish governmental responsibility for shelter, food, clothing, and medical care during the asylum process. Also, for school-age children, access to education is mandatory. This regulation, however, does not apply to preschool children (Asylum in Europe 2018d). Over the past three years, however, the welfare laws pertaining to asylum seekers and refugees were targeted for drastic changes, with cash benefits for refugees being lowered to approximately $650 per month. This is lower than the amount currently provided to low-income Austrian citizens, which is in violation with EU laws that require equal treatment of refugees (Asylum in Europe 2018e). Further changes planned include seizing migrants' cell phones and using the geo-data to get access to their travel routes, in an attempt to invoke Dublin restrictions or identify any irregularities (The Local 2018).

Asylum seekers are not authorized to work, and access to language-training programs is limited depending on the protection status. Most recent restrictions include abolishing apprenticeship programs for asylum seekers, thus taking away any opportunities to even prepare for employment while waiting on a decision regarding their status (Hefron 2018). These policies affect the asylum seekers' immediate ability to live autonomously and long-term ability to integrate and contribute to local economies.

One of the most immediate challenges faced by asylum seekers once they are assigned a protective status is housing. In 2015, the lack of adequate housing for asylum seekers led to more active networking between governmental and nongovernmental actors. Yet the housing challenge continued, being more acute for refugees or people holding alternate protection, and anti-immigrant sentiments escalated, with increased violent attacks of refugee housing facilities (Dearden 2017). Time constraints, due to ineffective processing of asylum cases, and a generalized housing shortage contributed to the problem. In the Austrian asylum system, once a final positive decision has been reached, people have a very limited time (in most cases, up to three months) to secure housing and move out of the asylum housing provided for them. During that time, they also must find employment, engage in language courses, and adapt to the communities they will continue to live in or relocate to. The lack of adequate housing to make this transition leads to overcrowding. Many immigrants try to stay with other family members or friends, which has repercussions on family reunification cases, especially for people with alternate protection status, who must prove the ability to pay for housing and living costs for their immediate family members. In a study conducted in Austria in 2016–2017, representatives of several NGOs raised this as one of the primary factors weakening integration efforts and leading to labor exploitation and increasing the risk of human trafficking (Popescu n.d.).

Vienna's Magdas Hotel aimed to address housing and employment and contribute to creating a safe space for refugees (Infomigrants 2017). Opened at the peak of the crisis, the hotel aimed to provide housing to newcomers; it soon transformed into an innovative best practice by hiring refugees and providing them a chance to build community in Austria. Thus, refugees were engaged in building, cleaning, and repurposing the space and now provide tourist services alongside Austrian workers. Magdas exemplifies the importance of working collaboratively with local authorities, NGOs, funders, as well as community activists, to foster recognition of the humanity of refugees and their contributions. In this case, opportunities benefited not only the refugees but also the local communities and economy. Such initiatives highlight the need for better housing and employment policies and offer a chance to educate local communities on current challenges and engage them in identifying alternative solutions.

Moving from Securitization to Safe Migration: Steps Forward in Regional and Global Migration Policies and Implications for Practice

One of the most essential positive outcomes of rapidly changing and increasingly restrictive migration policies at global levels, as well as in Europe and the United States, is the rise of the civil society, manifested at community levels and in global policy action. With all its limitations, the Global Compact for Safe Migration was formally adopted by the United Nations General Assembly on December 19, 2018. The civil society, including international and local NGOs, grassroots movements, and volunteers, was one of the important forces behind this historic moment. The Compact, although not legally binding, creates a global framework for the implementation of migration policies that will foster safety and purposefully create mechanisms to protect the rights of migrants. This is the first international agreement on migration that was reached through consultation between multilevel stakeholders and negotiation and collaboration between governments. Its significance goes beyond the disagreements that increased in the months prior to its final approval in December 2018. Support dropped from 192 of the 193 member countries as of July 2018 (with only the United States clearly in opposition) to 164 countries formally adopting the Compact, and only 152 final signatories (United Nations General Assembly 2018). Despite this reduction in support, the Compact establishes a clear strategy for international collaboration, with 23 objectives, aiming to ultimately shift the paradigm from aggressively protecting national borders to creating safe spaces within the migration landscape, through better data and improved legal pathways for migrants. It also potentially creates a balance between assisted returns and reintegration policies; targets negative drivers of migration; reduces vulnerability; and challenges injustice and discrimination (Newland 2018). This strategy could address the many issues discussed in this chapter, from reviewing and revising current international laws to create consistency and a new relevance for new migration contexts, to addressing the inconsistencies at regional and local levels, simplifying asylum processes, and improving access to existing benefits and protections for all migrants.

Economists indicate that population movements actually contribute to improving local and global economies. Yet the lack of consistent data and proper dissemination of such data between all migration actors, together with the manipulation of the masses by anti-immigrant movements and political interests, keep us from actually helping ourselves.

As practitioners, we are ethically responsible to continue to raise awareness, work with governments and civil society actors, and ensure an effective implementation of the Global Compact at all levels. It is also equally important to monitor the complementarity of the two compacts and work with policy makers and practitioners to create synergy between the Global

Compact on Safe Migration and the Global Compact on Refugees. As the GCR did not follow the same consultative process as the GCM, civil society, and particularly social workers working with asylum seekers and refugees, need to actively engage with state actors and international organizations and improve protection of this population.

The best practices presented in this chapter demonstrate that not only is it possible to promote and contribute to safe migration but that this has been already done. Through a consistent implementation of the two compacts and with the engagement of all relevant actors, we can shift the paradigm toward inclusion and safety, promoting sustainable models of practice that are centered on human rights.

Note

1. The Shengen space, established by the Shengen Agreement in 1995, originally included seven European countries. It was created to allow for the free movement of people among Shengen countries. Currently 26 countries belong to the Shengen Agreement, though conservative pressures call for reduction of the Shengen space.

Bibliography

Abramitzki, Ran, and Leah Boustan. 2017. "Immigration in American Economic History." *Journal of Economic Literature* 55, no. 4: 1311–1345.

Aloyo, Eamon, and Eugenio Cusumano. 2018. "Morally Evaluating Human Smuggling: The Case of Migration to Europe." *Critical Review of International Social and Political Philosophy*. https://www.tandfonline.com/doi/full/10.1080/13698230.2018.1525118.

Arendt, Hannah. 1949. *The Human Condition*. Chicago: University of Chicago Press.

Asylum in Europe. 2018a. *Introduction to Asylum System in Turkey*. https://www.asylumineurope.org/reports/country/turkey/introduction-asylum-context-turkey.

Asylum in Europe. 2018b. *Asylum Procedure Austria*. https://www.asylumineurope.org/reports/country/austria/asylum-procedure.

Asylum in Europe. 2018c. *Reception Conditions Austria*. https://www.asylumineurope.org/reports/country/austria/reception-conditions.

Asylum in Europe. 2018d. *Access to Education*. http://www.asylumineurope.org/reports/country/austria/reception-conditions/employment and-education/access-education.

Asylum in Europe. 2018e. *Austria: Social Welfare Restrictions on Refugees Contrary to EU Law*. November 21, 2018. https://www.asylumineurope.org/news/21-11-2018/austria-social-welfare-restrictions-refugees-contrary-eu-law.

Asylum Information Database (AIDA). 2018. https://www.asylumineurope.org/about-aida.

Benhabib, Seyla. 1999. "Citizens, Residents, and Aliens in a Changing World: Political Membership in the Global Era." *Social Research* 66, no. 3: 709–744.

Blitzer, Jonathan. 2018. "Trump's Public-Charge Rule Is a One-Two Punch against Immigrants and Public Assistance." *The New Yorker.* September 28, 2018. https://www.newyorker.com/news/dispatch/trumps-public-charge-rule-is-a-one-two-punch-against-immigrants-and-public-assistance.

Bloch, Alice, and Milena Chimienti. 2011. "Irregular Migration in a Globalizing World." *Ethnic and Racial Studies* 34, no. 8: 1271–1281.

Carrera, Sergio, Steven Blockmans, Daniel Gros, and Elspeth Guild. 2015. *The EU's Response to the Refugee Crisis: Taking Stock and Setting Policy Priorities.* December 16, 2015. https://www.ceps.eu/publications/eu%E2%80%99s-response-refugee-crisis-taking-stock-and setting-policy-priorities.

Ciobanu, Claudia. 2017. *Poland Follows Hungary's Footsteps in Corralling Migrants.* April 20, 2017. https://www.politico.eu/article/refugees-europe-poland-follows-hungarys footsteps-in-corralling-migrants/.

Collett, Elizabeth, and Camille Le Coz. 2018. "After the Storm: Learning from the EU Response to the Migration Crisis." Migration Policy Institute. https://www.migrationpolicy.org/research/after-storm-eu-response-migration-crisis.

Council of Europe. 1996. "European Social Charter (Revised)." *European Treaty Series 63,* May 3, 1996, 1–18. https://rm.coe.int/168007cf93

Davis, Jeffrey. 2018. US "Zero-Tolerance" Immigration Policy Still Violating Fundamental Human Rights Laws. *The Conversation.* June 27, 2018. https://theconversation.com/us-zero-tolerance-immigration-policy-still-violating-fundamental-human-rights-laws-98615.

Dearden, Lizzie. 2017. "Refugee Rescue Boat Sent to Help Far-Right Anti-Immigrant Ship Stranded in Mediterranean with Mechanical Failure." *Independent,* August 11, 2017. https://www.independent.co.uk/news/world/europe/refugee-rescue-boat-anti-immigrant-c-star-ship-mediterranean-defend-europe-mechanical-failure-far-a7887876.html.

The Economist. 2018. "Europe Is Moving towards the Tough Immigration Policies of Sebastian Kurz." July 5, 2018. https://www.economist.com/europe/2018/07/05/europe-is-moving-towards-the-tough-immigration-policies-of-sebastian-kurz.

Edwards, Lilian. 2005. *The New Legal Framework for E-Commerce in Europe.* Portland: Hart Publishing.

El-Hinnawi, Essam. 1985. *Environmental Refugees.* United Nations Environment Programme. https://digitallibrary.un.org/record/121267?ln=en.

European Asylum Support Office. 2016. *An Introduction to the Common European Asylum System for Courts and Tribunals: A Judicial Analysis.* https://www.easo.europa.eu/sites/default/files/public/BZ0216138ENN.PDF

European Commission. 1999. *Common European Asylum System.* https://ec.europa.eu/home-affairs/what-we-do/policies/asylum_en.

European Commission. 2017. *The Migration Crisis.* http://publications.europa.eu/webpub/com/factsheets/migration-crisis/en/.

European Commission. 2018. *EU-Turkey Statement: Two Years On.* April 2018. https://ec.europa.eu/home-affairs/sites/homeaffairs/files/what-we-do/policies/european-agenda-migration/20180314_eu-turkey-two-years-on_en.pdf.

European Council for Refugees and Exiles. 2018. *The Afghan Paradox: Chaos and Violence but Safe for Returns from Europe.* February 2, 2018. https://www.ecre.org/the-afghan-paradox-chaos-and-violence-but-safe-for-returns-from-europe/.

European Union Law. 2013. "Dublin III Regulation 604/2013." https://eur lex.europa.eu/LexUriServ/LexUriServ.do?uri=OJ:L:2013:180:0031:0059:EN:PDF.

Eurostat. 2018. *Asylum Quarterly Report.* September 2018. https://ec.europa.eu/eurostat/statistics-explained/index.php/Asylum_quarterly_report.

Federal Office for Migration and Refugees. 2018. *Initial Distribution of Asylum-Seekers (EASY).* http://www.bamf.de/EN/Fluechtlingsschutz/AblaufAsylv/Erstverteilung/erstverteilung node.html.

Garcés-Mascareñas, Bianca. 2015. "Why Dublin Doesn't Work." *CIDOB: Notes Internacionales,* 135. https://www.cidob.org/en/publications/publication_series/notes_internacionals/n1_135_por_que_dublin_no_funciona/why_dublin_doesn_t_work.

Gardos, Todor. 2018. *EU Court Rules on Blocking Extradition to Poland, Poland's Decimation of Its Justice System Raises Fair Trial Concerns.* Human Right Watch. https://www.hrw.org/news/2018/07/25/eu-court-rules-blocking-extradition-poland.

Gregg, Samuel. 2017. "National Sovereignty and the Challenge of Immigration." *Public Discourse: The Journal of the Witherspoon Institute.* August 22, 2017. https://www.thepublicdiscourse.com/2017/08/19911/.

Hathaway, James C. 2007. "Why Refugee Law Still Matters." *Melbourne Journal of International Law,* 8, no. 1: 89–103.

Hefron, Claire. 2018. "Asylum Seekers in Austria to Be Denied Apprenticeships." *Euronews.* August 28, 2018. https://www.euronews.com/2018/08/28/asylum-seekers-in-austria-to-be-denied-apprenticeships.

Horvath, Kenneth. 2014. "Securitization, Economization, and the Political Theory of Temporary Migration: The Making of the Austrian Seasonal Workers Scheme." *Migration Letters* 11, no. 2: 154–170.

Horvath, Kenneth, Anna Amelina, and Karin Peters. 2017. "Re-Thinking the Politics of Migration. On the Uses and Challenges of Regime Perspectives for Migration Research." *Migration Studies* 5, no. 3: 301–314.

Human Rights Watch. 2017. *Poland: Asylum Seekers Blocked at Border.* March 1, 2017. https://www.hrw.org/news/2017/03/01/poland-asylum-seekers-blocked-border#.

Huysmans, Jef. 2000. "The European Union and the Securitization of Migration." *Journal of Common Market Studies,* 38 (5):751–777.

Infomigrants. 2017. *Migrant Arrivals in Italy Down for First Time in 2017.* August 4, 2017. http://www.infomigrants.net/en/post/4451/migrant-arrivals-in-italy-down-for-first-time-in-2017.

Institute on Statelessness and Inclusion. 2017. *Stateless Persons in Europe*. http://www.worldsstateless.org/continents/europe/stateless-persons-in-europe.

Internal Displacement Monitoring Center. 2018. *Global Report on Internal Displacement 2018*. http://www.internal-displacement.org/global-report/grid2018/.

International Committee of the Red Cross (ICRC). 1949. "Convention (IV) Relative to the Protection of Civilian Persons in Time of War." August 12, 1949. https://ihl-databases.icrc.org/ihl/385ec082b509e76c41256739003e636d/6756482d86146898c125641e004aa3c5.

International Committee of the Red Cross (ICRC). 1977. "Protocol Additional to the Geneva Conventions of 12 August 1949, and Relating to the Protection of Victims from International Armed Conflicts (Protocol I)." June 8, 1977. https://ihl-databases.icrc.org/applic/ihl/ihl.nsf/Treaty.xsp?documentId=D9E6B6264D7723C3C12563CD002D6CE4&action=openDocument.

International Organization for Migration (IOM). 2018. *Missing Migrants Project*. https://missingmigrants.iom.int/.

Kirişci, Kemal, Jessica Brandt, and M. Murat Erdoğan. 2018. *Syrian Refugees in Turkey: Beyond the Numbers*. June 19, 2018. Brookings. https://www.brookings.edu/blog/order-from-chaos/2018/06/19/syrian-refugees-in-turkey-beyond-the-numbers/.

Klabunde, Anna and Frans Willekens. 2016. "Decision-Making in Agent-Based Models of Migration: State of the Art and Challenges." *European Journal of Population* 32, no. 1: 73–97.

Legal Centre Lesvos. 2017. *Syrian Kurds on Hunger Strike in Moria Refugee Camp*. April 21, 2017. http://legalcentrelesvos.org/2017/04/21/syrian-kurds-on-hunger-strike-in-moria-refugee-camp/.

Lendaro, Annalisa. 2016. "A 'European Migrant Crisis'? Some Thoughts on Mediterranean Borders." *Studies in Ethnicity and Nationalism* 16, no. 1: 148–157.

Léonard, Sarah. 2011. "EU Border Security and Migration into the European Union: FRONTEX and Securitisation through Practices." *European Security* 19, no. 2: 231–254.

The Local. 2018. *Austria to Seize Refugees' Mobiles and Demand Cash*. April 18, 2018. https://www.thelocal.at/20180418/austria-to-seize-refugees-mobiles-and-demand-cash.

Loewenstein, Antony. 2016. "Australia's Refugee Policy: A Global Inspiration for All the Wrong Reasons." *The Guardian*, January 17, 2016. https://www.theguardian.com/commentisfree/2016/jan/18/australias-refugee-policies-a-global-inspiration-for-all-the-wrong-reasons.

Médicins Sans Frontières. 2017. *EU Border Policies Fuel Mental Health Crisis for Asylum Seekers*. October 10, 2017. https://www.msf.org/greece-eu-border-policies-fuel-mental -health-crisis-asylum-seekers.

Migration Policy Institute. "Nearly Half of All Noncitizens in U.S. Could Be Affected by Proposed Trump Administration Public Charge Rule, Up from Current 3 Percent." June 12, 2018. https://www.migrationpolicy.org/news/

mpi-nearly-half-all-noncitizens-us-could-be-affected-proposed-trump-administration-public.

Moreno-Lax, Violeta. 2017. "The EU Humanitarian Border and the Securitization of Human Rights: The 'Rescue - through - Interdiction/Rescue - without - Protection' Paradigm.'" *Journal of Common Market Studies* 56, no. 2: 119–140.

Newland, Kathleen. 2018. "An Overheated Narrative Unanswered: How the Global Compact for Migration Became Controversial." Migration Policy Institute. https://www.migrationpolicy.org/news/overheated-narrative-unanswered-how-global-compact-became-controversial.

Ober, Kayly, and Patrick Sakdapolrak. 2017. "How Do Social Practices Shape Policy? Analysing the Field of 'Migration as Adaptation' with Bourdieu's 'Theory of Practice.'" *The Geographical Journal* 183, no. 6: 359–369.

Oberman, Kieran. 2016. "Immigration as a Human Right." In *Migration in Political Theory: The Ethics of Movement and Membership*. Edited by Lea Ypi Sarah Fine, 32–56. London: Oxford.

Official Journal of the European Union. 2010. "Charter of Fundamental Rights of the European Union, 83/02." March 30, 2010, 389–403.

Patel, Champa. 2017. "Root Causes of Rohingya Crisis Must Not Be Ignored." *Chatham House.* September 28, 2017. https://www.chathamhouse.org/expert/comment/root-causes-rohingya-crisis-must-not-be-ignored.

Perruchoud, Richard, and Jillyane Redpath-Cross (eds.). 2011. "Glossary on Migration." *International Migration Law Series 25.* IOM. https://publications.iom.int/system/files/pdf/iml25_1.pdf.

Popescu, Marciana. n.d. "From Global to Local: EU Migration Policies, Austrian Asylum Processes, and the NGO's Response." Unpublished manuscript.

Refugee Council of Australia. 2018. "Australia's Man-Made Crisis on Nauru." September 2018. https://www.refugeecouncil.org.au/wp-content/uploads/2018/09/Nauru_Manmade_Crisis.pdf.

Rietig, Victoria. 2016. *Moving beyond Crisis: Germany's New Approach to Integrating Refugees into the Labor Market.* Transatlantic Council on Migration. https://www.migrationpolicy.org/research/moving-beyond-crisis-germany-new-approaches-integrating-refugees-labor-market.

Rush, Nayla. 2018. *Refugee Resettlement Admissions in FY 2018.* Center for Immigration Studies. October 1, 2018. https://cis.org/Rush/Refugee-Resettlement-Admissions-FY-2018.

Ruttig, Thomas. 2018. *Afghanistan's Paradoxical Political Party System: A New AAN Report.* Afghanistan Analysts Network.

Romero, Simon and Miriam Jordan. 2018. "On the Border, a Discouraging New Message for Asylum Seekers: Wait." *New York Times*, June 12, 2018. https://www.nytimes.com/2018/06/12/us/asylum-seekers-mexico-border.html.

Scherer, Steve. 2018. "Saved but Still Suffering, Aquarius Migrants Head for Spain." *The Globe and Mail*, June 15, 2018. https://www.theglobeandmail.com/world/article-frances-macron-seeks-common-ground-with-italy-on-immigration/.

UNHCR. 1984. *Cartagena Declaration on Refugees.* https://www.unhcr.org/about-us/background/45dc19084/cartagena-declaration-refugees-adopted-colloquium-international-protection.html.

UNHCR. 2018a. *Figures at a Glance.* https://www.unhcr.org/en-us/figures-at-a-glance.html.

UNHCR. 2018b. *Mediterranean Situation.* January 2018. https://data2.unhcr.org/en/situations/mediterranean.

UNHCR. 2018c. *UNHCR Turkey Factsheet—August 2018.* August 31, 2018. https://reliefweb.int/report/turkey/unhcr-turkey-factsheet-august2018.

UNHCR. 2010. *Convention and Protocol Relating to the Status of Refugees.* https://www.unhcr.org/protection/basic/3b66c2aa10/convention-protocol-relating-status-refugees.html.

UNHCR. *The 1951 Refugee Convention.* https://www.unhcr.org/1951-refugee-convention.html.

UNHCR. 1969. *OAU Convention on Refugees.* https://www.unhcr.org/aboutus/background/45dc1a682/oau-convention-governing-specific-aspects-refugee-problems-africa-adopted.html.

UNICEF. 2018. *Children on the Move Key Facts & Figures.* https://data.unicef.org/wp-content/uploads/2018/02/Data-brief-children-on-the-move-key-facts-and-figures-1.pdf.

United Nations General Assembly. 2018. *General Assembly Endorses First Ever Global Compact on Migration Urging Cooperation among Member States in Protecting Migrants.* December 19, 2018. https://www.un.org/press/en/2018/ga12113.doc.htm.

United Nations Refugees and Migrants. 2016. *New York Declaration.* https://refugeesmigrants.un.org/declaration.

Universal Declaration of Human Rights (UDHR). 1948. http://www.un.org/en/universal-declaration-human-rights/.

Women's Refugee Commission. 2016. *Falling through the Cracks: Refugee Women and Girls in Germany and Sweden.* https://www.refworld.org/pdfid/56ef98954.pdf.

The World Bank. 2018. *Forced Displacement.* http://www.worldbank.org/en/topic/fragilityconflictviolence/brief/forced-displacement.

Zard, Monette. 2005. "Human Rights Strengthen Migration Policy Framework." Migration Policy Institute. https://www.migrationpolicy.org/article/human-rights-strengthen-migration-policy-framework.

PART 2

Health and Well-Being of Refugees

CHAPTER SIX

An Integrated Model of Interdisciplinary Care for Refugees

J. David Kinzie and Crystal Riley

This chapter describes the Intercultural Psychiatric Program (IPP) in Portland, Oregon. The program has treated refugees and asylum seekers for over 40 years, since 1977. It is a psychiatric program within the Department of Psychiatry at Oregon Health & Science University (OHSU). A major aspect of this program is the employment of ethnic mental health counselors who also serve as interpreters and case managers for patients from the same cultures as the counselors. The program has provided a model for patient care of psychiatrically impaired refugees. This model provides continuity of care in a culturally acceptable manner. Each psychiatrist-counselor team has an individual caseload and provides evaluation, education, medication, psychotherapy, and multiple types of case management. We will describe background information to provide context for the origin of the program, describe the roles of the psychiatrists and ethnic mental health counselors, and present the characteristics of the patients we treat. We will describe the system of care and treatment approach and provide case histories. We will also discuss administrative issues. We will present information on two specialty programs within the IPP: (1) the Intercultural Socialization Center and (2) the Torture Treatment Center of Oregon. We will also discuss the cost of care and outcomes of our model and address the integral role of teaching and research conducted by staff members of the IPP.

Background and Origin of the Intercultural Psychiatric Program

Originally, our clinic, started by the author J. David Kinzie[1] in 1977, was named the Indochinese Psychiatric Program, but as other groups of refugees came, the clinic was renamed as the Intercultural Psychiatric Program (IPP). The IPP served diverse refugee groups. These have included refugees from Bosnia, Somalia, Ethiopia, Russia, and Myanmar; Farsi-speaking individuals from Iran; Arabic-speaking patients from Iraq; and Spanish-speaking individuals from countries in Central and South America. Clearly, almost all of these refugees came from areas of political persecution, repression, and wars, including ethnic cleansing and torture. In January 2018, the clinic had about 1,000 active patients, most with severe psychiatric disorders. During its 40 years of existence, the program has been remarkably stable and yet flexible to adjust to serving new refugee groups coming to Oregon.

Administrative Structure

The IPP is an integral part of the Department of Psychiatry and reports to the chairman of the department who is responsible to the dean of the School of Medicine. There is no ambiguity about the lines of authority or responsibility. The psychiatrists are all faculty members of the Department of Psychiatry. Mental health counselors and administrative staff members are Oregon state employees, employed by the Department of Psychiatry. This provides administrative clarity about rules and regulations. The program is also a state-funded mental health clinic and, like any other mental health clinic in the state, needs to follow the rules and regulations of the state Mental Health Division. The payment for services is made from Medicaid and/or Medicare, and services are administrated through the Oregon Mental Health Division. The program serves two organizations—the School of Medicine and the Oregon State Mental Health Division. Despite possible conflicts that may arise due to having two administrative organizations, this arrangement has worked well for 40 years. The conflicts we have experienced were a result of multiple regulations of the Mental Health Division that are not required by the School of Medicine, such as mental health evaluations by the mental health counselors. The School of Medicine provided clarity for the physicians in charge of the medical care of patients related to their relationships with other physicians who were also taking care of the same patients, requiring electronic medical records and continuing medical education.

Clinic Development

In 1975, there were no culturally specific health services for refugees coming into the United States. The major mental health clinics were beginning to use interpreters, but these interpreters were not particularly helpful as they were often untrained and lacked psychiatric knowledge. Often, these interpreters were not emotionally accepted by the refugee patients. With the use of mental health counselors from the culture, our clinic had a rapidly growing clinic population to be described later. The United States also had no history of massive amounts of refugees from diverse cultures coming into the country at about the same time. Therefore, it was necessary to start a different kind of clinic, and we chose to develop one with counselors from the same countries as the patients themselves (see the following description). Soon after the clinic started, two faculty members joined, first Dr. Paul Leung and later Dr. James Boehnlein. Both are still working in the clinic. Originally, we took each patient in on their own turn, but this became too confusing, and we developed special times for each psychiatrist and counselor to see specific groups. For one afternoon the first author treated Cambodians and Dr. Leung treated Vietnamese. We then developed the concept of each psychiatrist working with one group of patients, and with one counselor, who spoke the language of the patients treated. This has been the model we have followed since that time (Kinzie et al. 1980; Kinzie and Manson 1983). The main impetus for this arrangement is to carefully and predictively provide a consistent treatment team for each patient. Each treatment team would consist of an IPP psychiatrist working in conjunction with a mental health counselor from the same culture and language group of the patient. Each ethnic counselor, then, would have the ability to help the psychiatrist understand both the language and culture of the patient in real time during treatment in the clinic setting. This model allows for continuity of long-term care and helps to facilitate development of a therapeutic and trusting relationship over time. This model also has proven to be cost effective.

Ongoing Developments

We never planned for the clinic to be long term, as we felt most of the patients from the various cultures would eventually settle into American society and become symptom free. What we did not initially consider was the increasing number of mass atrocities, wars, genocides, and chaotic disruptions in additional societies, which created many new refugee populations throughout the world. Subsequently, our clinic received refugees from multiple countries, as mentioned earlier. Our most recent new refugee patient groups have been from Iran and Afghanistan. We also see refugees from Nepal and Myanmar, both ethnic Burmese and Karen people. We have counselors who are from the culture and speak the language of all the groups we serve.

Roles of Interdisciplinary Team Members

Psychiatrists

The psychiatrists are all board-certified faculty members and have other duties in the department (i.e., teaching and administration). Currently, there is one full-time psychiatrist who is the clinic medical director and six other part-time psychiatrists. Three psychiatrists—J. David Kinzie, Paul Leung, and James Boehnlein—have been with the program for 40 years. Three others have been with the clinic for at least 10 years. Obviously, the psychiatrists who have stayed with the program are very dedicated to its mission and to the patients. Several psychiatrists have left over the years, but currently the staff is highly motivated and very competent and finds fulfillment in working with patients of different cultures. Although, in theory, all the IPP patients have primary care physicians (PCPs), many patients have not gone to their PCPs regularly, and a few patients, such as asylum seekers, are not eligible for services from primary care physicians because they have no medical insurance. Therefore, many psychiatrists have sometimes had to treat patients who are medically ill in addition to having major mental disorders. The roles of the psychiatrists include taking a history, making a diagnosis, providing health education, providing supportive psychotherapy, prescribing medicine, writing letters of support for Medical Certification for Disability Exception to obtain citizenship, evaluating psychiatric cases for court hearings related to asylum, and working with the ethnic mental health counselors to give the best patient care. For those patients without PCPs, the psychiatrists provide some medical care such as treating blood pressure, diabetes, and other medical problems.

Over the years, the medical problems of our patients have become more pronounced. With an aging population (many of our Vietnamese patients are now over 60), there is more hypertension and cardiovascular disease, and increasingly more dementia. These medical conditions do require specialty care, and most patients who have good insurance are able to be referred to primary care or other specialties. Many patients see obstetricians for delivery of their babies, and many have pediatricians. Those patients within the Oregon Health & Science University system, which uses electronic medical records, have good coordination of care. For those patients being treated outside this medical system, the care is sometimes not as well coordinated, such that it can be difficult to coordinate psychiatric and medical care. However, for most of our patients' situations, care is well managed and integrated.

Ethnic Mental Health Counselors

The model for hiring the ethnic counselors from the cultures of the patients as permanent staff members has its origin in the system that was developed to treat aborigines in Malaysia. About the time Vietnamese came into the country soon after 1975, a group of local counselors, mostly Vietnamese, were seeing refugee clients on their own. However, they realized that many of the patients had severe psychiatric problems and referred these patients to our program in the Department of Psychiatry. That is the origin of the first group of clinic patients we treated. Later, in addition to the Vietnamese, the patients included Cambodian and Laotian refugees. We obtained a grant to fund the Asian clinic counselors from a private foundation, and, when the grant ran out, it was necessary for the IPP to hire the counselors, as we needed them to fulfill our commitment to treating a large group of patients. At that time, we hired the counselors to be members of the Department of Psychiatry. This was possible through funding from the state Mental Health Division. The advantage of using counselors as permanent staff members seems obvious now. There are no unknown interpreters involved, the patients work with regular staff members who speak their languages and know their cultures, and the mental health counselors themselves gain knowledge of mental health and overall add a great stability to the program.

Originally, we sought counselors whose only qualifications were to exhibit warmth and empathy and demonstrate a commitment to maintaining confidentiality. We provided the counselors with psychiatric training and other specialty training that was needed. It was necessary for the state of Oregon to provide us dispensation for the counselors' lack of formal education. Over time the qualifications, however, became formerly required by the state. These requirements included a master's level degree in psychology or a related field, as well as certain specific training required by the county. As the IPP serves patients from a three-county area, the program had to meet the provider requirements for each of the three counties we serve. The IPP program gave our counselors paid time-off to complete undergraduate and graduate degrees. In 2018, we have 14 counselors, 10 with master's degrees in a health or counseling related field, and 4 who do not have a graduate degree but are supervised by a master's-level counselor. The counselors are a diverse group, and their numbers reflect the composition of IPP's patient populations. The IPP currently has two Vietnamese, two Somali, two Russian-speaking, and two Arabic-speaking counselors, and one counselor each for the Bosnian, Mien, Cambodian, Ethiopian, and Farsi-speaking patients. One counselor works with Nepalese and Burmese patients.

The role of the counselor can be very difficult. Many have their own personal traumas, and as they interpret for the psychiatrist taking a detailed history, they often have reexperiencing phenomena of their own traumas. This can cause some personal problems in their work, but usually with time, support, and further training, they are able to function quite well.

> *Example.* A psychiatrist and an already-trained IPP mental health counselor were interviewing a Cambodian patient, with a new counselor trainee observing. The patient described massive trauma during Pol Pot time and the death of many family members. The new trainee seemed not to pay any attention and picked up a newspaper and started to read during the session. The psychiatrist became very upset by his lack of respect. Later, it was learned that the trainee had lost many family members himself during the Pol Pot genocide. After further training and support, this new trainee became a very acceptable counselor.

In addition to interpretation, the counselor sometimes is asked to provide the psychiatrist with social and cultural background information about the patient and his or her own community. For example, the counselor may provide information about the role of women in their society, the fact that many patients have more than one wife, the necessary changes during Ramadan, a holy period for Muslims, and the frequent consultation that patients receive from native healers in the community. This helps inform the diagnostic process. The counselors are usually intimately involved in their communities and can provide other information such as family needs, financial stresses, or other problems of the patients. The counselor provides much case management, including arranging transportation, making medical appointments, contacting lawyers, explaining medicine, as well as explaining various expectations in American society related to school, childcare, and rent, and may help patients seeking to learn English and find jobs. The counselor provides a variety of services that gives the patient a sense of safety and security. It is a job of great responsibility that requires maturity, as well as the necessity of maintaining confidentiality for the counselors to be effective. This is particularly important when the counselor lives in or is involved in the patient's community.

The current counselors have a long history with the program; three have worked for IPP for 25 years and another for 17 years. Several other counselors had worked for the program for over 20 years, but now they have moved on or retired. Retaining counselors has been somewhat difficult based on the IPP's income and its requirement to pay OHSU for some financial needs of the entire university. The counselors, however, receive state employee benefits, which helps to partially compensate them for receiving a lower salary. Comparable mental health workers' salaries received in other mental health programs in the Portland Metropolitan Area are likely higher than the IPPs. For example, programs run directly by the Oregon Mental Health Division would pay higher salaries.

For many of our counselors, the job is quite meaningful in that it fulfills a mission most counselors feel toward their own ethnic group. However, the patient load is large. Each counselor is responsible for 50 to over 100 patients, with the average being about 80. This patient load is only possible because very few of the IPP patients have a history of drug or alcohol disorders and few have personality disorders, with suicidal ideations or threats, which would require more intensive services. The Muslim and Buddhist religions of many of our IPP patients prohibit suicide and alcohol abuse. The counselors, even with advanced degrees, need ongoing training. It takes about three years of clinical experience to be comfortable in the position, handling personal feelings and overcoming empathetic strain (i.e., countertransference reactions). A twice a month conference, which includes counselors reading and discussing their own cases, has been a learning and supportive environment, which helps keep morale high. Also counselors talk with their supervisors on a regular basis.

> *Example.* The patient, a young Cambodian woman, presented as mute and totally unable to speak. Her father said she's been like that for five years. With a Cambodian counselor, the psychiatrist began asking questions about symptoms. There was no response. A different approach was taken by asking simple questions about her name and where she lived. The counselor interrupted and said that was probably questions the Pol Pot Cadre asked and the answers would determine whether she lived or died. Under mild tranquilization, the psychiatrist began to touch the thighs and arms. Asking how she felt when he touched her mouth, she said, "I can't speak." Eventually, history was obtained. When she was in Cambodia, her husband was killed in front of her, and the cadre told her that if she said one word her tongue would be cut out.

The counselors facilitate group sessions with the patients. These are not therapy sessions per se, but a socialization group with emphasis on improving social relationships, maintaining cultural values, and providing basic education about American life (Kinzie et al. 1988). The issues include medicine and side effects, child rearing, getting medical care, and supporting each other at stressful times such as divorce, loss of income, problems with children, and serious medical illnesses. The groups celebrate both traditional holidays and American holidays. Traditional holidays include Vietnamese New Year and the Muslim religious time of Ramadan. Almost half of the patients attend some group. We have 11 ongoing groups. This includes five Vietnamese groups in one week and biweekly groups for Cambodian, Somali, Nepali and Burmese, Russian, Oromo (from Ethiopia), and Farsi-speaking clients.

Characteristics of the Patients Served

The clinic has about 1,000 currently active patients, a number that has remained stable for several years. The current patient population is shown in Table 6.1. From the table, one can see that the oldest clinics, Vietnamese, Cambodian, and Russian, have the highest percentage of patients over age 65. This represents an aging population who has been in the country the longest. Our latest data indicates that about 60 percent of the IPP patient population is female. Most of the patients have come from war-torn countries, and most have suffered from trauma and sometimes torture. Most of our patients were diagnosed with depression and anxiety, and sometimes with schizophrenia. Soon after the start of our clinic, the American Psychiatric Association's *Diagnostic and Statistical Manual*, 3rd ed. (*DSM-III*) came out in 1980 with a diagnosis of PTSD. We were struck by the severe suffering of Cambodians who experienced massive trauma, including starvation, death of relatives, and cruel punishment, at the hands of the Pol Pot Regime. It slowly occurred to us that they had possible PTSD, and we tested them with a structured checklist, which our clinic constructed based on symptoms of PTSD in the *DSM-III*, and found that they did have severe, multiple symptoms of PTSD (Kinzie et al. 1984). This work was one of the first publications of PTSD in a non-Western population using *DSM-III* criteria. We treated many of these patients for a year and many of them got better. We published an article saying that there was improvement in PTSD, and perhaps it was not as pessimistic a diagnosis as we were led to believe (Boehnlein, Kinzie, Rath, and Fleck 1985). However, we later found that all of our Cambodian patients relapsed and the chronic relapsing nature of the disorder became clear. Furthermore, we administered the structured PTSD checklist with other groups, particularly Vietnamese and Lao, and found that they had a high rate of PTSD as well. Now PTSD and major depression are the most common diagnoses of our patients. However, other diagnoses are present as well (see Table 6.2 for diagnoses of two patient groups, as diagnosed by the attending psychiatrist). Medical diagnoses are increasingly common, especially diabetes and hypertension, which are related to PTSD (Boehnlein et al. 1985; Kinzie 1989). These diagnoses and the incidence of dementia have increased over time as our patients have aged, probably related to a history of trauma (Kinzie 2001).

Table 6.1. Age and Country/Language of Origin Characteristics of Current Active Intercultural Psychiatric Program Patients

Clinics	Active Patients (N = 994)	Patients ≥ 60 years old (N = 382; 31% of total)	
	N	N	%
Arabic clinic	78	9	11
Bosnian clinic	113	51	45
Burmese clinic	51	8	16
Cambodian clinic	56	33	59
Ethiopian clinic	57	22	39
Farsi clinic	89	16	18
Mien clinic	29	5	17
Russian/Ukrainian clinic	70	35	50
Somali clinic	135	22	15
Spanish clinic	20	3	15
Vietnamese clinic	296	178	53

The sociocultural backgrounds of the patients are quite diverse; some have never been to school and others have graduate degrees. The average education level is having some high school education. Even within groups, there are subgroups, such as the Roma from Bosnia, the nomads from Somalia, and the various tribes from Ethiopia. The first groups from Indochina were predominantly Buddhist. The most recent groups from Somalia and Bosnia are Muslim. There are Christians from Vietnam, Ethiopia, and Guatemala.

The asylum seekers are a special group. Most are from quite repressive regimes, such as Iraq, Iran, and Ethiopia. Unlike refugees, they come without any support and must apply for asylum once in the United States, which is a lengthy and expensive process with no guarantee of success. In my experience in evaluation of over 40 asylum seekers, their asylum requests are genuine, and their lives are clearly in danger if they return to their former home. Our clinic has aided attorneys in presenting the cases for asylum by providing written reports and expert witness testimony.

Example. The patient is a 35-year-old woman from an African country. She is well educated and has traveled internationally in her profession. Once, 10 children were running away from the police. She let the children come into her house, and the police shot dead three children in front of her. She participated in multiple demonstrations against the government. For these she was jailed twice, once for a month and another time for two weeks. She was humiliated, pushed, and kicked in the back, and she shamefully admitted she was raped. The worst, she said, was seeing other people tortured. One of her sisters is in jail and a brother was jailed as well. The patient was told that if she was involved in any other demonstrations, she would be killed. Through her international contacts, the patient managed to come to America and apply for asylum. She obtained a work permit. The psychiatrist and counselor help with the asylum process by documenting each patient's traumas and symptoms. Based on the psychiatrist's evaluation of this patient, her case was considered to have adequate credibility. As of this writing, this patient has officially received asylum.

How the System of Care Works

Originally, most patients were referred to our clinic by refugee social service agencies. Now, most patients are referred for services by relatives. When patients call the clinic, they are immediately put in contact with the counselor who knows their language. The counselor is then the primary case manager for the patient; although there is a little switching among the several Vietnamese counselors, to accommodate both the patients' and the counselors' schedules and to provide the best possible fit between patient and counselor.

Counselors then meet with the patient to obtain a brief history, collect administrative information, and complete a few scales, the TTCO Symptom Checklist, which the Torture Treatment Center of Oregon (TTCO) staff created (unpublished) and the Sheehan Disability Scale (Sheehan and Sheehan 2008), which provides sub scores in three categories (work/school, social life, and family life) and an overall disability score. The counselor then makes an appointment with a psychiatrist, in which the evaluation is done with the counselor acting as interpreter (Kinzie et al. 1980). A counselor who speaks the primary language of the patient is always provided. Rarely, a patient will speak only a rare ethnic language, in which case, a special interpreter from OHSU or the community is hired to work with the patient–counselor–psychiatrist team. A treatment plan is given that includes follow-up with the psychiatrist and counselor, who work together long term. In other words, the triad of psychiatrist, counselor, and patient begins. This provides long-term continuity with language and cultural appropriateness, a factor that enhances the stability of the program.

There are no exclusion criteria, except that each patient must have some psychiatric disorder. All patients with all types of diagnoses are accepted. The basic premise is that the bar for refugees to seek psychiatric help is very high; because of cultural fears of psychiatric disorders and fears of being

Table 6.2. Current Psychiatric, Neurocognitive, and Medical Diagnoses (Sample of 2018 IPP Clinic Population Groups, $N = 100$)

	African Somali ($N = 28$) Ethiopian ($N = 22$) All $N = 50$	*Asian* Vietnamese All $N = 50$	Under 65 $N = 25$	65 and older $N = 25$
Psychiatric diagnoses*				
PTSD—all	34	11	2	9
PTSD with depression	31	10	2	8
PTSD without depression	3	1	0	1
Depression—all	48	20	4	16
Depression only	13	10	2	8
Depression with PTSD	31	10	2	8
Depression with psychotic features	4	0	0	0
Psychotic disorder—all	12	30	21	9
Schizophrenia	8	30	21	9
Schizoaffective disorder	4	0	0	0
Substance abuse	0	0	0	0
Neurocognitive diagnoses				
Traumatic brain disorder	4	0	0	0
Alzheimer probable	5	7	1	6
Dementia unknown type	1	0	0	0
Medical diagnoses				
Hypertension	20	12	5	7
Diabetes	9	10	6	4

Note: This nonrandom sample may give more weight to the Vietnamese patients with schizophrenia than a random sampling of the IPP clinic population, as a whole, would give.

* One of the psychiatric diagnoses appears in more than one category (i.e., PTSD with depression is in the PTSD and the depression categories).

labeled "crazy," the patient's needs are likely to be so great that an evaluation is always appropriate. There is a minimal waiting time. Patients are typically seen in two weeks, usually by the counselor, and if it's an urgent situation, the counselor can contact a psychiatrist for emergency treatment until there is a formal evaluation. Because there are no exclusion criteria, a sizable number of the clinic patients have psychotic symptoms. Because of a full psychiatric staff, the IPP medical staff members have the ability to treat almost all disorders. Usually only a few patients need hospitalization, and after hospitalization, the patients are referred again to our clinic.

Treatment Approach

The most important part of treatment is the respect given by the psychiatrist and the counselor to the patients. This involves empathetic listening, dependability, and continuity of the relationship over time in treatment (Kinzie 1989, 2001). This also involves flexibility in scheduling and in responding to the patients when they are experiencing emergency situations. Medicine has been very important in improving insomnia, nightmares, and agitation, all part of the trauma syndrome. We have made extensive recommendations regarding psychotropic medicine elsewhere (Kinzie 2016), but briefly, clonidine or prazosin for nightmares is very useful. A sedative antidepressant such as imipramine, or doxepin for depression and insomnia, provides rapid relief from insomnia and can greatly reduce depression symptoms. Nightmares can usually be reduced by half within a week or two, and sleep can be increased by several hours within the same time frame. Agitation is a disturbing symptom and can be treated by generic aripipozole or resperdone.

The therapy sessions deal with ongoing issues that frequently occur with refugees (e.g., relatives' trauma in their home country, illnesses in the family, loss of job and income, and children doing poorly in school). The symptoms and response to medicine are briefly discussed. Usually only minimal adjustments are required. Certain themes continue with each patient, and common topics include relationship challenges in the family, such as with children, spouses, parents, and within the entire community. In this respect, the type of psychotherapy we provide at the IPP is both supportive and interpersonal in nature. Therapy is not time limited, and no set discharge date is required. It is our experience that refugees with PTSD, depression, and other psychiatric illnesses have chronic disorders that remit and exacerbate over time. Of course, some patients drop out, but many return, usually with new stressors, as illustrated by the following case examples.

Example. The Cambodian female patient, who originally was seen at age 25 and who endured three years of severe torture under the Pol Pot regime, said her father was killed during the regime. She was in treatment with PTSD and depression for over two years and then dropped out. During the subsequent 13 years she had a steady job, was married, and then divorced. Then her sister found a picture of their father and sent it to her. Immediately, the patient had an intense flooding of memories that had been suppressed over those many years. Her father had been captured, tied up, and while he was still alive had his liver cut out in front of the patient. The PTSD symptoms totally returned, and she was unable to work. She returned to treatment and remained in treatment for the next several years.

The most challenging part of treatment for refugees, particularly in the beginning, is the acceptance of taking medicine. Although patients come regularly to their appointments and seem quite compliant, there are complaints that some American medicines are too strong for Asians. We began to test the blood levels of antidepressants in our patients whom we perceived to be quite compliant and found a shocking rate of noncompliance, almost all among Vietnamese, and very minimal antidepressant levels among Cambodians (Kinzie et al. 1987). There also was difficulty with patients' understanding that medicine needs to be taken every day rather than stopping as soon as they felt better. We discussed this with patients individually and in the groups and found that compliance greatly improved, and the patients' symptoms improved as well. However, the Mien ethnic group members were the exception, as they rarely took a therapeutic dose of medicine.

Critical Moments in Psychotherapy: Case Examples

The following examples describe critical moments in psychotherapy with refugees that are sometimes encountered. They illustrate the need for flexibility, maturity, and experience on the part of the clinician team members in order to handle these powerful moments.

> *Example.* During one session, the counselor was asked to leave the room. Julie, a well-educated woman from a country in Africa, told about when rebels from an unknown place came into her village and almost all the men, including her husband, were killed in front of her. She cried for several sessions and then asked the African counselor to leave and talked to the psychiatrist alone in fair English. She said that wasn't all that happened. "I was gang raped and felt so dirty." The psychiatrist gave her a hug, and they never spoke about it again, but her affect brightened in subsequent interviews.
> *Example.* Aman was an angry Somali man. He shouted at people as they passed his house and had no friends. He made several appointments in the clinic but didn't keep them. He finally did come but announced that he was not going to talk about it. We listened and listened, and finally he broke down and cried and blurted out his story. Militia had come into his village and lined up the men and began shooting them. Before he was shot, his eldest son stepped in front of him and took the bullet. The bullet killed

the son and lodged into the chest of the patient, who appeared to be dead at the time but actually did live. The patient cried and cried the entire session. Eventually, the psychiatrist said, "Your son must have had a good father to be so brave." His anger diminished over time, and he became a very helpful member in the community.

Example. Ivo was a good man. He raised good children, worked very hard at a demanding job, and taught Quran classes to children. He had severe losses and suffered personal deprivation as a prisoner of the Serbs when he was in Bosnia. One day after years of treatment, he said he needed to talk about the worst thing he had ever seen. His job as a political prisoner was to clean houses of dead Bosnians to keep from being shot by the Serbs. In one house there was a mass of bodies. A three-year-old blond girl emerged, hands up and crying. Ivo picked up the little girl and took her to the guard and asked what should be done. The guard grabbed the girl, threw her against a tree, and killed her. Later we learned that the patient had stopped giving Quran lessons because there was a blond girl in class. After hearing this heavily packed description from the patient, the psychiatrist and patient sat quietly together for a few minutes—honoring this powerful disclosure by the patient and the acceptance of this disclosure by the psychiatrist. At that moment in time, words were not necessary.

Two Specialty Programs within the IPP

The Intercultural Socialization Center

Group Therapy and Socialization Groups: Background

While patients' individual sessions with the psychiatrist and mental health counselor were very helpful in relieving psychiatric symptoms of poor sleep, nightmares, intrusive thoughts, and inability to concentrate, the IPP patients were also grappling with immediate, real-world problems of how to manage their everyday lives (i.e., how to rent an apartment, pay bills, travel around the city of Portland, shop for groceries, and speak English). In addition, many patients were experiencing social isolation in the community. To the extent that a lack of confidence in navigating the American system of everyday life in a busy city significantly added to their stress, it was important to address these problems.

We began to discuss group therapy and group activities for our patients. The counselors were very concerned that the patients would not see group therapy as a treatment because the psychiatrists would not come to the meetings. To encourage attendance, psychiatrists came to the Cambodian groups once a month, and psychiatrists also visited some of the other groups periodically. However, with language interpretation being necessary in order to include everyone, groups did not run smoothly. For the Cambodians, the group sessions were very difficult for the first couple of years. Although the counselors did not push for information, the group rapidly recounted the brutalities they suffered in Cambodia and some group sessions became overly tense. However, when the psychiatrist wasn't at the group session to lead the discussion, the counselors led socialization events, which went very well.

Patients' lack of social connectedness and isolation in the community led the psychiatrists and mental health staff to initiate socialization group therapy into the clinical program. This seemed to be a logical progression of the IPP's clinical offerings in terms of providing practical information and extra psychological support for patients to help them navigate their new surroundings and new ways of life in the United States. The initial goals of providing socialization group therapy were to provide a safe place to talk about problems of adapting to a new life in a new culture, opportunities to learn English in a very nonthreatening environment, and an opportunity for patients to socialize, helping each other build confidence. Regular informal English lessons were conducted, utilizing both the mental health counselors and the English-speaking staff.

Group Outings

Working with the Indochinese mental health counselors and the IPP administrative staff, author Crystal Riley[2] helped to plan an initial group outing for the IPP in about 1987. Several buses were needed to take our group of about 100 people (counselors and patients) on the 70-mile journey from OHSU to the Oregon coast. The goals of the trip included: enhancing socialization, building confidence in venturing around Oregon, the using of skills in planning a picnic outing, and learning about Oregon, their new home.

We did not have a picnic that day. We had four picnics. Each of the four ethnic groups (Cambodian, Lao, Mien, and Vietnamese) congregated with their own group members, who could speak their language, who were familiar with their foods and shared their culture. The four picnics were a tremendous success, with group members smiling, happy, and sharing the food each had brought from home with each other within their own cultural group. At the end of the day, the patients were asking for more similar experiences.

For many of the patients on this outing, this was their first or one of their very first opportunities to see the countryside and the coast of Oregon. Most of the patients did not own their own cars and thus had not been able to find their way to the coast. For the patients, many of whom were from small villages in their country, this trip felt like something they would do back home, in their own countries. It was familiar. It was enjoyable. It was comfortable.

The women enjoyed cooking and sharing, and the men enjoyed helping to organize certain aspects of the "campsite." There was a great deal of talking and laughter, as the patients within each group shared a meal and experiences with each other. They felt safe during this planned and supported group trip.

One of the main roles American staff members and volunteers filled in the socialization program for refugees was that of an American person saying "Welcome, we are glad you are here. What can I do to help you feel comfortable?" The other unexpected lesson, which we learned very quickly, was that these men and women from countries very distant from the United States had a great deal to teach us about their countries and about their ways of life. In the midst of working together and beginning to understand each other's way of life, the mental health counselor was not the teacher and the patient was not the student. Rather, we (mental health counselor and patients) were teachers and students for each other.

This method of working with the patients almost immediately became a comfortable process of learning and sharing, laughing together at our "goof ups," and lavishly praising each other for our successes. Out of this safe atmosphere, there was an automatic building of respect for the other person's feelings, gifts, talents, and frailties. American staff members, for example, have always had trouble learning languages other than English, but we tried hard to learn a few words of Vietnamese, Cambodian, Lao, and Mien. When American staff and volunteers tried to speak, using the words the patients had tried to teach us, everyone laughed, and it was OK. This helped to set an environment in which it was safe and OK to try and fail and to try again, and again, with support from each other.

With the success of several group trips, together with the positive responses of patients to the socialization groups held at the IPP clinic at OHSU, came an evolution of thinking among IPP psychiatrists and other mental health staff that we needed more opportunities to work with the patients on long-term projects (i.e., we needed a mechanism through which the patients and staff could continue to learn from each other and have an opportunity to build a new culture together). These ideas further evolved and we developed the Indochinese Socialization Center.

This was the late 1980s. The psychiatric literature of the 1970s and early 1980s was filled with many examples of the "Club House" model of treatment, especially for American patients who needed long-term psychiatric care, most of whom had psychotic illness. The Club House model described ways in which patients could gain confidence and learn to function more effectively by doing activities together with various members of a group of patients, each gradually taking more and more responsibility for carrying out certain activities, in a safe, supported group environment (McKay et al. 2017). The IPP psychiatrists and counselors and author Riley kept thinking of establishing a place that the Indochinese patients could consider a safe place to come, that is, "a Clubhouse" they could consider their own—a place where they could cook together, learn English, talk, plan trips, and learn together about ways of life in their new homeland.

The IPP secured a small grant from a religious foundation, and author Riley consulted with the then chair of OHSU's Community Psychiatry department, David Cutler, MD. Author Riley learned a main tenet of Community Psychiatry from Dr. Cutler: When you want to build support for a community project, get the community very involved and give ownership of the project to the community (David Cutler, personal communication, May 1989).

In 1989, the IPP opened the Indochinese Socialization Center (ISC) in a four-room house owned by a church (Cutler and Beigel 1978). The small house was located on the same block as the church in SE Portland, a 20-minute drive from OHSU. Author Riley served as the main half-time staff of the ISC, with IPP Vietnamese, Cambodia, and Mien mental health counselors as part-time staff. Members of the church served as volunteer staff with each group. A volunteer advisory board made up of church members, interested mental health professionals from the community, members of service organizations such as the local Lions Club, and others met monthly to help plan group activities and to help garner further and continued social acceptance toward the refugees and financial support from the surrounding SE Portland community. The anti-refugee sentiment in Portland was not very strong in 1989, but at the time, there were some concerns expressed in the community that the Asians coming in would take jobs away from American workers.

The initial plan of the Socialization Center was to hold four separate three-hour groups for each of the four ethnic groups the IPP then served (Cambodian, Lao, Mien, and Vietnamese). In addition, a Friday afternoon three-to-four-hour group was open to all Indochinese patients from the four ethnic groups. Coupled with the availability of groups held within the OHSU Department of Psychiatry, the above Socialization Center schedule provided additional treatment opportunities for any IPP patient who needed it due to the severity of his or her diagnoses (e.g., severe depression or psychosis) and/ or due to currently high levels of stress in his or her life. Patients who needed increased structure or support could participate in groups three times a week, that is, one group at OHSU, and two groups at the ISC.

The initial format of each group meeting at the ISC consisted of the patients and staff members planning, doing, and eating together. For example, we would almost always hold a meeting at the beginning of each group to discuss ideas for any long-term project, activity or trip the ISC was planning, debrief previous trips and activities, and complete planning for the educational or social activity of the day. We would always plan for a meal to be eaten together.

Planning the meal involved deciding on the menu, who would be the cooks and clean-up crew, and who would do the shopping. We almost always ate food from the culture of the participating group. Social activities at the ISC included picnics at a nearby park, bowling, art projects, and visits to local museums or the Portland Zoo. Examples of educational activities included learning and practicing English, problem solving related to paying of electric and other bills, or problem solving about how to find a new place to live. Sometimes we would have a guest come, for example, from the Portland water bureau, to talk with the group about water conservation. Sometimes we would spend time dreaming about and planning a future picnic or other type of outing or trip. Various professionals would come and talk about a specific topic, such as the importance of working toward U.S. citizenship. Sometimes medical professionals would come and discuss health issues.

Treatment Goals of ISC Groups

While treatment goals would vary for each individual, depending on their clinical diagnosis and their current conditions, the overall goals for each ISC group experience included encouraging participation of each group member and, as appropriate, the encouraging of group members to take leadership positions for the day, that is, take a lead role in planning the meal or serve as a shopper or as an assistant cook. Other specific treatment goals, relevant for some, included patients' being able to work on projects well with others, to express and discuss ideas clearly, and to follow plans and directions effectively. Intertwined with the previously mentioned social goals included the patients' learning of new skills, such as riding a bus and the building of patients' skill and confidence in speaking English.

Scope of ISC's Clinical and Rehabilitation Activities

The ISC continued to encourage involvement by the larger southeast Portland community, including: individual volunteers, such as from the church next door; local businesses, such as a bank; and local clubs, such as the Lions Club. This worked well to help us further develop dimensions of the ISC's scope of clinical activities available for patients and enabled patients, volunteers, and staff to work on projects together. The bank manager, for example, became involved with helping two men with psychotic illnesses to set up individual bank accounts, to which an ISC staff member was a co-signer.

With a grant from the Oregon Office of Vocational Rehabilitation, the ISC initiated a supported Employment Program in which patients could be supervised by an ISC staff member and be paid for doing yard, house, or office work. The grant monies helped us remodel the church-owned small house to create a new kitchen that met state health code requirements, which made it possible for ISC members to do catering for parties and events in the community. Working with the state health department, we encouraged ISC patients who were interested to study so they could take tests to receive food handlers' licenses. Rehabilitation activities also included organizing opportunities for patients to sell their handmade crafts and art work. The Mien patients showed enthusiasm for this activity. As the ISC activities continued to evolve, the ISC groups worked together with staff and volunteers to hold an annual ISC Dinner Auction for 10 years in the basement of the church, attended by the community. Proceeds from this activity were put back into ISC program activities, to help pay for group outings and for a special trip to visit the Asian food markets in Vancouver, British Columbia. This trip involved patients' staying at the YWCA.

Reflections on the Benefits of the Socialization Center

We operated a practical, successful model of psychosocial rehabilitation over 22 years for refugees coming to the IPP for treatment from across the world. The ISC provided IPP patients with services of additional emotional support and socialization from 1989 until 2011. Over the 22 years, approximately 100 to 150 patients participated in and benefited from ISC activities and groups each year. During the 22 years, the ISC served patients from over 10 population groups, including Cambodian, Vietnamese, Lao, Mien, Russian, Bosnian, Somali, Ethiopian, Bhutanese, and patients from Central and South America.

To track patients' progress in ISC's socialization groups, a brief 10-item ISC Socialization Scale was created to measure initiative, participation, ability to get along with others, ability to complete tasks, and capacity to assist or support others. This scale made it possible for mental health counselors to document improvements across time periods for the ISC patients. In addition, the using of the scale helped us to track how specific patients, whom staff members were particularly concerned about, were doing. Concerns about patients were usually related to their symptoms increasing, often due to a disappointment or bereavement. Analyzing outputs from the scale, we found these to correlate well with the Sheehan Disability Scale to assess functional impairment in three interrelated domains: work/school, social life, and family life (Sheehan, Harnett-Sheehan, and Raj 1996; Zimmerman et al. 2006).

The ISC served as a practicum placement for numerous students from several local colleges and universities in various clinical disciplines, including psychology, social work, medicine, occupational therapy, and vocational rehabilitation. The ISC also served as a vehicle to provide volunteers, students, and various community members the opportunity to participate with, get to know firsthand, and learn from refugees from all over the world, thus helping to dissolve cultural barriers for both the American helpers and the refugees. The students coming to the ISC also received training in interprofessional practice.

After operating 22 years off site of the main OHSU campus, the ISC closed in 2011 due to liability issues related to the risks of operating a clinical program with minimal staff located in the community, separate from the main program. These liability issues need to be addressed further, as without this further examination and resolution, many potential successful avenues of clinical treatment for refugees will be missed. One of the things increased funding would have made possible is increased professional staff to provide increased supervision and safety.

Currently in 2018, in the IPP, the group therapy sessions are run by counselors, and all the groups focus primarily on education and social activities and less on actual group therapy. The education and training that take place in the groups often relate to learning about and adjusting to life in the United States, such as learning to ride the bus, health education, how to apply for specific services, or how to register one's child in school. The groups are well attended, and there are groups for Vietnamese, Cambodian, Mien, Bosnians, Somalians, Russians, Farsi-speaking, Nepali, Burmese, and Ethiopian patients, providing solidarity and support among the members.

The Torture Treatment Center of Oregon

Treating Torture Survivors

In the late 1990s, we began not only to reconceptualize our work in terms of refugee trauma but also to recognize and identify the severely traumatic experiences of some of our patients as torture. This was specifically important for the Cambodians who experienced the Pol Pot Regime, the Mien from the hills of Laos, and for about half of the Vietnamese we were treating. Redefining the experiences of some or most of our patients as torture helped us to understand more fully the very traumatic stories of the refugee and immigrant groups who came for treatment in the late 1990s, such as the Somalis and some of the Bosnians we treated. In the late 1990s and early 2000s, the newer groups of refugees and asylum seekers coming to Oregon were from Ethiopia, Iran, Nepal, and Myanmar, and the traumas experienced by many of these individuals met the definition of torture.

The Oregon state government and the federal Office of Refugee Resettlement (ORR) around this time also became interested in assessing the impact of torture. In 1998, the Torture Victims Relief Act was signed into law, which made possible grant monies from the federal ORR to local programs providing mental health treatment to help relieve symptoms of PTSD and other psychiatric illnesses stemming from torture, and also to help with medical, legal, and social needs for torture survivors. In 1999, the IPP received funding from the state of Oregon for two years to initiate clinics for Bosnians and Somalis. In 2000, the IPP received a Survivors of Torture (SOT) grant from the federal ORR, which has continued since that time. The ORR SOT grant made it possible for the program to expand its services to refugees and asylum seekers who had been tortured. This was especially important for the asylum seekers, who, for the most part, do not qualify for state mental health funding.

During this period, we first designated part of our IPP program as the "Torture Treatment Center of Oregon" (TTCO). Staff members of the TTCO soon became active in the National Consortium of Torture Treatment Programs (NCTTP), both in terms of sharing clinical experiences and in terms of planning and carrying out research about torture and its impact on survivors with other treatment programs across the United States.

Experiences of Refugees and Asylum Seekers in Treatment in the United States

In our overall experience at the IPP, our refugee patients have been older at intake and have reported less education in their homelands than our asylum-seeking patients, similar to reports from some other treatment programs in the United States, which serve both refugees and asylum seekers (Member Centers of the National Consortium of Torture Treatment Programs 2015). For many of the refugees we have treated at the IPP, their traumas have been more elongated than those of the asylum-seeking patients. This is certainly true, for example, of the Cambodian refugee survivors of the Pol Pot Regime, which lasted nearly four years.

In general, for the IPP, many asylum seekers, perhaps because they are very focused on the goal of obtaining asylum, leave treatment soon after they have received asylum. The refugees in treatment in the IPP, on the other hand, have not had this same type of opportunity for a dramatically improved expectation of their future connected to moving from an undocumented to a legal status after arriving in the United States, and generally, refugee patients have stayed in treatment in the IPP longer than the asylum-seeking patients.

Life experiences of both refugees and asylum seekers interact with their social and medical needs during their trauma recovery and in their adjustment to their new home.

The contextual information relating to age and education mentioned earlier, rather than being applied directly to a specific refugee or asylum seeker, can be used to understand the slower progress of some refugees, perhaps especially those who are older or perhaps those who are finding it very challenging to learn a new language and a new way of life.

We never intended for the IPP clinic to be ongoing. Our expectation was that as patients organized and became more Americanized, they would fit into society and be able to be appropriately and adequately served by mainstream mental health agencies. What we did not recognize early on is that many patients have chronic illnesses, including psychosis, and that their PTSD often relapsed. Many of our patients have continued to receive services from our clinic for a very long time. A high percentage of the patient groups have populations over 60 years of age, who are more likely to have common medical problems, including hypertension, diabetes, and dementia. The breakdown of the diagnoses of our Somali and Ethiopian patients is shown in Table 6.2. This information is reflective of the entire IPP clinical population and shows the diverse diagnoses in the refugee population.

Reflections on Cost of the IPP Model of Care

One objection to our model has been the cost (i.e., salary costs for psychiatrists and counselors). This really is not an issue for us as the program is part of a state mental health clinic, which provides adequate funding for staff salaries for the main mental health services provided. Overall, our funding is 75 percent Medicaid and the remainder from Medicare, commercial insurance, and grants specifically to treat torture victims from the federal rehabilitation program for Survivors of Torture, which has given us flexibility in treating unfunded patients. The psychiatrist reimbursement is enough to pay for part of the doctors' academic salaries. The mental health counselors are paid a little less than MSWs in other mental health clinics, but they have good employment benefits and reduced fees for graduate school in local universities.

In general, it takes about 50 consistent patients to pay for the counselor and one-half day of psychiatrist time. This arrangement saves paying for an interpreter and a special case manager as the counselors do this work themselves. Pro bono immigration attorneys have represented many of our patients. Being part of a large university medical setting, billing is done through that organization. When needed by our program, legal assistance is provided by the university legal department, and the human resources department assists with personnel matters. There is much administrative rigidity and some slowness in the university bureaucracy, but, overall, its advantages outweigh the disadvantages. A key advantage of the IPP's being a part of a large university medical school is the provision of administrative stability and structure over time.

Outcomes of the IPP Model

The best outcome criteria are the simple facts that a refugee clinic has existed for over 40 years and has been able to adapt its services to a changing patient population. In evaluating attendance, we reviewed one random week of appointments. There were 101 MD appointments made and 82 percent were kept. This seems remarkable given that we serve a low-income minority psychiatric population. In a prospective study by our group, 22 torture victims were treated for one year, and at the end of that one year, 20 reported substantial improvement in both symptoms and social adjustment. However, two were unchanged, and there was no clear indication why this was so (Boehnlein et al. 2004; Kinzie et al. 2012). Having 22 out of 24 patients report substantial improvement was considered by our program as an excellent outcome. It is likely that the two who showed less successful outcomes than expected had specific other problems or issues holding them back.

Outcomes related to the ISC include that the IPP operated a practical, successful model of psychosocial rehabilitation for refugees for over 22 years (1989–2011), providing approximately 125–150 IPP patients each year with social support, skills training, work training, and the opportunity to feel safe and more comfortable in their new home, the United States. We created a brief, 10-item ISC Socialization Scale, which correlates well with the Sheehan Disability Scale to assess functional impairment in three dimensions: work–school, social life, and family life. The ISC also served as a vehicle to provide volunteers, students, and various members of the Portland, Oregon, community the opportunity to participate with, get to know firsthand, and learn from refugees from all over the world, thus helping to dissolve cultural barriers for the refugees, the American helpers, and the organizations and/or universities with which these helpers were affiliated.

In terms of collaboration with other programs treating refugees and asylum seekers, the IPP psychiatrists and mental health counselors have actively shared information and ideas with colleagues across the state of Oregon and the United States through numerous presentations at conferences, professional meetings, and professional publications in an effort to disseminate best practices with this specialized population. Several staff members of the IPP/TTCO have been active since 2000 in the National Consortium of Torture Treatment Programs, which currently has 33 member programs, a majority of which are funded by the Office of Refugee Resettlement's Survivors of Torture Program.

Teaching and Research: Integral to Our Medical School Responsibilities

Teaching

At any given time, one or two medical students spend part of their psychiatric rotation in our clinic. Most students have found this very helpful in learning about the lives of refugees and are often shocked about the severe trauma refugees have experienced. The students are also gratified to see how the patients can improve with treatment. Most years, a senior psychiatric resident spends time in the clinic, observing the faculty. They are mostly in an observer status as it is difficult to have a short-term psychiatrist take over part of the long-term established treatment relationship. The clinic provides experience in cross-cultural therapy and expands the residents' experience with people from other cultures, which is valuable foundational knowledge for all psychiatrists. The IPP, as well as the ISC, provided practicum placements for numerous students from several local colleges and universities in various clinical disciplines, including psychology, social work, medicine, occupational therapy, and vocational rehabilitation.

Research

Research and writing has been a major activity for our clinic since its founding. This is consistent with one of the goals of the university to expand the current knowledge base. Many of our publications have been done with great involvement from the counselors themselves. Papers written by our clinic staff that have not already been cited in the chapter address the development of a Vietnamese Depression Scale (Kinzie et al. 1982), Vietnamese in the criminal justice system (Bloom, Kinzie, and Manson 1985), the effects of massive trauma on children (Kinzie 1988; Kinzie et al. 1986), the use of Clonidine with Cambodians (Kinzie and Leung 1989), the prevalence of PTSD in Southeast Asian refugees (Kinzie et al. 1990) countertransference in the treatment of refugees (Kinzie 1994), ethical issues in the treatment of refugees (Boehnlein, Leung, and Kinzie 1998), the polysomnographic effects of Clonidine on Cambodians patients (Kinzie, Sack, and Riley 1994), cross-cultural treatment of refugee children (Kinzie et al. 1998), treatment of refugee children (Kinzie, Cheng, Tsai, and Riley 2006), and the high prevalence of diabetes and hypertension among refugee patients (Kinzie et al. 2008).

The IPP and TTCO's involvement and collaboration with the NCTTP has grown, especially in the area of research. The OHSU Institutional Review Board (IRB) has become the IRB of record for the NCTTP's 10-year study of refugees and asylum seekers who are torture survivors. The member centers of the NCTTP published a paper on this study in 2015 about descriptive, inferential, and functional outcomes on 9,025 torture survivors served over six years in the United States (Member Centers of the National Consortium of Torture Treatment Centers 2015).

There are many avenues that need to be explored with future research on refugees and asylum seekers. Among these are the relationship between trauma, torture, and later serious cardiovascular disease, especially in refugees and asylum seekers.

Conclusion

Psychiatric work with refugees is demanding. Clinicians gather difficult histories from patients who have survived inhumane acts perpetrated against them and their loved ones, including murder, starvation, rape, humiliation, and other torture. It is difficult to hear with empathy and yet provide therapeutic intervention. Training can help properly prepare a counselor or psychiatrist for the difficult involvements and encounters. A few psychiatrists have withdrawn from patients and dismissed the traumas described. Listening to descriptions of the inhumanity of man is quite difficult, and what is required is for the clinician to patiently listen and provide quiet, respectful empathy.

The point of a program like the IPP is the patient. "Burnout" or empathetic strain is a major problem for doctors and mental health counselors and others who work with torture survivors. These stories are very difficult to hear and yet remain therapeutically involved with patients. Indeed, with "burnout" there is irritability, with withdrawal from patients, and a loss of job satisfaction. "Burnout" has caused staff turnover and even overt hostility towards patients.

These cases require experience, empathy, and yet clinical competence and optimism that the patient can be helped. Our clinic has, with long experience, found that with our dedicated psychiatric staff and mental health counselors, we can provide treatment that is clinically competent and culturally sensitive.

This chapter addressed many issues (e.g., staff, finances, administration) which allow a refugee clinic to function. However, we must not lose sight of the goal—to help the patient live a better life and to decrease his or her suffering.

Notes

1. The senior author, J. David Kinzie, served as a general physician for Vietnamese patients in 1964 and 1965 in Vietnam during the war. Later he spent over a year treating aborigines in the jungles of Malaysia. After completing his psychiatric residency at the University of Washington in 1969 and a transcultural fellowship in Hawaii in 1970, Kinzie taught psychiatry at the University of Malaya and University of Hawaii. In 1976, he moved to the Oregon Health & Science University as the psychiatric residency training director. Following the Fall of Saigon a year earlier to the Việt Cộng, Oregon began receiving refugees from Vietnam in 1976 and, later, from Cambodia and Laos. Because of Kinzie's interest in Vietnamese refugees and the obvious psychiatric need for these refugees, the Indochinese Psychiatric Program clinic was started. The impetus for

starting the clinic for Kinzie was both personal (he was appalled by the war in Vietnam and what it did to the civilians) and academic (he wanted to see if an academic American setting could provide services for Vietnamese and other refugees and if this setting could effectively train psychiatrists to work with these populations).

2. Author Crystal Riley initially came to the IPP as a volunteer in 1986, where she worked with the IPP's ethnic mental health counselors and patients in various socialization group activities. She helped to plan and accompany mental health counselors and patients on group trips to the Oregon coast and other sites in Oregon. As an IPP staff member, beginning in late 1986, Riley and the counselors dreamed together about how nice it would be to have more space and time to carry out socialization activities with patients. A small grant from a local foundation and volunteers from a local church helped to bring the dreams of the Indochinese Socialization Center to fruition. Riley served as manager of three clinical programs for the IPP: The Indochinese Socialization Center (1989–2000), the Torture Treatment Center of Oregon (2000–2011), and the IPP's Child Psychiatric Program (2006–2011). Riley is currently vice president of the National Consortium of Torture Treatment Programs (NCTTP) and serves as chair of its Research & Data Committee.

References

Bloom, Joseph D., J. David Kinzie, and Spero Manson. 1985. "Halfway around the World to Prison, Vietnamese in Oregon's Criminal Justice System." *Medicine and Law* 4, no. 6: 563–572.

Boehnlein, James K., J. David Kinzie, Ben Rath, and Jennelle Fleck. 1985. "One-Year Follow-Up Study of Posttraumatic Stress Disorder among Survivors of Cambodian Concentration Camps." *American Journal of Psychiatry* 142, no. 8: 956–959.

Boehnlein, James K., J. David Kinzie, Uta Sekiya, Crystal Riley, Kanya Pou, and B. Rosborough. 2004. "A Ten-Year Treatment Outcome Study of Traumatized Cambodian Refugees." *Journal of Nervous and Mental Disease* 192, no. 10: 658–663.

Boehnlein, James K., Paul K. Leung, and J. David Kinzie. 1998. "Countertransference and Ethical Principles for Treatment of Torture Survivors." In *Caring for Victims of Torture*, edited by James M. Jaranson and Michael K. Popkin, 173–184. Washington, DC: American Psychiatric Press.

Cutler, David L., and A. Beigel. 1978. "A Church-Based Program of Community Activities for Chronic Patients." *Hospital Community Psychiatry* 29, no. 8: 497–501.

Kinzie, J. David. 1988. "The Psychiatric Effects of Massive Trauma on Cambodian Refugees." In *Human Adaptation to Extreme Stress: From the Holocaust to Vietnam*, edited by John P. Wilson, Zev Harel, and Boaz Kahana, 305–317. New York: Plenum Publishing Corporation.

Kinzie, J. David. 1989. "Therapeutic Approaches to Traumatized Cambodian Refugees." *Journal of Traumatic Stress* 2, no. 1: 75–91.

Kinzie, J. David. 1994. "Counter-transference in the Treatment of Southeast Asian Refugees." In *Beyond Empathy: Managing Affect and Counter-transference in Treatment of Posttraumatic Stress Disorder*, edited by J. P. Wilson and J. Lindy, 249–262. New York: Guilford Press.

Kinzie, J. David. 2001. "Psychotherapy for Massively Traumatized Refugees: The Therapist Variable." *American Journal of Psychotherapy* 55, no. 4: 475–490.

Kinzie, J. David. 2016. "Medical Approach to the Management of Traumatized Refugees." *Journal of Psychiatric Practice* 22: 76–83.

Kinzie, J. David, James D. Boehnlein, Paul K. Leung, Laura J. Moore, Crystal Riley, and Debra Smith. 1990. "The Prevalence of Posttraumatic Stress Disorder and Its Clinical Significance among Southeast Asian Refugees." *American Journal of Psychiatry* 147, no. 7: 913–917.

Kinzie, J. David, Keith Cheng, Jenny Tsai, and Crystal Riley. 2006. "Traumatized Refugee Children: The Case of Individualized Diagnosis and Treatment." *Journal of Nervous and Mental Disease* 194: 534–537.

Kinzie, J. David, D. Denny, Crystal Riley, James Boehnlein, Bentson McFarland, and Paul Leung. 1998. "A Cross-Cultural Study of Reactivation of Posttraumatic Stress Disorder Symptoms: American and Cambodian Psychophysiological response to Viewing Traumatic Video Scenes." *Journal of Nervous and Mental Disease* 186, no. 11: 670–676.

Kinzie, J. David, Richard H. Fredrickson, Ben Rath, Jennelle Fleck, and William Karls. 1984. "Posttraumatic Stress Disorder Among Survivors of Cambodian Concentration Camps." *American Journal of Psychiatry* 141, no. 5: 465–650.

Kinzie, J. David, J. Mark Kinzie, Behjat Sedighi, Abdella Woticha, Halima Mohamed, and Crystal Riley. 2012. "Prospective One-Year Treatment Outcomes of Tortured Refugees: A Psychiatric Approach." *Torture Journal* 22: 1–10.

Kinzie, J. David, and Paul Leung. 1989. "Clonidine in Cambodian Patients with Posttraumatic Stress Disorder." *Journal of Nervous and Mental Disease* 177, no. 9: 546–550.

Kinzie, J. David, Paul Leung, James K. Boehnlein, and Jennelle Fleck. 1987. "Antidepressant Blood Levels in Southeast Asians: Clinical and Cultural Implications." *Journal of Nervous and Mental Disease* 175, no. 8: 480–485.

Kinzie, J. David, Paul Leung, Anh Bui, Rath Ben, Kham One Keopraseuth, Crystal Riley, Jennelle Fleck, and Marie Ades. 1988. "Group Therapy with Southeast Asian Refugees." *Community Mental Health Journal* 24, no. 2: 157–166.

Kinzie, J. David, and Spero M. Manson. 1983. "Five-Years' Experience with Indochinese Refugee Patients." *Journal of Operational Psychiatry* 14, no. 2: 105–111.

Kinzie, J. David, Spero M. Manson, Vinh T. Do, N. T. Tolan, Anh Bui, and T. N. Pho. 1982. "Development and Validation of a Vietnamese-Language

Depression Rating Scale." *American Journal of Psychiatry* 139, no. 10: 1276–1281.

Kinzie, J. David, Crystal Riley, Bentson McFarland, Margaret Hayes, James Boehnlein, Paul Leung, and Greg Adams. 2008. "High Prevalence Rates of Diabetes and Hypertension Among Refugee Psychiatric Patients." *Journal of Nervous and Mental Disease* 196, no. 2: 108–112.

Kinzie, J. David, Robert L. Sack, and Crystal M. Riley. 1994. "The Polysomnographic Effects of Clonidine on Sleep Disorders in Posttraumatic Stress Disorder: A Pilot Study with Cambodian Patients." *Journal of Nervous and Mental Disease* 182, no. 10: 585–587.

Kinzie, J. David, William H. Sack, Richard H. Angell, Spero M. Manson, and Ben Rath. 1986. "The Psychiatric Effects of Massive Trauma on Cambodian Children. I. The Children." *Journal of American Academy of Child and Adolescent Psychiatry* 25, no. 3: 377–383.

Kinzie, J. David, Kiet A. Tran, A. Breckenridge, and Joseph D. Bloom. 1980. "An Indochinese Refugee Psychiatric Clinic: Culturally Accepted Treatment Approaches." *American Journal of Psychiatry* 137, no. 11: 1429–1432.

McKay, Colleen, Katie L. Nugent, Matthew Johnsen, William W. Eaton, and Charles W. Lidz. 2017. "A Systemic Review of Evidence for the Clubhouse Model of Psychosocial Rehabilitation." *Administration and Policy in Mental Health and Mental Health Services Research* 14, no. 6: 1–20.

Member Centers of the National Consortium of Torture Treatment Centers. 2015. "Descriptive, Inferential, Functional Outcome Data on 9,025 Torture Survivors over Six Years in the United States." *Torture Journal* 25, no. 2: 34–60.

Sheehan, David V., Kathy Harnett-Sheehan, and Anthony Baker Raj. 1996. "The Measurement of Disability." *International Clinical Psychopharmacology* 11, no. 6 (Suppl. 3): 89–95.

Sheehan, Kathy H., and Sheehan, David V. 2008. "Assessing Treatment Effects in Clinical Trials with the Discan Metric of the Sheehan Disability Scale." *International Clinical Psychopharmacology* 23, no. 2: 70–83. doi: 10.1097/YIC.0b013e3282f2b4d6.

Zimmerman, Mark, Camilo J. Ruggero, Iwona Chelminski, Diane Young, Michael A. Posternak, Michael Friedman, D. Boerescu, and N. Attiullah. 2006. "Developing Brief Scales for Use in Clinical Practice: The Reliability and Validity of Single-Item Self-Report Measures of Depression Symptom Severity, Psychosocial Impairment due to Depression, and Quality of Life." *Journal of Clinical Psychiatry* 67, no. 10: 1536–1541.

CHAPTER SEVEN

Refugee Resilience and Spirituality

Harnessing Social and Cultural Coping Strategies

Linda Piwowarczyk, Kathleen Flinton, and Fernando Ona

Introduction

Refugees and asylum seekers, some of whom are also survivors of torture, flee their homelands in search of safety and protection from persecution or fear of persecution based on race, religion, nationality, membership in a social group, or political opinion (UN Convention Related to the Status of Refugees 1951, Article 1). At the end of 2016, of the 65.6 million people displaced globally, 22.5 million were refugees (United Nations High Commissioner for Refugees 2017). Refugees are potentially subjected to traumatic events in their country of origin, during flight, and after arriving in a country of asylum.

Working with refugees and asylum seekers affords one the opportunity to be exposed to the worst of humanity, while also witnessing the extraordinary strength of the human spirit that can rise above the experienced trauma. This aspect of the work enhances the professional experience of working with survivors and contributes to the experience of "vicarious resilience" that stems from interaction with clients' stories of resilience (Hernandez, Gangsei, and

Engstrom 2007, 237). By reflecting on the survivor's ability to recover, providers can be influenced by such factors as witnessing and reflecting on human beings' immense capacity to heal, incorporating spirituality as a valuable dimension in treatment, developing hope and commitment, and developing the use of self in therapy (Hernandez, Gangsei, and Engstrom 2007).

Working within the dimension of spirituality is an important area of healing and resilience in recovery from the multifaceted experiences of trauma that refugees face. Spirituality—the understanding of one's self, one's place in the world, and one's humanity—is often disrupted. While spirituality can be disrupted, it is also a valuable resource for resiliency that those seeking to help survivors can utilize whatever their role as helper may be. Spirituality can also be a more familiar and comfortable arena for the survivor than the Western understandings of mental health. Unfortunately, few providers in the fields of medicine and mental health receive any training on how to incorporate spiritualty into their healing practices. This presents practice challenges to providers. Moreover, the provider's own spirituality may be challenged in this process.

In the literature, increasing attention is being paid to people's ability to endure life's challenges. Namely, resilience has been described as an "adaptive characteristic of an individual to cope with and recover from adversity" (Iacoviello and Charney 2014, 1). It has been viewed also as the ability to "bounce back" from adversity (Smith et al. 2008, 194). Resilience within individuals and populations is more ubiquitous than once appreciated (Bonanno 2004). In response to loss and trauma, "resilient individuals . . . may experience transient perturbations in normal functioning (e.g., several weeks of sporadic preoccupation or restless sleep) but generally exhibit a stable trajectory of healthy functioning across time, as well as capacity for generative experiences and positive emotions" (Bonanno 2004, 21). Litz (2005) also clarifies that much literature related to resilience is cross-sectional in nature and argues that what is also needed is research focusing on the long-term adaptation to trauma. Ungar reminds us that resilience is less an individual trait than it is an interplay between the individual, culture, and social and physical ecologies (Ungar 2011). Resilience is an interaction of both individual capacity as well as family/community/cultural capacity to provide support after adversity (Ungar 2008). Effective social support has been shown to minimize the experience of hopelessness while enhancing adaptive and active coping (Panzarella, Alloy, and Whitehouse 2006, 307). What distinguishes a resilience-promoting environment from one that thwarts development is its ability to provide the resources that support positive development in ways that are relevant to those needing help (Ungar and Liebenberg 2011).

This chapter seeks to illustrate the engagement of spirituality in refugees' recovery from trauma, examine a case (in this instance from a Christian perspective) that illustrates these challenges to both the client and the clinician, and address the practical considerations faced by providers.

Traumatic Exposure in Refugee Populations

It is important to examine the complexity of the impact of exposure to trauma, in part due to the fact that refugees can experience trauma in their countries of origin, during flight, and countries of first and second asylum. There is a tendency to focus exclusively upon traumatic events that occurred in the homeland that precipitated their decision to flee. There is an increased appreciation of the fact that postmigration factors can also be very significant in their impact upon health and well-being. For example, when evaluating a cohort of Iraqi refugees who had resettled in the United States at arrival and one year after migration, postmigratory exposure to daily stressors and less social support predicted worse one-year outcomes (LeMaster et al. 2017). Another example is provided by a group of migrants to Sweden, in which a low sense of coherence, poor acculturation (men only), poor sense of control, and economic difficulties in exile were found to be stronger risk factors for psychological distress than exposure to violence before migration (Sunquist 2000). Some argue that trauma-focused advocates tend to overemphasize the impact of direct war exposure on mental health and fail to consider the contribution of stressful social and material conditions (daily stressors in post-conflict areas) (Miller and Rasmussen 2010).

There are many examples from the refugee and postconflict literature that suggest there can be a range of responses to violence associated with armed conflict, as highlighted by the work of de Jong, Komproe, and Van Ommeren (2003). In a cross-sectional study of over 3,000 respondents ranging from 16 to 65 in age (depending on the group) assessing lifetime mental disorders from postconflict communities in Algeria, Cambodia, Ethiopia, and Palestine, there were differential responses to violence across countries with varying rates of posttraumatic stress disorder (PTSD), mood disorders, anxiety disorders, and somatoform disorders depending on the country (de Jong, Komproe, and Van Ommeren 2003). They assessed the prevalence of common mental disorders in these four samples and then analyzed the effect of violence associated with armed conflict on prevalence and comorbidity rates. Factors leading to depression and PTSD can differ in postconflict and refugee populations. A meta-analysis of 181 studies representing 81,866 refugees and other conflicted persons from 40 countries has shown that being a torture survivor was the strongest factor associated with PTSD (odds ratio [OR],[1] 2.01), followed by cumulative exposure to other potentially traumatic events (OR, 1.52), time since conflict (OR, 0.77), and assessed level of political terror (OR, 1.60). Depression was associated with other potentially traumatic events (OR, 1.64), time since conflict (OR, 0.80), reported torture (OR, 1.48), and residency status (OR, 1.30). The average rate of depression was 30.8 percent and the average rate of PTSD was 30.6 percent (Steel et al. 2009). Another example comes from a study conducted by the National Consortium of Torture Treatment Programs in the United States, representing a subset of its clients in which 69 percent of the 9,025 torture survivors studied had PTSD and 52.4 percent had major depressive disorder, with 35 percent with comorbid PTSD and major depression (National Consortium of Torture Treatment Programs 2015, 34). Why do some refugees develop PTSD and/or depression and others do not? Resilience appears to be an important contributing factor.

The Role of Resilience

In a nonrandom survey comparing Iraqi refugees (*n* = 75) and a control group of non-Iraqi Arab immigrants (*n* = 53) from a number of Iraqi/Arab community institutions in Michigan, resilience was found to be a protective factor against the development of psychopathology (Arnetz et al. 2013). Resilience was assessed using the 14-item Resilience Scale (RS-14) in an ethnic Muslim population internally displaced due to conflict 20 years prior (in 1990) from Northern Sri Lanka, aged 18 or above, and currently in the process of returning to their homes. Resilience was associated more strongly with economic and social factors (e.g., food security and social support) and negatively associated with the presence of mental disorder at one-year follow-up. The association between resilience and mental health was inconsistent in cross-sectional analyses and potentially confounded by social, demographic, and economic factors (Siriwardhana et al. 2015). Gender has also been shown to moderate and mediate sources of distress and resilience in a sample of 259 Afghan refugees in California (Stempel et al. 2017). Social, demographic, and economic factors more broadly have keen relevance to direct service and to social work practice that is strengths based and mobilizes "people's push toward growth, self-healing, health, and other natural forces" (Germain 1990, 138).

The Relationship between Faith and Resilience

Weber and Pargament (2014) argue that religion and spirituality have the capacity to promote mental health through "positive religious coping, community and support, and positive beliefs" and at the same time can also be damaging as a result of "negative religious coping, misunderstanding and miscommunication, and negative beliefs" (358). Can this be relevant to refugees, asylum seekers, and survivors of torture? In a chart review of 100 torture survivors using a convenience sample of a larger number of survivors who sought treatment at the Boston Center for Refugee Health and Human Rights (US), 88 percent described themselves as religious (i.e., I believe in God and practice a religion) and 9 percent spiritual (i.e., I believe in God, but

I'm not religious). When asked how often they thought about God, 81 percent responded once a day or more and 13 percent almost daily; 78 percent said they prayed once a day or more and 12 percent almost daily (Piwowarczyk 2013).

Religious belief and spirituality appear to have a positive impact on health and to be associated with increased self-esteem, a sense of well-being, meaning and purpose in life, increased social support, and a sense of community—all of which, as pointed out by Mawani (2014), have heightened the importance of religion in the context of migration. Qualitative work done with resettlement providers and refugee migrants also underscores that empathy, shared culture, and shared experiences from those who have successfully adapted to the new culture are critical to newcomers as they cope with the stresses of migration (Simich, Beiser, and Mawani 2003).

Political commitment, social support in exile, and prior knowledge of and preparedness for confinement and torture in an imprisoned cohort of Tibetan refugees served to foster resilience against psychological sequelae compared to a matched control of nontortured Tibetan refugees (Holtz 1998). Among 769 Tibetan refugees who sought safety in India, the psychological effects of trauma were mediated by coping strategies that were primarily religious (Sachs et al. 2008). In other works with a broad array of trauma survivors, including a prisoner of war, a number of psychosocial factors have been shown to contribute to resilience after disasters and other forms of trauma exposure including: optimism, cognitive flexibility, active versus passive coping skills, attending to one's physical health, maintaining a supportive social support network so as not to feel isolated or alone, and personal moral compass, which involves maintaining positive core beliefs about oneself and one's role in one's world (Iacoviello and Charney 2014). For many, having a moral compass can involve utilizing religion or spirituality to ask questions about life and personal meaning to construct personal narratives in the face of trauma (Iacoviello and Charney 2014). Factors that support higher resilience and positive mental health among populations that have been directly affected by war and conflict include strong family and social networks (from the same ethnic communities), coping (individual and communal), a sense of coherence, as well as religion, beliefs in resilience as an active and learned process, individual (personal) qualities and strengths, and community support (Siriwardhana et al. 2014).

Encounters with experiences of pain, distress, or hardship in the context of refugee trauma and torture have increasingly been a focus in clinical and academic settings (Burnett-Zeigler et. al. 2016; Hodge, Zidan, and Husain 2016). Academics and practitioners have defined such sustained ongoing encounters as suffering and describe suffering as multilevel realities that dynamically link the inner self with community, society, and culture. When these encounters are held up against faith, moral value systems, beliefs, or paradigms, suffering can lead to profound moral injuries and loss of meaning that may inform a spectrum of clinical presentations that are seemingly intractable within the clinical encounter (Kopacz et al. 2017). Research on the complex relationship between suffering and torture has emerged in part due to a quest to find meaningful intervention strategies to address loss of meaning. Additionally, this body of research seeks to attend to the spectrum of needs that include housing, access to food, and medical care among diverse communities, especially communities that are negatively impacted by war and conflict, economic disparities, structural violence, and poverty.

How Faith Can Inform the Experience of Trauma

Similarly, the literature includes various research approaches aimed at understanding the dynamic relationship between faith and trauma and how faith may play a role in shaping the context within which torture is experienced, and also, how faith may play a role in coping with torture (Anum and Dasti 2016; Best, Butow, and Olver 2016; Piwowarczyk 2005). Many researchers note how a spectrum of faith practices can often powerfully organize and make meaning of trauma and suffering (Park 2017). These systems of meaning can transform suffering into positive adaptive processes that support people who have experienced agony as a result of their traumas, promoting healing and effective coping with trauma in their everyday lives. Researchers have noted that frameworks of faith are a bedrock for meaning-making that can strengthen a person's belief systems and lead to personal and life-changing healing from traumatic experience and subsequent suffering. Thus, it is important to consider how faith is shaped by and informs the refugee trauma experience.

Such processes may also happen at ecological or community levels through activities such as storytelling, ritual/ceremony (see Chapter 13), and myth making that inform sociocultural practices that mitigate suffering through "collective trauma resolution," allowing community members to support traumatized members while mitigating victim blaming or self-blame (Kruizinga et al. 2016; Nolan 2016). Agger et al. (2012), for instance, demonstrate how culturally adapted spiritual ceremonies as part of testimony therapy can not only support an individual's capacity and faith to integrate, restore, and repair their traumatic memories, but also help them to powerfully engage in community support. For many communities, actively bridging the loss of meaning a traumatized person experiences with frameworks of faith can support the aspirations of people and communities to overcome the experience of suffering, thereby creating an avenue for individual and community resilience. Among refugees and asylum seekers, the turn toward faith in the wake of torture or community violence can offer liberation, strength, and motivation to find meaning in profound violation of the self or identity. This transformational process of utilizing strategies of faith is often grounded in culturally sanctioned, country-of-origin attitudes that refugees and asylum seekers must then adapt into new cultural landscapes (i.e., that of the country or location of resettlement) (Massey and Higgins 2011).

Renewal and reaffirmation of a flexible and dynamic integration of faith into a therapeutic intervention strategy, such as that found in testimony therapy, may provide an avenue for more effective response to a loss of meaning among refugees and asylum seekers. Additionally, reconnecting to socio-faith networks may reestablish seeds of hope and faith in a spiritual practice that provides solace in the face of trauma. Testimony, in its therapeutic capacity, might link to faith in its many forms, thereby opening up a different way to reflect upon one's experience of torture.

Spirituality has been identified as a factor associated with resilience across multiple settings and cultures. Among urban Pakistani and Somali refugees in Nepal, prayer and a belief in a higher being were noted to provide emotional support (Thomas et al. 2011). Similarly, a cohort of urban Congolese refugees living in Nairobi, Kenya, relied on faith in God's plan and their trust of religious community, in addition to establishing borrowing networks and compartmentalizing the past and present to help them cope (Tippins 2016). Sudanese resettled in Australia also relied on religious beliefs, social support, and personal qualities (Schweitzer, Jaimi, and Kagee 2007). Asylum seekers living with HIV in the UK have also turned to their personal faith, staying busy, as well as support received through their HIV care providers and voluntary organizations (Orton et al. 2012).

Spirituality can play an important role in trauma-informed practices. The beliefs, practices, and experiences of refugees and asylum seekers who have survived refugee trauma and torture may support therapeutic processes that seek to reestablish meaning-making in a person's life, especially if they have experienced a deep trauma. Understanding the spirituality of one's clients may enable providers to work with it to positively support a person's engagement in recovery and critically encourage providers to consider ways to intervene within this spiritual landscape. One way to consider this is through the use of ritual and ceremony within the therapeutic experience. Survivors of trauma may find it liberating to work with the wounds of their experience with the support of their faith tradition(s) through testimony directly rather than avoiding the pain. The utilization of the spiritual may provide helpful avenues to comprehend trauma that requires meaning-making while attending to and addressing feelings of loss, isolation, fear, and anxiety related to the traumatic experience. Furthermore, the integration of spirituality in trauma-informed clinical practice may allow a connection to a larger context that situates the wound of trauma in a different light, as a site for transforming the pain of trauma.

We present the case of Tola here and her testimony of torture and the ways in which spirituality in the clinical encounter provides an opening and a space for curiosity when engaging in what seems like an impossible space of suffering and pain. This takes seriously the challenge of prolonged trauma and how professionals can engage with spiritual practices and formally integrate them into a spectrum of therapeutic modalities. Additionally, engaging with spiritual approaches in practice encourages clinicians to ask questions about how this not only impacts clients but also affects themselves. If the site of the traumatic wound can be a transformative site of liberation for our clients, is there a possibility that the witnessing of a testimony as therapeutic process may provide an opening for liberation in the clinician? The engagement with spirituality in trauma practice may provide a shift for both the health professional and the client.

Case Study: Tola

Tola, a pseudonym, is a client at a torture treatment clinic located on the East Coast in the United States. Tola provided permission to share her case in this chapter. Tola has been seeing one of the author clinicians for psychotherapy for the past year. She has been engaged in an eclectic therapeutic strategy to address her mental health issues. These strategies have primarily included eye movement desensitization reprocessing (EMDR), cognitive behavioral therapy, and testimony therapy.

Tola is a woman in her early 30s from an African country. She was raised in a large Protestant family. Her family was active in the political opposition party of her country. She describes her childhood as "strictly religious, and loving," and she grew up with a conviction and orientation to improve her community through service. Tola characterized her childhood as "happy," and she often participated in Bible study after school and went to church "for much of the weekend." She shared that her friends came from her church or religious community, and she often associated only with families from her church.

Tola's father was "high up" in the political opposition and believed that the government in power was "not helping the people and so very corrupt." Tola's mother was supportive of her father's political activism but focused her energies on raising Tola and her four sisters and five brothers in a Christian household. In addition, her mother took care of both of Tola's grandmothers.

Tola shared that she was taught that the church was central to her faith. She said, "I fully trust my church leaders and my faith community." While Tola was attending university, military forces killed her father due to his prominent role in the opposition party. The assassination of her father emboldened Tola to become more active in the opposition party along with two of her brothers and her oldest sister. She immediately joined a group of Christians on campus that sought to organize Protestants to support the opposition party with the mission and vision of social justice and freedom from the corruption of the political party in power.

When Tola graduated from the national university with her degree in accounting and finance, she secured a position in the private sector as a junior accountant. After completing her master's degree in accounting, Tola quickly rose in the ranks of her company to hold a leading position for the country office of a company.

Tola testified that during her free time she engaged in two major activities that were meaningful for her. She continued to be active in her church and became a lay leader in her church by overseeing the management of tithes and how church funds were spent on programming. In addition to her weekend church duties, Tola used her accounting skills in her role as a volunteer with the political opposition to continue the political legacy of her father, stating, "This is not only what my father would have wanted but also what God sees as good." Due to her father's prior role in the main political opposition party, Tola, along with her siblings, took on important roles in the opposition party. Tola believed she was "doing God's work to help my people."

During the election year, Tola worked closely with opposition party leadership to ensure that the finances and accounting were managed well during the political campaigning. Tola reported that she worked many late hours to ensure that the flow of money was reconciled with campaign activities. She often attended high-level meetings with the leaders of the opposition party to discuss financial matters to make sure that political activities were funded and that the local campaigns were financially supported by the Central Office.

Immediately before the elections were held, Tola was on her way to a finance meeting of the opposition leadership. As she was approaching the building, armed military forces surrounded her, and arrested and detained her. During her more than two weeks of detention, Tola was physically, sexually, and psychologically tortured every day by military forces. Tola shared that during her experience of torture, "I was asking God, where are you? Where are you, God!?! Why is this happening to me?" One day after being brutally tortured for hours, she woke up in a hospital bed. Tola said that she did not know how she ended up in the hospital, but that a paper next to her told her to report to the police station after she was discharged.

Tola called her mother and oldest brother from the hospital. They were not allowed to see her because armed guards were outside her room, but they called the pastor of her church and asked if he could visit her. The pastor was able to visit her close to the time that she was discharged from the hospital. With a great deal of trepidation, Tola told her pastor that she was detained and beaten by military forces for the government. She did not fully disclose the details about what had happened to her. She also shared with the pastor that she was scared for the safety of her family. The pastor secured her safe passage to the church, telling the hospital staff that she "needed healing waters from the church."

While she was at the church, Tola heard from the pastor that military forces had burned her family's house down and that one of her brothers was missing. She also learned that two of her sisters had gone missing and that her mother was in the hospital. Tola expressed a deep sense of guilt. She felt that she put her family members at risk and wanted to go to her mother. However, the pastor and other members of the church leadership felt that her life was in danger, and, instead, they were able to secure her safe passage out of the country.

Tola left her country on a visa to attend a religious denominational conference in the United States. Upon arrival in the United States, she attended the conference, but, fearing for her life, declared herself as an asylum seeker. Through her pastor's network in the United States, she was able to connect to a church who referred her for treatment three months after her arrival in the United States.

Tola does not know what happened to her grandmothers and other family members. She experiences ambiguous loss, feelings of shame from the torture, and guilt for believing that she put her family in grave danger. She exhibits many symptoms of depression and PTSD, experiences frequent headaches, and suffers from the physiological and psychological toll of her torture experience. She feels a deep sense of abandonment from her God but has not withdrawn from her faith and participates in the local church community. She views herself as so unforgivable but also questions how God could do this to her.

Tola consistently asks, "How can there be a good God if He allows this? How can He do this to me?" She often resides in a space of moral ambiguity of blaming herself versus the faith she has held, which has clear boundaries about good and evil in the world. As she has stated in a session, "We [humans] should know what is good and what is bad. It's quite simple. It's black and white. I was taught this. I was taught what was right and what was wrong. It's a simple equation. I believe in good plus I believe in the Bible and this results in Jesus."

Tola's questioning of where God was during her torture experience has led her to feel that God abandoned her. Tola, however, did not abandon God as she continued to practice her faith. As Tola stated, "I want to know, I want to know why God wasn't there [during my torture]. What happened when He left me in this nightmare?" In a later testimonial, Tola asked, "Do you think God was there during my torture?" Over the course of the year, Tola has discussed her challenges with attending her church, often reflecting, "What does it matter that I go? Maybe I need to just read the Bible and study it for my answers."

Testimony therapy provides a space for people to share or provide a formal written or spoken statement of their traumatic experiences. According to van Dijk, Schoutrop, and Spinhoven (2003), this testimony is based on a person's experience and involves a person recounting his or her life stories, including the traumatic experiences. Through testimony therapy approaches, Tola was able to articulate her frustrations, expressing, "I can't be honest in these spaces [spaces where she practices faith]. I can't let people know what happened to me! They ask always, and I try, really try, to avoid this answer. Always!" These questions from her church community in turn have amplified Tola's symptomology and current mental health presentation, feeding into her hypervigilance and avoidant behaviors. Yet, Tola wants to share her uniqueness, including her torture narrative. Such disclosure, however, places her at risk within her faith community of being isolated or shamed. Hence, she states, "I must be there for our Savior Jesus Christ. I don't know, yes, how to be with my Lord and my people at the same time. [pause] But I am missing my people if I can't be myself at church. I grew up a certain way and being with church in a kind of way, but how can I here? Really, I can't tell people what happened to me! That's impossible."

Near the end of this session, Tola asked her therapist: "Do you know Mark?" After clarification, she meant the Book of Mark and specifically brought up Mark 4:35–41, "Jesus Stills the Storm." After reading this passage from the Bible she produced from her oversized bag, she set out to explain her storm in detail and ended saying, "The storm is really alive in me. I'm waiting for Jesus to still the storm." During the pause after her testimony, her therapist asked her, "In this passage you mention, is the storm in the disciples or was it around them?" Her eyes got big and she looked at her therapist with astonishment. The therapist went on. "I'm just curious, because when I hear you read this, I'm remembering someone preach that the storm is outside. It's outside of you. It's not in you. Jesus is calm amidst the storm that's all around them and says: 'Have you still no faith?' What do you think about that, Tola?"

Tola and her therapist ended their testimonial session that day, with Tola pondering the storm. They talked about the Light inside, within each of us. They spoke about Tola's faith as a way to help reinforce her inner Light and that her storm was around her, but she could be like Jesus: Breathe into the storm and hold it still, seek peace, remember her Light, and have faith.

Discussion: Radically Listening to the Testimony of Faith

Tola deeply suffers in her everyday life because of her torture experience. However, over the course of the year, Tola's ability to reflect upon her torture experience without feeling overwhelmed has improved in leaps and bounds. What is remarkable is how Tola engages with faith in this testimony and what, in turn, the testimony allows her to do as she and her therapist work through the suffering from her torture. At the end of this particular testimony, Tola comes to feel there is solace in her faith and remember who she is in this testimony of her Light.

Testimony and Personal History with Faith

The testimony itself is a reflection of her past faith. An aspect of Tola's faith was to read the Holy Scripture. In an earlier session, she speaks of her mother reading the Bible to her as a child. It is a powerful reminder of how faith can recall a positive resource that comes through as sacred text. It is in the process of testifying, however, that Tola rewrites her testimony upon reflecting about the storm's position. Is the storm within her or outside of her? The nature of the position shifts as her faith evolves with the interpretation she is using when rereading her sacred text.

Testimony: Faith and Loss

Tola is also questioning a spectrum of faith issues in this testimony. The constellation of losses due to her torture that Tola experiences amplifies the moral injuries and ambiguities that she struggles with as she continues to acclimatize and navigate through new sociocultural systems. Despite her ongoing practice of faith, her ability to draw strength and comfort from her faith is compromised due to the spectrum of violations to her self and personhood. She consistently asks herself profound moral questions that continue to destabilize her belief and value systems even when her faith persists. In order for others to understand her, Tola refers to what gets in the way of truly practicing her faith. Tola feels compelled to say something to her therapist and others about her torture experience. Yet, as she notes, it is hard to share with others how one has been sexually assaulted, brutally beaten, and almost killed. The disclosure is fraught with fears and anxieties, but the potential authenticity she may feel if she shares her experiences could be liberating, given the possibility of people truly seeing her and understanding her.

Renewing and reestablishing a sense of purpose through a client's testimony and how this testimony is shaped and reshaped over the course of the therapeutic encounter can restart and reclaim a refugee or asylum seeker's life in the face of profound violation and violence.

Challenges with Engaging with Faith Practices

On the other hand, for others, these strategies of faith can promote negative attributes of meaning-making that can cause a person to question his or her deeply held spiritual beliefs or values. In these cases, the loss of meaning expands and extends the traumatic experience for refugees and asylum seek-ers by enveloping and encasing them in a particularly knotty structure of suffering that may inform a loss of faith. In such challenging environments, refugees and asylum seekers who experience such traumas seek explanations for their suffering by attempting to search within their faith, or outside of their faith, in order to bridge their experience with evil (the source of their trauma) and goodness or belief in a higher power or God.

Tola struggled with a black-and-white reality of what is good and bad and what happens when you experience really bad things. For Tola, the violation that occurs becomes so embodied that it is a mark of badness that she feels she inherits. She is now dirty since her "purity" has been defiled because of the sexual and physical torture and her sacredness has been taken away. Early on, Tola was brought up in her church within the specific Christian norms and values of her denomination. It is this specific Christian tradition that characterizes her faith and also informs what is right and wrong in such stark polemics during and after her torture. Hence, the cascade of questions Tola has for God, as well as questions to herself about faith in relationship to her torture.

Challenges with the Process of Meaning-Making

In therapy, Tola works through some difficult questions about faith in relationship to her experience. She actually poses questions as to where God was during her torture and whether her God abandoned her. Subsequently, Tola is confronting the core issue of dissonance between her faith before the torture and afterward. Her security in faith is upended, and she must recon-sider and recast her relationship with faith that navigates this experience of profound violation.

For many refugees and asylum seekers, the struggle to reconcile the evil that has happened to them with their identity as people of faith or their faith in the goodness of the world becomes deeply overwhelming to them. Researchers have characterized this struggle in the reverberation of trauma conceptually as theodicy, where the individual seeks to understand evil within a belief system of a God who is good, all knowing, and powerful. The clinical work with Tola was to work with her torture narrative in this testi-monial space and to be curious about what comes up or emerges as she recounts what is going on with her and the questions that are raised as her boat steers through the storm in the sea.

Therefore, in the sea, a profound crisis of meaning that leads to an inabil-ity to maintain their faith in an all-knowing, benevolent God can emerge when people religiously or spiritually battle with their belief and value sys-tems in the context of their torture experience. Is this what is happening with Tola? In this testimonial, her boat is jostling in the storm but hasn't capsized. In other words, her faith is shaken, it is tested and battered, but hasn't been lost yet. Harris et al. (2015) characterize this existential crisis of faith as a moral injury that destabilizes the relationships between the individual, their faith group, and the society at large. Furthermore, these faith struggles may exacerbate and amplify existing trauma-related symptomology. In other words, the confluence of faith crises, suffering, and loss of meaning for refugees and asylum seekers who are survivors of torture or other forms of persecution must take into account the spectrum of losses. These may include losses of attachment to a belief and value system that highlights a benevolent God and their struggle to reconnect to their spiritual or religious past.

Role of Ritual and Faith Practices in Therapy

Increasingly, more focus has been placed on understanding the dynamic ways people engage with practicing faith to adjust, cope, withstand, and find healing from trauma and suffering by being open to healing rituals and practices. For Harris et al. (2015), clinically working within models of psychospiritual development may facilitate healing by reconstituting the self in relationship with faith practices that promote flexibility and strength in adaptive spiritual growth and conviction. Working with testimony therapy in this context has been helpful since it has actively provided a way to dynamically listen to the faith experience. In other words, as Tola testifies, a deeper relationship to her experience seems to emerge by iteratively and generatively interacting with her faith during the clinical counter. For example, it allows for the questioning of where her storm is located, and if it is truly in her or outside of her. Tola is able to reconsider these factors, and the possibility of reframing the experience is found within a reconceptualization of what all of this means to her.

Therapist as Spiritual Witness

Park et al. (2017) describe a process of reciprocal meaning-making that embeds spirituality in the clinical encounter and attunes the clinician to trauma-informed approaches in resolving loss of meaning and renewing a client's faith practice. Beyond testimony therapy, other treatment approaches call for understanding frameworks of theodicy and reconciliation with faith practices along with spiritual strength building (Hall and Johnson 2001; Harris et al. 2015). Further, de Castella and Simmonds (2013) call for a focus on posttraumatic growth in targeting trauma by strengthening religious and spiritual beliefs toward healing. What unites the array of psychospiritual approaches is a consistent focus on systematically incorporating faith in therapeutic and healing modalities in mental health.

As clinicians, an open orientation on safely facilitating or encouraging a client's dialogue with his or her faith may begin a process of systematically working with a client's beliefs, sense of purpose, goals, and values while reestablishing meaning as the client processes his or her trauma through any number of treatment modalities. This approach could reinforce and reframe a client's relationship to prayer or meditation potentially as a centering, safe resource for coping and emotional regulation.

Over time, Tola began not merely to question but also to be curious about the frames, schemas, and processes she employed to organize her faith experience and how this informed her challenges when engaging with her torture experience. Tola was able to iteratively identify and grapple with the myriad questions she had about her loss of meaning and faith. This was not an easy process, but through therapy, that was infused with an attention and attunement to her prior religious and spiritual sociocultural history, Tola was able to slowly reformulate her relationship with faith through a stance of facilitated curiosity and searching that was individually focused.

Through this process, Tola was able to begin to resolve and reconcile incongruities, inconsistencies, differences, and expectations in meaning to generatively create more plasticity in her approach to religious practice and spirituality. Again, this was not an easy process for her to work through. However, by facilitating intentional dialogue and respectful confrontation in a safe space of the clinical encounter, Tola was able to adopt more flexible adaptive spiritual and religious practices.

As clinicians, attuning and being present with suffering, loss of meaning, and torture can be exhausting work. These psychospiritual processes require endurance on the part of the clinician that absorbs his or her psychic, physical, and spiritual energy. Tola was both exhausted by the process of giving her testimonies and exhausting to the clinician in session, yet she was also inspired and inspiring. It is precisely these paradoxical experiences that we, as clinicians, find ourselves in within the clinical setting. How we attend to and address our own faith foundations along with the spectrum of self-care approaches we engage in can powerfully inform this therapeutic work. A renewal and regrounding in practicing faith and rearticulation with dynamic, adaptive, and flexible meaning-making processes may manifest an approach to engagement with faith for both the client and the clinician, which is dynamically alive within the clinical encounter.

The journey of engaging with Tola, and her testimony, in the clinical encounter perhaps is one of prophetic witness. West and Buschndorf (2014) describe prophetic witness as involving a profound engagement with the source of human pain and suffering through "human acts of justice and kindness" (12) in order to face, head on, personal and institutional evil. In a way, the clinical encounter thus can become a dynamic and radical force for faith renewal and reconnection in places of profound violation of the self in order to inspire and transform spiritual and religious practice to support healing and bearing witness.

Practice Challenges

Confronting the experience of trauma, suffering, and loss in the clinical space presents challenges to clinicians as we seek to navigate therapeutic interventions and the client's own impacted spiritual and cognitive understandings and worldviews. It may present challenges for our own spiritual frameworks and understandings, leaving us with vulnerabilities that can be similar to those of our clients at times. While our exposure to the traumatic events is distanced, it is an exposure nonetheless. Much as we look to the client's spiritual frameworks for resiliency, we must look to our own. Do our spiritual frameworks promote our own clinical resiliency? Or do they fail to provide a space to hold and make meaning of our clients' experiences, our own reactions, and our physical and psychological presence in sacred space and time?

One of the challenges clinicians may face is vicarious trauma. Pearlman and Caringi (2009) define vicarious trauma as a "negative transformation in the helper that results from the empathic engagement with trauma survivors and their trauma material, combined with a commitment or responsibility to help" (202). Furthermore, they identify the disruption in the clinician's systems of meaning-making as the mechanism at the heart of vicarious trauma. This mechanism of vicarious trauma calls for self-care that is "radical" in its approach. What is "radical" is the commitment to intentionality and the frequency and level of self-care needed to be fully engaged in trauma work (Pearlman and Caringi 2009, 216). When we turn our attention to our own presence in our clinical spaces, we are led to the heart of the experience of vicarious trauma. Our work places us on precarious ground, with vicarious trauma often being cited as an occupational hazard (Pearlman and Caringi 2009). In his work on moral injury, Shay (2011), in *Casualties,* brings in another perspective that is relevant to our thinking about ourselves and how our spirituality is impacted by working with survivors of trauma. Shay (2011) states that it is not the first injury that is fatal, the trauma itself, but the workarounds that are created by the survivor to deal with the sequalae of the primary injury. For example, nightmares may be experienced as a sequalae of a trauma experience, impacting the survivor's ability to sleep. The survivor may turn to substances to help him or her sleep, which in turn impact the survivor's ability to obtain the sleep cycles needed for reprocessing of the trauma experience. These workarounds can keep survivors stuck in cycles, which impede their inherent resiliency. It is in the space of our clinical interventions with the workarounds that we are engaged in the work of spirituality and resilience. We are overt that our clinical work addresses the primary injury in the clinical context, the trauma itself. But what is less recognized is that our clinical work is often to hold and manage the workarounds as well. These workarounds may include avoidance of places or people that remind the survivor of their trauma, potentially leaving the survivor with increased isolation, and thereby more reliant on the clinical relationship. Or the workaround may be the disrupted spirituality of the survivor, resulting in a loss of faith. As we manage the vicarious trauma that we may experience, we are experiencing a second layer of impact: our own moral injury. Our own spiritual frameworks may be tested as we seek to mend the spiritual frameworks of the survivor. If we are to allow ourselves to be truly present, how do we both tend to our own moral injury and engage in the "radical" self-care (Pearlman and Caringi 2009, 216) necessary to sustain ourselves in this work?

This radical self-care calls for many facets of tending to ourselves, prominent among them the charge to engage in processes of spiritual renewal. In spiritual renewal, we work to replenish and nourish ourselves on the spiritual level. As we cannot pour water from an empty cup, we cannot draw down our spiritual resources without finding ways to refill. We must tend to the mechanism of vicarious trauma as a spiritual injury. In doing so, we must replenish from a spiritual place in order to continue with the spiritual work with survivors. For some of us, our own belief systems provide the guidance for this. For others, this is a place where we may struggle. Briere (2012), in his work on mindfulness and spirituality, identifies our "center" as the space that we must identify and go back to in order to be mindfully present as trauma clinicians. Briere (2012) describes the center as "a mode that allows objective assessment and intervention, yet, at the same time, supports compassion and receptive attention" (271). Being at our center allows us to be regulated and fully present with ourselves in order to be fully present to our clients. The pathway to the center is different for each of us. It may come through meditation, exercise, or connecting with others. Regardless of our pathways, getting to our centers is engaging in spiritual practice. Finding the center is a shared skill, regardless of which path is followed. Our center also may hold for us the reasons why we do this work. When we return to our center, we reconnect with our reasons for being where we are and doing what we do. It is in our center that we find our own spiritual rationale for doing the work that we do and also our own resilience as clinicians.

Our professional identity and practice provide us with important tools for finding our center as trauma clinicians. The tradition of supervision is a hallmark of clinical practice. As the systems in which we practice place more stress on our limited resources, supervision has become a casualty.

When supervision does occur, it often focuses on case specifics or logistics. In its essence, it should be a space where clinicians can engage in examination of vicarious trauma and seek support around developing and strengthening their processes of spiritual renewal. Just as we are challenged to open the space of being fully present for the refugees with whom we work, we must engage in *all* aspects of our own experiences that parallel those of the client by creating those spaces for ourselves and others where resiliency is fostered for ourselves. In this framework, supervision becomes a foundation of ethical practice. In the case of Tola, clinical themes may surface and be sustained throughout ongoing supervision sessions. Foremost are the issues of exhaustion and endurance for both Tola and the clinician. The clinician is holding a space of healing and containment for Tola, and how does the clinician then find a similar space for himself or herself? This begins with making explicit the presence of spirituality work in the clinical space and welcoming it into the supervisory space. For the clinicians, being present with trauma takes a toll, and the clinician is left holding on to stories of suffering. Just as the client has passed to the clinician the work of their suffering, the clinician must also have a space to leave the suffering that has been passed to them, by passing it on to their supervisor in the space created in supervision. It is in this passing on through supervision that we can care for ourselves and, by doing so, create expanded spiritual spaces to hold the suffering. The supervisor then must engage with his or her own process to manage what he or she has accepted, paralleling the process of client and clinician. This cycle repeats itself, highlighting that the work of trauma and spirituality does not exist in isolation. We exist in communities of practice.

Our communities of practice with other providers who engage in similar work are also powerful spaces to be closely examined and shared. How do we hold the suffering of others and ourselves? How do we make our communities safe for us to be radically present with each other while confronting the reality of how hard this work can be and recognizing the effect it has on us? The encounter with Tola is an opportunity for us as clinicians to authentically share not only her suffering but the passing and transformation of her suffering into ours. The community of practice has a responsibility to name, acknowledge, and to hold this transformation as a real and vital piece of the clinical work. When the community of practice fails in this regard, we perpetuate the wound of trauma and silence, leaving the clinician vulnerable. The community of practice becomes an important factor in mitigating vicarious trauma and compassion fatigue so that the clinician can continue to integrate spirituality as a therapeutic strategy promoting resilience. Our community of practice must hold each of us to this very high standard, not leaving any clinician to seek healing on his or her own. Our places of practice and our colleagues are charged with responsibility for each other to ensure our practice settings are providing all that clinicians need to be supported in this work through access to supervision, support, and overt recognition of the impact the work may have on the clinician.

Conclusion

The case illustration mentioned earlier stemmed from a Christian perspective. As providers, it is important to understand the faith tradition observed by our clients (or the lack thereof). These beliefs often determine how we view the world and understand suffering. Spirituality as the ground for reclamation of meaning in a violated and traumatic space is a powerful therapeutic avenue that makes possible healing and transformation for both the client and clinician. These healing processes may be facilitated by the clinician by intentionally focusing on how the therapeutic encounter may encourage and promote the testifying about a traumatic narrative that is couched and grounded in a client's spiritual framework or approach.

In doing so, the opportunity for traumatic evolution, or the prospects that the client may wrestle with meaning within this spiritual plane, may provide a shift in how the client understands and views his or her suffering and trauma. Facilitating the testimony vis-à-vis a process of spiritual connection and renewal during the encounter may transform the suffering and represent a different way to work with the trauma.

In such a therapeutic collaboration between trauma survivor and clinician, the therapeutic encounter becomes a site for the survivor to engage with feelings of guilt and shame, isolation, anger, irritability, social withdrawal, physiological impacts, and challenges with feeling worthy of a future. Spiritual testimony may facilitate a survivor's rediscovery of meaning and purpose in his or her life. It may also provide a way to amplify spiritual practices that can mitigate symptomology while providing a space for considering issues of compassion, self-forgiveness, and healing.

Note

1. OR = odds ratio, which represents the odds that an outcome will occur given a particular exposure, compared to the odds of the outcome occurring without the exposure.

References

Agger, Inger, Victor Igreja, Rachel Kiehle, and Peter Polatin. 2012. "Testimony Ceremonies in Asia: Integrating Spirituality in Testimonial Therapy for Torture Survivors in India, Sri Lanka, Cambodia, and the Philippines." *Transcultural Psychiatry* 49, no. 3–4: 568–589.

Anum, Jawaria, and Rabia Dasti. 2016. "Caregiver Burden, Spirituality, and Psychological Well-Being of Parents Having Children with Thalassemia." *Journal of Religion & Health* 55, no. 3: 941–955.

Arnetz, Judith, Yoasif Rofa, Bengt Arnetz, Matthew Ventimiglia, and Hikmet Jamil. 2013. "Resilience as a Protective Factor against the Development of Psychopathology among Refugees." *Journal of Nervous and Mental Disease* 201, no. 3: 167–172.

Best, Megan, Phyllis Butow, and Ian Olver 2016. "Doctors Discussing Religion and Spirituality: A Systematic Literature Review." *Palliative Medicine* 30, no. 4: 327–337.

Bonanno, George A. 2004. "Loss, Trauma, and Human Resilience: Have We Underestimated the Human Capacity to Thrive after Extremely Aversive Events." *American Psychologist* 59, no. 1: 20–28.

Briere, John. 2012. "Working with Trauma: Mindfulness and Compassion." In *Compassion and Wisdom in Psychotherapy*, edited by Siegal Germerin, 265–279. New York: Guilford.

Burnett-Zeigler, Inger E., Stephanie S. Schuette, David E. Victorson, and Katherine L. Wisner. 2016. "Mind-Body Approaches to Treating Mental Health Symptoms among Disadvantaged Populations: A Comprehensive Review." *Journal of Alternative & Complementary Medicine* 22, no. 2: 115–124.

de Castella, Rosemary, and Janette G. Simmonds. 2013. "'There's a Deeper Level of Meaning as to What Suffering's All About': Experiences of Religious and Spiritual Growth Following Trauma." *Mental Health, Religion & Culture* 16, no. 5: 536–556.

de Jong, Joop TVM, Ivan H. Komproe, and Mark Van Ommeren. 2003. "Common Mental Disorders in Postconflict Settings." *Lancet* 361, no. 9375: 2128–2130.

Germain, Carel B. 1990. "Life Forces and the Anatomy of Practice." *Smith College Studies in Social Work* 60: 138–152.

Hall, M. Elizabeth Lewis, and Eric L. Johnson. 2001. "Theodicy and Therapy: Philosophical/Theological Contributions to the Problem of Suffering." *Journal of Psychology and Christianity* 20: 5–7.

Harris, Jeannette I., Crystal L. Park, Joseph M. Currier, Timothy J. Usset, and Cory D. Voecks. 2015. "Moral Injury and Psycho-spiritual Development: Considering the Developmental Context." *Spirituality in Clinical Practice* 2, no. 4: 256–266.

Hernandez, Pilar, David Gangsei, and David Engstrom. 2007. "Vicarious Resilience: A New Concept in Work with Those Who Survive Trauma." *Family Process* 46, no. 2: 229–241.

Hodge, David R., Tarek Zidan, and Altaf Husain. 2016. "Depression among Muslims in the United States: Examining the Role of Discrimination and Spirituality as Risk and Protective Factors." *Social Work* 61, no. 1: 45–52.

Holtz, Timothy H. 1998. "Refugee Trauma versus Torture Trauma: A Retrospective Controlled Cohort Study of Tibetan Refugees." *The Journal of Nervous & Mental Disease* 186, no. 1: 24–34.

Iacoviello, Brian M., and Dennis S. Charney. 2014. "Psychosocial Facets of Resilience: Implications for Preventing Posttraumatic Psychopathology, Treating Trauma Survivors, and Enhancing Community Resilience." *European Journal of Psychotraumatology* 5, no. 1. doi: 10.3402/ejpt.v5.23970. eCollection 2014.

Kopacz, Marek S., Courtney Ducharme, David Ani, and Ahmet Atlig. 2017. "Towards a Faith-Based Understanding of Moral Injury." *Journal of Pastoral Care & Counseling* 71, no. 4: 217–219.

Kruizinga, Renske, Iris D. Hartog, Mark Jacobs, Joose G. Daams, Michael Scherer-Rath, Johannes B. Schilderman, Mirjam A.G. Sprangers, and Hanneke W. Van Laahoven. 2016. "The Effect of Spiritual Interventions Addressing Existential Themes Using a Narrative Approach on Quality of Life of Cancer Patients: A Systematic Review and Meta-Analysis." *Psycho-Oncology* 25, no. 3: 253–265.

LeMaster, Joseph W., Carissa L. Broadbridge, Mark A. Lumley, Judith E. Arnetz, Cynthia Arfken, Michael D. Fetters, Jamil Hikmet, Nnamdi Pole, and Bengt B. Arnetz. 2017. "Acculturation and Post-Migration Psychological Symptoms among Iraqi Refugees: A Path Analysis." *American Journal of Orthopsychiatry* March 2. [Epub ahead of print]. doi: 10.1037/ort0000240.

Litz, Brett T. 2005. "Has Resilience to Severe Trauma Been Underestimated? *American Psychologist* 60, no. 3: 262; discussion 265–267.

Massey, Douglas S., and Monica Espinoza Higgins. 2011. "The Effect of Immigration on Religious Belief and Practice: A Theologizing or Alienating Experience?" *Social Science Research* 40, no. 5: 1371–1389.

Mawani, Farah N. 2014. "Social Determinants of Refugee Mental Health." In *Refugee and Resilience*, edited by Laura Simich and Lisa Andermann, 27–50. New York: Springer.

McLellan, Janet 2015. "Religious Responses to Bereavement, Grief, and Loss among Refugees." *Journal of Loss and Trauma* 20, no. 2: 131–138.

Miller, Kenneth E., and Andrew Rasmussen. 2010. "War Exposure, Daily Stressors, and Mental Health in Conflict and Post-Conflict Settings: Bridging the Divide between Trauma-Focused and Psychosocial Framework." *Social Science & Medicine* 70, no. 1: 7–16.

National Consortium of Torture Treatment Programs. 2015. "Descriptive, Inferential, Functional Outcome Data on 9,025 Torture Survivors over Six Years in the United States. *Torture* 25, no. 2: 34–60.

Nolan, Steve. 2016. "'He Needs to Talk!': A Chaplain's Case Study of Nonreligious Spiritual Care." *Journal of Health Care Chaplaincy* 22, no. 1: 1–16.

Orton, Lori, Jane Griffiths, Maia Green, and Healther Waterman. 2012. "Resilience among Asylum Seekers Living with HIV." *BMC Public Health* 12: 926.

Panzarella, Catherine, Lauren B. Alloy, and Wayne G. Whitehouse. 2006. "Expanded Hopelessness Theory of Depression and on the Mechanisms by Which Social Support Protects against Depression." *Cognitive Therapy and Research* 30: 307–333.

Park, Crystal, L. 2017. "Spiritual Well-Being after Trauma: Correlates with Appraisals, Coping, and Psychological Adjustment." *Journal of Prevention and Intervention in the Community* 45, no. 4: 297–307.

Park, Crystal L., Irene J. Harris, Jeanne M. Slattery, and Joseph M. Currier. 2017. *Trauma, Meaning, and Spirituality: Translating Research into Clinical Practice.* Washington, D.C.: American Psychological Association.

Pearlman, Laurie A., and James Caringi. 2009. "Living and Working Self-Reflectively to Address Vicarious Trauma." In *Treating Complex Traumatic Stress Disorders; an Evidence-Based Guide,* edited by Christine A. Courtois and Julian D. Ford, 202–224. New York: Guilford.

Piwowarczyk, Linda. 2005. "Torture and Spirituality: Engaging the Sacred in Treatment." *Torture* 15, no. 1: 1–8.

Piwowarczyk, Linda. 2013. "The Place of Spirituality in Treatment of Torture Survivors." Presentation at the 5th Annual Symposium of the National Consortium of Torture Treatment Programs, Washington, D.C., February 13, 2013.

Sachs, Emily, Barry Rosenfeld, Dechen Lhew, Andrew Rasmussen, and Allen Keller. 2008. "Entering Exile: Trauma, Mental Health, and Coping among Tibetan Refugees Arriving in Dharamsala, India." *Journal of Traumatic Stress* 21, no. 2: 199–208.

Schweitzer, Robert, Jaimi Greenslade Jaimi, and Ashraf Kagee. 2007. "Coping and Resilience in Refugees from the Sudan: A Narrative Account." *Australian and New Zealand Journal of Psychiatry* 41, no. 3 (March): 282–88.

Shay, Jonathon. 2011. "Casualties." *Daedalus* 140, no. 3: 179–188.

Simich, Laura, Morton Beiser, and Farah N. Mawani. 2003. "Social Support and the Significance of Shared Experience in Refugee Migration and Resettlement." *Western Journal of Nursing Research* 25, no. 7: 872–891.

Siriwardhana, Chesmal, Melanie Abas, Sisira Siribaddana, Athula Sumathipala, and Robert Stewart. 2015. "Dynamics of Resilience in Forced Migration: A 1-Year Follow-Up Longitudinal Associations with Mental Health in a Conflict-Affected, Ethnic Muslim Population." *BMJ Open* 5, no. 2: 1–10. https://bmjopen.bmj.com/content/bmjopen/5/2/e006000.full.pdf.

Siriwardhana, Chesmal, Shirwa S. Ali, Bayard Roberts, and Robert Stewart. 2014. "A Systematic Review of Resilience and Mental Health Outcomes of Conflict-Driven Adult Forced Migrants." *Conflict and Health* 8, no. 1: 13.

Smith, Bruce W., Jeanne Dalen, Kathryn Wiggins, Erin Tooley, Paulette Christopher, and Jennifer Bernard. 2008. "The Brief Resilience Scale: Assessing the Ability to Bounce Back." *International Journal of Behavioral Medicine* 15: 194–200.

Steel, Zachary, Tien Chev, Derrick Silove, Claire Marnane, Richard A. Bryant, and Mark van Ommeren. 2009. "Association of Torture and Other Potentially Traumatic Events with Mental Health Outcomes among Populations Exposed to Mass Conflict and Displacement: A Systematic Review and Meta-Analysis." *JAMA* 302, no. 5: 537–549.

Stempel, Carl, Nilofar Sami, Patrick M. Koga, Qais Alemi, Valerie Smith, and Aida Shirazi. 2017. "Gendered Sources of Distress and Resilience among Afghan Refugees in Northern California: A Cross-Sectional Study." *International Journal of Environmental Research and Public Health* 14, no. 1: 25. doi: 10.3390/ijerph14010025.

Sundquist, Jan, Louise Bayard-Burfield, Leena M. Johansson, and Sven Erick Johansson. 2000. "Impact of Ethnicity, Violence, and Acculturation on Displaced Migrants: Psychological Distress and Psychosomatic Complaints among Refugees in Sweden." *Journal of Nervous and Mental Disease* 188, no. 6: 357–365.

Thomas, Fiona C., Bayard Roberts, Nagendra P. Luitel, Nawaraj Upadhaya, and Wietse A. Tol. 2011. "Resilience of Refugees Displaced in the Developing World: A Qualitative Analysis of Strengths and Struggles of Urban Refugees in Nepal." *Conflict and Health* 5: 20. doi:10.1186/1752-1505-5-20.

Tippens, Julie A. 2016. "Urban Congolese Refugees in Kenya: The Contingencies of Coping and Resilience in a Context Marked by Structural Vulnerability." *Qualitative Health Research* 27, no. 7: 1090–1103.

Ungar, Michael. 2008. "Resilience across Cultures." *British Journal of Social Work* 38, no. 2: 218–235.

Ungar, Michael. 2011. "The Social Ecology of Resilience: Addressing Contextual and Cultural Ambiguity of a Nascent Construct." *American Journal of Orthopsychiatry* 81, no. 1: 1–17.

Ungar, Michael, and Linda Liebenberg. 2011. "Assessing Resilience across Cultures Using Mixed Methods: Construction of the Child and Youth Resilience Measure." *Journal of Mixed Methods Research* 5, no. 2: 126–149.

United Nations Convention related to the Status of Refugees. 1951. http://www.ohchr.org/EN/ProfessionalInterest/Pages/StatusOfRefugees.aspx.

United Nations High Commissioner for Refugees. 2017. *Global Trends: Forced Displacement in 2016*. UNHCR: Geneva, Switzerland.

Van Dijk, Janie A., Mirjam J. A. Schoutrop, and Philip Spinhoven. 2003. "Testimony Therapy: Treatment Method for Traumatized Victims of Organized Violence." *American Journal of Psychotherapy* 57, no. 3: 361–373.

Weber, Samuel R., and Kenneth I. Pargament. 2014. "The Role of Religion and Spirituality in Mental Health." *Current Opinion in Psychiatry* 27, no. 5: 358–363.

West, Cornel, and Crista Buschendorf. 2014. *Black Prophetic Fire*. Boston: Beacon Press.

CHAPTER EIGHT

Re-creating Family and Community Networks

Group Interventions with Forced Migrants

Adeyinka M. Akinsulure-Smith and Hawthorne E. Smith

Introduction

By the close of 2016, global forced migration had reached unprecedented levels, with over 65.3 million people around the world forced into flight due to conflict, persecution, human rights abuses, or generalized violence (United Nations High Commissioner for Refugees 2016). In their search for refuge, many forced migrants endure repeated multidimensional stressors in the forms of displacement, loss, deprivation, violence, and social upheaval (Drachman 2014; Fazel and Stein 2002; Lustig et al. 2004; Pumariega, Rothe, and Pumariega 2005; Yule 2002).

While individuals have variable reactions to being forced out of their homeland, there is significant evidence that such traumatic events can leave this population at risk for a range of physical and psychological disorders (Craig, Jajua, and Warfa 2009; Droždek and Bolwerk 2010; Fazel, Wheeler, and Danesh 2005; Keller et al. 2006; Ryan, Kelly, and Kelly 2009; Thomas and Thomas 2004; Turner and Herlihy 2009; Tribe 2002). Although there is well-documented evidence that trauma-informed interventions drawing on individual, family, and group modalities can alleviate symptomatology and improve emotional and physical well-being (Keller, Saul, and Eisenman 1998; Levers 2012; Nicholl and Thompson 2004; Pumariega, Rothe, and Pumariega 2005; Turner and Herlihy 2009), group treatment offers additional therapeutic factors. The group modality allows survivors to learn from and support one another in ways they could not do in individual therapy and may grant them the freedom to express deep feelings they would not necessarily share within the family context. This allows for therapeutic factors such as universality, information sharing, interpersonal learning opportunities, catharsis, rebuilding of community ties, and the fostering of hope (Bunn et al. 2016; Yalom and Leszcz 1995). Numerous scholars have documented the positive effects of group interventions with trauma survivors (Foy, Eriksson, and Trice 2001; Herman 1997; Kudler, Blank, and Krupnick 2000; Lubin et al. 1998). Increasingly, researchers and clinicians have acknowledged the efficacy of group interventions with forced migrants (Akinsulure-Smith 2009, 2012; Akinsulure-Smith, Ghiglione, and Wollmershauser 2009; Bunn et al. 2016; Droždek and Bolwerk 2010; Smith 2003; Smith and Impalli 2007; Tucker and Price 2007). Group therapy is particularly useful among forced migrant populations from collectivistic cultures where interpersonal relationships, along with community ties, social networks, and family connections, are prioritized (Bemak and Chung 2008; Chung et al. 2008; Smith 2003).

The primary goal of this chapter is to discuss the integral role of group interventions in caring for survivors of torture and refugee trauma at the Bellevue/NYU Program for Survivors of Torture (PSOT). Through this lens, we will highlight the many benefits, challenges, and lessons learned from incorporating therapeutic interventions developed in the context of working with forced migrants who face daunting challenges in overcoming the effects of their traumatic experiences, while adapting to life and normalizing their status in their adopted country.

Setting and Organization

The Bellevue/NYU PSOT is devoted to healing the bodies, minds, and spirits of people who have been tortured or otherwise persecuted. The program is located on the Lower East Side of Manhattan, one of the city's (and the nation's) most vibrant immigrant communities. PSOT is situated within two institutions of healing and training: the Bellevue Hospital Center (the nation's oldest existing public hospital) and the New York University School of Medicine. This partnership provides significant clinical resources as we strive to bring coordinated, interdisciplinary care to our client population (Akinsulure-Smith 2012; Keller, Saul, and Eisenman 1998). Since its founding in 1995, the program has served over 5,000 men, women, and children from over 100 countries who are survivors of torture and refugee trauma (Smith 2018).

PSOT has sustained itself through "in kind" support from both of its parent institutions since its inception and has received generous support from outside entities as well. In addition to contributions from private donors and community members, the program has been supported by the Office of Refugee Resettlement (through the Torture Victims Relief Act), the United Nations Voluntary Fund, and philanthropic organizations that prioritize issues regarding human rights, such as Human Rights First, the Robin Hood Foundation, the Langeloth Foundation, the Hope and Grace Foundation, and the Open Society Foundation.

PSOT's service provision model is based on two crucial tenets: We take a strength-based, resilience-focused approach to care, as opposed to an approach based on assumed pathology and dysfunction. We believe that our clients are "survivors," rather than simply "victims." They have already overcome many challenges and have undertaken many risks in order to flee their countries, make it to New York City, find our clinic, and engage in the healing process (Smith and Keller 2007). The focus on the survivors' own insights and understanding of their experiences and healing processes is consistent with the theory of human becoming, in which people are seen as the experts of their own lives, and their input can be a crucial factor in developing effective medical and mental health interventions (Green 2010; Smith and Akinsulure-Smith 2011).

At PSOT, we also take a holistic view of the survivors with whom we work, such that our clinical interventions are based on an integrated, interdisciplinary treatment philosophy (Smith and Akinsulure-Smith 2011). Our service provision team is comprised of primary care physicians (as well as other medical doctors operating in specialty areas, such as emergency medicine, obstetrics and gynecology, dermatology, and orthopedics), psychologists, psychiatrists, social workers, legal service and immigration specialists, art therapists, yoga instructors, English as second language tutors, administrative staff, and students. Our students include psychiatry and medical residents, psychology and social work interns, and psychology externs (Keller et al. 1998; Smith and Keller 2007). Great effort is taken to ensure that these various disciplines work together in a coordinated fashion through intake conferences, peer supervision sessions, six-month client follow-ups, care coordination meetings, and case conferences. Such an approach assures that we are truly an interdisciplinary team, as opposed to a multidisciplinary team, where a multitude of services may be provided, but without a coordinated approach to treatment planning and service provision (Smith 2018).

These dual tenets—of seeing our clients as survivors who have profound knowledge and insights as to their own needs and processes and working within an interdisciplinary team—were central to the development of our group interventions. Over time, PSOT has earned a reputation for being among the leaders in utilizing group modalities in culturally syntonic and adaptive ways. Before articulating the rationale for group treatment and describing the processes of developing effective group interventions, let us briefly touch upon the types of groups that PSOT has utilized.

PSOT's culturally driven support groups have proven to be clinically effective and sustainable over time. The initial group developed at PSOT, "La Famille Africaine" (the group for Francophone African survivors of torture), has just recently celebrated its 20th anniversary of continuous service provision and has touched the lives of hundreds of displaced torture survivors. Our groups for English-speaking African men and Tibetan-speaking survivors have each been active for over 15 years, while our therapy group for survivors of homophobic persecution and our geographically diverse support group for English-speaking survivors of torture have each been operating for a decade (Akinsulure-Smith 2012; Smith 2018).

PSOT has also conducted support groups for Albanian-speaking survivors, Fulani-speaking survivors, and female survivors of sexual violence. Our clinicians have collaborated with community groups to facilitate a short-term group for immigrants traumatized by the 9/11 terrorist attacks. PSOT co-created a community-based wellness group for African women in New York City fleeing the war in Sierra Leone (Akinsulure-Smith, Ghiglione, and Wollmerhauser 2009). We have also collaborated with legal advocacy groups, like the Center for Constitutional Rights, to design supportive, short-term group interventions for survivors of human rights abuses who were preparing to testify in high-profile legal proceedings regarding human rights abuses in their home countries of Bosnia and Uganda.

In addition to the ongoing, supportive group modalities, PSOT has developed a short-term, four-session psychoeducational and supportive intervention, known as "Orientation Groups." These manualized "O.R. groups" have been used with clients who have recently been accepted into the program. They have been developed to help clients learn about resources at the programmatic, hospital, and community levels. Clients learn and practice affect regulation skills, such as deep breathing, grounding, and progressive muscle relaxation, that largely come from a trauma-focused, cognitive, and behavioral perspective. Participants also learn about common psychological effects of trauma and the basics of the asylum process, and speak with one of our psychiatrists about psychopharmacology and the "meaning of medication" (Smith 2018). These orientation groups are linguistically based. We have run multinational orientation groups for English, French, and Tibetan speakers. These groups also serve as an opportunity for further triage; subsequent referrals for direct services are frequently made after clients have finished their orientation group participation (Smith 2018).

The orientation groups, as all groups at PSOT, are staffed and conducted from an interdisciplinary framework. These groups are frequently facilitated by staff from differing disciplines, and the group supervision may also be provided across disciplines, for reasons similar to those of the orientation groups. Research shows that effective clinical collaboration happens when there is a sense of similarity of mission and mutual dependence among disciplines (Berg-Weger and Schneider 2014). There is frequently cross-discipline supervision at PSOT, as our senior clinicians may work with trainees from outside their departments. Not only does this give us more flexibility in terms of scheduling and other logistics, but it also helps to deepen the training experience as our trainees have hands-on experience working with and being supervised by professionals from other disciplines. This allows them to broaden their perspectives on how to consider cases and intervene with specific clients.

PSOT also utilizes group modalities that are nonverbally based, such as art therapy and trauma-informed yoga (van der Kolk et al. 2014). These interventions have been shown to be quite effective with highly traumatized populations who may have difficulty expressing their feelings verbally. Interventions that are not so highly predicated on language proficiency are especially well suited to our program's extensive linguistic diversity, as clients who may not fit into one of our talk-oriented groups can still have meaningful client-to-client contact in a way that builds a sense of community and belonging. These group interventions are based on the notion that healing is an active process; it is not just the passive anticipation of things eventually getting better. It is an active engagement in the healing process that allows a victim to become a survivor. Artistic expression and communication, including both receptive and expressive modalities, are key in developing the capacity to engage in the healing process, as one learns to authentically engage with oneself and the world. A growing body of literature speaks to the intersection of artistic expression and healing. For example, researchers have detailed how expressive arts, such as dance, music, painting, and drawing, work by engaging the hypothalamus and activating the parasympathetic nervous system helping the body to simultaneously focus and relax (Ganim 1999; Samuels and Lane 1998). Such interventions have been shown to reduce hypertension, reduce anxiety, decrease the severity of pain, decrease the frequency of problematic behaviors, and help people to process traumatic memories (Benson 1975; Samuels and Lane 2000; Stuckey and Nobel 2010). These interventions are often included as part of the interdisciplinary treatment plan in conjunction with input from physicians, mental health service providers, and social service providers within the team.

Rationale for Group Interventions with Forced Migrants

Culturally Syntonic Interventions

PSOT's group services grew out of what we learned from our clients while providing individual therapy, medical services, social and legal service support, and educational services. Our initial group, the support group for French-speaking African survivors of torture, was developed after service providers were taught by their African clients that individual psychotherapy was basically unheard of in their home cultures. Traditionally, people in emotional distress were much more likely to turn to members of their extended family for guidance and support than to seek any kind of formalized mental health treatment. As this was a resource that no longer existed for survivors who had been forcibly extracted from their familial and social networks by the traumatic events they had experienced, they spoke about this gap in their coping resources. This led to the development of a group that would mimic some of the processes of an African extended family (Smith 2003).

As these groups are developed for traumatized individuals from many cultural and linguistic backgrounds, and since the group structures and norms vary among populations, cultural norms are taken into consideration as group facilitators and participants co-create the culture of each group (Smith and Impalli 2007). As such, this type of culturally derived group intervention, and its subsequent iterations, has frequently been found to be more culturally syntonic for our clients compared to individual psychotherapy or long courses of psychiatric medication (Smith 2003). This type of intervention has also helped to reduce the stigma associated with engaging in mental health services (Akinsulure-Smith 2012; Bunn et al. 2016; Smith and Akinsulure-Smith 2011; Smith and Impalli 2007). For example, the support group for English- and French-speaking African survivors draws heavily from the West and Central African traditions of the extended family and the communal support and discussion necessary to confront individual challenges. On the other hand, the group for people persecuted due to their sexual orientation tends to be more psychodynamic and process oriented (Akinsulure-Smith 2012; Smith 2018).

Another example of following the cultural lead of group participants occurred when PSOT's group for Tibetan survivors experienced an initial period when members were reticent to speak openly about the challenges they were facing. Upon further exploration, it turned out that their hesitation was not due to fear or issues of retraumatization; in fact, they were following their Buddhist beliefs and did not want to prioritize their personal suffering over the suffering of anyone else in the group. Once this was recognized, the group facilitators set up a plan by which each member would be "assigned" half of a session, during which they would be able to speak about whatever they would like to share about their lives. After three sessions, all six members had "shared," and from that point on, the group flowed in an open and supportive manner (Smith and Impalli 2007).

Reduction of Isolation

When conducting programmatic intake interviews with newly arrived survivors of torture and other forced migrants, we often hear that they are coping with significant challenges and pain that go beyond the particular traumatic events and torture they have experienced. They frequently talk of an overarching sense of isolation: of being adrift in this "cold society" where "everyone is busy," it's "dog eat dog," and it's "every man for himself." They have been forcibly pulled away from their usual sources of communal and emotional support, and they face significant barriers toward forming trusting interpersonal connections and social networks (Smith 2003). Group interventions have been shown to be useful in addressing vulnerabilities in social functioning and relationship development (Bunn et al. 2016; Kira et al. 2012; Stepakoff et al. 2006).

When survivors are placed in a context where their experiences, insights, and thoughts are received in a context of mutual respect, it helps them to find their voices in at least one environment, which may be a welcome respite from other social situations in which they may be too intimidated to speak up.

Normalization

"Am I crazy?" "How can anyone else understand what I've been through?" "I am damaged beyond repair." These are questions and statements that may be expressed by survivors of torture and refugee trauma as they confront their own physical, emotional, and cognitive reactions to their traumatic experiences. They may feel that their lives have limited value or utility. They may lose hope in terms of the possibility of healing or overcoming their painful experiences and circumstances. These negative self-perceptions can be just as detrimental to one's functioning and healing trajectory as the actual physical effects of torture. Many clients have concurred that the emotional impact of torture can be even more painful and long lasting than the physical pain (Smith and Keller 2007).

Many psychological interventions have been put in place to combat these negative self-assertions and cognitive distortions, especially in the context of trauma-focused cognitive behavioral therapy (Feeny et al. 2004). As effective as these therapist-based interventions have proven to be, we have found that the impact of hearing from others who have "walked the same path" has been extremely important in fostering the positive self-belief and encouragement necessary for a survivor to persist and travel the difficult road toward healing.

Our ongoing and open-ended groups tend to be more supportive in nature than traditional trauma-focused groups, in which survivors engage in guided exposure and processing (Bunn et al. 2016). However, group members will often share aspects of the challenges they have overcome on their journey toward healing, even if they do not describe their torture histories in detail. Members will share anecdotes that may carry messages like: "You should have seen me when I first got here . . ."; "Here's what I did when I found that I couldn't sleep . . ."; "I used to be so bright, but now it's like I can't remember anything"; and "I'm so scared about having to tell my story in front of an asylum officer."

Not only do these conversations carry pertinent information and psycho-educational content from people who have been engaged in similar struggles, but they are important in terms of process, where group members may learn that they are not alone in their suffering and that their struggles are not deviant or a sign of weakness. Members come to learn that they are not "sick" or "abnormal" people, but that they are traversing sick situations and abnormal circumstances (Smith 2003). In addition, as veteran group members are able to share their experiences and help to support newly arrived group members, they become part and parcel of someone else's healing process. They come to learn and internalize that they are not just people who are needy but they are also needed.

When survivors feel respected by others, it makes it less difficult for them to hold on to the notions of self-respect and self-esteem, which are necessary to combat the multiple occasions and levels of disempowerment they may be facing. Through these group processes of multidirectional empowerment, group members may begin to reclaim a positive sense of themselves as they take on some of the old roles, functions, and status that they once held in their homelands. Older members, who may be disempowered in terms of their current linguistic capacity or marginalized in terms of their academic or professional standing, may feel that at least they are being respected as a "community elder." Younger members who are separated from their families and who may feel socially isolated may experience the protective gaze of elders and hear their words of encouragement and advice as culturally syntonic interventions that situate them at the heart of a functioning family. This subsequently helps the younger members to orient themselves and persevere in their efforts to survive, advance, and thrive.

Clinical Efficiency and Sustainability

In addition to the therapeutic benefits for group members, there is also a practical argument for treatment programs to utilize group interventions. In this day of shrinking budgets and diminishing grant pools, treatment centers are obliged to do more with less. Group interventions allow programs to see and treat an expanded number of clients with the limited therapeutic and clinical resources they have (Bunn et al. 2016; Smith and Impalli 2007). Recently, as we have seen the amount of time that it takes to process an asylum claim increase, PSOT has seen an increase in clients who need ongoing supportive services. The length of time during which they need these services has also grown. Because our capacity to provide individual therapy services has not kept pace, our ongoing groups have become even more important as a sustainable vehicle for our programmatic functioning, as well as a supportive structure for clients facing these daunting challenges.

Practical Considerations for Group Interventions for Forced Migrants

Drawing from our experiences at PSOT and our work with the forced migrant population, we have learned that group treatment offers individuals from diverse cultures the opportunity to connect with others who have had similar experiences (e.g., loss, trauma, resettlement and acculturation, isolation, traumatic and depressive symptoms, and forced migration) in a safe and nurturing environment. This facilitates normalization of their experiences and healing while allowing them to develop strong community ties (Akinsulure-Smith 2009, 2012; Akinsulure-Smith, Ghiglione, and Wollmershauser 2009; Keller et al. 1998; Smith 2003; Smith and Impalli 2007).

To provide competent, trauma-informed group treatment, we suggest that service providers consider the following elements as they develop their group treatment. While our suggestions are not exhaustive, in our experience many of these factors have influenced the type of group services we have been able to offer and their success.

Clearly Define the Goals and Format of the Group Intervention

When implementing a group intervention, it is important to recognize that group treatment can take multiple formats (Bunn et al. 2016), including the following:

a) *Psychoeducational* ("Stage 1") groups, which are time limited and focus on providing information about a particular topic (e.g., information about the asylum process or different types and impact of psychotropic medications), such as the four-week orientation group described earlier. The informational aspect of these groups is particularly important for newly arrived forced migrants living in communities where a great deal of misinformation is spread throughout the community. Group members have stated that the only thing worse than a lack of information is misinformation (Smith 2003).

b) *Activity* groups, which bring people together to share a common activity and promote social connections and body based and creative ways to process trauma (e.g., yoga, art, music). Again, these groups and activities have been linked to positive health outcomes (Benson 1975; Samuel and Lane 2000; Stuckey and Nobel 2010) and have the advantage of being effective across linguistic dividing lines.

c) *Support* groups, with their emphasis on connecting, sharing, and learning about the kinds of problems members are experiencing and coping strategies, have been found to be successful. Members share what has helped them to successfully adapt to their new environments and what has not helped. These groups promote a supportive environment for sharing and developing new relationships (Kira et al. 2012; Stepakoff et al. 2006).

d) *Therapy and Trauma-Focused* ("Stage 2") groups, which tend to focus more on the sharing and processing of traumatic content. There is a focus on sharing, listening, and supporting. Allowing members to learn how to be with others who share common experiences and promoting acceptance helps to create a healing environment where it is safe to share and where trust of others can develop (Fischman and Ross 1990).

We recognize that the type of group intervention offered will be influenced by the training and availability of facilitators. While support groups and therapy groups are typically facilitated by trained and licensed clinicians, psychoeducational groups and activity groups do not necessarily require licensed mental health clinicians.

Define the Target Population of the Group to Be Offered

In order to develop a cohesive group, it is important to give thought to the target population and the overarching themes and commonalities that might be shared by group members. For instance, will the focus be demographic region, type of trauma, gender, or ethnicity (as in our Tibetan and Albanian groups)? Or is shared language more important (e.g., in our Francophone African group)? Cultural beliefs and taboos must also be considered, as potential group members may have cultural or religious injunctions against the mixing of gender within a group space. It is highly recommended that potential group members be consulted and given some input in terms of group composition and overarching group themes.

The balance between homogeneity and heterogeneity is dynamic and needs to be considered before launching a group and as the group develops. To that end, Yalom and Leszcz (1995) have taught that a heterogeneous group will find commonality, while a homogeneous group will find variation. Such has been our experience of the Francophone support group, which is heterogeneous in many ways. The group has had men and women from 22 different countries, including Muslims, Christians, and those who follow more traditional, indigenous belief systems. We have had highly educated government ministers, doctors, journalists, and lawyers, as well as escaped slaves, cattle herders, and street vendors who have never set foot in a formal class-room setting. But with this considerable heterogeneity, there is also a great deal of commonality regarding shared experiences of human rights abuses, torture, dislocation, and forced exile as a linguistic and racial minority (Smith 2003).

Historical events and societal movements may play a role in the way a group's target population is considered. Has there been a surge of forced migrants from a particular geographic region due to a rise in violence against that population? For example, as result of a surge of sexual violence in theaters of war around the world, our program saw a need to develop a group for women who had experienced sexual violence. When we saw an increase in individuals who were fleeing persecution due to their sexual orientation, we developed a group to address those needs.

Group Selection Criteria

Yalom and Leszcz (1995) state that much of a group's success is determined well before the first session. Determining inclusion criteria is a part of this. Some of the typical standards for group inclusion inform our screening processes, such as group participants being motivated and having positive expectations for the treatment. Members should have adequate fluency, in terms of expressive and receptive language skills, in a common language so that interpersonal communication is possible. If group members and the facilitators do not share a common language, how might interpreters be used in the group? If they are used, where will they come from and how will they be trained? How will trust be established (O'Hara and Akinsulure-Smith 2011)?

Over time, some factors have caused us to adjust our inclusion criteria and expectations to fit the realities that our clients are facing. For example, safety is a major concern, so we work diligently to screen potential members and make sure that there are no group members who have a past history of perpetrating human rights abuses. This information is queried and ascertained at various levels of the programmatic and group screening processes. Program applicants are asked directly if they have ever been involved in hurting others during their programmatic intake process. If there are aspects of their trauma history that cast doubt about their involvement in human rights abuses or violence, these aspects become an integral part of the semi-structured intake interview. These issues are revisited when someone who has been accepted into the program is being screened individually for potential group participation. In addition, we assess for comfort with being in a group with other people from the same country who may have differing experiences or hold different points of view regarding circumstances back home. Safety is a paramount issue in group functioning among people with significant trauma histories.

Group attendance is another issue that needs to be seen through the lens of the reality the participants are facing. Though we expect that group members attend sessions as frequently as they can, we also understand that there is precious little flexibility in the work schedules of disempowered, marginal, or informal laborers in the workforce. Often, they have no control over whether they can attend groups at a particular time.

We have also been obliged to revisit some of our notions regarding suicidal ideation or perceptual disturbances. Normally anyone expressing suicidal ideation or experiencing perceptual disturbances that could be construed as psychotic would be excluded from an outpatient group. However, we have found that clients who have expressed passive suicidal ideation (without active intent or plan) in a kind of philosophic "What is my life worth?" framework have been encouraged and helped by the supportive interventions of other group members who may have passed through a similar stage. Similarly, someone may report "hearing voices" when waking or falling asleep or say they receive messages from family members during their dreams. These survivors may find an accepting and supportive milieu among group members who may experience such phenomena as spiritually and culturally syntonic, as opposed to psychotic and sick. Such nuanced decisions and interventions should be considered carefully and should be done in conjunction with adequate and skilled psychiatric backup.

Group Rules/Norms

Thought must be given to how group rules and norms will be developed. Decisions must be made about how much influence members will have in determining the group rules. In our experience, engaging members in the co-construction of group norms has been a positive element in fostering a sense of ownership and engagement in the group. For example, when the Francophone support group was in its infancy, group members proposed that they should exchange phone numbers and be able to have outside contacts. This was in direct contradiction to the general group processes we had learned in our graduate training programs, so we were wary about "bending" this rule. It was through longer conversations with group members, in which we emphasized the need for confidentiality and maintaining a sense of safety for group members who chose to share their numbers, that we decided to move forward and allow outside group contacts. It has proven to be a very important aspect of the group over the years, as members have supported each other in times of crisis, passed along critical news, and created a supportive network that goes beyond the weekly group therapy sessions (Smith

2003). Similar findings have been identified in other groups with survivors of torture (Akinsulure-Smith 2012; Hubbard and Pearson 2004).

Client input has also been important in terms of other logistical concerns, such as the frequency and length of sessions, whether groups have open or closed membership, and whether the group is an ongoing versus a short-term group.

Roles of the Facilitator

When facilitating a group for traumatized, forced migrants, the responsibilities and considerations are complex. First and foremost, facilitators must create a safe and respectful environment that is conducive for mutual sharing and discussion. They must be able to identify and verbalize central themes put forth by group members, while calling attention to pertinent group processes. As group sessions can cover some painful or difficult terrain, it is incumbent upon facilitators to make sure that group members leave with a sense of shared growth and progress. This does not mean that facilitators should minimize the difficult content that was shared during the session, but they should emphasize the importance of being able to share in a context of mutual respect and shared growth, which may not openly exist in other aspects of their daily lives (Smith 2003; Smith and Impalli 2007). It is also necessary that the facilitator have enough cultural familiarity and dexterity to effectively manage and understand group processes (Akinsulure-Smith 2012; Fischman and Ross 1990; Smith and Akinsulure-Smith 2011).

Training and Use of Co-facilitators

There are important issues to keep in mind when working with trainees as co-facilitators. This is especially true for a client population that has experienced numerous losses. For example, trainee turnover might impact the sense of safety and trust among members within such a group setting if not discussed carefully with group members. Additionally, supervision must address the impact of such work on the trainees (Urlić 2005) and address the multicultural aspects of this work (Bemak and Chung 2004).

To this end, support for trainees at PSOT encompasses formal supervision as well as informal ways of facilitating communication and feelings of safety. Similar to our work with clients, trainees' experiences are normalized, and we strive to create an environment in which the expression of pain, doubt, or feelings of inadequacy is supported, respected, and attended to. We help to teach, and hopefully model to, our young clinicians that we need to attend to self-compassion and find creative ways to sublimate our experiences, so that we become "a conduit and not a container," in terms of the traumatic material and experiences to which we are exposed (Figley 1995; Figley and Kleber 1995; Murakami 2017; Smith 2007b).

At PSOT, we provide an intensive orientation training program to new trainees that provides both didactic and experiential learning opportunities regarding issues of service provision across and among cultures. During the training year, supervision is always used as a venue where issues of culture are central to the therapeutic and supervisory experience. We emphasize the notion that culture is an interpersonal, dynamic function and is not a simple study of the "cultural other." As such, it is also necessary to understand the clinician's reference group identities, feelings, and cultural conceptions in order to fully understand what is transpiring within the therapeutic relationship (Elsass 1997; Smith 2007a; Sue and Sue 1990).

Impact/Influence of Asylum Hearings and Their Outcomes

It is critical that all clinicians working with forced migrant populations are knowledgeable about the legal processes that their clients face and that they understand the differences between being a refugee, an asylee, an asylum seeker, or an undocumented person. The differing statuses can have a severe impact on the individual group members' willingness to access services, eligibility for services, and emotional functioning. Immigration status is often a central theme in group sessions (Drachman 1995; Wilkinson 2007). Clinicians who intend to demonstrate cultural competence and effective social justice advocacy (Arredondo, Tovar-Blank, and Parham 2008; Vera and Speight 2003) must be well informed and prepared to actively engage in the struggles and fears their clients will express and be faced with regarding their immigration status.

The concerns about U.S. immigration policies have been even more central to the groups we run at PSOT since the change of administration in January 2017. There are major concerns that people's immigration status, or their prospects for normalizing their status, are at risk. There are fears about increasing xenophobic reactions to immigrants in general and Muslim migrants in particular. Group conversations have confirmed that there are an incredible number of rumors gaining traction in various communities. It has been said, "The only thing worse than a lack of information, is misinformation" (Smith, Gangsei, and Lustig 2015). Our groups serve as an essential clearing house and sounding board for forced migrants to share their concerns and fears, as well as pertinent and valid information. This ensures that others are no longer walking alone, uninformed or without guidance.

Conclusion

A growing body of literature shows the enormous potential of group interventions to help treat and manage the multifaceted challenges and stressors that survivors of torture and other forced migrants face. Resources and bibliographies on group work with these populations exist through organizations such as the National Partnership for Community Training (managed by the Gulf Coast Jewish Family and Community Services in Miami, Florida) as well as the National Capacity Building Project (managed by the Center for Victims of Torture in Minneapolis, Minnesota). A recent literature review by Bunn et al. (2016) also points to many promising initiatives that exist in terms of group interventions for survivors of human rights abuses, whether in their countries of origin or after displacement. Though a significant number of qualitative case studies and testimonials do exist, there is a need for more empirical research about the impact and effectiveness of group treatment with refugees and other forced migrants.

That being said, it is important that we do not neglect the "practice-based evidence" we glean from practitioners around the world as we seek to strengthen our cadre of "evidence-based practice." It is often difficult (or potentially unethical) to withhold or delay treatment of survivors in need. As such, it is hard to set up randomized control studies or replicate the quantitative rigor of research lab conditions. We should acknowledge and respect these limitations while assessing the effectiveness of group interventions, but we should not ignore the hard-earned insights and testimonials from the survivors who animate and populate these groups.

We hear from many clients who give unsolicited confirmation that many of our goals for the groups have been achieved and that the underpinning rationale has been borne out. Many speak of "having a family again" or learning that "I'm not alone with my problems." We have seen members receive word-of-mouth referrals or jobs. We have seen group members provide housing for members in need who have recently arrived in the United States. We have seen group participants consoled after experiencing losses and supported and encouraged as they move forward with their asylum processes, or as they strive to reunite with their families (Akinsulure-Smith 2012; Smith and Akinsulure-Smith 2011; Smith and Impalli 2007).

It is striking when new members are welcomed into our ongoing groups and we hear long-standing group members describe their experience of the group and what they see as the value of participating. We hear them encourage the newcomers and describe how far they have come with the assistance of their fellow group members. We hear them normalize the newcomers' suffering and disorientation. We hear them say, "Nothing is easy, but everything is possible." We are privileged to witness the transformation as someone shifts from seeing only limitations to also seeing possibilities.

There is so much more to learn about group work with this population and so much more that needs to be done in terms of providing effective culturally informed group treatment. We are confident, however, that groups that are developed within the framework of a holistic and resilience-based view of the survivors, and that are formed within the context of an interdisciplinary approach to healing, will provide opportunities for further growth of the knowledge base of group work and innovation in terms of developing effective practices to assist this complexly challenged population. We hope that this chapter is a helpful beginning to this exploration, but we also encourage you to keep in mind that the true experts and innovators will be those clients with whom you will work.

References

Akinsulure-Smith, Adeyinka M. 2009. "Brief Psychoeducational Group Treatment with Re-traumatized Refugees and Asylum Seekers." *Journal for Specialists in Group Work* 34, no. 2: 137–150. doi:10.1080/01933920902798007.

Akinsulure-Smith, Adeyinka M. 2012. "Using Group Work to Rebuild Family and Community Ties among Displaced African Men." *The Journal for Specialists in Group Work* 37, no. 2: 95–112.

Akinsulure-Smith, Adeyinka M., Jessica B. Ghiglione, and Carrie Wollmershauser. 2009. "Healing in the Midst of Chaos: Nah We Yone's African Women's Wellness Group." *Women & Therapy* 32, no. 1: 105–120. doi:10.1080/02703140802384602.

Arredondo, Patricia, Zoila Tovar-Blank, and Thomas A. Parham. 2008. "Challenges and Promises of Becoming a Culturally Competent Counselor in a Sociopolitical Era of Change and Empowerment." *Journal of Counseling and Development* 86, no. 3: 261–268.

Bemak, Fred, and Rita C. Chung. 2004. "Teaching Multicultural Group Counseling: Perspectives for New Era." *The Journal for Specialists in Group Work* 29, no. 1: 31–41.

Benson, Herbert. 1975. *The Relaxation Response.* New York: HarperCollins Publishers.

Berg-Weger, Marla, and F. David Schneider. 2014. "Interdisciplinary Collaboration in Social Work Education." *Journal of Social Work Education*, 34, no. 1: 97–107, doi: 10.1080/10437797.1998.10778908.

Bunn, Mary, Charles Goesel, Mélodie Kinet, and Faith Ray. 2016. "Group Treatment for Survivors of Torture and Severe Violence: A Literature Review." *Torture* 26, no. 1: 45–67.

Chung, Rita C. Y., Fred Bemak, Diana P. Ortiz, and Paola A. Sandoval-Perez. 2008. "Promoting the Mental Health of Immigrants: A Multicultural/Social Justice Perspective." *Journal of Counseling & Development* 86, no. 3: 310–317.

Craig, Tom, Peter Mac Jajua, and Nasir Warfa. 2009. "Mental Health Care Needs of Refugees." *Psychiatry* 8, no. 9: 351–354.

Drachman, Diane. 1995. "Immigration Statuses and Their Influence on Service Provision, Access, and Use." *Social Work* 40, no. 2: 188–197.

Drachman, Diane. 2014. "Immigrants and Refugees." In *Handbook of Social Work Practice with Vulnerable and Resilient Populations*, edited by Alex Glitterman, 366–391. New York: Columbia University Press.

Drożdek, Boris, and Nina Bolwerk. 2010. "Evaluation of Group Therapy with Traumatized Asylum Seekers and Refugees—The Den Bosch Model." *Traumatology* 16, no. 4: 117.

Elsass, Peter. 1997. *Treating Victims of Torture and Violence: Theoretical, Cross-Cultural, and Clinical Implications*. New York and London: New York University Press.

Fazel, Mina, and Alan Stein. 2002. "The Mental Health of Refugee Children." *Archives of Disease in Childhood* 87, no. 5: 366–370.

Fazel, Mina, Jeremy Wheeler, and John Danesh. 2005. "Prevalence of Serious Mental Disorder in 7000 Refugees Resettled in Western Countries: A Systemic Review." *The Lancet* 365, no. 9467: 1309–1314. doi:10.1016/S0140-6736(05)61027-6.

Feeny, Norah, Edna Foa, Kimberli Treadwell, and John March. 2004. "Posttraumatic Stress Disorder in Youth: A Critical Review of the Cognitive and Behavioral Treatment Outcome Literature." *Professional Psychology: Research and Practice* 35, no. 5: 466–476.

Figley, Charles. 1995. "Compassion Fatigue as Secondary Traumatic Stress Disorder." In *Compassion Fatigue: Coping with Traumatic Stress Disorder in Those Who Treat the Traumatized*, edited by Charles Figley, 1–18. New York: Bruner/Mazel, Inc.

Figley, Charles, and Rolf Kleber. 1995. "Beyond the 'Victim': Secondary Traumatic Stress." In *Beyond Trauma: Cultural and Societal Dynamics*, edited by Rolf Kleber and Charles Figley, 75–98. New York: Plenum Press.

Fischman, Yael, and Jaime Ross. 1990. "Group Treatment of Exiled Survivors of Torture." *American Journal of Orthopsychiatry* 60, no. 1: 135–142. doi:10.1037/h0079191.

Foy, David W., Cynthia B. Eriksson, and Gary A. Trice. 2001. "Introduction to Group Interventions for Trauma Survivors." *Group Dynamics* 5: 246–251.

Ganim, Barbara. 1999. *Art and Healing: Using Expressive Art to Heal Your Body, Mind, and Spirit*. New York: Crown Publishing Group.

Green, Brenda L. 2010. "Applying Interdisciplinary Theory in the Care of Aboriginal Women's Mental Health." *Journal of Psychiatric and Mental Health Nursing* 17, no. 9: 797–803. doi: 10.1111/j.1365–2850.2010.01593.x.

Herman, Judith. L. 1997. *Trauma and Recovery: The Aftermath of Violence—From Domestic Abuse to Political Terror*. Vol. 551. New York: Basic Books.

Hubbard, John., and Nancy Pearson. 2004. "Sierra Leonean Refugees in Guinea: Addressing the Mental Health Effects of Massive Community Violence." In *The Mental Health of Refugees: Ecological Approaches to Healing and Adaptation*, edited by Kenneth E. Miller and Lisa M. Rasco, 95–132. Mahwah: Lawrence Earlbaum Associates.

Keller, Allen, Dechen Lhewa, Barry Rosenfeld, Emily Sachs, Asher Aladjem, Ilene Cohen, Hawthorne Smith, and Katherine Porterfield. 2006. "Traumatic Experiences and Psychological Distress in an Urban Refugee Population

Seeking Treatment Services." *Journal of Nervous and Mental Disease* 194, no. 3: 188–194. doi:10.1097/01.nmd.0000202494.75723.83.

Keller, Allen, Jack M. Saul, and David P. Eisenman. 1998. "Caring for Survivors of Torture in an Urban, Municipal Hospital." *The Journal of Ambulatory Care Management* 21, no. 2: 20–29.

Kira, Ibrahim A., Asha Ahmed, Fatima Wasim, Vanessa Mahmoud, Joanna Colrain, and Dhan Rai. 2012. "Group Therapy for Refugees and Torture Survivors: Treatment Model Innovations." *International Journal of Group Psychotherapy* 62, no. 1: 69–88.

Kudler, Harold S., Arthur S. Blank, and Janice Krupnick. 2000. "Psychodynamic Therapy." In *Effective Treatments for PTSD: Practical Guidelines from the International Society for Traumatic Stress Studies*, edited by Edna B. Foa, Terence M. Keane, and Matthew J. Friedman, 176–198. New York: Guilford Press.

Levers, Lisa L. 2012. *Trauma Counseling: Theories and Interventions*. New York: Springer Publishing Company.

Lubin, Hadar, Michelle Loris, John Burt, and David R. Johnson. 1998. "Efficacy of Psychoeducational Group Therapy in Reducing Symptoms of Posttraumatic Stress Disorder among Multiply Traumatized Women." *American Journal of Psychiatry* 155, no. 9: 1172–1177.

Lustig, Stuart L., Maryam Kia-Keating, Wanda G. Knight, Pau Geltman, Heidi Ellis, John D. Kinzie, Terence Keane, and Glenn N. Saxe. 2004. "Review of Child and Adolescent Refugee Mental Health." *Journal of the American Academy of Child and Adolescent Psychiatry* 43, no. 1: 24–36.

Murakami, Nancy. 2017. *Crossing Worlds, Intersecting Services: Practices for the Unique Needs of Forced Migrants and Survivors of Torture*. Full-day workshop for Catholic Charities of the Diocese of Cleveland and the Cleveland Center for Survivors of Torture, April 24, 2017. Cleveland, OH.

Nicholl, Catherine, and Andrew Thompson. 2004. "The Psychological Treatment of Posttraumatic Stress Disorder (PTSD) in Adult Refugees: A Review of the Current State of Psychological Therapies." *Journal of Mental Health* 13, no. 4: 351–362.

O'Hara, Maile, and Adeyinka M. Akinsulure-Smith. 2011. "Working with Interpreters: Tools for Clinicians Conducting Psychotherapy with Forced Immigrants." *International Journal of Migration, Health and Social Care* 7, no. 1: 33–43.

Pumariega, Andrés J., Eugenio Rothe, and JoAnne B. Pumariega. 2005. "Mental Health of Immigrants and Refugees." *Community Mental Health Journal* 41, no. 5: 581–597.

Ryan, Dermot A., Fiona E. Kelly, and Brendan D. Kelly. 2009. "Mental Health among Persons Awaiting an Asylum Outcome in Western Countries: A Literature Review." *International Journal of Mental Health* 38, no. 3: 88–111. doi:10.2753/IMH0020–7411380306.

Samuels, Mike, and Mary R. Lane. 1998. *Creative Healing: How to Heal Yourself by Tapping Your Hidden Creativity*. San Francisco: Harper.

Samuels, Mike, and Mary R. Lane. 2000. *Spirit Body Healing: Using Your Mind's Eye to Unlock the Medicine Within*. New York: John Wiley & Sons, Inc.

Smith, Hawthorne E. 2003. "Despair, Resilience, and the Meaning of Family: Group Therapy with French-Speaking African Survivors of Torture." In *Understanding and Dealing with Violence: A Multicultural Approach*, Winter roundtable series, edited by Barbara C. Wallace and Robert T. Carter, 291–316. Thousand Oaks, CA: Sage Publications.

Smith, Hawthorne, E. 2007a. "Multicultural Issues in the Treatment of Survivors of Torture and Refugee Trauma: Toward an Interactive Model." In *Like a Refugee Camp on First Avenue: Insights and Experiences from the Bellevue/NYU Program for Survivors of Torture*, edited by Hawthorne Smith, Allen Keller, and Dechen Lhewa, 38–64. New York: Jacob and Valeria Langeloth Foundation.

Smith, Hawthorne, E. 2007b. "Secondary Trauma, Compassion Fatigue, and Burnout: Risk Factors, Resilience, and Coping in Care Givers." In *Like a Refugee Camp on First Avenue: Insights and Experiences from the Bellevue/NYU Program for Survivors of Torture*, edited by Hawthorne Smith, Allen Keller, and Dechen Lhewa, 393–410. New York: Jacob and Valeria Langeloth Foundation.

Smith, Hawthorne, E. 2018. "Defining and Overcoming Trauma: Practical Applications with Trauma-Exposed Immigrants and Survivors of Torture." In *Models for Practice with Immigrants and Refugees: Collaboration, Cultural Awareness and Integrative Theory*, edited by Aimee Hilado and Marta Lundy, 275–295. Thousand Oaks, CA: SAGE Publications.

Smith, Hawthorne E., and Edna Impalli. 2007. "Supportive Group Treatment with Survivors of Torture and Refugee Trauma." In *Like a Refugee Camp on First Avenue: Insights and Experiences from the Bellevue/NYU Program for Survivors of Torture*, edited by Hawthorne Smith, Allen Keller, and Dechen Lhewa, 336–374. New York: Jacob and Valeria Langeloth Foundation.

Smith, Hawthorne E., Stuart Lustig, and David Gangsei. 2015. "Incredible until Proven Credible: Mental Health Expert Testimony and the Systemic and Cultural Challenges Facing Asylum Applicants." In *Adjudicating Refugee and Asylum Status: The Role of Witness, Expertise, and Testimony*, edited by B. Lawrence and G. Ruffer, 180–201. London: Cambridge University Press.

Stepakoff, Shanee, Jon Hubbard, Maki Katoh, Erika Falk, Jean-Baptiste Mikulu, Potiphar Nkhoma, and Yuvenalis Omagwa. 2006. "Trauma Healing in Refugee Camps in Guinea: A Psychosocial Program for Liberian and Sierra Leonean Survivors of Torture and War." *American Psychologist* 61, no. 8, 921–932.

Stuckey, Heather L., and Jeremy Nobel. 2010. "The Connection between Art, Healing, and Public Health: A Review of Current Literature." *American Journal of Public Health* 100, no. 2: 254–263.

Sue, Derald W., and David Sue. 1990. *Counseling the Culturally Different: Theory and Practice*. New York: Wiley.

Thomas, Samantha L., and Stuart D. Thomas. 2004. "Displacement and Health." *British Medical Bulletin* 69, no. 1: 115–127.

Tribe, Rachel. 2002. "Mental Health of Refugees and Asylum-Seekers." *Advances in Psychiatric Treatment* 8, no. 4: 240–247.

Tucker, Sarah, and Deidre Price. 2007. "Finding a Home: Group Psychotherapy for Traumatized Refugees and Asylum Seekers." *European Journal of Psychotherapy and Counselling* 9, no. 3: 277–287. doi:10.1080/13642530701 496880.

Turner, Stuart W., and Jane Herlihy. 2009. "Working with Refugees and Asylum Seekers." *Psychiatry* 8, no. 8: 322–324.

United Nations High Commissioner for Refugees. 2016. "Figures at a Glance." Retrieved from http://www.unhcr.org/figures-at-a-glance.html.

Urlić, Ivan. 2005. "Recognizing Inner and Outer Realities as a Process: On Some Countertransferential Issues of the Group Conductor." *Group Analysis* 38, no. 2, 249–263.

van der Kolk, Bessel A., Laura Stone, Jennifer West, Alison Rhodes, David Emerson, Michael Suvak, and Joseph Spinazzola. 2014. "Original Research Yoga as an Adjunctive Treatment for Posttraumatic Stress Disorder: A Randomized Controlled Trial." *Journal of Clinical Psychiatry* 75, no. 6: e559–e565.

Vera, Elizabeth M., and Suzette L. Speight. 2003. "Multicultural Competence, Social Justice, and Counseling Psychology: Expanding Our Roles." *The Counseling Psychologist* 31, no. 3, 253–272.

Wilkinson, John. 2007. "Immigration Dynamics: Processes, Challenges, and Benefits." In *Like a Refugee Camp on First Avenue: Insights and Experiences from the Bellevue/NYU Program for Survivors of Torture*, edited by Hawthorne Smith, Allen Keller, and Dechen Lhewa, 65–81. New York: Jacob and Valeria Langeloth Foundation.

Yalom, Irvin D., and Molyn Leszcz. 1995. *The Theory and Practice of Group Psychotherapy*, 5th ed. New York: Basic Books.

Yule, William. 2002. "Alleviating the Effects of War and Displacement on Children." *Traumatology* 8, no. 3, 160–180.

CHAPTER NINE

Child Migrants in the United States

Challenges to the Promotion of Their Rights and Best Interests

S. Megan Berthold and Alysse M. Loomis

Introduction

The rights and best interests of children who have sought refuge and safety in recent years by migrating to the United States have been compromised and violated on a massive scale. This has been true whether they have come alone or with family members. Investigative reports by media, human rights, and legal institutions have documented these realities and called for the halting of abusive practices and the promotion of the rights of child migrants.

The case of Helen, a five-year-old asylum seeker from Honduras, profiled in a recent *New Yorker* story (Stillman 2018), illustrates some of the rights violations, including how children were forcibly separated from guardians at the U.S.-Mexican border. Helen, her grandmother Noehmi, and other relatives fled from Honduras in July 2018 after gang members threatened Noehmi's son. After thousands of miles of travel, they crossed the Rio Grande river in a raft.

> Helen slipped from their raft and risked drowning. Her grandmother grabbed her hand and cried, "Hang on, Helen!" When the family reached the scrubland of southern Texas, U.S. Border Patrol agents apprehended them and moved them through a series of detention centers. A month

earlier, the Trump Administration had announced, amid public outcry over its systemic separation of migrant families at the border, that it would halt the practice. But, . . . [an official] pulled Helen from her [Noehmi's] arms. "The girl will stay here," he said, "and you'll be deported." Helen cried as he escorted her from the room and out of sight. (Stillman 2018, para. 2 and 3)

Long before Helen arrived in the United States, legal precedent established by the *Flores Settlement* (Stipulated Settlement Agreement, *Flores v. Reno* 1997) set guidelines for when and for how long migrant children could be held in immigration detention and determined their right to a bond hearing. Helen was put in a federally contracted unaccompanied minors' shelter. Had she appeared before a judge for a bond hearing, she may well have been let out of government custody and allowed to reunite with her family. Helen and other young migrant children, unable to understand or make informed decisions for themselves in complex immigration court proceedings, were required by the federal government to do so.

At the time of her apprehension, in fact, Helen checked a box on a line that read, "I do request an immigration judge," asserting her legal right to have her custody reviewed. But, in early August, an unknown official handed Helen a legal document, a "Request for a Flores Bond Hearing," which described a set of legal proceedings and rights that would have been difficult for Helen to comprehend. ("In a Flores bond hearing, an immigration judge reviews your case to determine whether you pose a danger to the community," the document began.) On Helen's form, which was filled out with assistance from officials, there is a checked box next to a line that says, "I withdraw my previous request for a Flores bond hearing." Beneath that line, the five-year-old signed her name in wobbly letters. (Stillman 2018, para. 9)

It is hard to imagine that five-year-old Helen, without the assistance of an attorney to represent her, understood what she was doing when she asserted and later withdrew her request for a Flores bond hearing. Developmentally, it is implausible. Helen and all children under international law are rights-holders, and parents, governments, and society are obligated to secure these rights (UN CMW and CRC 2017; United Nations General Assembly 1989). Children who are migrating are widely seen under international law as warranting extra protection and care (UN CMW and CRC 2017). Instead, in recent years, migrant children in the United States have been held in jail-like detention facilities, subjected to numerous other rights violations (e.g., lack of access to legal, social, and health services), and traumatized by forcible separation from their parents and other family members (Amnesty International 2018; Cumming-Bruce 2018).

In a joint statement, a group of UN human rights experts[1] on racism, torture, and the rights of migrants noted in response to the large-scale migration of children, many of whom were unaccompanied by a guardian, migration should not be criminalized and children who are migrating must always have their best interests observed.

> Migration is not a crime, and migrants in irregular situations should not be treated as criminals or deprived of their liberty and security. . . . The criminalisation and detention of migrants exceed the legitimate interests of States in protecting their territories and regulating migration. . . . Children must never be detained because of their or their parents' migration status. It goes against the best interests of the child, is a clear violation of child rights, and causes irreparable harm that can amount to torture. (Office of the United Nations High Commissioner for Human Rights [OHCHR] 2018b, para. 6 and 7)

The UN experts who met to negotiate, draft, and adopt the historic Global Compact for Safe, Orderly and Regular Migration (OHCHR 2018a; adopted in December 2018) called attention to the particular and severe harms that child migrants were experiencing in the context of the criminalization and detention of migrants. The compact sought to establish global cooperation and promote a framework to address international migration, while adhering to international legal obligations and human rights. It affirmed that no state actor can solve the issues of migration on its own and highlighted the special situation of separated and otherwise unaccompanied migrant children.

This chapter will explore the experiences of child and adolescent migrants in the United States, with a particular focus on those separated from their family members and in detention (see Chapter 3 for more on detention and deportation). We will define refugee status and other legal forms of relief for children who flee from danger and seek refuge outside of their homelands in the United States. The experiences of child migrants during the Obama and Trump administrations will be framed within a human rights lens, and relevant international and U.S. human rights mechanisms and treaties will be identified. Finally, priority recommendations for advocacy and policy efforts will be explored consonant with obligations to promote and protect child migrant rights. This information not only is important for policy, health, and human rights professionals but also can be used by the general public to effect change and promote a more welcoming and just society.

Definitions

Language matters. The terms "refugee" or "immigrant" are often used to refer to persons who leave their home countries and move to another country to live permanently. These terms, however, may not be accurate descriptions of a person's legal status (see Chapter 2 for an in-depth discussion of legal statuses). Some children come to the United States having already been screened and designated as a *refugee* prior to their arrival, adhering to the U.S. definition of refugee that requires that the person has been persecuted on account of at least one of five protected grounds (i.e., race, nationality, political opinion, religion, or membership in a particular social group) and/ or has a "well-founded fear" of future persecution (Refugee Act of 1980). Others enter the United States without any legal status or with a temporary visa and apply for *asylum* after arrival. If they are granted asylum, they are referred to as an *asylee* (or a *derivative asylee* if they were named on their parent's successful asylum application). Some migrant children come to the United States with family members or guardians, while others come alone to the United States and are referred to as *unaccompanied minors*. There are also children *trafficked* to the United States, or trafficked by criminal enterprises or enslaved into forced sexual and/or other labor (UN General Assembly 2000). We are using the term "child migrant" in this chapter to refer to all of these children. Other children affected by immigration policies described in this chapter are U.S. citizens, born in the United States to undocumented parents, who live in mixed-status families (with at least one migrant parent without legal status) (Zayas 2015).

Statistics Regarding Migrant Children

It is impossible to precisely measure the number of children who move across borders as some do not come to the attention of authorities. The United Nations High Commissioner for Refugees estimates that children comprise more than half of all the world's 25.4 million refugees (UNHCR n.d.a, n.d.b). There were 12 million children seeking refuge in 2016 alone (UNICEF 2017). The number of separated and unaccompanied children who registered as such has grown in recent years, reaching at least 300,000 in 2015–2016 in 80 countries (approximately five times the number registered in 2010–2011) (UNICEF 2017). Of all refugees who entered the United States from 2002 to 2017, 40 to 50 percent were 20 years old or younger each year (Connor 2017). In FY2018 (October 2017 through September 2018), the U.S. Customs and Border Protection (CBP) apprehended 396,579 persons at Southwest Border ports of entry, up from 303,916 the year before (U.S. Customs and Border Protection 2018). The FY2018 figure included 50,036 unaccompanied children and 107,212 family units, higher than the previous record number of 77,857 family units taken into custody in 2016 (Miroff and Dawsey 2018). In addition, 124,511 persons were deemed inadmissible to the United States in FY2018 (including 53,901 family units and 8,624 unaccompanied children) at these same Southwest Border ports of entry, up slightly from 111,601 in FY2017 (U.S. Customs and Border Protection 2018).

Forms of Immigration Relief for Undocumented Children in the United States

For those undocumented children already in the United States, a number of forms of immigration relief are available to prevent their "removal" or deportation from the United States. These include the Deferred Action for Childhood Arrivals (DACA) program (for temporary relief from removal), asylum, Special Immigrant Juvenile Status (SIJS, a humanitarian form of relief available to noncitizen minors who were abused, neglected, or abandoned by one or both parents), U visa (for victims of some crimes), T visa (for victims of severe forms of human trafficking), or other humanitarian relief (American Immigration Council 2015). Some of these forms of relief, including DACA, have been under recent attack by the Trump administration. In 2018 concerted efforts by the Trump administration were made, and fought in court, to deny migrant children and their families the right to claim asylum in the United States if they did not enter through a port of entry. All of these children are the concern of this chapter and should be the concern of our government, which is charged with safeguarding and promoting the rights of all children.

Care and Custody of Unaccompanied Children (UACs)

Once in the United States, most UACs are detained by U.S. Customs and Border Protection (CBP) officers initially (Seghetti, Siskin, and Wasem 2014). While apprehended undocumented adults or families can be put into expedited removal proceedings, this is not the case for UACs (Pub. L. No. 110–457, 122 Stat. 5044). Those UACs from countries other than Mexico or Canada are currently placed into regular removal proceedings in federal immigration court, and within 72 hours of apprehension, their custody is transferred to the Office of Refugee Resettlement (ORR). If the UAC is from a continuous country (i.e., Canada or Mexico), he or she is immediately sent back by CBP under the "voluntary return" program (if the receiving country agrees to the repatriation), unless screening by CBP finds the child to be a victim of trafficking, in fear of persecution if back in his or her homeland, or unable to independently make his or her own decisions (Seghetti, Siskin, and Wasem 2014). Questions about the CBP's ability to appropriately identify children who have been persecuted, abused, or traumatized were raised by various nongovernmental organizations (American Immigration Council 2015). As with many of the immigration policies and laws, policies regarding UACs evolved over time. Starting in the summer of 2014, UACs who entered the United States over the southwest border on or after May 1, 2014, were given priority for processing in immigration court and were scheduled for a first hearing within 21 days after the court obtained the case on its docket (American Immigration Council 2015). These "rocket docket" cases, as they came to be known, gave children less time to obtain a lawyer, compromising their ability to win their case and avoid being "voluntarily removed" from the United States (American Immigration Council 2015).

With the Homeland Security Act of 2002 (United States of America 2002), Congress transferred the responsibility for the care and custody of unaccompanied migrant minors to the U.S. Office of Refugee Resettlement (ORR). ORR established a continuum of care for those children whom they were not able to place with a family member or sponsor with whom they have a relationship. This included foster care, group homes, shelters, and staff-secure (for children who do not need to be in a secure facility but do need close supervision by staff members), secure, and residential treatment facilities. What became apparent, however, was that once transferred to the care and custody of ORR, the safety of these children was not assured.

Abuses and Other Experiences of Migrant Children and Families Once in the United States

Once they arrive at the U.S. border, the traumas are not all behind them (U.S. Senate Committee on Homeland Security & Governmental Affairs 2016). Many migrant children have been subjected to systematic violations under at least the last two administrations (Obama and Trump administrations), during an era of increasing scrutiny, distrust, racism, and fear of migrants from some in the United States, including from some in positions of political power. The Trump administration not only detained and abused unaccompanied children, it expanded its focus to migrant families. Civil society, legislators, and the courts have responded. Hallmarks of each of these eras are described in the following text.

Experiences during the Obama Administration

The American Civil Liberties Union ([ACLU] 2018) concluded that the CBP had a culture of impunity and lack of adequate external or internal agency accountability or oversight. Based on interviews with children and over 30,000 U.S. government documents dating from 2009 through 2014 during the Obama administration, the ACLU found that the CBP engaged in abuse and neglect of unaccompanied children (UACs) it detained (ACLU 2018).

Among the numerous types of abuse, children reported harassment and intimidation; physical, psychological, and sexual abuse; threats (including of sexual abuse and death); the use of stress positions; separation from family members; denial of access to legal and medical services; and unsanitary and inhumane conditions of detention (including inadequate provision of food and water and being kept in "hieleras," which are iceboxes or freezers). Such conditions and depriving children of their liberty amount to cruel, inhuman, and degrading treatment (UN Committee on the Protection of the Rights of All Migrant Workers and Members of Their Families 2017).

An ACLU investigation documented the words of some of the detained UACs. One 15-year-old, who was denied medical care when found by CBP officers in a state of ill health, reported, "They called derogatory names such as 'i***** pendejo' (f****** idiot) and 'mierda' [piece of crap] as they each pushed me from one side to the other" (ACLU 2018, 14). Other UACs reported that CBP agents called them dehumanizing names, such as "dogs" or "she-males" who had come to the United States to get a sex change operation (ACLU 2018, 15). Another 15-year-old reported being hit with a thorny branch and punched by a CBP officer. "I yelled at the officer after he hit me, I told him that I was a minor. He replied by saying that he didn't care. Our conversation was in Spanish. He said, 'No me importa, hijo de tu p**** madre' ('I don't care you son of a b****')" (ACLU 2018, 15). An adolescent mother described how her daughter became ill and dehydrated after drinking spoiled milk supplied by CBP agents. After receiving treatment at the hospital, the child's medicine was taken away. The mother wrote, "We went back to the hielera and the agents took the medicine for my child away. The agents in the second hielera did not give the medicine to my child and would not let me give it to her. She went about two days without medicine" (ACLU 2018, 22).

Documents from the Department of Homeland Security's Office for Civil Rights and Civil Liberties (CRCL) were obtained by the ACLU after it launched a Freedom of Information Act (FOIA) lawsuit. These documents provided accounts of U.S. CBP officers threatening to place minors with unrelated adults in order for them to be raped or otherwise sexually abused. One such document recounted the report of a 16-year-old boy:

> They threatened to place a false age on his paperwork so that they can send him to adult detention and get raped by the other men inside. He recalls one agent telling him "Te vamos a poner de 23 para mandarte a la carcel para que los otros te hagan su vieja" (translation: We're going to put that you are 23yo to send you to jail so that the others can make you their lady). They also stated to him, "te vamos a pintar la cara tambien" (translation: We're going to put makeup on you too). They continued to make inappropriate sexual comments to him he reported as they went on referring to what can happen to him in the jail cells with the other men such as grabbing him from behind and forcing oral sex on him. (ACLU 2018, 25)

Sometimes, according to CRCL documents, the CBP officers sexually abused child detainees themselves. In regard to a 15-year-old female UAC,

> During her 7 days in Border Patrol custody at the Weslaco Station in Texas (Rio Grande Valley Sector), she witnessed a male Border Patrol Agent sexually abuse another female detainee by placing his hand in between the pants and stomach and stating inappropriate comments about her physical appearance. In addition, a few days later the same male agent touched her thigh in an inappropriate manner. (ACLU 2018, 26)

A 16-year-old mother detained with her infant recounted that a CBP agent stood near her holding cell's door and said in Spanish, "Right now, we close the door, we rape you and f*** you" (2015-CRFO-0000800007, as cited in ACLU 2018, 26). In response to this ACLU report, the CBP promptly issued a statement claiming that the ACLU's report of child abuse and neglect in CBP detention facilities were unfounded (American Immigration Lawyers Association 2018). The evidence collected by the ACLU from U.S. government agencies suggests otherwise.

During the Obama administration, a Department of Homeland Security (DHS) Advisory Committee on Family Residential Centers was convened. Its first recommendation included the position that the separation and detention of migrant families is never in children's best interest and is furthermore usually not necessary or appropriate (Department of Homeland Security 2016). The Advisory Committee argued that family detention should only rarely be used, in situations

> of danger or flight risk that cannot be mitigated by conditions of release. If such an assessment determines that continued custody is absolutely necessary, families should be detained for the shortest amount of time and in the least restrictive setting possible; all detention facilities should be licensed, non-secure and family-friendly. If necessary to mitigate individualized flight risk or danger, every effort should be made to place families in community-based case-management programs that offer medical, mental health, legal, social, and other services and supports, so that families may live together within a community. (Department of Homeland Security 2016, 2)

This recommendation to use family detention only as a last resort and to prioritize community-based solutions did not receive traction during the Trump administration. Instead, in the years following this recommendation, a ramping up of practices and policy changes were made that were hostile to migrants, including children. This in turn galvanized legal and community-based efforts in opposition.

Experiences during the Trump Administration

The neglect and abuses of child migrants have continued under the Trump administration. Steven Wagner, a high-ranking U.S. official from the Department of Health and Human Services (DHHS) charged with the care and protection of unaccompanied minors, testified in a Senate Permanent Subcommittee on Investigations hearing in April 2018 that his agency had lost approximately 1,500 of the children under its care to follow up, having been unable to make contact with the relatives or other individuals who they had been placed with (Miller, L. 2018). This amounted to more than 19 percent of all children the DHHS attempted to reach between October and December 2017. The ORR is the DHHS agency responsible for the care, custody, and placing of some of these children with family or other sponsors. A report by the Subcommittee documented that some of these children were released by ORR to sponsors who trafficked them (Miller, L. 2018). In his testimony, Wagner stressed, "I understand that it has been HHS's long-standing interpretation of the law that ORR is not legally responsible for children after they are released from ORR care" (Andone 2018). An effective mechanism must be put in place to ensure that all children under the care of U.S. authorities are accounted for. The difficulty the authorities had in making contact with relatives of children they released from their custody may be because those relatives themselves might be undocumented and fearful of responding to any attempts to be contacted. Obviously, this poses a serious issue in terms of follow-up and making sure kids are cared for and not being further abused.

Detained children have reported being demeaned, assaulted, and forcibly injected with drugs, and court filings claim that the conditions in which many of the facilities keep migrant children are unconstitutional (Ellis, Hicken, and Ortega 2018). As Holly Cooper, an immigration attorney challenging the detention of the minors, stated, "There seems to be a level of cruel intent I've never seen before and a real indifference to the well-being of a child" (Ellis, Hicken, and Ortega 2018, para. 8).

CNN reported on the case of *John Doe 2*, a migrant youth who, after multiple fights and incidents of harming himself while in a shelter, was transferred to the Shenandoah Valley Juvenile Center, a public detention center in Virginia for migrant youth deemed to be dangerous. He described in a declaration how he was treated there when he reacted to abuse from staff. "They will grab my hands and put them behind my back so I can't move. Sometimes they will use pens to poke me in the ribs, sometimes they grab my jaw with their hands," he wrote. "They are bigger than me. Sometimes there will be three or four of them using force against me at the same time. The force used by staff has left bruises on my wrists, on my ribs, and on my shoulder. The doctor here gave me ibuprofen for the pain" (Ellis, Hicken, and Ortega 2018, para. 13). John Doe 2 also recounted being handcuffed and tied to a chair, with a restraint with air holes put over his face. Other children reported similar punishment at the facility, and one wrote about being tied to a chair naked for over two days (Ellis, Hicken, and Ortega 2018, para. 14). Another child recalled being put in the restraint chair when detained at Shenandoah. "You feel suffocated with the bag on," he recounted. "They just grab the left side of your head and they force it over you. You can't move to resist. The first thing that came to my head when they put it on me was, 'They are going to suffocate me. They are going to kill me'" (Ellis, Hicken, and Ortega 2018, para. 52). A 15-year-old reported being assaulted by staff at the same facility, stressing, "I want us to be treated as human beings" (Ellis, Hicken, and Ortega 2018, paras. 53). A lawsuit was filed against the facility, and Governor Ralph Northam of Virginia launched an investigation into the allegations. Investigative reporting has revealed that these are not isolated incidents.

Allegations of sexual abuse of UACs have emerged in more than one facility (Neuman 2018). Some of the youth, such as 11-year-old Maricela (a pseudonym used in court documents) who is being given 10 medications a day in Shiloh Treatment Center in Manvel, Texas, would rather go home. "I do not feel safe here," said Maricela. "I would rather go back to Honduras and live on the streets than be at Shiloh" (Ellis, Hicken, and Ortega 2018, para. 48).

The Trump administration has also engaged in the widespread practice of separating children from their parents at the border when they enforced its "zero-tolerance" initiative, criminally prosecuting those who violated 8 U.S.C. § 1325(a) by attempting or making an illegal entry into the United States (Cheng 2018a; U.S. Department of Justice 2018). This initiative by the U.S. Department of Justice and the U.S. Department of Homeland Security is known as Operation Streamline. The U.S. CBP came up with a new designation for the over 2,600 children that they took from their families: *deleted family units* (Miroff, Goldstein, and Sacchetti 2018).

Perceptions of the Trump administration's immigration policies and practices are polarized, with supporters and critics alike. Zeid Ra'ad al-Hussein, the United Nations High Commissioner for Human Rights, called for an immediate halt to the United States' separation of migrant families. Further, citing the president of the American Association of Pediatrics, he called the separation of children from their parents and locking the children up as "government-sanctioned child abuse" and stated, "The thought that any state would seek to deter parents by inflicting such abuse on children is unconscionable" (Cumming-Bruce 2018, paras. 3 and 4). In what has been called a scathing report of E. Scott Lloyd, the ORR director under President Trump, Bob Carey (who was ORR director during the Obama administration) remarked: "They're turning ORR into a detention agency. . . . It does not reflect the intent of Congress. They are not equipped to become a juvenile detention agency" (as quoted in Planas 2018, para. 20).

The practice by U.S. authorities of "disappearing" children by forcibly separating them from their parent(s) and rendering them unaccompanied is reminiscent of the forced disappearances that took place in Argentina and other repressive regimes, including some countries from which the migrants fled. Health and mental health professionals have widely warned that depriving already-vulnerable and traumatized children of the presence and caregiving from their parent(s) can lead to severe suffering and lifelong and irreparable harm (Linton, Griffin, and Shapiro 2017). It has been called cruel, inhumane, and degrading treatment and, by some, torture (Gray 2018). According to a group of eleven UN human rights experts serving as UN Special Rapporteurs, the U.S. practice of detaining migrant children "severely hampers their development and in some cases, may amount to torture" (United Nations 2018).

The Hope Border Institute (2018) reported that, in an effort to deter asylum seekers, "ICE and CBP wrench children from parents arriving at the border, dividing families and creating situations where children are lost in the system" (p. 2). In response, U.S. Immigration and Customs Enforcement (ICE) claimed that the U.S. government does not have a blanket policy of routinely removing children from their parents, but that such actions are a result of increased prosecution of immigration-related crimes (Donaldson 2017), including efforts to protect children from being smuggled or trafficked to the United States (Kennedy 2018). Analysis by the Vera Institute of Justice (2018) "found no evidence to suggest that Operation Streamline had any impact on migrants' decisions to enter the United States. Operation Streamline succeeded only in clogging federal courts, eroding due process, and incarcerating tens of thousands of people" (para. 2). Border Patrol arrest rates of families were unaffected (9,652 family members arrested in April 2018; 9,485 in May 2018; and 9,449 in June 2018; Hesson 2018).

In an interview with National Public Radio, John Kelly (White House chief of staff) defended taking children away from their mothers at the border, indicating that it could be a strong deterrent for immigrants illegally crossing the border. When the reporter asked him what he thought about some calling the administration's policy heartless and cruel, Kelly stated, "The children will be taken care of—put into foster care or whatever" (Mark 2018).

The treatment of migrant children and their families described here represents clear violations of U.S. law and international human rights norms. Over the course of several months in late spring and summer of 2018, reports and images of detained children and infants separated from their parents, some in cages, made national news on a near daily basis in the United States. In the face of ramped-up family separation, a series of class-action and other lawsuits were filed by lawyers, and a significant part of the public protested against the Trump administration policies and actions.

Lawsuits and Protests in Response to Administration Policies and Actions

The ACLU initiated a national class-action lawsuit against ICE for its alleged separation of hundreds of children from their parents (Kennedy 2018). *The New York Times* reported in April 2018 that ORR data indicated that in the previous six months more than 700 children (including more than 100 under the age of four) had been taken from adults who stated they were the children's parents (Dickerson 2018a). In the ensuing weeks and months, the documented number of separated family units reported by the U.S. CBP rose to approximately 8,000 (Amnesty International 2018). While some children were separated from their families during the Obama administration, this was on a much smaller scale and was not a systematic practice or policy (Qiu 2018). The size and scope of separations during the Trump administration were unprecedented. Equally disturbing, the Trump administration failed to keep track of who the children were related to and where their family members were, compromising later efforts to reunite them (Dickerson 2018b).

The range of issues targeted by protests and lawsuits by the ACLU and others included, in part, violating the *Flores Settlement* by separating migrant children and their parent(s); conditions of detention; drugging detained migrant children with psychotropic medications without parental consent or court order; sexual abuse; assault; and torture (Cheng 2018b; Yoon-Hendricks and Greenberg 2018). Detained migrant children reported being subjected to various abuses, including girls who shared that they were forced to strip naked by guards who leered at them (Jordan 2018b). Reports of widespread abuse that amount to torture have been made in lawsuit filings such as that by attorney Peter Schey of the Center for Human Rights and Constitutional Law.

> "The treatment of these children amounts to torture," Schey told HuffPost, adding that the situation has become worse under the Trump administration. "We see a policy of enforced hunger, enforced dehydration and enforced sleeplessness coupled with routine insults and physical assaults." (Chapin 2018, para. 7)

In response to Schey's filing, U.S. district judge Dolly Gee appointed an independent monitor to investigate and report directly to her regarding conditions in Rio Grande valley Customs and Border Protection detention facilities in Texas (Watt and Kravarik 2018). This action came during a status hearing of a lawsuit regarding the 1997 *Flores v. Reno* settlement agreement concerning standards of care for immigrant children who are in the custody of the U.S. government.

A number of notable court rulings resulted. U.S. district judge Dana Sabraw, in an important judicial ruling, ordered the Trump administration to reunite families who it had separated at the U.S.-Mexico border (Barrett, DeBonis, Miroff, and Stanley-Becker 2018). Judge Dana M. Sabraw, a U.S. district judge of the U.S. District Court for the Southern District of California, granted a preliminary injunction on June 26, 2018, ordering that the Trump administration reunite all separated migrant children with their parents. The administration was given 14 days to reunite children under the age of five and 30 days to reunite the older children. After "deleting" the family unit in their databases, and separating the children from the parents, the authorities lacked adequate records to locate and reunite many (Miroff, Goldstein, and Sacchetti 2018).

In response, the Trump administration developed a reunification plan (U.S. DHHS, DHS, and DOJ 2018) which proved to be inadequate. While the Trump administration did reunite many families by the July 26, 2018, court deadline, 711 children were not reunited with their parents by this date (Hals 2018). These families were deemed "ineligible" to reunite by the Trump administration as follows: the parent(s) of 431 of the children were outside the United States (i.e., had already been deported), the parents of 120 children waived their right to reunify with their child (according to the ACLU these parents were misled into doing so), the parent(s) of 79 children had been released into the United States and their location was unknown, the location of parents of 94 of the children were under review, 67 parents had a "red flag" concern raised by the government, and the remaining 7 were undergoing litigation on other matters (Jordan 2018a; Schmidt 2018a). Furthermore, the ACLU reported that the U.S. government was making great efforts to quickly deport the reunified families (Cheng 2018c).

After his 30-day deadline to reunite the "deleted" families passed, U.S. district judge Dana M. Sabraw lambasted the government for its lack of preparation and coordination. The judge stated, "There were three agencies, and each was like its own stovepipe. Each had its own boss, and they did not communicate" (Miroff, Goldstein, and Sacchetti 2018, para. 9). He underscored the harms to family and children: "What was lost in the process was the family. The parents didn't know where the children were, and the children didn't know where the parents were. And the government didn't know either" (Miroff, Goldstein, and Sacchetti 2018, para. 9). In a subsequent status hearing in early August 2018, Judge Sabraw rejected the Trump administration's claim that groups that advocate for immigrants such as the ACLU should be responsible for locating the nearly 500 parents separated from their children by the administration (Kopan 2018). Judge Sabraw declared, "And the reality is that for every parent who is not located, there will be a permanently orphaned child, and that is 100% the responsibility of the administration" (Kopan 2018, para. 5).

U.S. district judge Dolly Gee in Los Angeles ruled that the Trump administration was violating state child welfare laws by giving migrant children psychotropic medications without parental or custodial consent. She ordered that, before the administration could continue administering such medications, it must obtain such consent or a court order unless the situation was an emergency (Schmidt 2018b). Judge Gee also ordered all children not assessed to be a danger to self or others by a licensed professional moved out of Shiloh, the residential treatment facility where Maricela was being medicated and abused. U.S. district judge John Bates in Washington, DC, ordered the full reinstatement of DACA, including allowing for new applications (Chung 2018). At the time of this writing, the number of migrant children detained in federal facilities is at a record high of over 14,000 (Vongkiatkajorn 2018). Many detained migrant children have been released, with no services to make room for others who are expected to arrive (Miroff 2018). Migrant children are being housed in tents in the desert at Tornillo in El Paso county in Texas, a temporary camp with a capacity to house 3,800 children (Ainsley and Ramos 2018).

The Trump administration is considering detaining children and their asylum-seeking families together (Miroff, Dawsey, and Sacchetti 2018), and thousands of mostly Central American migrants, including migrant children, are amassed in Mexico near the U.S. border, waiting to hear if they will be allowed to apply for asylum in the United States (Miroff, Partlow, and Dawsey 2018). In a decision by the Ninth Circuit Court of Appeals, Judge Jon Tigar ordered a preliminary injunction preventing the Trump administration's policy that prevents all asylum seekers from entering the United States from being implemented. Judge Tigar ruled, "Whatever the scope of the President's authority, he may not rewrite the immigration laws to impose a condition that Congress has expressly forbidden" (Khoury 2018). It is unclear at present how these legal proceedings, policies, and practices will develop. Concerted efforts have been made by grassroots actors, attorneys, and legal organizations, such as the ACLU, to fight these actions and policies. Given the wide-scale nature of the legal and human rights violations, however, the challenges they have faced have been enormous.

Other important judicial rulings and perhaps Congressional legislative actions are likely to occur regarding immigration issues in the coming months and years, hopefully ones that will stop harms and rights violations and prevent new ones from occurring. In the meantime, migrant children are suffering (Miller, D. 2018). It is important to understand that many migrant children have faced cumulative traumas and to hold accountable those who have contributed to those harms through their actions or inactions. This is part of what is needed to promote the rule of law and ensure that the human rights of all children are promoted.

Protecting the Key Rights of Child Migrants

All children, regardless of their migration or legal status, have a right to be protected and have their well-being and best interests promoted. International and domestic laws and standards mandate that we do. We will outline key human rights treaties, standards, and principles relevant to the protection of child migrants.

International Mechanisms

All member United Nations states, with the exception of the United States (Office of the United Nations High Commissioner for Human Rights 2017), have ratified the United Nations Convention on the Rights of the Child (CRC, United Nations General Assembly 1989). State parties are obligated to ensure that the rights of all children, including migrant children, to protection are realized and secured. Even though the United States has only signed but not ratified the CRC, it's framework can and is being used by advocates to promote child rights in the United States (Libal, Mapp, Ihrig, and Ron 2011). Fundamentally:

Children on the move are children, first and foremost—they need protection

The Convention on the Rights of the Child protects every child, everywhere. All children, regardless of legal status, nationality or statelessness, have the right to be protected from harm, obtain such essential services as health care and education, be with their families, and have their best interests guide decisions that affect them. (UNICEF 2017, 7)

The United Nations has established principles and safeguards to ensure the protection of refugee children and at-risk adolescents who were being resettled. These are compiled in Table 9.1, along with key UN treaties relevant to the protection of child migrants and a link to various UN treaty body committees that are monitoring whether states comply with their obligations concerning migrant rights, including the rights of child migrants. Of particular note is a general comment from the Committee on Migrant Workers and the Committee on the Rights of the Child, stressing:

Every child, at all times, has a fundamental right to liberty and freedom from immigration detention. The Committee on the Rights of the Child has asserted that the detention of any child because of their or their parents' migration status constitutes a child rights violation and contravenes the principle of the best interests of the child. . . . States should expeditiously and completely cease or eradicate the immigration detention of children. Any kind of child immigration detention should be forbidden by law and such prohibition should be fully implemented in practice. (UN Committee on the Protection of the Rights of All Migrant Workers and Members of Their Families 2017, Article B.5)

These UN Committees also declared that the breakup of a family unit by deporting one or both parents while the child remains in the United States "is disproportionate, as the sacrifice inherent in the restriction of family life

Table 9.1. Key International Treaties, Standards, and Principles Relevant to the Protection of Child Migrants

Treaty Body/Mechanism	Principles/Standards	Citation/links
UN Protection Principles and Safeguards Relating to the Resettlement of Refugee Children and Adolescents at Risk	• the best interests of the child; • family unity; • not focusing only on unaccompanied children (due to unintended consequences of encouraging children to migrate alone or parents to abandon them in the hopes that they will be eligible for resettlement); and • a permanent and durable solution.	UNHCR 2016
UN Convention on the Rights of the Child (CRC). Note: The United States has signed but not yet ratified.	• obligates countries to provide protection and care for unaccompanied children, and • to take into account a child's best interests in every action affecting the child. Art. 37 of the CRC: "States Parties shall ensure that: (a) No child shall be subjected to torture or other cruel, inhuman or degrading treatment or punishment. . . . (b) No child shall be deprived of his or her liberty unlawfully or arbitrarily. The arrest, detention or imprisonment of a child shall be in conformity with the law and shall be used only as a measure of last resort and for the shortest appropriate period of time; (c) Every child deprived of liberty shall be treated with humanity and respect for the inherent dignity of the human person, and in a manner which takes into account the needs of persons of his or her age. In particular, every child . . . shall have the right to maintain contact with his or her family through correspondence and visits, save in exceptional circumstances; (d) Every child deprived of his or her liberty shall have the right to prompt access to legal and other appropriate assistance, as well as the right to challenge the legality of the deprivation of his or her liberty before a court or other competent, independent and impartial authority, and to a prompt decision on any such action."	United Nations General Assembly 1989

(Continued)

Table 9.1. (*Continued*)

Treaty Body/Mechanism	Principles/Standards	Citation/links
UN Committee on the Protection of the Rights of All Migrant Workers and Members of Their Families, Joint General Comment No. 4 of the CMW and No. 23 of the CRC on the Rights of the Child during Migration	All migrant children have the right to: • liberty and freedom from immigration detention (Article B5); • child-sensitive due process guarantees and access to justice (Article B 14 and 15); • family life (Article E); • nonseparation/family unity (Article E, 1); • family reunification (Article E, 2); • protection from violence and abuse (Article F); • an adequate standard of living (Article H); and • health (Article I).	UN CMW 2017
United Nations Children's Emergency Fund's (UNICEF) six-point agenda for action in relation to uprooted child migrants and refugees	It calls for: (1) the protection of uprooted children from violence and exploitation; (2) an end to the detention of migrant and refugee children through the creation of practical alternatives; (3) giving children legal status and keeping families together; (4) facilitating uprooted children's access to health services and education; (5) promoting action on the root causes (e.g., poverty, violence) of the uprooting of children from their homes; and (6) combating discrimination and xenophobia.	UNICEF 2017, 8
New York Declaration for Refugees and Migrants	• agreement to establish, in 2018, a global compact for safe, orderly, and regular migration; and • recognition that nonrefugee child migrants needed urgent protection.	Office of the President of the United Nations General Assembly 2016, para. 4
Initiative for Child Rights in the Global Compacts (civil society-led steering committee, co-convened by Save the Children and Terre des Hommes)	Six key areas of child rights: • nondiscrimination and integration; • best interests of the child; • children's access to services; • ending child immigration detention; • durable solutions; and • child protection.	Initiative for Child Rights n.d.

Treaty Body/Mechanism	Principles/Standards	Citation/links
Global Compact for Safe, Orderly and Regular Migration	• first-ever UN global agreement on a common approach to international migration; • nonlegally binding; and • 23 objectives aimed at improved management of migration at all levels (i.e., local, national, regional, and global).	OHCHR 2018a

Universal Periodic Review, special procedures, and treaty bodies	• Monitoring of states' compliance with their obligations related to migrants' rights (including the rights of child migrants) through various treaty body committees:
	
	  o Committee on Migrant Workers (CMW)
	
	  o Committee on the Elimination of Racial Discrimination (CERD)
	
	  o Committee against Torture (CAT)
	
	  o Human Rights Committee (HRC)—monitoring the International Covenant on Civil and Political Rights (ICCPR)
		• CMW: https://www.ohchr.org/EN/HRBodies/CMW/Pages/CMWIndex.aspx
		
		• CERD: https://www.ohchr.org/en/hrbodies/cerd/pages/cerdindex.aspx
		
		• CAT: https://www.ohchr.org/en/hrbodies/cat/pages/catindex.aspx
		• HRC monitoring
		
		• ICCPR: https://www.ohchr.org/EN/HRBodies/CCPR/Pages/CCPRIndex.aspx

and the impact on the life and development of the child is not outweighed by the advantages obtained by forcing the parent to leave the territory because of an immigration-related offence" (UN Committee on the Protection of the Rights of All Migrant Workers and Members of Their Families 2017, Article E.1.29).

State parties who have ratified UN treaties are reviewed periodically by the UN Committee associated with each treaty regarding if they are meeting their obligations under the treaty. Key child rights outlined in Table 9.1 have yet to be realized in the United States. For example, the rights to liberty from immigration detention, due process, nonseparation and family unity, health, and an adequate standard of living (to name a few) as per the recent Joint General Comment No. 4 and 23 of the UN Committee on the Protection of the Rights of All Migrant Workers and Members of Their Families (2017) are clearly being violated, as described in this chapter.

A positive development was the adoption in September 2016 by all Member UN States of the *New York Declaration for Refugees and Migrants*, which, in part, included an agreement to establish a "global compact for safe, orderly and regular migration in 2018" (Office of the President of the United Nations General Assembly 2016, para. 4) and recognition that nonrefugee child migrants needed urgent protection. The Trump administration withdrew the United States from the Compact, stating that it was incompatible with U.S. sovereignty and its ability to secure its borders and implement U.S. immigration laws (Karimi 2017). In July 2018, the Global Compact was finalized (OHCHR 2018a) and it was adopted in Marrakesh, Morocco, and then endorsed by the UN General Assembly in December 2018 (International Organization for Migration Office to the United Nations n.d.). It remains to be seen as to what extent the provisions of the compact (also known as the Marrakesh Compact on Migration) are implemented and the impact this has on child migrants and their families.

U.S. Safeguards

There are four key legal protections in place in the United States that are cornerstones to protecting the dignity and safety of child migrants and ensuring that their special concerns and rights are safeguarded. These are: (1) the *Flores Settlement*, which set forth nationwide standards governing the detention, treatment, and release of child migrants in U.S. custody (Stipulated Settlement Agreement, *Flores v. Reno* 1997); (2) the Victims of Child Abuse Act (VCAA) of 1990, which requires the reporting of alleged or suspected child abuse by all federal law enforcement personnel, including those working in immigration detention centers (Victims of Child Abuse Act 1990); (3) the 2003 Prison Rape Elimination Act (PREA), which mandates the reporting, investigation of allegations, and efforts to prevent sexual abuse and assault for those in federal custody (the Department of Homeland Security adopted PREA regulations in 2014 for its detention facilities, calling for "zero tolerance") (Department of Homeland Security 2014); and (4) the William Wilberforce Trafficking Victims Protection Reauthorization Act of 2008 (TVPRA), which increased protections for UACs and directed the establishment of policies and protocols for safe repatriation when appropriate (USA TVPRA 2008).

Some of the official policies in place relevant to the care and protection of child migrants are appropriate. For example, CBP policy states that officers and agents "should recognize that juveniles experience situations differently than adults" (US CBP 2015, ¶ 1.6). Further, CBP policy classifies children and UACs as "at-risk populations" and acknowledges that additional oversight or care of these minors may be required (US CBP 2015, ¶ 5.1). A key problem is that these policies are not always or systematically implemented. Additionally, those CBP officers charged with making determinations in the case of child minors do not have the appropriate professional background or training needed to assess and recommend what is in the best interest of individual child migrants.

Investigation of alleged violations of the human rights of migrant children by our government is essential to a functioning democracy and to adhering to international human rights standards. Amid troubling reports of efforts by ICE to destroy records showing their abuse of child migrants (Lopez 2017; Thomas 2018), it is vital to ensure transparency and a rule of law in our country. Putting in place effective and transparent monitoring mechanisms to ensure that we are adhering to and implementing the *Flores Settlement*, VCAA and PREA requirements, and TVPRA provisions is essential.

Conclusion

Despite international and domestic legal obligations, the rights of migrant children are often not protected due to inconsistent implementation across states, antimigrant national or state laws or practices, and the relative lack of resources of the less wealthy countries that receive the most refugees along with competing demands to care for their own nationals. A structural analysis is essential to a fuller understanding of forced migration and in order to address the root causes. While this is beyond the scope of this chapter, it is important to acknowledge that Central America's regional migration crisis is connected to current and past U.S. policies, such as its development and free trade policies (Akram 2018). Frequently absent from the narrative is any discussion of Mexican migration policy and the persecution of Central American migrants in transit through Mexico. The unique circumstances and persecution of Indigenous peoples are often left out as well.

At present, the United States is a long way from ensuring that its immigration policies are in keeping with what is in the best interest of the child or that migrant children's right to liberty and to not be subjected to torture or other cruel, inhuman, or degrading treatment or punishment are being realized. The U.S. treatment of child migrants is not "based on an ethic of care and protection" (UN CMW 2017, para. 12) but rather on enforcement. The antimigrant policies of the Trump administration, such as the detention and separation of children from their parents and efforts to change the impact of the use of public benefits by noncitizens (Department of Homeland Security 2018), have instilled fear in many of those already in the United States. This has deterred many migrants from seeking needed health care and other services for fear of being reported to the authorities and deported (Chapter 10 addresses this in more depth), thereby compromising their well-being.

Given the realities of life experienced by child migrants and their families in the United States as described in this chapter, including outright abuse and ongoing human rights violations, there is an urgent need for immediate action. What we know about the current situation of child migrants should be used to guide and set priorities for advocacy efforts and policy reform. For example, as stated by the Office of the United Nations High Commissioner for Human Rights (2018b), "Detention for the purposes of migration control should be a measure of last resort" (para. 7). This UN principle, in keeping with human rights, is relevant for children and adults alike.

Among the most pressing priorities are to stop detaining and separating migrant children and families. Community-based alternatives that are noncustodial should be used instead. Further, those who have been separated must be reunified, including connecting children with their family members who have been deported. The rights of asylum seekers to a credible fear interview must be ensured and the right to apply for asylum safeguarded (see Chapter 2 for an elaboration of these rights). Migrant children facing legal proceedings must be provided with legal representation and child-sensitive due process. The particular needs of mixed-status families must be a priority as well, such as ensuring access to education for the children; health for all; and the right to family unity, which is destroyed when parents are separated and deported from their U.S. citizen children.

Much work remains to be done to make sure that migrant children are not dehumanized and that they are treated with dignity and respect, their rights are protected, and their health and well-being are realized. Absent adequate oversight, reform, and new initiatives, these vulnerable children are likely to continue to be lost and abused by the governmental representatives and systems entrusted to care for them. Transformative actions must be taken to promote child rights, enhance assessment and treatment efforts, and develop a larger and more appropriately trained workforce, topics covered in Chapter 10.

Ordinary people in the United States can play an important role by being in solidarity with refugee and asylum-seeking children and their families. Awareness and understanding of the realities faced by migrant children and families, such as those addressed in this chapter, is the first step. This task can be a difficult one, however, given the array of misleading and distorted news from some outlets and some of those in power, including the Trump administration. Armed with accurate facts, we all can make a difference by contacting our local, state, and federal representatives to advocate for change to bring about humane laws and policies that promote the rights and best interests of migrant children and their families. We can volunteer with agencies and legal organizations working to document the situation of migrants on the ground and resettle refugees (Hennessy-Fiske 2018; see also Chapter 4 in this book). And we can educate others in our communities to have a more accurate understanding of and be more welcoming to migrants, thereby combating prejudice, discrimination, and, in some cases, violence against them.

In light of reports of migrant children harming themselves and giving up hope that they will ever get out of detention where they suffer enumerable abuses, migrant children need to know that there are people and organizations beyond the walls of the detention facilities that encage them that are fighting for them and their rights.

Note

1. These UN experts were Mr. Felipe González Morales, special rapporteur on the human rights of migrants; Mr. Nils Melzer, special rapporteur on torture and other cruel, inhuman, or degrading treatment or punishment; and Ms. E. Tendayi Achiume, special rapporteur on contemporary forms of racism.

References

Ainsley, Julia, and Annie Rose Ramos. 2018. "Inside Tornillo: The Expanded Tent City for Migrant Children." *NBC News*, October 12, 2018. https://www.nbcnews.com/politics/immigration/inside-tornillo-expanded-tent-city-migrant-children-n919431.

Akram, Susan M. 2018. "What's Driving the Migration Crisis at Our Southern Border?" *WBUR*, August 8, 2018. www.wbur.org/cognoscenti/2018/08/08/why-do-migrants-flee-central-america-susan-akram.

American Civil Liberties Union. 2018. *Neglect and Abuse of Unaccompanied Immigrant Children by U.S. Customs and Border Protection.* University of Chicago School of Law's International Human Rights Clinic (IHRC) and the ACLU (San Diego and Imperial Counties) Border Litigation Project. New York: ACLU. https://www.aclusandiego.org/civil-rights-civil-liberties/.

American Immigration Council. 2015. *A Guide to Children Arriving at the Border: Laws, Policies and Responses.* Washington, DC: American Immigration Council. https://www.americanimmigrationcouncil.org/research/guide-children-arriving-border-laws-policies-and-responses.

American Immigration Lawyers Association. 2018. *CBP Response to ACLU Report on Abuses against UACs. AILA Doc. No. 18052349.* Washington, DC: AILA. http://www.aila.org/infonet/cbp-response-to-aclu-report.

Amnesty International. 2018. *USA: "You Don't Have Any Rights Here": Illegal Pushbacks, Arbitrary Detention & Ill-Treatment of Asylum-Seekers in the United States.* London: Amnesty International. https://www.amnesty.org/download/Documents/AMR5191012018ENGLISH.PDF.

Andone, Dakin. 2018. "US Lost Track of 1,500 Immigrant Children, but Says It's Not 'Legally Responsible.'" *CNN,* May 27, 2018. https://www.cnn.com/2018/05/26/politics/hhs-lost-track-1500-immigrant-children/index.html.

Barrett, Devlin, Mike DeBonis, Nick Miroff, and Isaac Stanley-Becker. 2018. "Congress, Courts Stymie Trump Border Crackdown." *Washington Post,* June 27, 2018. https://www.washingtonpost.com/news/morning-mix/wp/2018/06/27/federal-judge-enjoins-separation-of-migrant-children-orders-family-reunification/?noredirect=on&utm_term=.133cd806d95b.

Chapin, Angelina. 2018. "Drinking Toilet Water, Widespread Abuse: Report Details 'Torture' for Child Detainees." *HuffPost,* July 17, 2018. https://www.huffingtonpost.com/entry/migrant-children-detail-experiences-border-patrol-stations-detention-centers_us_5b4d13ffe4b0de86f485ade8.

Cheng, Amrit. 2018a. "ICE Separates 18-Month-Old from Mother for Months." *ACLU Blog,* April 23, 2018. https://www.aclu.org/blog/immigrants-rights/ice-and-border-patrol-abuses/ice-separates-18-month-old-mother-months.

Cheng, Amrit. 2018b. "More Than 500 Children Are Still Separated. Here's What Comes Next." *ACLU Blog,* August 21, 2018. https://www.aclu.org/blog/immigrants-rights/immigrants-rights-and-detention/more-500-children-are-still-separated-heres.

Cheng, Amrit. 2018c. "The Government's Rush to Deport Reunited Families." *ACLU Blog,* July 25, 2018. https://www.aclu.org/blog/immigrants-rights/deportation-and-due-process/governments-rush-deport-reunited-families.

Chung, Andrew. 2018. "U.S. Court Orders Trump Administration to Fully Reinstate DACA Program." *Reuters,* August 3, 2018. https://www.reuters.com/article/us-usa-immigration-daca/us-court-orders-trump-administration-to-fully-reinstate-daca-program-idUSKBN1KP014.

Connor, Phillip. 2017. *U.S. Resettles Fewer Refugees, Even as Global Number of Displaced People Grows: Break with Past Responses to Global Refugee Surges.* Washington, DC: Pew Research Center. http://www.pewglobal.org/wp-content/uploads/sites/2/2017/10/Pew-Research-Center_U.S.-Refugees-Report_2017.10.12.pdf.

Cumming-Bruce, Nick. 2018. "U.N. Rights Chief Tells U.S. to Stop Taking Migrant Children from Parents." *The New York Times*, June 18, 2018. https://www.nytimes.com/2018/06/18/world/europe/trump-migrant-children-un.html.

Department of Homeland Security. 2014 "Standards to Prevent, Detect, and Respond to Sexual Abuse and Assault in Confinement Facilities; Final Rule." *Federal Register* 79, no. 45. 6 C.F.R. 115, March 7, 2014. https://www.gpo.gov/fdsys/pkg/FR-2014-03-07/pdf/2014-04675.pdf.

Department of Homeland Security. 2016. *Report of the DHS Advisory Committee on Family Residential Centers*. Washington, DC: US Department of Homeland Security. https://www.ice.gov/sites/default/files/documents/Report/2016/ACFRC-sc-16093.pdf.

Department of Homeland Security. 2018. "Inadmissibility on Public Charge Grounds." *Federal Register* 83, no. 196: 51114, October 10. Proposed Rules. https://www.gpo.gov/fdsys/pkg/FR-2018-10-10/pdf/2018-21106.pdf.

Dickerson, Caitlin. 2018a. "Hundreds of Immigrant Children Have Been Taken from Parents at U.S. Border." *The New York Times*, April 20, 2018. https://www.nytimes.com/2018/04/20/us/immigrant-children-separation-ice.html.

Dickerson, Caitlin. 2018b. "Trump Administration in Chaotic Scramble to Reunify Migrant Families." *The New York Times*, July 5, 2018. https://www.nytimes.com/2018/07/05/us/migrant-children-chaos-family-separation.html.

Donaldson, Lisa R. 2017. October 24, 2017 meeting clarification. Appendix 3: Email from US Border Patrol regarding family separation. In *Sealing the Border: The Criminalization of Asylum Seekers in the Trump Era*. El Paso, TX: Hope Border Institute, October 25, 2017, 38. https://www.hopeborder.org/sealing-the-border.

Ellis, Blake, Melanie Hicken, and Bob Ortega. 2018. "Handcuffs, Assaults, and Drugs Called 'Vitamins': Children Allege Grave Abuse at Migrant Detention Facilities." *CNN*, June 21, 2018. https://www.cnn.com/2018/06/21/us/undocumented-migrant-children-detention-facilities-abuse-invs/index.html.

Gray, Gerald. 2018. "Children 'Disappeared' at the United States/Mexico Border: A Symptom with Consequences for the United States." *Intervention* 16, no. 2: 66–68.

Hals, Tom. 2018. "Most Children, Parents Separated at U.S.-Mexican Border Reunited: Court Filing." *Reuters,* July 26, 2018. https://www.reuters.com/article/us-usa-immigration/most-children-parents-separated-at-u-s-mexican-border-reunited-court-filing-idUSKBN1KG19B.

Hennessy-Fiske, Molly. 2018. "Down on the Border, Texas Volunteers Open Their Homes and Hearts to Asylum Seekers." *Los Angeles Times*, November 21, 2018. https://www.latimes.com/nation/la-na-texas-asylum-volunteers-20181121-story.html?fbclid=IwAR1NlqVEdesHXE2pEeqCgcIBKu8GG0M0zipoceMkZXPGDNIT7Z2KIQMCveU.

Hesson, Ted. 2018. "Family Border Arrest Levels Remain Unchanged Despite 'Zero Tolerance.'" *Politico*, August 3, 2018. https://www.politico.com/story/2018/08/03/family-border-arrests-zero-tolerance-721536.

Hope Border Institute. 2018. *Sealing the Border: The Criminalization of Asylum Seekers in the Trump Era*. El Paso, TX: Hope Border Institute. https://www.hopeborder.org/sealing-the-border.

Initiative for Child Rights. n.d. *Initiative for Child Rights in the Global Compacts*. https://www.childrenonthemove.org/.

International Organization for Migration Office to the United Nations. n.d. *Global Compact for Migration*. https://unofficeny.iom.int/global-compact-migration.

Jordan, Miriam. 2018a. "'Why Did You Leave Me?' The Migrant Children Left behind as Parents Are Deported." *The New York Times*, July 27, 2018. https://www.nytimes.com/2018/07/27/us/migrant-families-deportations.html.

Jordan, Miriam. 2018b. "Whistle-Blowers Say Detaining Migrant Families 'Poses High Risk of Harm.'" *The New York Times*, July 18, 2018. https://www.nytimes.com/2018/07/18/us/migrant-children-family-detention-doctors.html.

Karimi, Faith. 2017. "US Quits UN Global Compact on Migration, Says It'll Set Its Own Policy." *CNN*, December 3, 2017. https://www.cnn.com/2017/12/03/politics/us-global-compact-migration/index.html.

Kennedy, Merrit. 2018. "ACLU Sues ICE for Allegedly Separating 'Hundreds' of Migrant Families." *NPR*, March 9, 2018. https://www.npr.org/sections/thetwo-way/2018/03/09/592374637/aclu-sues-ice-for-allegedly-separating-hundreds-of-migrant-families.

Khoury, George. 2018. "Trump Administration Anti-Asylum Policy Enjoined." *U.S. Ninth Circuit, The FindLaw 9th Circuit News and Information Blog*, November 20, 2018. https://blogs.findlaw.com/ninth_circuit/2018/11/trump-administration-anti-asylum-policy-enjoined.html#more.

Kopan, Tal. 2018. "Judge Slams Trump Admin for Suggesting ACLU, Others Should Find Deported Parents." *CNN*, August 3, 2018. https://www.cnn.com/2018/08/03/politics/trump-administration-aclu-deported-parents/index.html.

Libal, Kathryn, Susan C. Mapp, Eileen Ihrig, and Aviva Ron. 2011. "The United Nations Convention on the Rights of the Child: Children Can Wait No Longer for Their Rights." *Social Work* 56, no. 4: 367–370. https://doi.org/10.1093/sw/56.4.367.

Linton, Julie M., Marsha Griffin, and Alan J. Shapiro. 2017. "Detention of Immigrant Children." *Pediatrics* 139, no. 5: e 20170483. From the American Academy of Pediatrics Policy Statement. http://pediatrics.aappublications.org/content/139/5/e20170483.

Lopez, Victoria. 2017. "ICE Plans to Start Destroying Records of Immigrant Abuse, Including Sexual Assault and Deaths in Custody." *ACLU Blog*, August 28, 2018. https://www.aclu.org/blog/immigrants-rights/ice-and-border-patrol-abuses/ice-plans-start-destroying-records-immigrant.

Mark, Michelle. 2018. "John Kelly: It's Not 'Cruel' to Separate Families at the Border—Children Will Be 'Put into Foster Care or Whatever.'" *Business Insider*, May 11, 2018. http://www.businessinsider.com/john-kelly-family-separation-policy-illegal-border-crossing-2018-5.

Miller, Devin. 2018. "Pediatricians Speak Out: Detention Is Not the Answer to Family Separation." *AAP News*, July 24, 2018. http://www.aap publications.org/news/2018/07/24/washington072418.

Miller, Leila. 2018. "Trafficked in America: HHS Official Says Agency Lost Track of Nearly 1,500 Unaccompanied Minors." *Frontline*, April 26, 2018. https://www.pbs.org/wgbh/frontline/article/hhs-official-says-agency-lost-track-of-nearly-1500-unaccompanied-minors/.

Miroff, Nick. 2018. "Hundreds of Migrant Families Released from ICE Detention Centers." *Washington Post*, October 9, 2018. https://www.pressherald.com/2018/10/09/hundreds-of-migrant-families-released-from-ice-detention-centers/.

Miroff, Nick, and Josh Dawsey. 2018. "Record Number of Families Crossing U.S. Border as Trump Threatens New Crackdown." *Washington Post*, October 17, 2018. https://www.washingtonpost.com/world/national-security/record-number-of-families-crossing-us-border-as-trump-threatens-new-crackdown/2018/10/17/fe422800-c73a-11e8-b2b5-79270f9cce17_story.html?noredirect=on&utm_term=.addb4bede0a9.

Miroff, Nick, Josh Dawsey, and Maria Sacchetti. 2018. "Trump Administration Weighs New Family-Separation Effort at Border." *Washington Post*, October 12, 2018. https://www.washingtonpost.com/local/immigration/trump-administration-weighs-new-family-separation-effort-at-border/2018/10/12/45895cce-cd7b-11e8-920f-dd52e1ae4570_story.html?noredirect=on&utm_term=.1e29b0854d0b.

Miroff, Nick, Amy Goldstein, and Maria Sacchetti. 2018. "'Deleted' Families: What Went Wrong with Trump's Family-Separation Effort." *Washington Post*, July 28, 2018. https://www.washingtonpost.com/local/social-issues/deleted-families-what-went-wrong-with-trumps-family-separation-effort/2018/07/28/54bcdcc6-90cb-11e8-8322-b5482bf5e0f5_story.html?utm_term=.3b6876f94f30.

Miroff, Nick, Joshua Partlow, and Josh Dawsey. 2018. "Trump Plan Would Force Asylum Seekers to Wait in Mexico as Cases Are Processed, a Major Break with Current Policy." *Washington Post*, November 21, 2018. https://www.washingtonpost.com/world/national-security/trump-plan-would-force-asylum-seekers-to-wait-in-mexico-as-cases-are-processed-a-major-break-with-current-policy/2018/11/21/5ad47e82-ede8-11e8-9236-bb94154151d2_story.html?noredirect=on&utm_term=.a6aa16e273d9.

Neuman, Scott. 2018. "Allegations of Sexual Abuse Surface at Arizona Shelters for Migrant Children." *NPR News*, August 3, 2018. https://www.npr.org/2018/08/03/635203037/allegations-of-sexual-abuse-surface-at-arizona-shelters-for-migrant-children.

Office of the President of the United Nations General Assembly. 2016. *Press Release: New York Declaration for Refugees and Migrants Adopted by all Member States at Historic UN Summit*. New York: United Nations. https://refugeesmigrants. un.org/sites/default/files/un_press_release_-_new_york_declaration_-_ 19_september_2016.pdf.

Office of the United Nations High Commissioner for Human Rights (OHCHR). 2017. *Status of Ratification: Interactive Dashboard*. Geneva, Switzerland: OHCHR. http://indicators.ohchr.org/.

Office of the United Nations High Commissioner for Human Rights (OHCHR). 2018a. *Global Compact for Migration*. Geneva, Switzerland: OHCHR. https://refugeesmigrants.un.org/sites/default/files/180713_agreed_out come_global_compact_for_migration.pdf.

Office of the United Nations High Commissioner for Human Rights (OHCHR). 2018b. *Global Compact for Migration: UN Experts Call on States to Ensure Protection of Migrants' Rights*. Geneva, Switzerland: OHCHR. https://www. ohchr.org/EN/NewsEvents/Pages/DisplayNews.aspx?NewsID=23359& LangID=E.Planas, Roque. 2018. "A Single Trump Appointee Was Respon sible for Keeping Hundreds of Kids Locked up Longer." *HuffPost*, July 26, 2018. https://www.huffingtonpost.com/entry/scott-lloyd-refugee- resettlement_us_5b58cd0fe4b0fd5c73cb3c1a.

Qiu, Linda. 2018. "Fact-Checking the Trump Administration's Case for Child Separation at the Border." *The New York Times*, June 19, 2018. https:// www.nytimes.com/2018/06/19/us/fact-check-trump-child-separation. html.

Refugee Act of 1980. 1980. Pub. L. No. 96-212, 94 Stat. 102.

Schmidt, Samantha. 2018a. "Migrant Parents Were Misled into Waiving Rights to Family Reunification, ACLU Tells Court." *Washington Post*, July 26, 2018. https://www.washingtonpost.com/news/morning-mix/wp/2018/07/26/ migrant-parents-were-mislead-into-waiving-rights-to-family-reunifica tion-aclu-tells-court/?utm_term=.d7f44aeff931.

Schmidt, Samantha. 2018b. "Trump Administration Must Stop Giving Psychotro pic Drugs to Migrant Children without Consent, Judge Rules." *Washington Post*, July 31, 2018. https://www.washingtonpost.com/news/morning- mix/wp/2018/07/31/trump-administration-must-seek-consent-before- giving-drugs-to-migrant-children-judge-rules/?noredirect=on&utm_ term=.2a4bd07c2eac.

Seghetti, Lisa, Siskin, Alison, and Wasem, Ruth Ellen. 2014. *Unaccompanied Alien Children: An Overview*. Washington, DC: Congressional Research Service. http://fas.org/sgp/crs/homesec/R43599.pdf.

Stillman, Sarah. 2018. "The Five-Year-Old Who Was Detained at the Border and Persuaded to Sign Away Her Rights." *The New Yorker*, October 11, 2018. https://www.newyorker.com/news/news-desk/the-five-year-old-who-was- detained-at-the-border-and-convinced-to-sign-away-her-rights.

Stipulated Settlement Agreement, *Flores v. Reno*, No. CV 85–4544-RJK (Px) (C.D. Cal). 1997. January 17. https://www.aclu.org/sites/default/files/field_doc- ument/flores_settlement_final_plus_extension_of_settlement011797.pdf.

Thomas, Jake. 2018. "ACLU: ICE to Destroy Records Showing Their Sexual Abuse of Immigrants." *The Intellectualist*, May 28, 2018. https://www.themaven. net/theintellectualist/news/aclu-ice-to-destroy-records-showing-their-sexual-abuse-of-immigrants-KGqAQ0CMbEeCZ2W16_WSVw/.

United Nations. 2018. "US Migrant Children Policy Reversal, Still 'Fails' Thousands of Detained Youngsters: UN Rights Experts." *UN News*, June 22, 2018. https://news.un.org/en/story/2018/06/1012832.

United Nations Children's Emergency Fund (UNICEF). 2017. *A Child Is a Child: Protecting Children on the Move from Violence, Abuse and Exploitation.* New York: UNICEF. https://www.unicef.org/publications/files/UNICEF_A_child_is_a_child_May_2017_EN.pdf.

United Nations Committee on the Protection of the Rights of All Migrant Workers and Members of Their Families. 2017. *Joint General Comment No. 4 (2017) of the Committee on the Protection of the Rights of All Migrant Workers and Members of Their Families and No. 23 (2017) of the Committee on the Rights of the Child on State Obligations Regarding the Human Rights of Children in the Context of International Migration in Countries of Origin, Transit, Destination and Return* (UN CMW and CRC), November 16, 2017. CMW/C/GC/4-CRC/C/GC/23. http://www.refworld.org/docid/5a12942a2b.html.

United Nations General Assembly. 1989. *Convention on the Rights of the Child*, November 20, 1989. United Nations Treaty Series, vol. 1577, p. 3. http://www.refworld.org/docid/3ae6b38f0.html.

United Nations General Assembly. 2000. *Protocol to Prevent, Suppress and Punish Trafficking in Persons, Especially Women and Children, Supplementing the United Nations Convention against Transnational Organized Crime*, November 15, 2000. http://www.refworld.org/docid/4720706c0.html.

United Nations High Commissioner for Refugees (UNHCR). n.d.a. "Children." http://www.unhcr.org/children-49c3646c1e8.html.

United Nations High Commissioner for Refugees (UNHCR). n.d.b. "Figures at a Glance." http://www.unhcr.org/figures-at-a-glance.html.

United Nations High Commissioner for Refugees (UNHCR). 2016. "Resettlement of Children and Adolescents at Risk." http://www.refworld.org/docid/58344f244.html.

United States of America: Homeland Security Act of 2002 [United States of America]. 2002. 107th Congress; 2nd Session. November 25. http://www.refworld.org/docid/3deba3364.html.

United States of America: William Wilberforce Trafficking Victims Protection Reauthorization Act of 2008 (USA TVPRA 2008). 2008. Pub. L. No. 110–457. December 23. http://www.refworld.org/docid/49805ae72.html.

U.S. Customs and Border Protection (US CBP). 2015. *National Standards on Transport, Escort, Detention, & Search.* Washington, DC: US CBP. https://www.cbp.gov/document/directives/cbp-national-standards-transport-escort-detention-and-search.

U.S. Customs and Border Protection. 2018. *Southwest Border Migration FY2018.* Washington, DC: US CBP. https://www.cbp.gov/newsroom/stats/sw-border-migration.

U.S. Department of Health and Human Services, U.S. Department of Homeland Security, and U.S. Department of Justice (U.S. DHHS, DHS, and DOJ). 2018. *The Tri-Department Plan for Stage II of Family Reunification.* Washington, DC: U.S. DHHS, DHS, and DOJ. https://www.hhs.gov/sites/default/files/UAC-Tri-Department-Process.pdf.

U.S. Department of Justice. 2018. "Attorney General Announces Zero-Tolerance Policy for Criminal Illegal Entry." *Press Release Number 18–417.* April 6, 2018. https://www.justice.gov/opa/pr/attorney-general-announces-zero-tolerance-policy-criminal-illegal-entry.

U.S. Senate Committee on Homeland Security & Governmental Affairs. 2016. "GAO Confirms Negative, Unintended Consequences of Flawed UAC Policies." Washington, DC: U.S. Senate Committee on Homeland Security & Governmental Affairs. https://www.hsgac.senate.gov/media/majority-media/gao-confirms-negative-unintended-consequences-of-flawed-uac-policies.

Vera Institute of Justice. 2018. *Operation Streamline: No Evidence That Criminal Prosecution Deters Migration.* New York: Vera Institute of Justice. https://www.vera.org/publications/operation-streamline.

Victims of Child Abuse Act. 1990. 34 U.S.C. § 20341 (b) (6). *Child Abuse Reporting,* http://uscode.house.gov/view.xhtml?req=(title:34%20section:20341%20edition:prelim).

Vongkiatkajorn, Kanyakrit. 2018. "There Are Now More Than 14,000 Immigrant Kids in Federal Custody—A New Record: And It's Likely to Get Worse." *Mother Jones,* November 17, 2018. https://www.motherjones.com/politics/2018/11/there-are-now-more-than-14000-immigrant-kids-in-federal-custody-a-new-record/.

Watt, Nick, and Jason Kravarik. 2018. "Federal Judge to Appoint Independent Monitor for Detained Migrant Children." *CNN,* July 27, 2018. https://www.cnn.com/2018/07/27/us/federal-judge-independent-monitor-migrant-children/index.html.

William Wilberforce Trafficking Victims Protection Reauthorization Act of 2008. Pub. L. No. 110-457, 122 Stat. 5044. https://www.congress.gov/110/plaws/publ457/PLAW-110publ457.pdf.

Yoon-Hendricks, Alexandra, and Zoe Greenberg. 2018. "Protests across U.S. Call for End to Migrant Family Separations." *The New York Times,* June 30, 2018. https://www.nytimes.com/2018/06/30/us/politics/trump-protests-family-separation.html.

Zayas, Luis H. 2015. *Forgotten Citizens: Deportation, Children, and the Making of American Exiles and Orphans.* Oxford: Oxford University Press.

CHAPTER TEN

Promoting the Health and Well-Being of Child Migrants in the United States through Holistic Practice

Alysse M. Loomis and S. Megan Berthold

Millions of children are on the move across international borders—fleeing violence and conflict, disaster or poverty, in pursuit of a better life. Hundreds of thousands move on their own. When they encounter few opportunities to move legally, children resort to dangerous routes and engage smugglers to help them cross borders. Serious gaps in the laws, policies and services meant to protect children on the move further leave them bereft of protection and care. Deprived, unprotected, and often alone, children on the move can become easy prey for traffickers and others who abuse and exploit them. (UNICEF 2017, 6)

Introduction

Promoting the well-being of migrant children requires a culturally humble and holistic lens that seeks to promote these children's well-being across a constellation of domains and takes into account a child's range of potential experiences, family dynamics, and culture. This chapter explores the potential experiences that child migrants may face, including experiences pre-, during, and post-resettlement in the United States. This chapter also identifies the potential impact of these experiences on children's development, physical health, mental health, education, and family dynamics. Practice considerations are made for each domain that identify ways that professionals interacting with child migrants (such as medical doctors, psychologists, mental health clinicians, social workers, and teachers) can support their well-being. From advocating for increased access to health care resources to screening for trauma experiences, there are a number of ways that professionals and other individuals who interact with child migrants can support their well-being and future development.

Contexts for Leaving Homeland

Varied contexts surround the migration of children. Children often experience little to no choice in the matter of whether to leave their country or not because of decisions made by their parents or guardians, unsustainable living conditions (e.g., poverty, food insecurity, homelessness, forced child marriage), or safety concerns outside their control (e.g., war, disasters, trafficking, child abuse, domestic violence, drug cartel, and/or gang violence) (UNICEF 2017). Given how arduous it generally is for children to leave their country, and dangerous for those forced to flee, children often experience compelling reasons for migration (UNICEF 2017).

Such was the case for a 9-year-old boy from Honduras (J.S.R.) and a 14-year-old girl from El Salvador (V.F.B.), who arrived at the U.S.-Mexico border after the Trump administration's "zero-tolerance" policy went into effect. This policy sought to intensify efforts to criminally prosecute those who entered the United States without authorization. The parents of J.S.R. and V.F.B. were separated from their children, detained, and criminally prosecuted. J.S.R. and V.F.B. were sent to Connecticut, where they were detained and placed in a group home by the federal Office of Refugee Resettlement (ORR). The children have experienced significant trauma and were diagnosed with PTSD, anxiety, and depression (Johnson 2018). J.S.R.'s grandparents were murdered by gang members before he fled with his father to the United States. He saw his grandmother's dead body tossed in a river and witnessed additional gang violence in Honduras. During his detention at the border, J.S.R.'s father was taken away to sign some documents and never returned. J.S.R. reported that he was kept in a "hielera" (ice box/cooler) with other children. V.F.B.'s stepfather was killed by a gang in El Salvador before she and her mother fled to the United States. V.F.B. also was detained in freezing circumstances. One day, when V.F.B. returned from taking a shower at the detention center, her mother was gone (Altimari 2018).

The vulnerable (e.g., families with young children, disabled individuals, and those with serious health conditions) and those deemed to have the best chances of successfully integrating into society usually receive priority for resettlement in the United States (Zong and Batalova 2017). Some children are part of a planned migration with their families who move to the United States as refugees, immigrants with valid work or other visas, or immigrants without documentation. Other child migrants join family members already in the United States as part of family reunification, either through sponsorship by a relative or as undocumented migrants. Some children come as unaccompanied minors (UAM) and, with inadequate protections and few routes to legalization of their immigration status in the United States, are particularly vulnerable to exploitation and abuse from smugglers or traffickers, or to being recruited into gangs. Between FY2012 and FY2017, the Office of Refugee Resettlement received 229,495 unaccompanied child referrals for placement from the Department of Homeland Security as part of its Unaccompanied Refugee Minor Program (Office of Refugee Resettlement 2018).

Continued Risk for Danger and Trauma after Leaving Homeland

Living conditions for child migrants, in transit and once arrived in a country of exile such as the United States, are often dangerous, insufficiently secure, and/or unstable such that the children experience additional traumas and deprivation. Child migrants may live in temporary displaced persons or refugee camps, crowded shelters, or the streets. Unaccompanied migrant children or children separated from parents at the U.S.-Mexico border are increasingly being placed in "tent camps." The tent city of Tornillo near El Paso, Texas, has the capacity to hold over 3,800 children and houses children for an average of 59 days (Ainsley and Ramos 2018). Some child migrants, including those in the United States, are detained by immigration authorities and subjected to deportation or harsh and abusive treatment in detention (see Chapter 9).

Dangers en Route to the United States

Independent government reports, including by the U.S. Government Accountability Office, have described the traumatizing nature of the journey taken by Central American children to the United States (U.S. Senate Committee on Homeland Security & Governmental Affairs 2016). The dangers include such experiences as injuries or death from falling off freight trains, being caught by traffickers and sold into brothels, rape, assault, kidnapping, extortion by crime syndicates or cartels, and exploitation by smugglers (UNICEF 2017). Some children never make it to the United States. Gender differences have been observed, with girl migrants worldwide especially at risk for discrimination, sexual exploitation, and gender-based violence (UNICEF 2017).

Boy migrants have been found to be at risk for torture, sexual violence, and forced conscription in times of wars or other conflicts such as in Syria (Davis, Taylor, and Murphy 2014).

Dangerous Refugee Camps

Many children migrating to the United States have spent time in refugee camps in transit from their home country. Children may also have spent time in the "tent camps" for unaccompanied or separated minors at the U.S.-Mexico border. Refugee camps themselves are often not safe places. Some camps are at the edge of war zones and children may be particularly vulnerable to recruitment as child soldiers or being harmed as civilians caught in the cross fire and subjected to human rights violations (Janmyr 2014). In addition to the official camp administrators, unofficial or even criminal power brokers may wield great power, leaving children at risk of being exploited by drug dealers, traffickers, or others in power (Crisp 2000).

Stressors upon Entry in the United States

Common misconceptions purport that once children are resettled in the United States, the dangers that they previously faced are behind them. However, although children may not face the exact dangers that prompted their departure from their home country, they may experience similar or new types of dangers in the United States. Migrant families often resettle where their ethnic community enclave is, which can be an important source of social and emotional support. However, due, in large part, to a lack of access to adequate social and financial resources, these ethnic enclaves or other areas in which migrant families may resettle may be in high-poverty, high-violence neighborhoods, where children are at risk of exposure to community violence and victimization (Berthold 1999; Kula and Paik 2016). Children who arrive at the U.S.-Mexico border seeking asylum or entry may also experience unique traumas due to border policies and practices. For example, under the Trump administration, children who arrive at the border seeking asylum are currently in danger of not being allowed to apply for asylum (Dominguez and Seifert 2018) or of being subjected to such harsh conditions and abuse in detention that their parent(s) contemplate volunteering to return to their country of origin just to get out of detention (Hope Border Institute 2018). If they are somehow able to apply for asylum, and this is not granted, they are at risk of being deported back to their homeland, where their lives are typically in danger.

Undocumented children in the United States also face being deported once they turn 18, particularly under the current Trump administration (Stewart 2018). Currently there are almost 700,000 children in the United

States who qualify as recipients of Deferred Actions for Childhood Arrivals (DACA), due to being brought to the United States without documentation as children (López and Krogstad 2017). Children who qualify for DACA are, in theory, granted deferred action and can be authorized for work. They are not granted legal status, however, which may bar them from other types of support, such as financial aid for pursuing higher education. In recent months under the Trump administration, DACA is on unstable grounds, as it has been rescinded and reinstated in a matter of months (Chung 2018). Currently, courts are considering renewals of children's DACA status; however, new requests for DACA are not being considered. Despite the benefits that DACA can provide some children, the lack of permanent legal status and the current sociopolitical climate means that children's future under DACA is not guaranteed. In fact, interviews with children who qualify as DACA recipients find that children report feeling a sense of "non-belonging" and stressors related to worries about finding work and not being able to access financial aid (Benuto et al. 2018), which can negatively impact children's well-being.

Those U.S. citizen children who live in mixed-status families, in which members of their family have different immigration statuses, have in recent years been at increased risk for having their parents, and sometimes other relatives, deported (Zayas 2015). This violates children's right to family unity, and if their parent(s) are deported back to their home country, it places children at risk of separation from their parents or going with their parent to their parent(s)'s homeland, where they may never have been before (United Nations Committee on the Protection of the Rights of All Migrant Workers and Members of Their Families 2017). Children are exposed to narratives about deportation and raids by Immigration and Customs Enforcement (ICE) on the television and through other outlets and may experience fear and anxiety about their parents' ability to stay in the United States and may have distorted beliefs about the cause of their parents' deportation (Zayas et al. 2015). For example, children may believe that the parent is being deported because the child has been bad, or that the child can prevent the parent from being removed from the country. Children may experience hypervigilance and be "on the lookout" for ICE agents who may remove their parents or be fearful and clingy with parents (Dreby 2015), which may disrupt their concentration at school and expose them to high levels of stress for long periods of time. Distress associated with a parent's detainment or deportation is potentially harmful to children's mental health (Zayas et al. 2015) and should be assessed and addressed in order to promote migrant children's well-being.

Promoting the Well-Being of Migrant Children

Refugee children have been found to have higher rates of trauma exposure compared to immigrant or U.S. origin children (Betancourt et al. 2017). Just as the *types* of traumas that refugee and other migrant children and adults experience vary considerably, children's individual *responses* to traumatic events also differ (Dreby 2015; Zayas et al. 2015). Trauma can affect a child's normal developmental processes, not only at the biological level but also at the psychological and social level (Brabeck, Lykes, and Hunter 2014). Research with nonrefugee children has also pointed to the need to consider children's experiences in utero when their mother is traumatized or subjected to intense stress (Yehuda et al. 2005). Clinicians and others working with child migrants should thoroughly and holistically assess the experiences of these children across their life span but also be aware of the number of factors that can pose risks to a child's well-being upon resettlement in the United States (Berthold and Libal 2016; Evans, Diebold, and Calvo 2018). When assessing for and addressing the effects of trauma on a child with migration experience, it is important to consider the child's attachment and stage of development (Zayas et al. 2015), as a child's age and developmental capacities will inform the child's understanding of the traumatic experiences and the treatment approach. Maintaining such a holistic frame when beginning clinical work with trauma-exposed children is good practice for *all* children; however, with migrant children and their families, it is particularly critical (Brabeck, Lykes, and Hunter 2014). Effects of migration experiences on several domains of child well-being and considerations for professionals working with child migrants are discussed in the following section.

Child Development

The foundation of healthy child development is a child's attachment to a caregiver; attachment relationships also help to buffer the effects of stressful experiences (Bowlby 1969). When migrant children are separated from their parent/caregivers, due to a parent immigrating to the United States or more so through forced separations on the U.S. border or deportation, children are at risk developmentally. Lacking a caregiver to meet a child's needs, stimulate the child, or comfort the child when distressed all place the child at risk for developmental delays and other issues.

Trauma can have a negative effect on developmental trajectories for all children (Font and Berger 2015). When children and their parents are in a state of crisis due to trauma or focused on the aftermath of trauma and needs associated with resettlement, children's developmental progress may slow or be halted. Children may not receive age-appropriate stimulation, and developmental needs may go unmet. Consider a toddler being detained in a family detention center who may not have access to toys or space to explore, thus limiting access to developmentally appropriate stimulation. Living in a socio-economically deprived area or a locale with a lot of community violence, which is the case for many families following resettlement (Berthold 1999; Kula and Paik 2016), may also contribute to developmental delays for children (Najman et al. 2009). Children may also regress to earlier developmental states as a way to cope with trauma. For example, a child who was previously toilet trained may regress in the face of ongoing trauma, such as separation from his or her parents, and no longer be toilet trained.

Particularly, high rates of developmental delays have been found in numerous low- and middle-income countries around the world, from which many migrant children in the United States come from (Scherzer et al. 2012). This is thought to be in part due to public health responses that have reduced child mortality in many countries but left children affected by the aftermath of complications related to diseases such as HIV/AIDS and malaria (Scherzer et al. 2012). However, the prevalence rate of developmental delays in migrant children is not known (Abdullahi et al. 2018). This is likely due in large part to the lack of access to assessment and diagnosis in many developing countries, from which families may migrate; the lack of access to these services in exile; and the lack of access to professionals for detained migrant children. This is a concern as, in part, it is a missed opportunity to formally document migrant children's developmental needs and places children at risk of not getting identified for services that they may be in need of.

Upon entry into the United States, early intervention supports for migrant children and families often fail to assess for and subsequently attend to children's developmental delays. This means that in addition to being at elevated risk for entering the United States with untreated developmental delays, migrant children may continue to not have adequate supports and services to promote their development upon resettlement. Families with refugee status have limited access (less than a year) to medical care, which may already not be enough support to address a child's developmental need. Generally, families seeking asylum or without legal status do not have access to medical care at all, with the exception of pro-bono or low-cost clinics with programs that serve these populations.

Professionals assessing for developmental delays among refugee families must tread carefully. Even if asked by professionals, parents may be fearful to disclose a child's known developmental delays or disabilities or express concerns about the child's development for fear of being refused entry in the country or deportation. For some families, this has been a reality. In some countries, such as Australia, children's developmental disabilities have been used as grounds for refusal of entry or deportation (Zwi et al. 2017), as these children were considered to be a "burden" to the resettling country. Recent legislation proposed by the Trump administration (U.S. Citizenship and Immigration Services 2018) would allow the federal government to consider the use of health and other service programs, such as Medicaid, or food stamps when making public charge determinations that could be used to deny "green cards" or adjustment of status to Lawful Permanent Resident status (Artiga, Damico, and Garfield 2018). While refugees and asylees are exempt, children in mixed-status families may be affected by this legislation, which could result in children with developmental delays or other health- or service-related needs being denied legal status or an increased reluctance of parents seeking Lawful Permanent Residence status to disclose their child's developmental delays. This repercussion of discriminatory refugee policies may limit the collection of prevalence rates of developmental delays, the allocation of resources for early-intervention services for refugee children, as well as the provision of services for migrant children with needs related to a developmental delay.

If left unassessed and untreated, developmental delays may hinder children's well-being long term by affecting their socioemotional development, learning, and mental health, to name a few areas of impact. Migrant children's development must be considered through the lens of their culture, as well as within the context of exposure to traumatic experiences, departure from their home country, separation from social and familial networks, and integration within the U.S. society. What qualifies as or is interpreted by parents as a developmental delay may differ vastly by culture, and culture may also play a role in how treatment for developmental delays is viewed by parents (Mandell and Novak 2005). For example, religion and faith have been found to be particularly important as a support for Latino parents of a child with developmental delays (Skinner et al. 2001). When working with child migrants and their parents, clinicians should not assume to know the parents' views on normative child development or treatment approaches but rather should engage in an open dialogue to solicit the parents' perspective.

Practice Recommendations

First and foremost, immigration and refugee policies that discriminate against children with developmental delays and disabilities should be adamantly opposed. Legislation that considers children's health or service use needs as part of a determination for entry and/or permanent legal status in the United States can only serve to deter families from seeking services that children need and, thus, will result in poor outcomes for children. Caregivers in mixed-status families may also be concerned that if they seek services, ICE will apprehend and deport them, which can result in untreated illnesses for children and their caregivers. Clinicians can provide valuable input toward advocacy efforts as to the importance and effectiveness of early-intervention supports and services and to the detrimental impact of untreated developmental delays on children's well-being. Clinicians should also be prepared to address cultural stigma or shame surrounding children's development and provide parents with appropriate resources about services and supports available to young children that they will be able to access. Specialized services for migrants may be more available and linguistically accessible in urban areas in the United States.

Agencies supporting refugee and migrant children upon resettlement into the United States should integrate brief developmental screenings into current health screenings. *The Ages and Stages Questionnaire*, third edition, is a developmental assessment used with children up to 66 months, takes 10–15 minutes to administer, and is administered with the child and parent (Squires et al. 2009). This questionnaire, or others conducted in similar ways with assessors, children, and caregivers, provides an opportunity to both educate and elicit parent concerns about children's development in addition to screening. If screenings are universally administered, this can also set the foundation for the collection of prevalence data that may be helpful in assessing the need related to developmental supports for migrant children.

Physical Health

Currently the CDC recommends that refugee children are screened for elevated blood levels, anemia, hepatitis B virus, tuberculosis, and *Strongloides* when entering the United States (Yun et al. 2016). In addition to screening for communicable diseases, health professionals are advised to screen for trauma exposure. This is because adversity in childhood has overwhelmingly been linked in a dose–response relationship to a number of long-term physical health outcomes in adulthood, such as obesity and diabetes, as well as health-risk behaviors, such as smoking. The relationship between childhood adversity and health is seen for adults with migrant experience (Opaas and Varvin 2015) as well as adults without migrant experience (Felitti et al. 1998). Adverse childhood experiences may cumulatively contribute to a constellation of health outcomes for children that last far into adulthood.

There are other salient physical health issues to consider for migrant children beyond the health risks that communicable diseases as well as trauma and adverse events may pose. Anemia and malnutrition are commonly found among children in refugee camps (Lutfy et al. 2014), and household food insecurity is common among refugees living in the United States (Anderson et al. 2014). Estimates suggest that nearly half of refugee children are malnourished upon entering the United States according to World Health Organization (WHO) standards, including children who are over- and undernourished (Dawson-Hahn et al. 2016a). Children who enter the United States undernourished may gain weight rapidly and subsequently become overweight or obese. In fact, refugees have qualitatively reported higher intakes of meat, soda, and dairy upon resettling in the United States (Dharod et al. 2013). Prior studies in the United States suggest that children who are overweight at arrival are more likely to be overweight 6 to 24 months after arrival (Hervey et al. 2000) and that over a similar time frame, refugee children, particularly older refugee children, had greater increases in body-mass-index and obesity prevalence than nonrefugee low-income peers (E. Dawson-Hahn et al. 2016b). Such studies suggest that nutrition interventions require targeted approaches to address both under- and overnutrition.

Sexual health also plays an integral role in children's development and health outcomes. Some migrant children experience sexual abuse and/or assault prior to coming to the United States, either in their homeland or in transit. Additionally, children may not have had prior exposure to sexual health information, placing them at risk for sexually transmitted diseases and unwanted pregnancy. Refugee youth have qualitatively described a lack of access to information about sexual health and sexually transmitted infections, aside from information related to HIV/AIDS (Dhar et al. 2017; McMichael and Gifford 2010, 2009). Youth have identified barriers to accessing sexual health information, including a lack of resources, shame, concerns about confidentiality, and the competing demands of other issues related to resettlement, such as the meeting of their basic needs (McMichael and Gifford 2009).

Finally, discrimination is a contributing factor to both physical and mental health. In a study of Asian American immigrants, racial discrimination and language discrimination were found to be associated with increased risk of chronic conditions (Yoo, Gee, and Takeuchi 2009). In another study of Latino immigrant adolescents, youth who perceived higher discrimination generally in society and personally also reported more symptoms of depression (Ríos-Salas and Larson 2015), indicating that it is important to consider not only individual experiences of being discriminated against but also what messages youth pick up about society overall.

Practice Recommendations

Supporting the physical health of migrant children includes screening, education, and targeted interventions. Screening for health risks during children's resettlement should include not only communicable diseases but also factors that contribute to health risks, such as trauma exposure. Health screenings should address experiences the parent and child may have had not only in their host country but also in transit, which may include time spent in a refugee camp. Professionals screening children should also discuss the impact of deprivation, malnutrition, or overnutrition. These types of screening questions should be asked during intake health-screening interviews. Of course, opportunities for recommended screening in the United States likely only apply to children with legal refugee status, compared to children who are undocumented or seeking asylum who may not have access to screening and/or health services.

Opportunities for screening also facilitate opportunities for education of youth. One area of identified need for migrant youth is sexual and reproductive health education. Lack of access to reproductive health education and stigma around such education are barriers for many migrant youth (Dhar et al. 2017; McMichael and Gifford 2009). Providers working with youth and their families can provide universal and culturally and linguistically appropriate heath education that can support youth awareness of their own reproductive health and health practices (Dhar et al. 2017). Communities can also take part in promoting reproductive health education for migrant youth by supporting the education of parents and connection between youth and parents, which can reduce risky sexual practices (McMichael and Gifford 2009).

Services that address household food insecurity and child hunger and malnutrition are also important components of promoting the well-being of migrant children. Community centers and schools can promote access to food and nutrition education for migrant children and families through specific education about nutrition and local food, by providing access to healthy food during the day, and supporting community efforts such as community gardens (Smith and Cuesta 2018). As food insecurity does not seem to be lessened with increased duration in the United States, it is also important to consider how financial supports for families that help families access food can be extended beyond the short initial period of time for refugees (Anderson et al. 2014) and can be implemented for children who may not traditionally have access, such as UAM children.

Migrant children's rights to health and rehabilitation must be vigorously promoted (Berthold and Libal 2016). At a time in the United States when the Trump administration has sought to "repeal and replace" the Affordable Care Act, which would eliminate health insurance for millions (Patashnik and Oberlander 2018), is considering changes to the "public charge" regulations (including for the use of health care) that would limit admissibility to the United States and adjustment of status from a nonimmigrant visa status to a legal permanent resident status (Miroff 2018), is implementing restrictive immigration Executive Orders, and is stepping up efforts to deport undocumented immigrants (Wang 2018), this obligation is under attack.

The recent "public charge" legislation proposed by the Trump administration may also deter parents from seeking out health care for themselves and their children. In fact, estimates suggest that as a result of this proposed legislation, parents of 875,000 to two million U.S. citizen children may choose to drop Medicaid/CHIP funding for their child for fear of being deemed a public charge (and possibly without any alternative source of health insurance coverage) despite being eligible for services (Artiga, Damico, and Garfield 2018). Clinicians and social service professionals should advocate against the government considering health program usage when making determinations about residency or entry into the United States, as these will only serve to undermine the health and well-being of children and families and deprive them of their right to health care.

Mental Health

Most mental health clinicians are well-versed in addressing the effects of trauma on their client's well-being. However, unique skills are needed when working with migrant children. Children who have experienced trauma (pre-, during, and/or postmigration) may be at increased risk for mental health difficulties, such as anxiety and posttraumatic stress symptoms (Betancourt et al. 2017). One recent study found that more than half of a sample of refugee children from Syria had a possible anxiety disorder (Javanbakht et al. 2018). Also, compared to immigrant or U.S.-born children who have experienced trauma, refugee children have been shown to have different profiles of trauma symptoms (Betancourt et al. 2017), which means that typical trauma-informed psychoeducation or interventions may not be appropriate for these youth.

Children with refugee and other migrant statuses often have experienced a range of types of traumas, which may include violence directed toward them, such as assault by police or torture, or nondirect violence, such as witnessing a family member or close relative being assaulted or killed (Oras, De Ezpeleta, and Ahmad 2004). A review of studies of refugee children found that children who were directly exposed to violence as part of their experience, such as through physical assault or torture, have more poor mental health outcomes than children who were not directly exposed to violence, but perhaps heard about or witnessed violence (Fazel et al. 2012). However, it is important to consider developmental periods when considering risk and exposure with migrant children. The review included refugee children ages two and up, whereas a study done with infants in war time found harm directed toward an infant's caregiver was more traumatic, and related to more posttraumatic symptoms than harm directed toward the infants themselves (Feldman and Vengrober 2011). Overall, however, migrant children's risk of developing mental health symptoms is likely to be associated with their caregiver's symptoms (Javanbakht et al. 2018), demonstrating that it is important to consider work with the whole family rather than only with the migrant child.

When thinking about the impact of trauma experienced by migrant and refugee children, it is important to also think about the effects of interpersonal experiences such as abuse and/or neglect. In fact, adult's experience of childhood maltreatment was shown to have more of an impact on their adjustment than their experiences of trauma linked to war and human rights violations (Opaas and Varvin 2015). Child abuse and neglect may also be a driving force in some cases for the child to migrate and/or may occur in tandem with other traumatic events. This has important implications for screening for trauma with migrant children and highlights that not only the refugee-related traumas and postmigration experiences but also the child's lifetime experiences of child maltreatment and household dysfunction must be considered.

Children are affected not only by the traumatic experiences they and their families face but also by policies and conversations about policies related to migrant experiences (Rubio-Hernandez and Ayón 2016). Following the passage of anti-immigration legislation in Arizona, immigrant parents described that their children were hypervigilant and had an increased fear of authority figures (Rubio-Hernandez and Ayón 2016). Parents also shared that children had a sense of responsibility following the passage of the legislation, such as feeling as though they could prevent their parent's deportation or were responsible for ensuring their parent was safe. Words and legislation matter in the health and well-being of migrant children.

Practice Recommendations

While migrant children are screened for physical health issues upon entering the country, screening for mental health needs is rare to nonexistent. Additionally, there are not adequate trauma- and mental health–screening tools for refugee children, particularly children under six years old (Gadeberg et al. 2017). In a positive shift, guidelines from the Center for Disease Control on mental health screening for children are forthcoming. Guidelines for appropriate mental health and trauma screenings, particularly for children, are important to develop to identify the needs for mental health services among child migrants.

Screening is helpful for measuring the scope of children's responses to their migration experiences, but it is inadequate in and of itself if not paired with access to needed services. Trauma-focused interventions may be helpful for addressing trauma and mental health symptoms associated with migrant children's experiences, and it is important that agencies serving migrant children are able to refer these children and families to mental health clinicians trained in trauma-focused interventions that are culturally responsive. The evidence-base on such interventions is sparse with this population. For example, a review of studies of interventions to address sexual and gender-based violence following armed conflict found that there was not a single study that considered an intervention for children under age 14 (Tol et al. 2013). However, there are some interventions being researched with children in other countries that may be applied to migrant youth in the United States.

In a randomized study, Betancourt et al. (2014) explored the effects of a trauma-based intervention that included psychoeducation, relaxation, and problem-solving with war-exposed youth in Sierra Leone. The intervention was associated with significantly improved levels of emotion regulation, social support, as well as school outcomes, such as attendance, compared to children who did not receive the intervention (Betancourt et al. 2014). Other interventions that have been used successfully with refugee children include eye movement desensitization and reprocessing (EMDR) and cognitive behavioral therapy (CBT) (Oras, De Ezpeleta, and Ahmad 2004; Tyrer and Fazel 2014). Group-based treatment may also be very helpful for young migrant children, particularly because group treatments celebrate the role that each child's culture can play in promoting healing and support the development of social ties (Akinsulure-Smith 2009). Mental health practitioners working with migrant children should also be attuned to the influence of the sociopolitical context on children's levels of fear and well-being.

Education

The majority of children entering the United States as migrants, refugee or otherwise, will have to quickly integrate within the educational system, which can provide children opportunities for both additional stress and/or protective supports. Some children entering the United States may have had no formal education before (particularly girls), and others may have missed substantial amounts of school because of disruptions due to war; a lack of schooling in refugee camps; as well as poverty, high costs of education, or the need for children to work rather than go to school. Upon entering the United States, refugee children may be placed in schools based on their age, with little regard to prior education and English literacy (Bettmann et al. 2017). Teachers may be unaware of cultural norms, may have low expectations of migrant students, or may place cultural stereotypes on migrant students, which all contribute to children's learning difficulties (Graham, Minhas, and Paxton 2016). For migrant children, educational expectations that are too high (e.g., children being placed in a grade based on age only) or too low (e.g., placing with no regard for past experience or current capacity) put migrant children at risk for learning difficulties (Graham et al. 2016). Experiencing discrimination may also harm migrant children's educational outcomes, such as increasing their risk of dropping out of high school (Correa-Velez et al. 2017).

Some children may already know English (the dominant language in the United States), other children may settle in communities with native-speaking neighbors and service providers, and still other children may settle into communities with little supports for interpretation with service providers.

Children may learn English more quickly than their parent/caregivers based on their exposure to English as a Second Language through the education system and may be enlisted as interpreters for their parents. This practice has been identified as damaging to children and to their parents' health, as this practice may change family dynamics when children are gatekeepers for their parents' health and/or parents may leave out important information for the doctor because they do not want their children to know (Juckett and Unger 2014). Additionally, it may be damaging for children to hear about their parents' serious illnesses or private health matters.

The educational system is also important to children's developing social relationships with peers. Migrant children often have to reengage with a new set of social peers, which may be challenging based on literacy and cultural factors. Refugee and other migrant children may experience bullying from peers based on their inability to speak English or based on different cultural norms that make engaging with other peers and adults difficult (Bettmann et al. 2017). Parents may also disapprove of their children associating with American peers or taking on American values/norms. Such experiences may lead to social isolation, family conflict, stress, and other difficulties.

Children's access to education may also be affected by the social context around immigration. Increased efforts have been made in recent years by the authorities to apprehend and deport undocumented individuals in the United States. This has left some undocumented children and their family members fearful to attend schools, court houses, and health facilities (Cervantes, Ullrich, and Matthews 2018). The U.S. Supreme Court (in *Plyler v. Doe*) ruled that all children in America, regardless of immigration status, have a right to a basic education (*Plyler v. Doe*, 457 U.S. 202 (1982)). This ruling has been undermined at the time of this writing by comments from Secretary of Education DeVos that schools can make a choice to contact ICE to come for students or their parents who may be undocumented (Klein 2018). Due to the current political context, parents who are undocumented may isolate themselves in their homes, not placing their child in school or publicly funded programs, for fear that they will encounter immigration officials (Cervantes, Ullrich, and Matthews 2018).

Practice Recommendations

First and foremost, all migrant children have a right to access to education. Unfortunately, this right has been denied for many migrant children, including children with UAM status and children being detained at the border. UAM who seek access to schools may not have the required paperwork to enroll, such as birth or immunization records, which may delay or prevent them from accessing education (Evans, Diebold, and Calvo 2018). Education for children being detained in the "tent camp" in Tornillo has, until recently, been comprised of workbooks that children have an option of working on (Ainsley and Ramos 2018) rather than structured classes appropriate for children's age and ability. This disregard for children's right to education should be remedied through more flexible policies that allow UAM children to attend school without formal transcripts and advocacy for quality educational supports for children being detained in "tent camps" at the border.

For all migrant children, educational approaches should be: (1) culturally tailored, (2) informed by children's resettlement experiences, (3) community-engaged (linking parents, schools, and communities), and (4) multisystematic (Reynolds and Bacon 2018). Supporting the well-being of migrant children in schools requires an approach that values the child's culture and potential traumatic experiences prior to entering school in the United States and that engages parents, community members, and schools in a wrap-around approach to education. Schools in which migrant children are placed should expect and support positive school outcomes for students while providing a trauma-informed context for children and adequate supports for families.

School-based interventions have been found to be of use for helping refugee and other migrant children to settle into a new environment and may provide opportunities to integrate mental health services as well (Tyrer and Fazel 2014). School-based interventions to support refugee children should seek to support children within the school context as well as to make teachers more aware of the child's unique culture and individual learning needs. Further, collaboration between the school and parent(s) is particularly important for migrant children, to support parents not only in understanding the U.S. school system but in facilitating communication about the child to the parent and collaborating to ensure child success. Questions to consider when working with refugee children in the educational context are whether to place children in the grade with their age peers or based on their educational level. Additionally, it is necessary to consider the impact of English literacy on children's placement in classrooms as well as the unique needs of very young migrant children, namely those in preschool and primary school (Bettmann et al. 2017).

Maintaining a positive and safe environment for migrant children also includes providing training for parents through schools or community groups on their rights and advocating that ICE officials should not be allowed in educational settings. An example of such resources for teachers and parents is the *Education & Immigration Resource Guide for Staff, Educators, & Principals*, developed by the Los Angeles Unified Board of Education (L.A. Unified Board of Education 2018). This resource conveys the message "we are one" and gives information to school staff for migrant parents related to their rights and resources related to access to education.

Family Dynamics

Among the many violations of the rights of child migrants currently taking place in the United States is the right to the integrity of the family unit, which "can be undermined both by the forced physical separation of members of the family, by its division according to immigration status and by processes of detention, removal and deportation" (Hope Border Institute 2018, 12). Family dynamics and roles may be impacted by family separation, whether due to parents migrating before children, forced separation as seen on the U.S. border, or deportation. Children whose parents migrated before them may have resentment toward their parents, even following reunification (Dreby 2015). Forced separations and detainment of children and/or families can impact family roles, by replacing parents as the authority figure with detention center staff. Family detention can make it difficult for parents to meet the needs of their children, such as being able to make them food, play with them, or comfort them (Schochet 2018).

In the case of J.S.R. and V.F.B., discussed earlier, attorneys for the two children sued the federal government (*J.S.R. v. Sessions* and *V.F.B. v. Sessions*), seeking reunification with their parents. U.S. district court judge Victor A. Bolden, a federal judge in Connecticut, ruled in July 2018 that the separation of two migrant children from their parents at the U.S.-Mexico border is unconstitutional (Altimari 2018). The parents were granted parole, and the children and their parents were reunited in Connecticut on July 16, 2018. The legal battles for these two families are not over. As part of a settlement with the government, the children were granted humanitarian parole for one year, a temporary form of legal status to allow them time to obtain treatment to address their traumas before their asylum hearings. Their treatment will be paid by Medicaid. The parents still have pending immigration cases, and it is possible that they may still be deported, perhaps even before their children's asylum cases are heard in court (Fertig 2018).

Additionally, migration may differentially impact children and their parents and may result in acculturative stress based on navigating the differences between the parent's culture and that of the United States. Communication is identified as a significant struggle in refugee families, as children and their parents may speak different languages or have different cultural expectations (Betancourt et al. 2015). Many refugee families identify leveraging their cultural community or outside organizations, such as schools, to support parents and children in navigating these challenges (Betancourt et al. 2015).

Interviews with refugee families and their service providers also uncovered that refugee children may be at higher risk of encountering problems with the law and child welfare, based on different norms and customs (Bettmann et al. 2017) and family stressors associated with immigration/

deportation. For example, rules/laws around children's truancy from school and around what constitutes child abuse and neglect (such as leaving a child unattended in the house) may differ wildly from a refugee family's home country to the United States (Kolhatkar and Berkowitz 2014; Rhee et al. 2012). Additionally, parents who are being detained who have child welfare involvement may not be able to be accessed by child welfare workers and may be barred from participating in child welfare hearings (Finno-Velasquez and Dettlaff 2018).

Practice Recommendations

Developing a structurally competent approach is particularly important for clinicians working with migrant children. A structurally competent approach will help clinicians keep in mind the life experiences and systemic forces (economic, political, and social) that affect child migrants and their families (Ostrander, Melville, and Berthold 2017). Structurally competent practices can help practitioners hold in mind the potential ways that family members have been affected by migration and the ways that family dynamics can affect the child. The Center on Immigration and Child Welfare in New Mexico is an example of an organization working to meet unique needs of immigrant families in the child welfare system with a structural lens that considers the unique needs of immigrant families interacting with child welfare (Finno-Velasquez and Dettlaff 2018). Family therapy can be another particularly useful tool that helps to promote connectedness and shared meaning-making around trauma experiences within families (De Haene et al. 2018).

Structurally competent practices will also help clinicians in navigating cultural differences around child abuse and neglect definitions and their duties as mandated reporters. There are country-level differences in definitions of child abuse and neglect (Kolhatkar and Berkowitz 2014), which may vary between a parent's country of origin, a country in which they were in a refugee camp (if applicable), and the United States. Stereotyping, difficulties in communication (e.g., language barriers), and cultural biases can negatively influence clinicians when assessing for child maltreatment in migrant families (Kolhatkar and Berkowitz 2014). Providing psychoeducation on U.S. laws and definitions related to child maltreatment may provide a good context for having discussions about use of discipline (such as corporal punishment) as well as other parenting practices. Although clinicians in the United States are mandated to report abuse or neglect, and failing to do so can result in fines or lost licenses, clinicians must also be culturally respectful and assess cultural practices that may be different from their own from a child-centric perspective when they assess for harm (Kolhatkar and Berkowitz 2014).

Despite the many risks associated with the trauma experienced by many children entering the United States as migrants, there are many protective cultural and other factors that may promote resilience among refugee children. As noted previously, migrating to "resource rich" environments can help to buffer or repair the effects of trauma, both for children and for their families. This points to the need to effectively support migrant families during the resettlement process through supports in meeting basic needs for housing, food, health care, and education as well as in supporting the development of rich social networks. Factors that are protective against child abuse and neglect, such as social connections, concrete support for families, parent-child attachment, and psychoeducation about parenting in the United States (Kolhatkar and Berkowitz 2014), should be supported by clinicians. Putting the experiences of migration within the context of a child's life and future experiences may support children and families in moving forward following migration.

Conclusion

It is critical to consider the potential influences of children's experiences pre-, during-, and post-resettlement. It is important to develop a continuum of care to promote the well-being of migrant children that includes trauma-informed, developmentally appropriate screening tools (e.g., health, mental health, child development, family needs) and evidence-based practices to address trauma and mental health symptoms. Such interventions should take place across a number of child-serving systems, including education, medical, mental health, legal, and social service systems. Other settings, such as libraries, that potentially encounter migrant children and families should also be provided with resources to facilitate connecting with such families. Providers that come into contact with migrant families and providers across all of these systems should have access to resources and education that can support them in meeting the needs of migrant children and families. One potential resource would be professionally and specially trained interpreters. Finally, it is critical that we continue to advocate for migrant children's rights, including advocating to maintain family structures and reduce practices that rupture family bonds, promoting the financial stability of migrant children and families through adequate social services, and reducing discrimination and stigma by challenging rhetoric that breeds fear within migrant children and their families. We recognize that the United States, like states all over the world, has an interest in protecting its borders and controlling the influx of migrants. This interest must, however, not impinge upon its international and domestic obligation to ensure the best interests of the children are met and protected.

References

Abdullahi, Ifrah, Helen Leonard, Sarah Cherian, Raewyn Mutch, Emma J. Glasson, Nicholas de Klerk, and Jenny Downs. 2018. "The Risk of Neurodevelopmental Disabilities in Children of Immigrant and Refugee Parents: Current Knowledge and Directions for Future Research." *Review Journal of Autism and Developmental Disorders* 5, no. 1: 29–42. doi:10.1007/s40489-017-0121-5.

Ainsley, Julia, and Annie Rose Ramos. 2018. "Inside Tornillo: The Expanded Tent City for Migrant Children." *NBC News*, October 12, 2018. https://www.nbcnews.com/politics/immigration/inside-tornillo-expanded-tent-city-migrant-children-n919431.

Akinsulure-Smith, Adeyinka M. 2009. "Brief Psychoeducational Group Treatment with Re-Traumatized Refugees and Asylum Seekers." *Journal for Specialists in Group Work* 34, no. 2: 137–150. doi:10.1080/01933920902798007.

Altimari, Daniela. 2018. "Judge Rules Separation of Immigrant Children Living in Connecticut from Their Parents Is Unconstitutional." February 14, 2018. http://www.courant.com/politics/hc-pol-judge-rules-detention-unconstitutional-20180714-story.html.

Anderson, Laura, Diana S. Hadzibegovic, Jeanne M. Moseley, and Daniel W. Sellen. 2014. "Household Food Insecurity Shows Associations with Food Intake, Social Support Utilization and Dietary Change among Refugee Adult Caregivers Resettled in the United States." *Ecology of Food and Nutrition* 53, no. 3: 312–332. doi:10.1080/03670244.2013.831762.

Artiga, Samantha, Anthony Damico, and Rachel Garfield. 2018. "Potential Effects of Public Charge Changes on Health Coverage for Citizen Children." *Issue Brief*, May. http://files.kff.org/attachment/Issue-Brief-Potential-Effects-of-Public-Charge-Changes-on-Health-Coverage-for-Citizen-Children.

Benuto, Lorraine T., Jena B. Casas, Caroline Cummings, and Rory Newlands. 2018. "Undocumented, to DACAmented, to DACAlimited: Narratives of Latino Students with DACA Status." *Hispanic Journal of Behavioral Sciences* 40, no. 3: 259–278. doi:10.1177/0739986318776941.

Berthold, S. Megan. 1999. "The Effects of Exposure to Community Violence on Khmer Refugee Adolescents." *Journal of Traumatic Stress Studies* 12, no. 3: 455–471.

Berthold, S. Megan, and Kathryn Libal. 2016. "Migrant Children's Rights to Health and Rehabilitation: A Primer for US Social Workers." *Journal of Human Rights and Social Work* 1, no. 2: 85–95. doi:10.1007/s41134-016-0010-3 (Erratum, *Journal of Human Rights and Social Work*, Published online July 6, 2016. doi:10.1007/s41134–016–0015-y).

Betancourt, Theresa S., Rochelle Frounfelker, Tej Mishra, Aweis Hussein, and Rita Falzarano. 2015. "Addressing Health Disparities in the Mental Health of Refugee Children through Community Based Participatory Research: A Study in Two Communities." *American Journal of Public Health* 105, no. S3: S475–S482. doi:10.2105/AJPH.2014.302504.

Betancourt, Theresa S., Ryan McBain, Elizabeth A. Newnham, Adeyinka M. Akinsulure-Smith, Robert T. Brennan, John R. Weisz, and Nathan B. Hansen. 2014. "A Behavioral Intervention for War-Affected Youth in Sierra Leone: A Randomized Controlled Trial." *Journal of the American Academy of Child and Adolescent Psychiatry* 53, no. 12: 1288–1297. doi:10.1016/j.jaac.2014.09.011.

Betancourt, Theresa S., Elizabeth A. Newnham, Dina Birman, Robert Lee, B. Heidi Ellis, and Christopher M. Layne. 2017. "Comparing Trauma Exposure, Mental Health Needs, and Service Utilization across Clinical Samples of Refugee, Immigrant, and U.S.-Origin Children." *Journal of Traumatic Stress* 30, no. 3: 209–218. doi:10.1002/jts.22186.

Bettmann, Joanna E., Mary Jane Taylor, Elizabeth Gamarra, Rachel L. Wright, and Trinh Mai. 2017. "Resettlement Experiences of Children Who Entered the United States as Refugees." *Social Development Issues* 39, no. 3: 1–18.

Bowlby, J. 1969. *Attachment and Loss v. 3*. London: Random House. doi:10.1177/000306518403200125.

Brabeck, Kalina M., M. Brinton Lykes, and Cristina Hunter. 2014. "The Psychosocial Impact of Detention and Deportation on U.S. Migrant Children and Families." *The American Journal of Orthopsychiatry* 84, no. 5: 496–505. doi:10.1037/ort0000011.

Cervantes, Wendy, Rebecca Ullrich, and Hannah Matthews. 2018. "Our Children's Fear: Immigration Policy's Effects on Young Children." Washington, D.C. https://www.clasp.org/sites/default/files/publications/2018/03/2018_ourchildrensfears.pdf.

Chung, Andrew. 2018. "U.S. Court Orders Trump Administration to Fully Reinstate DACA Program." *Reuters*, August 3. https://www.reuters.com/article/us-usa-immigration-daca/us-court-orders-trump-administration-to-fully-reinstate-daca-program-idUSKBN1KP014.

Correa-Velez, Ignacio, Sandra M. Gifford, Celia McMichael, and Robyn Sampson. 2017. "Predictors of Secondary School Completion among Refugee Youth 8 to 9 Years after Resettlement in Melbourne, Australia." *Journal of International Migration and Integration* 18, no. 3: 791–805. doi:10.1007/s12134-016-0503-z.

Crisp, Jeff. 2000. "A State of Insecurity: The Political Economy of Violence in Kenya's Refugee Camps." *African Affairs* 99, no. 397: 601–632. doi:10.1093/afraf/99.397.601.

Davis, Rochelle, Abbie Taylor, and Emma Murphy. 2014. "Gender, Conscription and Protection, and the War in Syria." *Forced Migration Review* 47: 36–37.

Dawson-Hahn, Elizabeth E., Suzinne Pak-Gorstein, Jasmine Matheson, Chuan Zhou, Katherine Yun, Kevin Scott, Colleen Payton, et al. 2016a. "Growth Trajectories of Refugee and Nonrefugee Children in the United States." *Pediatrics* 138, no. 6: e20160953–e20160953. doi:10.1542/peds.2016–0953.

Dawson-Hahn, Elizabeth E., Suzinne Pak-Gorstein, Andrea J. Hoopes, and Jasmine Matheson. 2016b. "Comparison of the Nutritional Status of Overseas Refugee Children with Low Income Children in Washington State." *PLoS ONE* 11, no. 1. doi:10.1371/journal.pone.0147854.

De Haene, Lucia, Cécile Rousseau, Ruth Kevers, Nele Deruddere, and Peter Rober. 2018. "Stories of Trauma in Family Therapy with Refugees: Supporting Safe Relational Spaces of Narration and Silence." *Clinical Child Psychology and Psychiatry* 23, no. 2: 258–278. doi:10.1177/1359104518756717.

Dhar, Cherie Priya, Dilu Kaflay, Nadia Dowshen, Victoria A. Miller, Kenneth R. Ginsburg, Frances K. Barg, and Katherine Yun. 2017. "Attitudes and Beliefs Pertaining to Sexual and Reproductive Health among Unmarried, Female Bhutanese Refugee Youth in Philadelphia." *Journal of Adolescent Health* 61, no. 6: 791–794. doi:10.1016/j.jadohealth.2017.06.011.

Dharod, Jigna M., Huaibo Xin, Sharon D. Morrison, Andrew Young, and Maura Nsonwu. 2013. "Lifestyle and Food-Related Challenges Refugee Groups Face Upon Resettlement: Do We Have to Move beyond Job and Language Training Programs?" *Journal of Hunger & Environmental Nutrition* 8, no. 2: 187–199. doi:10.1080/19320248.2012.761574.

Dominguez, Astrid, and Mike Seifert. 2018. "At US Ports of Entry, the Government Is Denying Asylum to Those Seeking Refuge." *ACLU blog*. July 31, 2018. https://www.aclu.org/blog/immigrants-rights/ice-and-border-patrol-abuses/us-ports-entry-government-denying-asylum-those.

Dreby, Joanna. 2015. "U.S. Immigration Policy and Family Separation: The Consequences for Children's Well-Being." *Social Science and Medicine* 132: 245–251. doi:10.1016/j.socscimed.2014.08.041.

Evans, Kerri, Kylie Diebold, and Rocío Calvo. 2018. "A Call to Action: Reimagining Social Work Practice with Unaccompanied Minors." *Advances in Social Work* 18, no. 3: 788–807. doi:10.18060/21643.

Fazel, Mina, Ruth V. Reed, Catherine Panter-Brick, and Alan Stein. 2012. "Mental Health of Displaced and Refugee Children Resettled in High-Income Countries: Risk and Protective Factors." *The Lancet* 379, no. 9812: 266–282. doi:10.1016/S0140–6736(11)60051–2.

Feldman, Ruth, and Adva Vengrober. 2011. "Posttraumatic Stress Disorder in Infants and Young Children Exposed to War-Related Trauma." *Journal of the American Academy of Child and Adolescent Psychiatry* 50, no. 7: 645–658. doi:10.1016/j.jaac.2011.03.001.

Felitti, Vincent J., Robert F. Anda, Dale Nordenberg, David F. Williamson, Alison M. Spitz, Valerie Edwards, Mary P. Koss, and James S. Marks. 1998. "Relationship of Childhood Abuse and Household Dysfunction to Many of the Leading Causes of Death in Adults." *American Journal of Preventive Medicine* 14, no. 4: 245–258. doi:10.1016/S0749–3797(98)00017–8.

Fertig, Beth. 2018. "Two Immigrant Children in Connecticut Get Temporary Legal Status after Separation from Parents." *WNYC News*. August 30, 2018. https://www.wnyc.org/story/two-immigrant-children-connecticut-get-temporary-legal-status-after-being-separated-parents/.

Finno-Velasquez, Megan, and Alan J Dettlaff. 2018. "Challenges to Family Unity and Opportunities for Promoting Child Welfare in an Increasingly Punitive Immigration Landscape." *Advances in Social Work* 18, no. 3: 727–744. doi:10.18060/21716.

Font, Sarah A., and Lawrence M. Berger. 2015. "Child Maltreatment and Children's Developmental Trajectories in Early to Middle Childhood." *Child Development* 86, no. 2: 536–556. doi:10.1111/cdev.12322.

Gadeberg, A. K., E. Montgomery, H. W. Frederiksen, and M. Norredam. 2017. "Assessing Trauma and Mental Health in Refugee Children and Youth: A Systematic Review of Validated Screening and Measurement Tools." *European Journal of Public Health* 27, no. 3: 439–446. doi:10.1093/eurpub/ckx034.

Graham, Hamish R., Ripudaman S. Minhas, and Georgia Paxton. 2016. "Learning Problems in Children of Refugee Background: A Systematic Review." *Pediatrics* 137, no. 6: e20153994–e20153994. doi:10.1542/peds.2015–3994.

Hervey, Katrina, Delfino Vargas, Lisa Klesges, Philip R. Fischer, Sally Trippel, and Young J. Juhn. 2000. "Overweight among Refugee Children after Arrival in the United States." *Journal of Health Care for the Poor and Underserved* 20, no. 1: 246–256. doi:10.1353/hpu.0.0118.

Hope Border Institute. 2018. *Sealing the Border: The Criminalization of Asylum Seekers in the Trump Era.* El Paso. https://www.hopeborder.org/sealing-the-border.

Janmyr, Maja. 2014. "Attributing Wrongful Conduct of Implementing Partners to UNCHR: International Responsibility and Human Rights Violations in Refugee Camps." *Journal of International Humanitarian Legal Studies* 5, no. 1–2: 42–69. doi:10.1163/18781527–00501013.

Javanbakht, Arash, David Rosenberg, Luay Haddad, and Cynthia L. Arfken. 2018. "Mental Health in Syrian Refugee Children Resettling in the United States: War Trauma, Migration, and the Role of Parental Stress." *Journal of the American Academy of Child and Adolescent Psychiatry* 57, no. 3: 209–211. e2. doi:10.1016/j.jaac.2018.01.013.

Johnson, K. 2018. "Children Separated from Parents at Border Testify at Hearing in Bridgeport." July 11, 2018. https://www.nbcconnecticut.com/news/local/Rally-to-Reunite-Migrant-Children-With-Parents-Held-Ahead-of-Court-Hearing-487878281.html.

Juckett, Gregory, and Kendra Unger. 2014. "Appropriate Use of Medical Interpreters." *American Family Physician* 90, no. 7: 476–480.

Klein, Rebecca. 2018. "Betsy DeVos Stirs Uproar by Saying Schools Can Call ICE on Undocumented Kids." *HuffPost.* May 23, 2018. https://www.huffingtonpost.com/entry/betsy-devos-uproar-schools-call-ice-undocumented-kids_us_5b05a297e4b05f0fc8441ce3.

Kolhatkar, Gauri, and Carol Berkowitz. 2014. "Cultural Considerations and Child Maltreatment. in Search of Universal Principles." *Pediatric Clinics of North America* 61, no. 5: 1007–1022. doi:10.1016/j.pcl.2014.06.005.

Kula, Stacy M., and Susan J. Paik. 2016. "A Historical Analysis of Southeast Asian Refugee Communities: Post-War Acculturation and Education in the U.S." *Journal of Southeast Asian American Education and Advancement* 11, no. 1. doi:10.7771/2153–8999.1127.

L.A. Unified Board of Education. 2018. "Education & Immigration Resource Guide for Staff, Educators, & Principals." https://achieve.lausd.net/cms/lib/CA01000043/Centricity/domain/818/pdfs/We%20Are%20One_Booklet_Staff%20Educators_Principals.pdf.

López, Gustavo, and Jens Manuel Krogstad. 2017. "Key Facts about Unauthorized Immigrants Enrolled in DACA." *Pew Research Center.* September 25, 2017. http://www.pewresearch.org/fact-tank/2017/09/25/key-facts-about-unauthorized-immigrants-enrolled-in-daca/.

Lutfy, Caitlin, Susan T. Cookson, Leisel Talley, and Roger Rochat. 2014. "Malnourished Children in Refugee Camps and Lack of Connection with Services after US Resettlement." *Journal of Immigrant and Minority Health* 16, no. 5: 1016–1022. doi:10.1038/nn.3945.Dopaminergic.

Mandell, David S., and Maytali Novak. 2005. "The Role of Culture in Families' Treatment Decisions for Children with Autism Spectrum Disorders." *Mental Retardation and Developmental Disabilities Research Reviews* 11, no. 2: 110–115. doi:10.1002/mrdd.20061.

McMichael, Celia, and Sandra Gifford. 2009. " 'It Is Good to Know Now . . . before It's Too Late': Promoting Sexual Health Literacy amongst Resettled Young People with Refugee Backgrounds." *Sexuality and Culture* 13, no. 4: 218–236. doi:10.1007/s12119-009-9055-0.

McMichael, Celia, and Sandra Gifford. 2010. "Narratives of Sexual Health Risk and Protection amongst Young People from Refugee Backgrounds in Melbourne, Australia." *Culture, Health and Sexuality* 12, no. 3: 263–277. doi:10.1080/13691050903359265.

Miroff, Nick. 2018. "Trump Proposal Would Penalize Immigrants Who Use Tax Credits and Other Benefits." *Washington Post*, March 28, 2018. https://www.washingtonpost.com/world/national-security/trump-proposal-would-penalize-immigrants-who-use-tax-credits-and-other-benefits/2018/03/28/4c6392e0-2924-11e8-bc72-077aa4dab9ef_story.html?noredirect=on&utm_term=.707f65b13091.

Najman, Jake M., Mohammad R. Hayatbakhsh, Michelle A. Heron, William Bor, Michael J. O'Callaghan, and Gail M. Williams. 2009. "The Impact of Episodic and Chronic Poverty on Child Cognitive Development." *Journal of Pediatrics* 154, no. 2: 284–289. doi:10.1016/j.jpeds.2008.08.052.

Office of Refugee Resettlement. 2018. "Facts and Data: General Statistics." https://www.acf.hhs.gov/orr/about/ucs/facts-and-data.

Opaas, Marianne, and Sverre Varvin. 2015. "Relationships of Childhood Adverse Experiences with Mental Health and Quality of Life at Treatment Start for Adult Refugees Traumatized by Pre-Flight Experiences of War and Human Rights Violations." *The Journal of Nervous and Mental Disease* 203, no. 9: 684–695. doi:10.1097/NMD.0000000000000330.

Oras, Reet, Susana Cancela De Ezpeleta, and Abdulbaghi Ahmad. 2004. "Treatment of Traumatized Refugee Children with Eye Movement Desensitization and Reprocessing in a Psychodynamic Context." *Nordic Journal of Psychiatry* 58, no. 3: 199–203. doi:10.1080/08039480410006232.

Ostrander, Jason, Alysse Melville, and S. Megan Berthold. 2017. "Working with Refugees in the U.S.: Trauma-Informed and Structurally Competent Social Work Approaches." *Advances in Social Work* 18, no. 1: 66. doi:10.18060/21282.

Patashnik, Eric, and Jonathan Oberlander. 2018. "Republicans Are Still Trying to Repeal Obamacare. Here's Why They Are Not Likely to Succeed." *Washington Post*, June 13, 2018. https://www.washingtonpost.com/news/monkey-cage/wp/2018/06/13/republicans-are-still-trying-to-repeal-obamacare-heres-why-they-are-not-likely-to-succeed/?noredirect=on&utm_term=.30f79b17799b.

Plyler v. Doe, 457 U.S. 202 (1982).

Reynolds, Andrew D., and Rachel Bacon. 2018. "Interventions Supporting the Social Integration of Refugee Children and Youth in School Communities: A Review of the Literature Refugee Children." *Advances in Social Work* 18, no. 3: 745–766. doi:10.18060/21664.

Rhee, Siyon, Janet Chang, S. Megan Berthold, and Glorianne Mar. 2012. "Child Maltreatment among Immigrant Vietnamese Families: Characteristics and Implications for Practice." *Child and Adolescent Social Work Journal* 29, no. 2: 85–101. doi:10.1007/s10560–011–0253.

Ríos-Salas, Vanessa, and Andrea Larson. 2015. "Perceived Discrimination, Socio-economic Status, and Mental Health among Latino Adolescents in US Immigrant Families." *Children and Youth Services Review* 56: 116–125. doi:10.1016/j.childyouth.2015.07.011.

Rubio-Hernandez, Sandy P., and Cecilia Ayón. 2016. "Pobrecitos Los Niños: The Emotional Impact of Anti-Immigration Policies on Latino Children." *Children and Youth Services Review* 60: 20–26. doi:10.1016/j.childyouth.2015.11.013.

Scherzer, Alfred L., Meera Chhagan, Shuaib Kauchali, and Ezra Susser. 2012. "Global Perspective on Early Diagnosis and Intervention for Children with Developmental Delays and Disabilities." *Developmental Medicine and Child Neurology* 54, no. 12: 1079–1084. doi:10.1111/j.1469–8749.2012.04348.x.

Schochet, Leila. 2018. "Trump's Family Incarceration Policy Threatens Healthy Child Development." *Center for American Progress*, July 12, 2018. https://www.americanprogress.org/issues/early-childhood/reports/2018/07/12/453378/trumps-family-incarceration-policy-threatens-healthy-child-development/.

Skinner, D. G., V. Correa, M. Skinner, and Jr. Bailey D. B. 2001. "Role of Religion in the Lives of Latino Families of Young Children with Developmental Delays." *American Journal on Mental Retardation* 106, no. 4: 297–313. doi:10.1352/0895–8017(2001)106<0297:RORITL>2.0.CO;2.

Smith, Julia, and Guadalupe Cuesta. 2018. "Hunger in the Fields: Food Insecurity and Food Access among Farmworker Families in Migrant and Seasonal Head Start." *Journal of Latinos and Education*. doi:10.1080/15348431.2018.1500291.

Squires, Jane, Elizabeth Twombly, Diane Bricker, and LaWanda Potter. 2009. "Ages and Stages Questionnaires—Third Edition." In *ASQ-3 User's Guide*. doi:10.1037/t11523–000.

Stewart, Emily. 2018. "Immigrant Children Can Be Detained, Prosecuted, and Deported Once They Turn 18: Kids in Shelters Get Handed Back over to

ICE Once They're Legal Adults." *VOX*, June 21, 2018. https://www.vox. com/2018/6/21/17489320/unaccompanied-minors-ice-detention-family-separation-18.

Tol, Wietse A., Vivi Stavrou, M. Claire Greene, Christina Mergenthaler, Claudia Garcia-Moreno, and Mark Van Ommeren. 2013. "Mental Health and Psychosocial Support Interventions for Survivors of Sexual and Gender-Based Violence during Armed Conflict: A Systematic Review." *World Psychiatry* 12, no. 2: 179–180. doi:10.1002/wps.20054.

Tyrer, Rebecca A., and Mina Fazel. 2014. "School and Community-Based Interventions for Refugee and Asylum Seeking Children: A Systematic Review." *PLoS ONE* 9, no. 2. doi:10.1371/journal.pone.0089359.

United Nations Children's Emergency Fund (UNICEF). 2017. *A Child Is a Child: Protecting Children on the Move from Violence, Abuse and Exploitation*. New York: UNICEF. https://www.unicef.org/publications/files/UNICEF_A_child_is_a_child_May_2017_EN.pdf.

United Nations Committee on the Protection of the Rights of All Migrant Workers and Members of Their Families, *Joint General Comment No. 4 (2017) of the Committee on the Protection of the Rights of All Migrant Workers and Members of Their Families and No. 23 (2017) of the Committee on the Rights of the Child on State Obligations Regarding the Human Rights of Children in the Context of International Migration in Countries of Origin, Transit, Destination and Return* (UN CMW and CRC). November 16, 2017, CMW/C/GC/4-CRC/C/GC/23. http://www.refworld.org/docid/5a12942a2b.html.

U.S. Citizenship and Immigration Services. 2018. "Inadmissibility on Public Charge Grounds: A Proposed Rule by the Homeland Security Department." https://www.federalregister.gov/documents/2018/10/10/2018-21106/inadmissibility-on-public-charge-grounds.

U.S. Senate Committee on Homeland Security & Governmental Affairs. 2016. GAO Confirms Negative, Unintended Consequences of Flawed UAC Policies. February 22, 2016. https://www.hsgac.senate.gov/media/majority-media/gao-confirms-negative-unintended-consequences-of-flawed-uac-policies.

Wang, Cecillia. 2018. "In Its Zeal to Deport Immigrants, the Justice Department Scraps Due Process." *ACLU Blog*, April 19, 2018. https://www.aclu.org/blog/immigrants-rights/deportation-and-due-process/its-zeal-deport-immigrants-justice-department.

Yehuda, Rachel, Stephanie Mulherin Engel, Sarah R. Brand, Jonathan Seckl, Sue M. Marcus, and Gertrud S. Berkowitz. 2005. "Transgenerational Effects of Posttraumatic Stress Disorder in Babies of Mothers Exposed to the World Trade Center Attacks during Pregnancy." *Journal of Clinical Endocrinology and Metabolism* 90, no. 7: 4115–4118. doi:10.1210/jc.2005–0550.

Yoo, Hyung Chol, Gilbert C. Gee, and David Takeuchi. 2009. "Discrimination and Health among Asian American Immigrants: Disentangling Racial from Language Discrimination." *Social Science and Medicine* 68, no. 4: 726–732. doi:10.1016/j.socscimed.2008.11.013.

Yun, Katherine, Jasmine Matheson, Colleen Payton, Kevin C. Scott, Barbara L. Stone, Lihai Song, William M. Stauffer, Kailey Urban, Janine Young, and Blain Mamo. 2016. "Health Profiles of Newly Arrived Refugee Children in the United States, 2006–2012." *American Journal of Public Health* 106, no. 1: 128–135. doi:10.2105/AJPH.2015.302873.

Zayas, Luis H. 2015. *Forgotten Citizens: Deportation, Children, and the Making of American Exiles and Orphans.* Oxford: Oxford University Press.

Zayas, Luis H., Sergio Aguilar-Gaxiola, Hyunwoo Yoon, and Guillermina Natera Rey. 2015. "The Distress of Citizen-Children with Detained and Deported Parents." *Journal of Child and Family Studies* 24, no. 11: 3213–3223. doi:10.1007/s10826-015-0124-8.

Zong, Jie, and Jeanne Batalova. 2017. "Refugees and Asylees in the United States." *Migration Information Source.* http://www.migrationpolicy.org/article/refugees-and-asylees-united-states/.

Zwi, Karen, Santuri Rungan, Susan Woolfenden, Lisa Woodland, Pamela Palasan-thiran, and Katrina Williams. 2017. "Refugee Children and Their Health, Development and Well-Being over the First Year of Settlement: A Longitu-dinal Study." *Journal of Paediatrics and Child Health* 53, no. 9: 841–849. doi:10.1111/jpc.13551.

PART 3

Cultural Considerations and Refugee-Informed Perspectives

CHAPTER ELEVEN

Transcultural Mental Health Services for Refugees

Two Service Models from Montreal, Canada

Toby Measham, Jaswant Guzder, G. Eric Jarvis, Rayanne Elias, Cécile Rousseau, Lucie Nadeau, and Ghayda Hassan

Introduction

Refugees as a group have strong capacities of resilience to mental health difficulties despite their experience of highly stressful and traumatic experiences. At the same time, however, people fleeing their countries of origin and seeking refuge in new homelands as refugees are a population with an increased risk of specific mental health difficulties related to their exposure to war, violence, torture, forced migration, and exile, as well as to the stressors of an uncertain resettlement and its attendant legal, social, political, and economic predicaments (Kirmayer et al. 2011). Adult refugees resettled in Western countries could be about 10 times more likely to have posttraumatic stress disorder than age-matched general populations in those countries, and refugee children have also been found to have similarly high rates of posttraumatic stress disorder in Western countries. Major depression is also a common mental health concern for refugee populations, while its prevalence rate of 1 in 20 adults is similar to that in several host country populations

(Fazel, Wheeler, and Danesh 2005). Postmigration stressors, including structural barriers and inequalities, aggravated by exclusionary policies, racism, and discrimination, pose additional risks to mental health (Kirmayer et al. 2011). The corollary of risk factors is protective factors, and decreasing stressors by promoting a warm welcome with access to education, health, work, and initiatives to support social inclusion promotes mental health (Agic et al. 2016). Despite the research findings showing a risk for mental health difficulties, refugee populations, nevertheless, face barriers receiving appropriate health care, including mental health care (Kirmayer et al. 2011).

This chapter will focus largely on two clinical service models developed within the McGill University Division of Social and Transcultural Psychiatry and related community health networks in Montreal, Quebec, which provide a cultural orientation to mental health care services as they address the particular needs of patients from refugee and minority backgrounds. One is a child- and family-oriented cultural psychiatry service working with community-based primary health care services in a collaborative care setting, and the other is a tertiary care, regional hospital–based psychiatry cultural consultation service that provides psychiatric consultation and treatment planning for children, adults, and their families.

The Division of Social and Transcultural Psychiatry at McGill University in Montreal, Quebec, supports research, training, and mental health care consultation and treatment within a diverse urban context. Social and cultural factors affecting the mental health and well-being of minorities, whether individuals or communities, are considered by our staff, researchers, clinicians, and students at the intersection of disciplines that embrace the cultural, historical, neuropsychiatric, psychopharmacological, psychological, political, religious, spiritual, and social realms, reflecting the broad range of participating academic disciplines. The division networks with local, national, and international colleagues and institutions to promote research and training in cultural psychiatry. The work of our network has been detailed in a recent book: *Cultural Consultation, Encountering the Other in Mental Health Care* (Kirmayer, Guzder, and Rousseau 2014). This chapter will describe our group's clinical and community work with refugees who are experiencing mental health care concerns.

We begin with a brief description of the Canadian, Quebec, and Montreal populations, followed by a history of Canadian refugee and mental health policy, and then a description of the Quebec context. We review the theoretical underpinnings of culturally responsive mental health care assessment and treatment as practiced in our network. We will illustrate two dimensions of this work by describing, first, the collaborative mental health care community-based services provided in local community clinics in the Montreal area, and second, the specialized Jewish General Hospital (JGH) tertiary care Cultural Consultation Service (CCS).

Canadian Context

Canada is a diverse country. The 2016 National Census of Canada recorded a population of 35,151,728 people (Statistics Canada n.d.a). More than one-fifth of Canadians are foreign-born, and two-fifths of Canadian children are of the first (born outside of Canada) or second generation (having a parent born outside of Canada) (Statistics Canada 2017). Recent immigrants represent 3.5 percent of Canada's population, defined as obtaining their immigrant or permanent resident status in the five years prior to the 2016 census, and 1 in 10 recent immigrants to Canada were admitted to Canada as refugees (Statistics Canada 2017). Toronto, Ontario; Vancouver, British Columbia; and Montreal, Quebec, are the cities of residence for over half of all immigrants and recent immigrants to Canada. Quebec is home to the second largest number of recent immigrants (17.8 %) after Ontario, and immigrants represented 23.4 percent of Montreal's population in 2016 (Statistics Canada 2017).

English and French are the official languages of Canada, and French is the official language of the Province of Quebec. The 2016 census found that the percentage of immigrants with English or French as a mother tongue decreased from 71.2 percent in 1921 to 27.5 percent in 2016, mirroring changes in countries of origin over the same period (Statistics Canada 2017). In terms of language proficiency, 6.8 percent of immigrants reported not being able to conduct a conversation in English or French (Statistics Canada 2017). Canada has a diverse and rich cultural heritage; over 250 ethnic origins or ancestries were reported by Canadians in the 2016 census, along with 40 percent reporting more than one ancestry, and 6.2 percent of Canadians reporting Aboriginal ancestry (Statistics Canada 2017). The 2016 census also asked about visible minority status, using the definition referred to by the Employment Equity Act, which defines visible minorities as "persons, other than Aboriginal peoples, who are non-Caucasian in race or non-white in colour" (Statistics Canada n.d.b). Nearly 20 percent of the Canadian population identified as a member of a visible minority group. Of those who identified in this manner, 61 percent identified as South Asian, Chinese, or black, with individuals of South Asian origin constituting the largest visible minority group living in Canada (Statistics Canada 2017). The term "racialized group" will replace the term "visible minority" for the remainder of this chapter, as "racialized group" is the term of choice used in the Mental Health Commission of Canada's *Case for Diversity* report about service provision because it acknowledges race as a social construct (McKenzie et al. 2016), while "Indigenous peoples" is the terminology now most widely used in Canada in reference to Canada's first inhabitants. Canada welcomes a significant number of newcomers yearly, with more than 200,000 immigrants and 25,000 refugees coming to Canada each year (McKenzie et al. 2016). Canada resettled a historic number of refugees in 2016, welcoming over 46,000 persons and completing its commitment to resettle 25,000 Syrian refugees by the end of February 2016 (Government of Canada n.d.a).

Canadian Refugee and Mental Health Policy

Canada is a signatory of the United Nations 1951 Convention and 1967 Protocol Relating to the Status of Refugees (UNHCR 2010). The Convention defines refugees as people who have fled their country because of a well-founded fear of persecution related to their political opinion, race, religion, nationality, or membership in a particular social group. Canada signed the UN Convention in 1969 after revising discriminatory Canadian immigration policies toward non-Europeans.

The Canadian Immigration Act of 1976 recognized refugees as a distinct class of persons eligible for landed immigrant status as defined by the UN Convention definition of refugees and, in addition, included persecuted and displaced persons eligible for humanitarian reasons who did not qualify under the UN definition (Knowles 2016). It was positively regarded as a progressive piece of legislation establishing Canada's commitment to fulfill its legal obligation as a signatory to the UN Convention (Canadian Museum of Immigration at Pier 21 n.d.a).

The current Canadian refugee system has two main parts. The first is the Refugee and Humanitarian Resettlement Program for people who need protection from outside of Canada, and the second, the In-Canada Asylum Program, for people making refugee claims in Canada (Government of Canada n.d.b). Resettled refugees are accorded refugee status following an overseas screening process and receive permanent resident status before arriving in Canada. They may either be sponsored by the Government of Canada or be sponsored privately. Refugee claimants, on the other hand, enter the country by their own means and claim refugee status in Canada. Their claims are heard by the Immigration and Refugee Board, which determines whether they meet the legal criteria for refugee status.

Canada has laws respecting its diversity. In 1988, Canada became the first country to pass official multiculturalism legislation. The Multiculturalism Act of 1988 guaranteed the free expression of languages and cultures other than English and French in Canadian society and promoted multiculturalism as a fundamental characteristic of Canadian heritage and identity (Canadian Museum of Immigration at Pier 21 n.d.b). Multiculturalism in this context refers to placing a high value on ethnic diversity and encouraging the preservation of languages other than the two official Canadian languages, French and English. These attitudes have influenced policies affecting refugees in matters of health and mental health in subsequent decades.

In order to support immigrant and refugee mental health and well-being, the Canadian Task Force on Mental Health Issues Affecting Immigrants and Refugees (1988) was commissioned to identify factors influencing the mental health of immigrants and refugees in Canada and to make recommendations to improve their well-being and promote their adjustment to a full life in Canada. The task force found significant barriers to mental health care in Canada's immigrant and refugee populations and made 27 recommendations to the federal government in the areas of education, health, social services, immigration, research, and training to support adaptation and well-being. These recommendations have been summarized in a report by Hansson et al. (2010). While visionary, the task force's recommendations were difficult to implement, in part because Canada has provincial health jurisdictions, and also because Canada did not have a national mental health care strategy at that time.

A little less than a decade later, in 2007, the federal government founded the Mental Health Commission of Canada (MHCC). Since that time, the commission has championed mental health care in Canada, with a holistic approach that includes addressing the social determinants of mental health, with refugee mental health being one of its areas of focus. In 2008, it established a Diversity Task Group to examine mental health service improvement for immigrant, refugee, ethnocultural, and racialized (IRER) groups in Canada. Their report, *Improving Mental Health Services for Immigrant, Refugee, Ethno-cultural and Racialized groups: Issues and Options for Service Improvement*, determined that six of the recommendations from the 1988 task force had been fully implemented (Hansson et al. 2010). This new Diversity Task Group returned with 16 recommendations for improved planning and provision of services, with involvement of communities highlighted as an important goal. Among their recommendations were improvements for cultural and linguistic competence in mental health services, including a comprehensive linguistic competence strategy with language support and interpretation services with funding for these services from service providers. They noted that very few jurisdictions in Canada provided linguistic support in health or mental health services at the time of their report, in contrast to interpreter availability in the legal system.

Canada had its first national mental health strategy in 2012, when the Mental Health Commission of Canada produced *Changing Directions, Changing Lives: The Mental Health Strategy for Canada* (Mental Health Commission of Canada 2012). The document has a wide scope and attempts to address the needs of a diverse and geographically sprawling nation by introducing six overarching strategic directions, which include 26 priorities and 109 recommendations. The aim of Strategic Direction 4: Disparities and Diversity is to "reduce disparities in risk factors and access to mental health services, and strengthen the response to the needs of diverse communities and Northern-ers" (Mental Health Commission of Canada 2012, 78). This direction aims at addressing risk factors for developing mental health problems, including socioeconomic risk, low education and lack of social support, disparities in access to appropriate mental health programs and services because of socio-economic status, ethnocultural background, experience of racism and reasons for emigrating, living in a Northern or remote community, being part of an official language minority (Francophone or Anglophone) community, and gender and sexual orientation (Mental Health Commission of Canada 2012). Priority 4.2 of this Strategic Direction addresses the mental health needs of immigrants, refugees, ethnocultural, and racialized groups. It makes recommendations for services to be more welcoming; to use standards of cultural competence and safety; to increase access to services in diverse languages; to better evaluate the potential of traditional knowledge, customs, and practices to address mental health problems and illnesses and to improve access to those that work; to support community organizations; and to develop and implement mental health plans in all jurisdictions to meet these needs with full involvement of community members (Mental Health Commission of Canada 2012). The Multicultural Mental Health Resource Centre, developed by the MHCC Science Advisory Committee as a part of this initiative, is at McGill University (Multicultural Mental Health Resource Centre n.d.a). This website provides resources with the aim of improving the quality and avail-ability of appropriate mental health services for people of diverse cultural and ethnic backgrounds.

The Mental Health Commission of Canada continues to be at the fore-front of improving mental health care access and addressing the social determinants of mental health in Canada. Its *Case for Diversity* report pro-vides powerful arguments and evidence to support investing in culturally and linguistically appropriate and diverse mental health services in Canada (McKenzie et al. 2016). Again in 2016, the Mental Health Commission of Canada published *Supporting the Mental Health of Refugees* in the context of Canada's commitment to resettle Syrian refugees displaced by war (Agic et al. 2016). This report paid particular attention to the resilience, protec-tive factors, and unique needs of refugees. The goal of the report was to promote wellness in refugees by calling on decision makers at all levels of government as well as organizations and service providers to make a coor-dinated effort to support the adaptation and well-being of these newest arrivals to Canada, including recommending adequate funding to achieve these goals.

While the Mental Health Commission of Canada defines a national men-tal health strategy, it neither provides nor funds mental health services. The provision of health services in Canada, including mental health services, remains under provincial jurisdiction. The federal government, through its

Interim Federal Health Program (IFHP), first established in 1957, does have a direct role in providing limited, temporary coverage of health care benefits, including mental health care, for specific eligible persons who aren't eligible for provincial or territorial coverage (Government of Canada n.d.c). Before 2012, IFHP coverage was equivalent to provincial health insurance combined with social assistance health benefits and included almost all medical services as well as certain supplemental services for all resettled refugees as well as refugee claimants until acceptance as refugees, or if not accepted, until their date of removal (Ruiz-Casares et al. 2016).

In 2012, the federal government introduced major amendments to the IFHP, rescinding this previously receptive policy. These amendments created a differential mode of health coverages, where the type and extent of coverage depended on refugee categories. It also eliminated health coverage (except in cases of public health or public safety risk) to refused refugee claimants and also to refugee claimants from a list of countries termed Designated Countries of Origin (Government of Canada n.d.d), which were considered to be safe in that they did not normally produce refugees and they respected human rights and offered state protection. Qualitative research findings documented the adverse effects of these health care changes (Marwah 2014). Some examples of adverse effects included: increased risks to pregnant refugees when prenatal health care was no longer available; health conditions worsening due to delayed health seeking behavior as well as a lack of access to preventative and/or early intervention care; inability to access some prescription medications to treat health conditions; some clinics no longer accepting refugee patients; and some refugees sometimes being asked to pay even for services that they were entitled to.

In Quebec, the provincial government reacted swiftly by stepping in to compensate for the gaps opened up by the cuts in federal coverage, so that medical services and medications for all refugee claimants and refused claimants with an IFHP certificate were funded. Despite this quick response to mitigate the effects of these funding cuts, a survey of health service providers in Montreal documented a high level of confusion among health care providers about health care coverage for refugee claimants, raising concerns that these rapid and administratively complex changes brought increased barriers to health care access to an already-vulnerable population (Ruiz-Casares et al. 2016). On November 5, 2014, following a federal court decision that the 2012 IFHP cuts violated the Canadian Charter of Rights and Freedoms, the federal government adopted a new but still complex version of the IFHP program (Ruiz-Casares et al. 2016). Most recently, in January 2016, a newly elected federal government announced that it would fully restore refugee health care benefits to pre-2012 levels (CBC News 2016), which has since taken place.

The Quebec Context

Quebec has a unique historical and cultural context as a francophone province in Canada and has adopted an intercultural approach focused on adaptive adjustment centered in a unique francophone cultural heritage. Quebec was the first province to have a provincial mental health policy (Gouvernement de Quebec 1989), and a number of reports and books have addressed the importance of culture to mental health in Quebec, underscoring an appreciation of culture in Quebec's mental health policies (see, e.g., Bibeau et al. 1992). Quebec's "Plan d'action en santé mentale Quebec" (Ministère de la Santé et des Services Sociaux 2005–2010, 2015–2020) guides Quebec's mental health policies. Quebec also established a provincial bank of interpreters in 1993, providing trained interpreters for languages other than French and English for the health and social services sectors, significantly meeting the language needs in service access and mental health care for many people living in an increasingly diverse Quebec.

Quebec's and Canada's approaches to cultural diversity have shifted over the years, with collective tensions emerging over cultural diversity, which have had potential impact on both mental health and mental health care delivery to citizens and refugees. The elected government of Quebec in 2013 proposed the Charter Affirming the Values of State Secularism and Religious Neutrality and of Equality between Women and Men, and Providing a Framework for Accommodation Requests (National Assembly 2013). The charter recommended, in the interests of state neutrality, secular values, and gender equality, that "ostentatious" religious symbols should be forbidden in public institutions. The charter sparked intense debate, and proponents of divergent sociopolitical agendas had difficulty finding common ground. Many professionals at McGill and in the Division of Social and Transcultural Psychiatry were deeply concerned by the proposed charter and reached out through media to express their concern about the charter's erosion of human rights and its negative effects on mental health, well-being, and social integration (Kirmayer et al. 2013). The bill did not pass into law as a new government was elected in 2014.

This new government passed Bill 62, requiring face coverings to be removed when giving or receiving public services, including health care services, for purposes of identification, communication, or security reasons. The bill included the possibility of applying for exemptions to the law on religious grounds and is currently undergoing a constitutional challenge in regard to freedom of religion (Shingler 2017). In 2017 a Quebec superior court judge granted a temporary suspension of the section of the law that dealt with face coverings until Quebec released criteria for requesting and granting religious accommodation, which Quebec subsequently provided in 2018; however, that section of the law was suspended for a second time in

June 2018 until the challenge to the law is heard in court (Shingler 2018). A new provincial government was elected in October 2018 and is expected to table a new bill in 2019 to address the ongoing debate over religious symbols (Shingler 2019). A climate of distrust toward migrants and refugees continues, and there is a current upsurge in tensions around ethnic and religious identities.

In summary, over the last several decades, the general trend in Quebec and Canada, with relatively widespread popular support, has been to aid, accept, and settle diverse peoples suffering persecution in their countries of origin. At the same time, there are increasing local and global tensions and discriminatory discourse and policies (Schain 2018) that risk generating a climate of stigma and discrimination that could undermine the positive adjustment of various immigrant, refugee, ethnocultural, and racialized populations (IRER). Of enormous concern is the recent upsurge of hate crimes in Canada and Quebec, with police-reported hate crimes jumping sharply in 2017 with a 47 percent increase (Statistics Canada 2018).

Culturally Informed and Responsive Care

As clinical services acknowledged issues of barriers to care, training and clinical approaches shifted to explicitly address the importance of cultural safety of both patient and therapist as they co-constructed encounters across social realities in culturally safe therapeutic settings. These issues became more explicit both in Canada and internationally, as clinicians became increasingly aware of both the need for therapist training and the shifting demographics and ethnicities in recent waves of global migration. Cultural formulation is a clinical tool (Multicultural Mental Health Resource Centre n.d.b.) developed in response to the increasing awareness that our clinical assessment, training, and treatment models need to encompass variations of culture on development, identity, the family life cycle, spirituality, coping and help-seeking, social networks, and interpersonal agendas. Programs, policies, treatments, and supports are now being developed to better address diversity in mental health care, and the MHCC's *Case for Diversity* identifies many promising examples both locally and globally (McKenzie et al. 2016). For example, ethno-specific clinics are one such approach, where culturally adapted services are provided for communities that especially use their services, while also serving the wider population who request them. Some community clinics may have mental health providers who are bicultural and may provide ethnic match or experience identifications with certain ethnic groups in the community or from a culture with closer affiliations than European or dominant cultural staff. As an example, the Hong Fook Mental Health Association in Toronto, Ontario, developed a promising practice model for community engagement by providing language-specific intake services in Cantonese,

English, Khmer, Korean, Mandarin, and Vietnamese, and ethno-specific assessment and consultation of clients from East and Southeast Asian cultural communities in Toronto (Hong Fook Mental Health Association n.d.). Taking a different approach, Nafsiyat in the United Kingdom (Kareem and Littlewood 1999) pioneered a service model taking an interest in client choice and in particular to considerations of language, ethnicity, and sexual orientation as a basic cultural ground to be acknowledged, especially for marginalized communities in London.

There are also specialized care clinics addressing a diverse IRER population, where there is not a particular community in any great number using the clinic's services. These clinics typically have a multicultural, multidisciplinary mental health care team that works collaboratively with interpreters, culture brokers, community agencies, and other support systems in highly multiethnic areas. These clinics can be either community-based or hospital-based, and organized to provide consultation or consultation and treatment. Our focus here will be with the Montreal proximity-based collaborative child psychiatry community mental health care team, which provides assessment and treatment in partnership within neighborhood community health clinics at the CSSS de la Montagne—CIUSSS West Central Montreal health care network, in collaboration with the McGill University teaching hospitals of the Montreal Children's Hospital and the Jewish General Hospital. The Cultural Consultation Service is housed at the Jewish General Hospital, where it provides specialized cultural consultations for the greater Montreal and provincial regions (Kirmayer, Guzder, and Rousseau 2014). In both services the consultation process has tried to promote systemic and culturally informed approaches to clinical work. Cultural formulation, the use of interpreters and culture brokers, ongoing training seminars, and research initiatives have been developed in both settings. The Cultural Consultation Service submitted its work to the call for promising practices included in the *Case for Diversity* report. The proximity-based collaborative child psychiatry community mental health team is not specialized and promotes team supervision in cultural mental health. It has a research and clinical orientation based in a network of community clinics, which also houses the SHERPA Research Program (a research, immigration, and society-oriented research team of which some of the authors of this chapter are members). The Regional Program for the Settlement and Integration of Asylum Seekers (PRAIDA), the center for triaging social work and primary care for refugees, including interfacing with the refugee board hearing process, is part of the community health clinic network where the proximity-based collaborative child psychiatry community mental health team is located. PRAIDA is included in the *Case for Diversity* report. Cultural consultation services are elaborated and covered financially within a public medicare setting in Canada and often located in urban community clinics or teaching hospitals, but remain fragile and sometimes contested even in these settings.

Proximity-Based Collaborative Child Psychiatry and Community Mental Health Care Team

The Consultation Process

The proximity-based collaborative child psychiatry team model was developed following collaborative work between child psychiatrists involved in transcultural work and first-line community health and social service clinicians working in community clinics in highly culturally diverse Montreal neighborhoods. Child psychiatrists trained in transcultural psychiatry join the community clinics' Youth Mental Health (YMH) teams and are on site at the clinics for part of the week. This allows for direct patient consultations with first-line clinicians in the community clinics and also for many occasions of both formal and informal clinical exchanges with community clinic clinicians. These proximity-based services appear to allow for improved access to mental health care for the community clinic's clientele. Referrals to child psychiatrists and the YMH team within the model of collaborative care are made by community health and social service providers who are already working with a child and his or her family. An intake triage clinician prioritizes referrals first, on the basis of urgency, and second, on date of referral. They may be provided a direct assessment, which includes meeting the patient and his or her family, together with their primary community worker. Alternately, an indirect consultation may be provided, where the team discusses the case with the patient's referring community health and social service professional and provides recommendations. The collaborative care model allows this proximity-based mental health team to provide ongoing support and collaboration with the primary care clinicians. When appropriate, other professionals within the child's network participate in systemic problem solving and consultation (e.g., professionals from the child's school or child welfare professionals).

The consulting mental health team includes a child psychiatrist (who can be accompanied by trainees from health, mental health, and social services fields) and community-based clinician(s) including social workers, psychologists, creative arts therapists, psychoeducators, nurses, and physicians. The patient's referring clinician or physician is encouraged to attend. The team first meets with the referring professional and community-based team to review the referral information and to discuss the plan for the interview. The referring team members are encouraged to stay for the subsequent interview with the patient and his or her family and their community-based team. Consultations often include a professionally trained language interpreter and may include a cultural broker as well.

The assessment includes an orientation to the cultural axis, and the team explores the mental health concerns that brought the family to seek care. Integration of developmental and systemic issues includes cultural aspects of the patient, family, and community, along with cultural conceptualizations of distress and issues of vulnerability and resilience, and the assessment builds on supporting a connection between the individual and the health care team. Premigratory, migratory, and postmigratory stressors are especially explored. Emphasis is placed on assessing current stressors and barriers to care that can be addressed in order to promote mental health and well-being. Experience of trauma is explored with a modulated approach to avoid retraumatization in this setting (Measham and Rousseau 2010). Social and academic difficulties, medical symptoms as well as unexplained somatic symptoms, and mental health symptoms, including sleep problems, internalizing and externalizing symptoms, unusual thoughts, suicidality, and post-traumatic or dissociative phenomena are all carefully reviewed. Protective factors and resilience promotion as well as risk factors are explored to assess possibilities of individual, family, community, and cultural support systems and interventions to create the conditions for coping, adaptation, and treatment.

The interview takes into account that family members and individuals often have different experiences that they may not have disclosed to each other, as well as divergent views on the meaning of difficulties and treatment, and shifting and multiple acculturation experiences, cultural identities, and generational differences. Systemic exploration includes taking care to follow the family's lead in defining distress and focuses on problem solving, as opposed to intrusive uncovering. The interview also lays the foundation for possibilities for engagement with additional resources when needed, both with the clinic as well as with their primary care or school resources. A review of the team and family's work together over time is performed to support continuity in care.

A clinical history interview is conducted with families and complemented with individual play assessments with children, including separate interviews with adolescents and with some child patients. Observations about the process of the interview, the interaction with the team, as well as collateral information from the family interview are all useful in the team's formulation, clinical diagnostic impressions using the *Diagnostic and Statistical Manual of Mental Disorders*, 5th edition, diagnostic classification system (American Psychiatric Association 2013), and proposed treatment plan. This approach allows the team to have an overall systemic assessment and to include the impact of culture and postmigratory context before proposing diagnostic impressions and deciding on possible treatment approaches and recommendations.

After the assessment, the patient and their family are invited to step out of the meeting room for a few minutes. During this brief interlude, the team, including the referring professionals, seek to reach a shared understanding of the main difficulties, intervention frameworks, networking possibilities, and possible treatment options either in the community or in the clinic. The patient and his or her family are then invited back to discuss these impressions and recommendations. The ensuing discussion with the patient and family then reaches a shared agreement on a proposed treatment plan.

Special Considerations in the Consultation Process

Interpreters are key members of the team, and families are offered interpreters for their maternal tongue as an option, regardless of their mastery of their host country's official languages. This provides an explicit respect for a family's cultural background, lessens the burden on children or family members who may have been acting as interpreters previously, and additionally may help to address power imbalances in situations where the health care team or the family's children may have a greater mastery of the host country's languages than a youth's parents (Rousseau, Measham, and Moro 2011), or where trauma or gendered hierarchy issues have created silencing (Jack and Ali 2010). Interpreters and culture brokers can contribute valuable insight in evaluating issues involving child development by offering their observations on culturally normative developmental milestones and offering a context of familiar language to evaluate language, motor, play, and social interaction during the assessment. Some interpreters can also serve in the role of culture broker and mediator by bringing their perspectives on social and cultural issues and thus helping to elaborate the cultural formulation. The health team also may need to give some consideration to their own responses, biases, or blind spots as a part of the peer supervision and intervention discussion to reduce the risk of institutional racism (Guzder 2014).

Clinicians working in a transcultural team give consideration to acknowledging the impact of power differentials in their clinical approach. In addition to the presence of an interpreter or culture broker to facilitate communication and understanding, the alliance-building efforts are focused on safety in building dialogue, with due consideration given to issues of power in communication, including the right to be silent. Joining the family is reinforced throughout the process by using a circular seating arrangement of the family with the team of clinicians, by the introductory statement of some self-disclosure acknowledging the presence of team members from different backgrounds who have different perspectives (i.e., recognizing the multiplicity of perspectives that are all valuable), and by conveying an attitude of genuine interest and humility (Tervalon and Murray-Garcia 1998). In formulating treatment recommendations, the consultation aims to explore the attitudes of individuals and families, both positive and negative, and their expectations and experiences with the host country's mental health and other services. At times the family or individual may be involved with religious institutions, social service agencies, mentors, and community-based resources, or as technology allows, there may be frequent contact with family or significant others who live elsewhere, and these experiences are sought out. The relational or isolated state of these and other social networks plays a role in deciding on supports for building well-being and mental health for children and their families. Knowledge sharing between the primary health and social services care team, family, and the collaborative care consultation team is fundamental to the cultural consultation process. This communication allows co-construction of a meaningful care plan with care partners and families, exchange of knowledge, and acknowledgment of social or cultural ingredients in the context of mental health or illness. The team reviews feedback from the team providing care in an ongoing collaborative care process to review which recommendations have been helpful, which are less feasible, and which are either not useful or even detrimental. After the assessment, the collaborative care consultation team writes a child and family psychiatric assessment report with diagnostic impressions and recommendations for treatment. The cultural formulation outline (Lewis-Fernández et al. 2016) and other cultural formulation tools (Multicultural Mental Health Resource Centre n.d.b) are used in interviewing and as a guide to the interviewer, enhancing diagnosis and treatment planning. Cultural issues are included in this report, and cultural formulation is integrated and does not form a separate part of the report. The networking aspect of the consultation is used as an opportunity for sharing information and for knowledge transfer, network building, and peer development in this collaborative community and clinic setting.

Special Considerations in Treatment

Exploring cultural representations of mental health and illness provides context to the experience of illness as lived experience in individuals within a family system, as well as elaborations of cultural, collective, and social narratives relevant to the individual, family, and team. Unravelling the internal experience of mental distress facilitates the patient's potential to define, clarify, and/or reframe their difficulties in a narrative. Interviewing and storytelling, including the play and drawings by children during the interview, may help to promote, shift, contain, or define the meaning of presenting symptoms or suffering. These interviews may evoke or uncover relevant emotional responses, especially of unresolved and unexpressed grief and feelings of loss for cherished love objects, home, and aspects of belonging, as well as bring forth themes of protective responses, identity process, or possible social stigma preoccupations that the child or family may have experienced. Exploring representations of mental health difficulties can evoke memories and can open a family reflection on experiences that the children and their families may have encountered in their premigratory journeys. The team must be prepared to create a holding environment and cultural safety to support modulation of the disclosure process if needed. Treatment recommendations take into account what is most meaningful and supportive to well-being, as the patient and family formulate narratives in treatment that will offer more hope, and support identity processes and capacity for adaptation. The team hopes to encourage the patient and his or her family to approach his or her needs in the interview in a manner that draws on multiple and culturally diverse avenues of support and transformation.

In some cases, discussion about the diagnostic or clinical impression and treatment recommendations is sufficient, and the team bridges the referral back to their primary health and social services care team, with backup consultation available as needed to support community teams and resources. At other times, a brief clinical crisis intervention provided by the consulting team may be warranted to address acute child mental health symptoms, crises, high levels of distress in parent-child relational problems, or explicitly serious parental mental health issues. Since child and family well-being is promoted by helping to support children's sense of belonging at school and in the community, the team will foster connection to the network of psychosocial support provided by community clinic teams, extended family members (who sometimes are not in Canada), and associated community organizations as needed.

The goal in the acute setting for providing care to refugee youth presenting with mental health difficulties is to strengthen individual and family protective factors and resilience and to address mental health difficulties. Before exploring fragile or emotionally reactive subjects, it is necessary to engage the patient and his or her family by seeking and promoting strengths at an individual and systemic level, including by exploring nontraumatic elements of the family's past and current functioning and by mobilizing supports that can promote well-being. The therapist may wish to build on family traditions and cultural or spiritual practices that historically have promoted healing by welcoming the patient and family to share their views on a route to healing mental distress, including religious or spiritual avenues, or inviting traditional healers or spiritual supporters if needed. Supporting the patient and family to share their cultural, internal, and collective worlds, especially when these interiorities or collective narratives are not familiar or are misinterpreted or misunderstood, can be helpful. Preferences for treatment are also explored, and Western-based treatments can be recommended and traditional treatments valued simultaneously. The therapist needs to be flexible and ready to explore treatments that have not been considered compatible with host culture treatment frames. Family networks and other persons of support for the child and family are also included in the treatment, either in person or else symbolically or by telephone, when this is considered helpful. Part of understanding a family is to know who is interested in a therapeutic encounter, what it means to be sent to a clinic, what can or should be kept secret or unspoken, and how connection can be made to open a culturally safe discourse in the broadest sense of the interiority as well as the social construction of the person of the therapist and of the patient.

Expressive and supportive mental health therapies are integrated in this systemic approach. A systemic orientation is crucial, whether with a single patient or with an entire system, a point first made by Bowen (Bowen 1978). Initial treatment recommendations include a multidisciplinary approach, with supportive individual and family involvement and expressive creative arts therapies predominating. The orientation is pragmatic, resilience-focused, and also narrative-focused, with psychodynamic principles and family therapy basic to the initial clinical work of assessment and stabilization of mental health difficulties. Usually an interpreter (if needed and wished for) and sometimes also a culture broker (the latter, if possible, represented by clinicians with cultural knowledge and expertise in clinical psychiatry, psychology, or social work) are present to help with assessment and also delivery of these treatment modalities. Once a child and family's well-being are supported, additional depression, anxiety, or trauma-specific treatments, such as cognitive-behavioral therapy, are introduced as needed. Forming a positive first meeting (Minuchin 1974) and treatment is an engagement that also helps the family and sometimes other individuals within the family to seek further help in the future from care providers if needed.

Finally, the team takes into account that patients can be at risk of receiving insufficient or inadequate care because of language barriers, cultural distance, stigma, poverty, belief systems, discriminatory attitudes and social exclusion, distrust, and/or a lack of information about services. These issues are explored during the consultation process, though some issues may become clear only after knowing a family over a period of time. Finally, accepting that therapeutic knowledge is co-constructed and comes in stages is important to alliance building and to helping patients and their families develop skills to master affective distress, grief, and protection from the revival of toxic memories.

Community-based practitioners who refer their patients for assessment are generally strong advocates for their patients and families, and they foster a sense of belonging for clients to their geographically based community clinic and neighborhood. Families may become disorganized or distressed when dealing with such increased social stressors as school problems and refugee board hearings, and may need additional support at this time. There may be issues of trauma or domestic violence in the past or present that may be evident or secret, and the consulting team needs to be vigilant and think of broad considerations to decrease stressors and promote mental health and well-being. The team can actively support advocacy efforts and mediate around patient's needs with institutions, such as schools, legal services, health care, social services, and housing, and this can considerably decrease stressors and promote mental health and well-being. Finally, the cultural consultation space may provide a place for reflection for all partners around planning, needs, attitudes and practices that can support child and family well-being.

Clinical Vignette: Proximity-Based Collaborative Child Psychiatry and Community Mental Health Care Team

All clinical vignettes in this chapter use pseudonyms and are otherwise altered to protect anonymity.

Malika is an eight-year-old girl from Sub-Saharan Africa, brought to consultation by her social worker because her mother does not accept her daughter's diagnosis of an autistic spectrum disorder (ASD) and does not consent to her receiving specialized services at school to support youth with Autism Spectrum Disorder difficulties. As a result, Malika cannot receive specialized services at school to support her learning needs. During the assessment it is evident that Malika has a severe ASD, which interferes with her functioning. When the child psychiatrist inquiries about what people in Malika's mother's village would say about Malika, she becomes anxious and confides, "They would say she is a child of the river, this is very bad. You have to abandon them on the river side and walk away." She also evokes the fact that other people could suggest that Malika is possessed, which is also a frightening perspective. Finally, she recounts that Malika sings beautifully at church, and that she is very proud of this. The psychiatrist then suggests, smilingly, "Maybe Malika is an angel." Malika, who was until that moment mute and staring, begins to sing.

This brief vignette illustrates the complex work of meaning-making around mental health problems. Both our psychiatric diagnostic categories and traditional categories were perceived as harmful by Malika's mother. An alliance was established around co-constructing an alternate narrative, which centered on the recognition of her child's positive gift. Malika's mother was then able to trust the team and mediate a position of accepting the utility of an Autism Spectrum Disorder diagnosis and allowing her daughter to access school services, while asserting that the diagnosis did not describe her child, without any challenge by the team to force another narrative at this point in the bridge building.

Refugee Support on a Cultural Consultation Service (CCS)

The Cultural Consultation Service (CCS) was founded in 1999 at JGH in Montreal, Quebec, in one of the most diverse population regions of the city (Kirmayer, Guzder, and Rousseau 2014). The CCS was formed by a group of transcultural psychiatry practitioners with the crucial support of the JGH and its Department of Psychiatry as a pilot project offering consulting services for referring practitioners, agencies, or institutions seeking a consultation for individual patients, couples, families, groups, or communities on issues involving cultural factors in mental health care assessment and treatment. Most referrals came from family medicine clinics, refugee clinics, and hospital-based teams, although a significant number also came from social workers in child protection services and clinicians helping refugees going before the Immigration and Refugee Board, or community workers involved in removing legal barriers or repairing the effects of detention. Issues of language, ethnicity, racism, and religion often confused the diagnosis and treatment of patients with medical and mental health concerns. Of the first 401 referrals to the CCS, 164 (41%) were refugee claimants from Africa, the Caribbean, Latin America, South Asia, the Middle East, and East or Southeast Asia. Referring clinicians mostly had concerns about diagnosis, culturally appropriate treatment, and how to advance the refugee application process by helping the patient to meet the requirements of the Immigration and Refugee Board process. The refugees referred to the CCS were in a highly precarious position of constant uncertainty: they were often separated from family members who were left behind in dangerous circumstances and unable to reunite with them until the hearing process was resolved. Many reported being put into detention (either in the home country or in Canada), refused official refugee status, threatened with deportation, or stopped by the police. Refugees reported a wide range of traumatic experiences before arriving in Canada: persecution due to religion, political opinion or sexual orientation, and the experience of war atrocities. Many presented with acute depressive or posttraumatic stress disorder states related to sexual or physical victimization prior to arrival. For some, the migration route was lengthy and dangerous, travelling thousands of miles before reaching safety. Many of the patients had limited exposure to secular education and could not speak English or French, which created barriers to finding meaningful employment, thus impacting levels of poverty and undermining competency and creating shame and role dislocation, as well as creating barriers to accessing timely medical care and securing reasonable education for their children in Canada. Unemployment of fathers was a frequent stressor and created attendant issues of shame and vulnerability to depression. Male mental health issues and engagement of fathers presented additional challenges in offering care or treatment. Many women refugees had the additional burden of having endured gender-based violence (GBV) and had varied responses to past and present trauma. Silence was common within a context of complex cultural and collective oppression. Depression during pregnancy and postpartum depression were significant concerns, with refugee women being at higher risk of these disorders (Zelkowitz 1996). Of the 91 female refugee claimants assessed from 2000 to 2013, 80 percent reported GBV, with 39 percent of these making GBV their principal reason for seeking asylum.

Evaluating refugees is one of the principle mandates of the CCS. Cultural consultation requires collaborating with many other professionals, including in the triage process prior to the first meeting with the client, when the service prepares the referring file, gathers consents, decides with staff who should be at the interview, and records clinical information. The service has an experienced triage secretary who books interpreters and coordinates the setting of the interview. The team may meet with the patient or his or her family only once, but up to three evaluative sessions may be needed, depending on the complexity of the consultation. Members of the referring clinical team are strongly encouraged to attend, and patients usually come with a referring agency or therapist, with appointments made to accommodate the referring source and family. When available, linguistic interpreters from the CCSs and the official Quebec government banks of interpreters as well as culture brokers (from the CCS's own network of culture interpreters, also known as culture brokers) situate beliefs and behaviors in family, social, and cultural context. The collaboration with an interpreter and meeting with the interpreter is a necessary foundational aspect of this service provision model. Once any given clinical evaluation is complete, the CCS team meets with the referring team, often accompanied by students from family therapy, interdisciplinary researchers, clinical observers, and others, for a discussion and clinical case conference. At this time the CCS consultant and the referring clinician work collaboratively to refine the diagnosis, clarify cultural aspects of the case, and finalize treatment recommendations. Summaries of all stages of the evaluation are typed and sent to the referring clinical team. On rare occasions, a patient's situation remains problematic over the long-term and is referred to the CCS for a second or third evaluation (Kirmayer et al. 2014).

While the CCS consultation places the patient at the center of the clinical encounter, there is a parallel focus on supporting the referring clinician's alliance with the patient and promoting a knowledge transfer model informed from multiple sources including the *DSM-5* version of the cultural formulation (APA 2013). Knowledge transfer in this context refers to exchanging knowledge with the referring clinician and attendees of the CCS joint meeting about their patient's culture and worldview, ways to address their concerns, and empowerment strategies for their continued progress providing care in the community. The clinical interview does not follow a structured inquiry, but rather covers a flexible outline of topics, including aspects of development, identity, countertransference, treatment alliance, social well-being of patients and families, avoidance of stereotyping, and informing multiple aspects of beliefs and of social, systemic, and collective aspects impinging on familial systems, identity and cultural parameters. Each patient's unique cultural formulation is relevant to a complex generational and social context of the patient, family, and community. It typically takes considerable time to model and teach this approach and its core skills. Some consultations may be lengthy clinical evaluations, with each new case usually requiring two to three hours, not necessarily over one session, depending on the needs of the patient and referring source. With children or families, a longer period than this may be needed. Research to evaluate the outcome of these consultations is built into the assessment (Kirmayer et al. 2015).

A fundamental role of the CCS is a focus on advocacy for refugee applicants, accepted refugees, and persons of precarious status and their families, to improve access to the basic necessities of life, such as food, shelter, work permits or welfare, medical care, legal counsel, and designated representatives (assigned individuals who represent a person's best interests in court when mental illness is of such severity that it precludes an understanding of the legal process or participation in the hearing), access to critical interventions, and language-specific counseling or therapy. Part of the advocacy intention is to remove impediments to safety, connect with social networks, support adaptation and skill acquisition, and address impediments to accessing care, such as language barriers or cultural distance and differences. The CCS links patients to social supports, writes letters for immigration hearings, and sometimes does home visits to evaluate how patients are functioning in their real-life settings.

There is a need to spend time to allow a careful review of migration trauma and dilemmas, with the clinician managing the interview to avoid intrusive interviewing that could retraumatize the patient or provoke a detrimental response. For many patients, speaking through a professional interpreter is a new experience, which facilitates cultural safety and communication in their mother tongue and removes their family members from the complex role of interpreter. Since the presence of an interpreter may increase patient anxiety about confidentiality, especially in small communities where the interpreter might be encountered in their circle, the patient is always asked permission to proceed with the interpreter, and interpreter confidentiality is discussed prior to the onset of interviews and then with the patient. These steps reinforce cultural safety, build the therapeutic alliance and gain trust, and facilitate the disclosure of difficult issues, permitting a richer understanding of the patient's predicament, and contributing to directing the team to steps that may alleviate the patient's distress (Jarvis 2014).

Other problems facing refugees transcend any single setting and arise more generally from the historical fabric of the society and culture in Canada, including institutional racism and acculturation challenges (Jarvis 2017). The assessment explores how patients negotiate cultural diversity, religious orientations in a Quebec currently in the midst of a debate regarding secularism, and their perceptions of the host society's response to their cultural difference or their difficulties adjusting to their new country. Despite historical legacies of slavery and colonialism being embedded in modern Euro-American societies, this is largely neglected in noncultural psychiatry-oriented psychiatric evaluations (Miles and Torres 2007). In contrast, these issues are a fundamental part of the CCS focus on cultural safety as a complex agenda, especially for refugees and immigrants. Despite the positive adjustment of the majority of immigrants to Canada and the highly integrated diversity of Canadians, the CCS often serves immigrants or refugees at risk as they proceed in the complex psychosocial process linked with immigration, especially as all immigration involves a progressive generational acculturation and identity process that Akhtar has described in the framework of a "third individuation" (Akhtar 1995).

In addition, some referrals are requested by schools or other institutions that are themselves grappling with broader issues of individual and collective identity and generational transitions in a contemporary francophone secular Quebec in Canada. Minority clients are processing agendas of generational transition as well as dynamics of individual and collective identities. The interplay of these broader issues of social strength and vulnerability and their effects on patient well-being requires careful attention in the clinical setting.

The key issues of intolerance, racism, or power differentials are opened if the patient allows this to emerge in the assessment interview, whether around the refugee child and/or family's experiences coping with the dissonances of acculturation or with racism impacting power and gender relations. These agendas sometimes compound or overlap as impediments to healing their pre- or postmigration experiences of violence, trauma, and loss. Additionally, while strong voices within the dominant culture of Quebec may define its well-being in secular contexts, many refugees with strong religious worldviews and gender roles inherent to their strengths or embedded as cultural values and identity formation have to negotiate their integration with a society in the process of affirming gender equality and questioning the place of religious practice and symbols within the public sphere (Jarvis 2017). These are the ingredients that also sustain many societies, and in any case are private and individual, yet socially define agendas of families and individuals. Many immigrants have been sustained by strong religious values; others have additional internalized family roles or identities and beliefs that help to cope or frame their suffering. Finally, the healer is also part of this connectivity, and talking to a doctor under any circumstance involves inherent power imbalance in the clinical relationship. There are additional resistances to disclosure that may place an additional burden on refugees seeking care. These may involve their experiences of negative reception from the host society or devaluation of their background, language, culture or religion, as well as refugees' precarious status of belonging and legal struggles. These experiences may undermine their willingness to disclose and ability to trust the professionals, impeding their actively participating in the evaluation. Striving in the therapeutic space for a sense of cultural safety remains fundamental to the consulting process. When a rapport is built, the care team may be able to access and understand the patient's migration trajectories, premigration trauma, and family or trauma issues, including issues of racism or power differentials. Disclosure may present an opportunity for healing or shifting emotional states, reframing, and building a more hopeful narrative. The CCS strives to open rather than to restrict access to these delicate issues of religion, identity, racism, acculturation strain, and trauma by acknowledging historical inequalities that may exist and attempting to find a ground where the power differential in the evaluation is more equitable. The acknowledgment by the clinical interviewer of these aspects of experience and of cultural strain is fundamental to cultural formulation and alliance building and is a the goal of the CCS consultation. The Cultural Consultation formulation and recommendations in the service of patients in distress are made with recommendations to support safety, resilience, adaptive capacity, and coping with mental health issues, identity, systemic conflict, grief, and trauma. In addition, once refugees achieve refugee status and the attendant stress associated with this uncertainty and precarity is resolved, a new chapter of life and a positive shift in well-being can be nurtured.

Cultural Consultation Service Vignette

A mother of South Asian origin with school-aged children presented with her referring community social worker for an evaluation of her acute deterioration in mental health, which included threats to kill her children and herself. Her decompensation occurred after the Immigration and Refugee Board refused to grant her asylum. She initially refused to speak when seen for consultation by a male CCS psychiatrist. She also refused an interpreter, as her prior disclosure of her rape to a community helper had undermined her trust and reputation in her community. Her lawyer was appealing her case, but her fears of deportation had reawakened other fears, which she eventually shared in a second consultation with a female CCS clinician who spoke one of her mother tongues.

During the consultation, she disclosed premigratory marital rape and gender violence, as well as postmigratory rape while in detention in the United States on her way to Canada, and stigma as a result of these experiences within her own ethnic group. She was also experiencing complex unresolved grief as both of her beloved parents had died since sending her to North America. Since their deaths, she had remained in a dissociated "unreal" state in relation to her parents' deaths. Her suicide and murder threats represented in part her thoughts and wishes to reunite with her parents at times, as well as a reflection of her response to the Immigration and Refugee Board deportation decision, which precipitated her acute fear, rage, panic, and anguish. She had lost any belief in her religious community, and her social isolation compounded her sense of panic and alienation, which had subsequently progressed to homicide and suicide threats.

The consultation team approached her mourning and lack of a sense of safety by reinforcing her systemic and collective identifications, which included positive messages of her parents. They organized a plan to keep her children safe with a goal of avoiding the additional catastrophic reaction, which she would likely experience if her children were removed to placement in child welfare services. The interview proceeded with a focus on her family, including her parents as "ghosts," who entered into dialogue with the patient on her current predicament. As they had been a source of refuge during her flight from domestic violence and rape in her country of origin, the interview was in part a dialogue seeking their advice as internalized parts of herself.

During a subsequent consultation visit, the team focused also on her therapeutic alliance with her referring worker with whom she had a good relationship. In addition, the intervention included advice on the adjustment and monitoring by her primary care clinician of her antidepressant medication for the acute treatment of her depression and posttraumatic stress disorder (PTSD) symptoms, and bearing witness to her narrative of trauma and grief. Part of the intervention was coming up with ways to support and contain her grief, using a ritual of remembering her deceased parents in order to reinforce hope and to strengthen her positive identification with their nurturing role. School and daycare supports were put in place to increase supervision and support her parenting burden and to reduce the isolation of her children. Legal consultation by referring the patient to an attorney who could help her with her appeal to remain in Canada on humanitarian grounds was part of the CCS advocacy role.

This vignette illustrates the complex and often high-stakes clinical challenges of a cultural consultation. The consultant intervenes to reinforce a preexisting positive therapeutic alliance and build on cultural safety parameters, assists the patient to therapeutically disclose her traumatic events in a modulated fashion, formulates a treatment plan to support the patient's and children's mental health and safety, and advocates for the patient and her family's continued safety and well-being.

Conclusion

This chapter presents the work of two culturally responsive mental health care services in Montreal, a tertiary care setting based in the Jewish General Hospital (the Cultural Consultation Service), and a primary care setting in community mental health clinics (the Proximity-Based Collaborative Child Psychiatry and Community Mental Health Care Team). These two models of cultural consultation are part of a network of Montreal-based clinical, research, and teaching services aimed at addressing mental health and social well-being in a culturally diverse society and offering training and knowledge transfer to referring clinicians and their teams. Both services have required individual "champions" and institutional support to sustain their existence.

The CCS started as a clinical service with a research structure supported by a federal government health research grant administered by Health Canada, which provided the resources to initially develop the CCS so that intake and follow-up questionnaires and a process evaluation of the process of consultation could be conducted. Patient care was provided by clinicians who were also researchers, and a formative evaluation was conducted on service delivery and implementation, reviewing the outcomes of the first 100 cases referred to the service. Ongoing challenges included sustaining funding for the service within its institutional base, as is the case for other cultural programs in mental health around the world, as well as ongoing efforts to incorporate the use of the cultural axis in mainstream psychiatric clinical approaches. The service's supraregional status allows it to provide services to patients regardless of their geographical location. Successful implementation of a service like the CCS requires a skilled intake coordinator, who will schedule consultation appointments and reach out to and maintain contact with the network of linguistic interpreters and culture brokers. Funding requirements are modest in the Quebec setting if the key position of intake coordinator is funded by the home institution, as institutional space, clinician, and linguistic services are covered by public health care services, and culture brokers who are not otherwise employed as professional interpreters volunteer their services to the CCS.

The proximity-based collaborative child psychiatry and community mental health care team is currently evaluating its youth mental health collaborative care model as part of a larger multisite grant supporting culturally informed and responsive mental health care services in Montreal, Quebec (Nadeau et al. 2009). These proximity-based services appear to allow for improved access to mental health care for a community clinic's multiethnic clientele. Promoting proximity-based, accessible, and culturally safe mental health services for children, youth, and families is an ongoing focus of their work.

The objective benefits of models of mental health care services that embrace sociocultural factors need further evaluation and documentation. Evidence and research on the inclusion of cultural formulation–based models of cultural psychiatry and mental health will allow stakeholders in mental health care service delivery to make informed decisions about the provision of adequate mental health care services for refugees, as well as ways to reduce barriers to care and to promote the well-being of minorities at risk in our diverse society. A significant effort to this end has been started by the MHCC *Case for Diversity* report (McKenzie et al. 2016). Advocacy by, and collaboration between, multiple partners in care remains fundamental to the policy approaches and teaching orientation promoted by these services (Kirmayer, Kronick, and Rousseau 2018).

References

Agic, Branka, Kwame McKenzie, Andrew Tuck, and Michael Antwi. 2016. "Supporting the Mental Health of Refugees to Canada." Ottawa: Mental Health Commission of Canada. https://www.mentalhealthcommission.ca/sites/default/files/2016-01-25_refugee_mental_health_backgrounder_0.pdf.

Akhtar, Salman. 1995. "A Third Individuation: Immigration, Identity and the Psychoanalytic Process." *Journal of the American Psychoanalytic Association.* 43, no. 4: 1051–1084.

American Psychiatric Association. 2013. *Diagnostic and Statistical Manual of Mental Disorders.* 5th ed. Arlington: American Psychiatric Association.

Bibeau, Gilles, Alice M. Chan-Yip, Margaret Lock, Cécile Rousseau, and Carlo Sterlin. 1992. *La Santé Mentale et Ses Visages: Un Québec Pluriethnique au Quotidien.* Chicoutimi: Gaetan Morin.

Bowen, Murray. 1978. *Family Therapy in Clinical Practice.* New York: Aranson.

Canadian Museum of Immigration at Pier 21. n.d.a. "Immigration Act, 1976." https://pier21.ca/research/immigration-history/immigration-act-1976.

Canadian Museum of Immigration at Pier 21. n.d.b. "Multiculturalism Act. 1988." https://pier21.ca/research/immigration-history/canadian-multiculturalism-act-1988.

Canadian Task Force on Mental Health Issues Affecting Immigrants and Refugees. 1988. *After the Door Has Been Opened: Mental Health Issues Affecting Immigrants and Refugees in Canada.* Ottawa: Multiculturalism and Citizenship Canada.

CBC News. 2016. "Liberal Government Fully Restores Refugee Health Care Program." February 18, 2016. http://www.cbc.ca/news/politics/mcallum-philpott-interim-federal-health-program-refugees-1.3453397.

Fazel, Mina, Jeremy Wheeler, and John Danesh. 2005. "Prevalence of Serious Mental Disorders in 7,000 Refugees Resettled in Western Countries: A Systematic Review." *Lancet* 365, no. 9467: 1309–1314.

Government of Canada. n.d.a. "Canada, a History of Refuge." https://www.canada.ca/en/immigration-refugees-citizenship/services/refugees/canada-role/timeline.html.

Government of Canada. n.d.b. "How Canada's Refugee System Work." https://www.canada.ca/en/immigration-refugees-citizenship/services/refugees/canada-role.html.

Government of Canada. n.d.c. "Health Care-Refugees." https://www.canada.ca/en/immigration-refugees-citizenship/services/refugees/help-within-canada/health-care.html.

Government of Canada. n.d.d. "Designated Countries of Origin Policy." https://www.canada.ca/en/immigration-refugees-citizenship/services/refugees/claim-protection-inside-canada/apply/designated-countries-policy.html.

Gouvernement du Quebec, Ministère de la Santé et des Services Sociaux. 1989. *Politique de Santé Mentale.* Québec: Gouvernement du Québec. http://publications.msss.gouv.qc.ca/msss/document-001741/?&date=DESC&type=politique&critere=type.

Guzder, Jaswant. 2014. "Institutional Racism as a Seminal Concept of Cultural Competency Training." In *Critical Psychiatry and Mental Health: Exploring the Work of Suman Fernando in Clinical Practice,* edited by Roy Moodley and Martha Ocampo, 111–123. London: Routledge.

Hansson, Emily, Andrew Tuck, Steve Lurie, and Kwame McKenzie for the Task Group of the Services Systems Advisory Committee, Mental Health Commission of Canada. 2010. *Improving Mental Health Services for Immigrant, Refugee, Ethno-cultural and Racialized Groups: Issues and Options for Service Improvement.* https://www.mentalhealthcommission.ca/English/document/457/improving-mental-health-services-immigrant-refugee-ethno-cultural-and-racialized-groups.

Hong Fook Mental Health Association. n.d. "Hong Fook." http://www.hongfook.ca.

Jack, Dana C., and Alisha Ali, eds. 2010. *Silencing the Self across Cultures: Depression and Gender in the Social World,* 1st ed. Oxford: Oxford University Press.

Jarvis, G. Eric. 2014. "Cultural Consultation in General Hospital Psychiatry." In *Cultural Consultation: Encountering the Other in Mental Health Care,* edited by Laurence J. Kirmayer, Jaswant Guzder, and Cécile Rousseau, 293–314. New York: Springer.

Jarvis, G. Eric. 2017. "Negotiating Differences of Culture and Language in the Hospital Setting." *Annales Medico-psychologiques* 175, no. 6: 567–572.

Kareem, Jafar, and Ronald Littlewood, eds. 1999. *Intercultural Therapy: Themes, Interpretations and Practice,* 2nd ed. Hoboken: Wiley Blackwell.

Kirmayer, Laurence J., Jaswant Guzder, Mimi Israel, Suparna Choudhury, Nathalie Dinh, Nancy Frasure-Smith, Ian Gold, et al. G. 2013. "Letter: The Values Charter Would Be Unhealthy." *The Gazette,* October 15, 2013. http://www.montrealgazette.com/health/Letter+values+charter+would+unhealthy/9033600/story.html.

Kirmayer, Laurence J., Jaswant Guzder, and Cécile Rousseau, eds. 2014. *Cultural Consultation: Encountering the Other in Mental Health Care.* New York: Springer.

Kirmayer Laurence J., Rachel Kronich, and Cécile Rousseau. 2018. "Advocacy as Key to Structural Competency in Psychiatry." *JAMA Psychiatry* 75, no. 2: 119–120.

Kirmayer, Laurence J., Lavanya Narasiah, Marie Muñoz, Meb Rashid, Andrew G. Ryder, Jaswant Guzder, Ghayda Hassan, Cécile Rousseau, and Kevin Pottie, for the Canadian Collaboration for Immigrant and Refugee Health.

2011. "Common Mental Health Problems in Immigrants and Refugees: General Approach in Primary Care." *Canadian Medical Association Journal* 183, no. 12: E959–E967.

Kirmayer, Laurence J., Cécile Rousseau, G. Eric Jarvis, and Jaswant Guzder. 2015. "The Cultural Context of Clinical Assessment." In *Psychiatry*, 4th ed., edited by Allan Tasman, Jerald Kay, Jeffrey A. Lieberman, Michael B. First, and Michelle R. Riba, 56–70. New York: John Wiley & Sons.

Knowles, Valerie. 2016. *Strangers at Our Gates: Canadian Immigration and Immigration Policy, 1540–2015*, 4th ed. Toronto: Dundern Press.

Lewis-Fernández, Roberto, Neil K. Aggarwal, Ladson Hinton, Devon E. Hinton, and Laurence J. Kirmayer. 2016. *DSM-5 Handbook on the Cultural Formulation Interview*. Washington, DC: American Psychiatric Press.

Marwah, Sonal. 2014. *Refugee Health Care Cuts in Canada: System Level Costs, Risks and Responses*. Wellesley Institute Advancing Urban Health. http://www.wellesleyinstitute.com/publications/refugee-health-care-cuts-in-canada-system-level-costs-risks-and-responses/.

McKenzie, Kwame, Branka Agic, Andrew Tuck, and Michael Anywi. 2016. *The Case for Diversity: Building the Case to Improve Mental Health Services for Immigrant, Refugee, Ethnocultural and Racialized Populations*. Report to the Mental Health Commission of Canada. https://www.mentalhealthcommission.ca/sites/default/files/2016-10/case_for_diversity_oct_2016_eng.pdf.

Measham, Toby, and Cécile Rousseau. 2010. "Family Disclosure of War Trauma to Children." *Traumatology* 16, no. 4: 85–96.

Mental Health Commission of Canada. 2012. *Changing Directions, Changing Lives: The Mental Health Strategy for Canada*. Calgary, AB: Author. https://www.mentalhealthcommission.ca/sites/default/files/MHStrategy_Strategy_ENG.pdf.

Mental Health Resource Centre. n.d.b. "Cultural Formulation." http://www.multiculturalmentalhealth.ca/clinical-tools/cultural-formulation/.

Miles, Robert, and Rudy Torres. 2007. "Does 'Race' Matter? Transatlantic Perspectives on Racism after 'Race Relations.'" In *Race and Racialization: Essential Readings*, edited by Tania Das Gupta, Carl E. James, Roger C.A. Maaka, Grace-Edward Galabuzi, and Chris Andersen, 65–73. Toronto: Canadian Scholar's Press Inc.

Ministère de la Santé et des Services Sociaux, Gouvernement du Québec, *Plan d'Action en Santé Mentale 2005–2010: la Force des Liens*. http://publications.msss.gouv.qc.ca/msss/document-000786/.

Ministère de la Santé et des Services Sociaux, Gouvernement du Québec, *Faire Ensemble et Autrement, Plan d'Action en Santé Mentale 2015–2020*. http://publications.msss.gouv.qc.ca/msss/fichiers/2015/15-914-04W.pdf.

Minuchin, Salvador. 1974. *Families and Family Therapy*. Cambridge: Harvard University Press.

Multicultural Mental Health Resource Centre. n.d.a. "Welcome to the MMHRC: Responding to Cultural Diversity in Mental Health." http://www.multiculturalmentalhealth.ca.

Multicultural Mental Health Resource Centre. n.d.b. "Cultural Formulation." http://www.multiculturalmentalhealth.ca/clinical-tools/cultural-formulation/.

Nadeau, Lucie, Cécile Rousseau, Yves Séguin, and Nicolas Moreau. 2009. "Évaluation Préliminaire d'un Projet de Soins Concerté en Santé Mentale Jeunesse à Montréal: Faire Face à l'Incertitude Institutionelle et Culturelle." *Santé Mentale au Québec* 34, no. 1: 127–142.

National Assembly. 2013. *Bill 60: Charter Affirming the Values of State Secularism and Religious Neutrality and of Equality between Women and Men, and Providing a Framework for Accommodation Requests.* Québec Official Publisher. http://www.assnat.qc.ca/en/travaux-parlementaires/projets-loi/projet-loi-60-40-1.html?appelant=MC.

Rousseau, Cécile, Toby Measham, and Marie-Rose Moro. 2011. "Working with Interpreters in Child Mental Health." *Child and Adolescent Mental Health* 16, no. 1: 55–59.

Ruiz-Casares, Monica, Janet Cleveland, Youssef Oulhote, Catherine Dunkley-Hickin, and Cécile Rousseau. 2016. "Knowledge of Healthcare Coverage for Refugee Claimants: Results from a Survey of Health Service Providers in Montreal." *PLoS One* 11, no. 1. doi: 10.1371/journal.pone.0146798.

Schain, Martin A. 2018. "Shifting Tides: Radical-Right Populism and Immigration Policy in Europe and the United States." Migration Policy Institute. https://www.migrationpolicy.org/research/radical-right-immigration-europe-united-states.

Shingler, Benjamin. 2017. "Quebec's Face-Covering Law Heads for Constitutional Challenge." *CBC News*, November 7, 2017. https://www.cbc.ca/news/canada/montreal/quebec-niqab-bill-62-legal-challenge-face-covering-1.4390962.

Shingler, Benjamin. 2018. "Judge Suspends Face-Covering Ban, Says It Appears to Violate the Charter." *CBC News*, June 28, 2018. https://www.cbc.ca/news/canada/montreal/quebec-bill-62-face-covering-july1-1.4724863.

Shingler, Benjamin. 2019. "Ban on Religious Symbols, Education Reforms Top Agenda as National Assembly Resumes." *CBC News*, February 5, 2019. https://www.cbc.ca/news/canada/montreal/caq-legault-national-assembly-1.5005263.

Statistics Canada. n.d.a. "Census Program." https://www12.statcan.gc.ca/census-recensement/index-eng.cfm.

Statistics Canada. n.d.b. "Visible Minority and Population Group Reference Guide, Census of population, 2016." https://www12.statcan.gc.ca/census-recensement/2016/ref/guides/006/98-500-x2016006-eng.cfm.

Statistics Canada. 2017. "October 25, The Daily, Immigration and Ethnocultural Diversity: Key Results from the 2016 Census." https://www150.statcan.gc.ca/n1/daily-quotidien/171025/dq171025b-eng.htm.

Statistics Canada. 2018. "The Daily, Police-Reported Hate Crime, 2017." https://www150.statcan.gc.ca/n1/daily-quotidien/181129/dq181129a-eng.htm.

Tervalon, Melanie, and Jann Murray-García. 1998. "Cultural Humility versus Cultural Competence: A Critical Distinction in Defining Physician Training

Outcomes in Multicultural Education." *Journal of Health Care for the Poor and Underserved* 9, no. 2: 117–125.

United Nations High Commissioner for Refugees (UNHCR). 2010. *Convention and Protocol Relating to the Status of Refugees.* https://www.unhcr.org/protection/basic/3b66c2aa10/convention-protocol-relating-status-refugees.html.

Zelkowitz, Phyllis. 1996. "Childbearing and Women's Mental Health." *Transcultural Psychiatry* 33: 391–412. https://doi.org/10.1177/136346159603300402.

"We're Not Asking for Handouts!" Voices of Women Refugees from Africa on Rapid Economic Self-Sufficiency in the United States

Badiah Haffejee and Jean F. East

Introduction

Forced displacement resulting from war, persecution, and political conflict is devastating and leaves women refugees, including women refugees from Africa, especially vulnerable. The United States has a history of providing refuge for those fleeing dire situations, and in recent years, it resettled between 70,000 and 80,000 refugees every year (Refugee Admissions Report 2017). In fact, in response to the global refugee crisis, President Barack Obama increased the admissions ceiling from 85,000 in fiscal year (FY) 2016 to 110,000 in FY 2017 (Zong and Batalova 2017). This chapter qualitatively examines the lived experiences of 20 African women refugees attempting to meet the demands of economic self-sufficiency in Colorado.

The availability of gender disaggregated data by country of origin is limited (Martin and Yankay 2012); however, in FY 2015, a total of 69,933 refugees were resettled in the United States (Refugee Admissions Report 2016). Of these, 22,472 (32%) refugees were from various parts of the African continent. In FY 2016, a total of 84,995 refugees were admitted, of which 31,625 (37%) were from Africa (Refugee Admissions Report 2016). Of the 84,995 resettled in FY 2016, Colorado resettled a total of 2,420 refugees, including women refugees from Africa (Refugee Admissions Report 2016). While the increase in the admissions ceiling by the Obama administration marked the largest yearly increase since 1990, in January 2017, the new administration issued Executive Order 13780 ("Protecting the Nation from Foreign Terrorist Entry into the United States") to reduce the admission ceiling from 110,000 to 50,000, and to halt refugee resettlement for 120 days (Zong and Batalova 2017). Within the first few months of FY 2017, 42,414 refugees were admitted—a few thousand short of the new admissions ceiling (Zong and Batalova 2017). Of these admitted refugees, 13,612 (32%) were from the Democratic Republic of the Congo, Somalia, and Eritrea (Refugee Admissions Report 2017). Following several months of winding through the federal court, Executive Order 13780 took effect. These policy changes significantly curtailed U.S. resettlement efforts, especially from Muslim majority countries, which include Libya, Somalia, and Sudan (Zong and Batalova 2017).

Resettlement offers African women refugees and their families a sense of security and an opportunity to live to their full human potential. However, the task of resettlement is immense and poses daunting challenges for these women refugees who have experienced unimaginable horrors of war, poverty, gender-based violence, and entrapment in refugee camps for protracted periods. Yet relatively little is understood about the ways that African women refugees, who have limited resources when they first resettle to the United States, are attempting to move to economic self-sufficiency, adjust, and cope in their new setting. Critical race theory (CRT) is used to elucidate the lived and racialized experiences, as well as the multiple dimensions and complexities of the resettlement context as experienced by 20 women refugees from Africa.

Critical Race Theory

Critical race theory has its origins in radical feminism and critical legal studies, both of which draw from critical theory (Delgado and Stefancic 2001). Critical race theorists/scholars such as Derrick Bell were "deeply distressed over the slow pace of racial reform in the United States" (Delgado and Stefancic 2000, xvi). In 1989, gaining intellectual insight from the Civil Rights Movement, critical legal studies, and feminist studies, critical race scholars began organizing. Unified by the belief that racism is permanent and deeply embedded in U.S. society, CRT contests the legitimization of ahistoricism, meritocracy, neutrality, and objectivity.

As a theoretical framework, CRT opposes the experiences of the dominant group as normative and is anchored in the unique histories and experiences of persons of color (Crenshaw et al. 1995). Additionally, it amplifies the ongoing pursuit for racial equity (Delgado and Stefancic 2001), which, in the United States, challenges racial stratification and racial oppression in society (Howard-Hamilton 2003).

While not exhaustive, according to Delgado and Stefancic (2001), the six central tenets of CRT are as follows: (1) "Racism is a normal part of American life," despite espoused, institutional ideals regarding social justice and equity; (2) "colorblindness and meritocracy systematically disadvantage people of color"; (3) legitimizing of "voices of color" and their unique perspectives, their understanding of being racially minoritized, and their insights into the operation of racism; (4) and emphasis on "intersectionality," which allows for the exploration of difference within and between groups and takes into account issues such as historical and sociopolitical context while maintaining awareness of racial inequalities; (5) "interests convergence," which is the process whereby the dominant group will encourage and tolerate "racial advances" for persons of color only when they support "white self-interests"; and (6) "revisionist history," or the idea that American history should be closely analyzed and reinterpreted instead of accepting it as truth and at face value (Delgado and Stefancic 2001, 7–9).

The lived experiences of African women refugees who have resettled in the United States can be contextualized through theories such as CRT. CRT explains the experiences of group invisibility, feelings of marginality, and the powerlessness that African women refugees experience while integrating into life in the United States. Second, CRT is one vehicle with which professionals can look beyond the world as it is experienced by dominant society and consider the lived and racialized experiences of African women refugees, whose perspectives are often left out or pushed to the margins. This is important to consider when examining these women's histories and public policy and is key when contextualizing the experience of African women refugees who depend on government provisions to survive (Haffejee 2016; Haffejee and East 2016). Third, CRT utilizes counternarrative to challenge the hegemonic knowledge (Delgado and Stefancic 2001) of African women refugees. Through these counter narratives, African women refugees' untold stories are elucidated—a powerful means to create meaning and challenge the myths (Howard-Hamilton 2003) about African women refugees. Listening to those stories and drawing on this knowledge informs the development of culturally appropriate policies, interventions, and practices. Fourth, CRT provides insight into the social, economic, and political inequities as experienced by

African women refugees. Fifth, CRT exposes the underlying oppressive structures and the racist ideologies endemic in refugee policy, those that continue to adversely impact African women refugees. Lastly, CRT reveals how racialized refugee policy and citizenship distinctions (i.e., refugee classification) serve as a means of controlling and relegating African women refugees to the fringes of U.S. society.

A Qualitative Study of Women Refugees from Africa

This chapter is based on a qualitative study carried out in 2015 of 20 women refugees from Africa. Purposive and snowball sampling were employed. The principal selection criteria included African women refugees who: (1) had lived in a refugee camp, (2) had a moderate understanding of English, (3) had lived in the United States for a minimum of nine months and a maximum of 36 months, and (4) had feasible means of communication (i.e., a private phone) with the researcher (the first author) as an interviewee. The time frame criteria for being in the United States ensured that participants had some experience navigating the demands of refugee policy for early economic self-sufficiency.

Data were collected with Institutional Review Board approval. The study involved an in-depth, minimally structured interview that lasted approximately 1.5 to 2 hours at a location that allowed for privacy. All participants received $25 for their time.

Transcripts were analyzed utilizing Interpretative Phenomenological Analysis (IPA) and followed the IPA guidelines outlined by Smith and colleagues (2009). IPA is concerned with the subjective meanings rather than objective accounts and is a dynamic process in which the interpretations and analysis of the researcher are vital (Smith et al. 2009). The data analysis resulted in two core categories: premigration and postmigration lived experiences. We report on the themes that relate most specifically to the challenges in meeting the demands of refugee policy.

Refugee Policy

As covered in Part 1 of this book, refugee policy has played a critical role in the experience of refugees in this country. The Refugee Act of 1980 provides funding to states, which then contract with local nonprofit organizations. The provisions provided by the Act include: (1) cash assistance for eight months, (2) employment training and job placement, and (3) funds to the agency for case management/support for provision of social services, including programs fostering English-language acquisition. In addition, the Refugee Act states that cash assistance is suspended if the refugee refuses to participate in either a social service program or an appropriate employment offer.

In a broad sense, U.S. refugee policy aims to rapidly integrate refugees into life in the United States. Case management and social services are provided to help in the transition, acknowledging the many potential barriers, such as language and employability. In reality, the policy's main focus is to promote the economic independence of refugees (Kramer 2011). As Eleanor Ott points out, "Economic self-sufficiency is the first point mentioned in the Act and its reauthorization in 2002, and the idea of self-sufficiency is reiterated eleven more times in the legislation" (Ott 2002,10). Not only is economic self-sufficiency foundational in current refugee policy but also attaining such "self-sufficiency" is unrealistically expected to be accomplished in a short period of time, eight months. The eligibility period for assistance has gone from 36 months prior to 1988 to 8 months as of 1992 (Office of Refugee Resettlement [ORR] 2012). Adult refugees are expected to gain human capital and language skills and to earn enough money to move away from dependency and public funds (Haffejee and East 2016). Moreover, refugee policy mandates that refugees enter the workforce within 90 days after their arrival (Sossou et al. 2008). In addition to the provisions aimed to support self-sufficiency, there is also a provision in the policy that refugees must pay back their travel expenses to this country within 42 months, an added burden to enter the job market quickly and become economically stable.

Economic Self-Sufficiency from a Critical Race Theory Lens

In the United States, fostering economic self-sufficiency is the cornerstone of much social welfare policy, including refugee policy. This is most evident in the Personal Responsibility and Work Reconciliation Act of 1996 and in the implementation of the corresponding program, Temporary Assistance to Needy Families (TANF). Adults who receive TANF have a maximum time limit of five years to draw on services and cash assistance, though in some states, these limits are even more stringent. Welfare policy is embedded in the values of the United States, which include meritocracy, personal responsibility, and success as defined in economic terms. While one intent of refugee policy is humanitarian, the policy provisions clearly delineate that a refugee or refugee family's primary responsibility is to gain employment so as not to be dependent on government assistance. Whether it is refugee policy or welfare policy, the primary framework is "market justice" (Kneipp 2000, 262); that is, the market economy is where someone succeeds. Little attention is given to social or personal conditions that can influence economic outcomes. As noted in CRT, a market justice framework negates the reality of the presence and influence of racism. The focus on workforce participation and market-oriented logic in this case becomes a means of further subjugating women refugees from Africa by not taking into account the structural and racial barriers they may face. This oppressive system is especially evident in the mandates to economic self-sufficiency that require adult refugees, including African women refugees, to enter the workforce 30–90 days after arrival. The system continues to view women refugees from Africa as a homogenous group and fails to consider the historical (e.g., precolonial and colonial), gender, cultural, and political (e.g., the conflict and violence) oppression of these women.

It is also important to recognize that economic self-sufficiency is a myth (East 1998). To explore this myth, we need to examine the concept of dependency, the counterpart of self-reliance or self-sufficiency. The construction of dependency carries multiple meanings (Fraser and Gordon 1994). Dependency is considered a natural part of the development process; for example, children are expected to be dependent on adults. In the psychological literature, dependency was often applied to women as a psychological trait (Stiver 1991). In the discourse of public welfare and refugee policy, dependency is the economic state of needing government assistance. It is this dependency that refugee policy aims to avoid. From a CRT perspective, the interests of the dominant group are maintained in that refugees are serving the needs of the low-wage labor market. What this construction of dependency ignores is that many U.S. citizens need government benefits for survival (Benson 2016). Some of these benefits are mainstream and based on previous engagement in the market economy, like Social Security. These are regarded as acceptable by the broader society. Other benefits, like health care, are more suspect: Do those who do not have access to health benefits really deserve these benefits and at what cost? Dependence on cash assistance or Supplemental Nutrition Assistance Program (SNAP)/Food Stamps for those who cannot work is vilified. Women refugees, who face multiple barriers to economic security, encounter a long-standing economic self-sufficiency myth in the United States; that is, those with economic security are not dependent on multiple benefit systems, family, social networks, and social capital that contribute to their success (Fineman 2000).

Moreover, self-sufficiency for refugees is so much more than economic self-sufficiency. Parallel to the research and literature on the complexity of economic self-sufficiency for many women in the United States (Edin and Lein 1997), the refugee experience, and specifically the experience of women refugees from Africa, encompasses a set of complex circumstances and challenges that make attaining economic self-sufficiency a difficult process (Opoku-dapaah 2017), and certainly not one to be achieved within a few months of arrival in the United States. Furthermore, due to the extensive work participation commitments of TANF, women refugees (in this case, African women refugees) will likely have less time to focus on English acquisition (Haffejee 2016), resulting in significantly reduced earnings, since English is often a requirement for higher job positions and wages (Opoku-dapaah 2017).

Lived Experiences of African Women Refugees

The study sample was comprised of African women refugees (N = 20) between the ages 23 and 57 years old, with an average age of 33 years. Four participants lived in public housing. Sixteen paid rent independently and lived mostly in privately owned one-bedroom apartments concentrated in predominantly low-income and underserved neighborhoods in a greater metropolitan area of the mid-west. Countries of origin included the following: Democratic Republic of the Congo (DRC), Ethiopia, Eritrea, Somalia, and Sudan.

All 20 women lived in refugee camps in Africa ranging from 3 to 22 years and were proficient in two to five native languages, such as Amharic, Arabic, French, Kinyarwanda, Lingala, Somali, Swahili, and Tigrinya. Thirteen women were from rural (e.g., agricultural and cattle farming) communities, and seven women grew up in urban areas. Of the 20 women, only 3 women had professional careers, but with little-to-no English, before being forcibly displaced from their homes. One woman was a teacher, a second woman held a high-level government position, and a third woman was a pharmaceutical assistant. Of the remaining 17 women, 15 reported that they were teenagers when they were displaced from their homes to live in refugee camps.

At the time of the study, 18 women had 1 to 6 children, ranging from 3 months to 18 years old. Of the 18 women, 4 (who were widowed) had children still living in Africa awaiting reunification with their families. Six women were single, five were widowed, five lived with their husbands, three were divorced, and one was separated from her husband due to him being denied resettlement in the United States. Fifteen were female heads of households and minimum-wage earners. Eight of the twenty women were also proficient in English. The length of time in the United States varied from nine months to three years, with an average time of approximately two years. Thus, none of the participants had active/open cases with their respective resettlement agencies (i.e., they were no longer receiving resettlement benefits). Of the 20 women, 16 were accessing public benefits, such as TANF, Medicaid, and SNAP.

The lived experiences of women refugees from Africa present a picture of trauma that continues to hinder the women's ability to become economically self-sufficient. The analysis of the first author's dissertation findings revealed the emergence of six major themes under the core category *postmigration*. The six major themes were: "The Psychological Toll of War," "The Pathways to Move towards Economic Self-Sufficiency," "Structural Barriers to Economic Self-Sufficiency," "Resettlement Stressors," "Resilience," and "Resistance." This chapter focuses on (1) trauma experiences and war, (2) employment barriers, and (3) policy barriers.

Trauma Experiences and War

One experience common to many refugee groups, both men and women, is war and the violence related to war. Gender-based violence both en route and in refugee camps is particularly relevant for women refugees. In order to fully understand the lives of refugees in the United States in the context of refugee policy that demands economic self-sufficiency, an understanding of the lived experience of trauma as experienced by many refugee populations, including women from Africa, is essential. Based on the findings presented in this chapter and the available literature (Bhui et al. 2006; Craig et al. 2009), the trauma experiences of women refugees premigration are ever present in their memories and have a profound effect on their lives and ability to meet the demands of economic self-sufficiency policy postmigration.

The women in this study recounted their experiences with great intensity. They described their lives as being destroyed "in an instant." One woman said, "We [mother and 8 siblings] fled my country in 2000, but the war broke out in 1996—I was 13 years old . . . gunshots were always going off. I remember sitting in school [being caught in the cross fire] and we have to run quickly and hide for safety. The next day it is the same thing. Sometimes you . . . miss so much school . . . they shoot anytime, no warning—they [rebels] don't worry about our education."

Another woman, a widower with five children who lived in Darfur, told of how the rebels came into her home and attacked her. "I saw friends die and I had to just walk over the dead bodies," she added. A woman from Eritrea narrated the experience of being recruited for the military. "The government was looking for [us] to fight in the military. [As a result] of these circumstances [their lives] were a big secret. It was hard to tell anybody that we were trying to escape—it was like we had to live [underground]. It was hard. We could not even tell our sister or our parents because they would come to [our homes] and interrogate or kill every one of them. They didn't care."

When it came time to leave their home countries, women were often forced to "[flee] with only the clothes [they] were wearing and some dry food [like porridge] to mix with some water and sugar. The water we got from the river—even if it was dirty we would have to drink it." One participant described watching her father and brother being killed. Feeling desperate, she left Rwanda in terror, wearing a single piece of cloth wrapped around her. The women in this study told stories of their escapes, which often entailed walking across countries with their children and being aware that at any time they could be killed.

For some women, sexual violence also became a part of their daily experience as they waited for approval of their refugee status from UN High Commissioner for Refugees authorities prior to entry into the camp. One refugee depicted her experience as follows:

> I was just 17 years old. We [mother and children] slept on the streets for a month. My father [a former General in the military] was in jail. Kabila's people put him there—they change everything. . . . My mother asked a soldier to help us. He agreed! So we stayed in the barracks. . . . I will never forget his name. He [interrogated] me about my father and treated me like I was his property, like a dog. All I did was lie there because I was afraid he would kill us. My mom couldn't say anything—she cannot protect me from the military men. I got my first pregnancy by him but lost my baby . . . he was raping me every night. When I left the hospital, I run away to the refugee camp. I never saw my family after that. Up to now, I have not seen my family since.

While these experiences took place during premigration, the trauma and memories do not go away.

Trauma and Its Impact

One cannot understand the stories of the African women refugees who were interviewed for the study described in this chapter without being keenly aware of the effects of trauma. The traumatic responses experienced by these women include not only their personal responses to the horrific events they faced but also the communal effects of trauma, as the women refugees in this study collectively have experienced the cumulative effect of the refugee experience. The violence and trauma experienced by many refugees, and confirmed in the stories of the women presented in this chapter, represent a wide range of trauma types and symptoms of traumatic stress. One possible impact of severe trauma is "multiple disrupted attachment," which "eloquently speaks to the myriad and fundamental ways in which . . . individuals and . . . communities . . . have been traumatized" (Haskell and Randall 2009, 49). The experiences of the African women refugees in this study often epitomized multiple disrupted attachments: loss of roles; loss of family, including husbands and children; loss of country; loss of safety; loss of basic necessities; loss of privacy; and loss of owning their own bodies and more. Many women described the ongoing emotional and cognitive challenges they faced associated with these traumatic experiences as they tried to integrate into U.S. society and move to rapid economic self-sufficiency.

The *emotional* impact of past trauma lives in the present. Several women said they still "worried all the time" and were afraid. One woman refugee shared that she was afraid to walk outside by herself and that she lost her first job at an airport because of a fear of riding the bus by herself. Others talked about feeling sad and crying often. Of the 20 women interviewed, 13 women were sole providers for the family. They worried about not being able to adequately provide for their families on a daily basis.

In addition to strong emotional consequences of trauma, women described substantial *cognitive* impacts. The intrusion of the past and memories was commonplace, despite trying to forget. As one woman said, "When I think about that [referring to her trauma experiences] my heart is in pain." These sentiments were echoed by another woman, who said, "Initially it was good here, but as time went by, all the memories from back home came back. The hardships [in America] make it worse. So it is difficult here now." Memory loss and difficulty processing information can be cognitive consequences of trauma and commonly associated conditions of depression and PTSD. This may make economic self-sufficiency more difficult to attain. As one woman stated, "My mind is absent; my memory is not remembering anything; it's delete, you know." This experience made it particularly difficult to retain information in formal learning or job-training environments.

In addition to the emotional and cognitive impacts of trauma, the presence of *physical* impacts of trauma on the body was reported. These included "[rapid] heartbeat," "high blood pressure," "diabetes," feeling "low energy," and sometimes "loss of appetite." Several women disclosed that they experienced "nightmares" most nights, which often resulted in "sleeping problems." In fact, the women linked their insomnia and nightmares to thinking about their past and present problems "all the time." For other women, "chronic pain," "heart problems," "suffering headaches," and excessive menstrual "bleeding" related to postsexual trauma impeded their ability to maintain and/or work in jobs such as "housekeeping," because such jobs are physically demanding and requires them to work "long hours." This is exemplified in one story: "I was beaten very badly. Sometimes I get very bad back pain, and when that happens, I struggle to get out of bed or walk—it's painful. That is why I asked [name of agency] for any job [besides] lifting heavy objects."

Another woman's story is a poignant example of the physical challenges that adversely affect some women's ability to meet the demands of rapid economic self-sufficiency. During her 18 years in the Gihembe refugee camp in Rwanda, one woman suffered a "massive heart attack." She underwent "[major] surgery" that left a very noticeable scar. As a result, she was "not able to ever work," especially work that was physically demanding. At the time of the interview, she had not yet met with a cardiologist to obtain either medical approval to work or an exemption from work to access disability benefits.

She called for an appointment at the local public hospital but did not understand how to proceed, as the automated voice spoke too fast. Consequently, she only works part-time and makes and sells handmade goods to supplement her family income. As she aptly pointed out, "[America] is not really the heaven that I heard about because life is a big struggle here."

While refugees have access to physical and mental health services through the resettlement agencies, using these services is not an easy process. Two women reported that limited mental health services were made available to them. One woman went to an agency "to talk about [her] sad feelings" but had to use an interpreter, who was a man from her community. Talking about her trauma, especially her experiences of sexual violence in the presence of a male from her community, was "too difficult" to be helpful. Another woman shared similar sentiments, but she also noted that due to work obligations, she was unable to meet regularly with her therapist. In her words, "I had to go to work to support my children and pay the rent, you know."

Workplace Barriers as a Challenge to Achieving Economic Self-Sufficiency

As mandated by refugee policy, employment is an integral component for a *successful* transition to rapid economic self-sufficiency. Thus, resettlement agencies are required to provide job-training programs to assist African women refugees to search for employment, most often in sectors requiring few skills or an extensive educational background and that pay low wages.

Little-to-no transferable skills. Of the 20 women, only 2 utilized a formal support system to find employment. Soon after their arrival, two women completed a six-week formal hospitality job-training program offered by one of the local resettlement agencies. This job-training program included job interview and hands-on-food safety skills, but not English comprehension. With the help of the employment coordinator at the agency, the two women were placed in jobs shortly after completing the training, although these jobs were not directly related to the training received. It is important to note that successful completion of job training does not necessarily guarantee employment, especially when the women have limited English skills. For example, one woman talked about why she was not doing the work that she was trained in: "The interview was difficult because of the language and [her low-level reading skills]. . . . I am an aide to the cook in the kitchen. The cook puts the food on the plate . . . I must make sure not to give [patients with diabetes and various food allergies the wrong tray of food]."

The ability to speak English afforded more job opportunities and potentially greater economic advancement, since English is the primary language and a prerequisite for most educational settings, services, and jobs. One woman said, "[I]t's like insurance for the job." Another expressed, "If the US was [multilingual], finding a job and communicating with people would also be so much easier." Another woman's sentiments were that "these rules are keeping us down. If you don't speak English, then you can't live your dream. . . . it stops you from doing things. . . [like studying] to be a CNA . . . feel[s] like you are handicapped—you want to stand up and walk but you're stuck in a wheelchair."

Clearly, an emphasis on rapid economic self-sufficiency conflicts with the *successful* integration of women refugees from Africa, who bring with them unique life circumstances and are "harder to help or employ"—especially recent arrivals who are from mostly agricultural and cattle-farming communities who have languished in under-resourced refugee camps across Africa, with little-to-no English and formal education, limited native language literacy, and few economic resources or transferable skills.

Marginalized and invisible. The women spoke powerfully and poignantly about the ways in which they experienced racism, discrimination, and Islamophobia in the workplace in the United States. They talked about being dismissed at work or denied employment based on their skin color, age, and religion because they were perceived as different from those in mainstream U.S. society. One respondent described how, even with English proficiency and a job-training certificate, she could not find employment. She said, "The recruitment [specialist] would arrange an interview . . . I would go and do very well. I also answered all the questions, you know." Regardless, "Everyone [three companies] called me to say I didn't get the job." The repeated rejection from prospective employers resulted in her feeling that she "might be too old . . . and didn't look right. My color is not right." Not only did she feel like she did not "fit" the profile because of her skin color but she also thought that wearing clothing typical of her ethnic/cultural heritage exacerbated the situation: "I always wear my African clothes. In my culture, I am [considered] an elder so I wear the African head wrap. Maybe that is not good enough."

One of the most poignant responses indicating racial discrimination came in one participant's response: "I survived the war, people dying everywhere, but it is hard to survive how the white people at my work are treating me." This was powerful to hear, and there was anger and helplessness in her voice. When asked what made her say this, she answered, "I cannot survive because it is making me sick." She elaborated about her experience at work: "My supervisor treats me different. . . . He is very rude and talks to me with an angry voice. Like I am stupid. Everyone I work with has gloves and a mask to do their job. When I asked for my own, he said, 'You don't need it.' Now, I am getting chest pain and my hands are peeling because [of] . . . the chemical. I [must tolerate] it before I get into trouble or lose my job."

In addition to race, 9 out of a total of 11 Muslim women expressed that they were treated differently because of their religion. A 33-year-old Somali woman explained that her "burqa [long veil with full face exposed] is always a problem at work." In fact, she has been told on several occasions to wear a "hijab [the headscarf]" instead of a "burqa." Supposedly, wearing a burqa jeopardizes her job security. Although she emphasized the significance of her dress, out of fear of being perceived as a terrorist, losing her job, and out of respect for authority, she instead tries her "best to [wear] hijab."

The dominant narrative in the United States is that of a color-blind *postracial* society driven by meritocracy. This ideology, as women reported hearing in the camps, is that the United States is the land of limitless opportunity in which African women refugees can go as far as their own merit (which includes innate abilities, working hard, having the right attitude, and having high moral character and integrity) takes them. Arguably, these were all characteristics that African women refugees in this study embodied, hence the women were devoted to this narrative and believed that through hard work, they would achieve the *American dream*. As demonstrated in this part (and throughout this chapter), African women refugees are not living the American dream, because the racist system is stacked against them. Moreover, their minority status and *othering* (a way of reminding a group of their outsider status or perceiving them as fundamentally different due to language, history, ethnicity/culture, religion, and traditions) separates them from historically underrepresented groups such as African Americans in mainstream U.S. society (Haffejee 2016). These women represent several oppressed or marginalized identities and are also targets for multiple forms of discrimination. Consequently, they not only endure compounding effects of overt and subtle degrees of discrimination from those in positions of power but also from mainstream society.

Policy Barriers as a Challenge to Economic Self-Sufficiency

"We are not asking for handouts." Refugees are eligible to receive an array of resettlement services and benefits, many of which are provided by resettlement agencies. These agencies are aware of the newly arrived refugees' needs, for example, family size, housing, and income, before they are resettled. Upon arrival, African women refugees are greeted by a caseworker/manager, taken to housing, and immediately immersed in the fast-paced U.S. society far removed from their natal land. Nineteen out of twenty women expressed extreme disappointment in the way that refugee service agencies provide services and support. One respondent shared some of her experiences as a newcomer, which included feeling abandoned and the lack of preparedness by the resettlement agency. In her words: "[The case manager] just dropped us [her and her six-month old baby] off and told me [that] this is where we will sleep. I was handed a card [Electronic Benefits Transfer] and told to go buy food at King Soopers." Almost two years had passed since she arrived, and still she became emotional as she recalled the lack of preparedness of the resettlement agency. She further articulated: "I now live in a one-bedroom apartment with my two children, but I want you to know that this was not always [the case]. When I came here, the agency did not have a [single

family] home available for me so I had to share with two Congolese families for almost six months." Not only was this decision made for her, but also this living arrangement proved to be quite challenging because of the language, ethnic, and cultural differences: "It was really hard because we were not from the same tribe and we didn't speak the same [native] language."

Poor living conditions in low-resource neighborhoods and high apartment rents were additional service provision issues reported by several women. A 36-year-old mother of three children talked about being resettled in a low-resource neighborhood and school district. First, though, she felt it extremely important to emphasize the following: "African [women] refugees are not asking for handouts! But, surely, [the agency] cannot expect us to live in such a bad apartment. It was very dirty and roach infested. At night, we'd be sleeping and the roaches would crawl over us." Another woman further highlighted, the high monthly rent for such "bad" apartments became their financial responsibility immediately after their 90-day cash assistance ran out: "Why do [agencies] put us in such expensive apartments. It is not right to do that—they must think. But they don't care." The women hoped for a life that included a bright future for their children, which "is [their] duty towards their children." Yet, they had limited access to resources that might help them thrive and they lived in substandard housing and in "[areas] that are not very safe." As one respondent expressed, "Even the schools for our children are also not good—there are no school buses, but what can we do. We are far from everything." For this woman, it seemed both un-American and incomprehensible that they resettled in the United States to "feel safe" and to have "a better life" but found that "maybe if you are a refugee you must be happy with how things are here."

Navigators. In terms of service provision, community navigators are key people in the resettlement process as they help newcomers navigate complex U.S. systems (i.e., TANF, school districts, health care) and language barriers to access resources (Haffejee 2016). For several women, language barriers and a lack of information and connection to cultural brokers, such as navigators, left them feeling "alone" and "isolated." For example, one woman said that she envisioned "life to be different here in America." Instead, on the first day, "[her] case manager told her to report to their office within a few days to [complete the necessary] paperwork for her welcome [i.e., Food Stamps, cash assistance] money." She was "very confused but did not know how to ask for an [explanation]," resulting in her feeling "alone" and "frustrated." Despite feeling this way, she felt compelled to meet with her case manager. The following statement powerfully represents the participant's sentiments trying to navigate complex systems and access resources with little-to-no English: "[T]hey didn't care that I got lost like a dog in the street and that I felt unsafe while trying to find their office. It took me a long time to find and figure out the bus system . . . I couldn't even ask anyone on the street for [directions] because I could not speak any English . . . I asked the police officer but he also couldn't understand me." Because navigators have several shared experiences with the women (such as culture, language, are former refugees or currently refugees), they are trusted and are therefore able to provide support in times of extreme stress that extend far beyond initial resettlement (Haffejee 2016). Thus, for the overwhelming majority of the women, navigators are a highly valued resource to help bridge the cultural/language divide, regardless of the length of time living in the United States.

Cultural responsiveness. The lack of culturally responsive services (such as translators and interpreters) often resulted in women not fully understanding resettlement benefits. Since the women are "expected to [enter the workforce] with less developed English," and within 30–90 days after arrival, the women felt it important that interpretation and translation services be provided to them. The women expressed that agencies are explicit in demonstrating (through visuals and role-play) some of the basic etiquette rules according to American culture, including "what to say when [they] greet Americans" and "what to do when [they] visit American homes." For example, "We must first knock or tell American people before we visit them." The same does not apply to mandatory provisions. On the contrary, refugee providers provide little-to-no interpretive services that explain the resettlement benefits process to the women. Especially, key resettlement benefits such as TANF represent "our first time [that] we have paperwork like this to do. It is important that we understand it. Our [livelihood] depends on it." For example, one woman felt strongly about these experiences and remarked: "[The agencies] don't make us feel like we are [valued]. They should provide someone that can interpret and explain the rules of the [resettlement provisions]. . . . we don't understand English. They just expect us to understand." Another woman echoed similar sentiments, stating that sometimes the agency "just sends a letter to explain things [such as social security], but we don't understand what the hell is going on. We can't read it. Makes me feel like even here refugees are still treated differently—like we are still refugees."

For most of our women participants, not understanding how their work support or benefits were structured was especially frustrating. For example, resettlement supports are incrementally lost as a woman's income increases, but often before sufficient income can be sustained to replace that support, which is problematic. Two women reported that when they received their "first paycheck," their "Food Stamps" and TANF were significantly reduced. These deductions came as a huge surprise and impacted the women's ability to provide for their families and pay their high apartment rent, not to mention the interest accrued on late payments. When the women inquired with their "case manager, [they] were just told—but you signed the paper!" Stunned and in absolute disbelief, they commented: "We didn't know what to do. We just [cried] because we didn't have an interpreter." Most of the women in this study are traditionally from oral societies where one's word is binding. "Here [in America] if you . . . sign a paper that you did not understand—you stand to face repercussions." Another woman's powerful words underscore sentiments related to signing paperwork without fully understanding the content therein. In fact, she described it as deceitful and disempowering, saying: "If you just sign and you did not understand—then what are you signing? Why don't they [the agency] just do things in a dignified manner. Provide an interpreter or someone that will spend time with us to help us through all of this." The researcher, also the first author, was struck by the sense of powerlessness in this statement, further noting that they "can't argue" for an increase in benefits; however, the women felt that service providers should provide "someone to help and explain things. . . . We want to have jobs but [the agencies] are still violating African [women] refugees."

The loss or reduction of resettlement benefits and high costs of childcare are especially stressful for women. One woman said, "I am not happy because my rent is $679 and my paycheck is $320. How am I supposed to pay rent and electric out of my money? If I pay late, then my rent is like $700." Another woman expressed similar sentiments: "I have sleepless nights because I am worried about my children and how we will live. If I can't pay my rent, I will be living on the street. Also, I pay $250 per month from my wages for child-care . . . I cry every day again [like life in the camp]."

Filled with a profound sense of hopelessness, some women turn to the resettlement agency to explore more affordable housing options. For example, one woman articulated that she asked "to move into a cheaper one-bedroom apartment with her three children" or apply for low-income housing. Unfortunately, the "agency was not able" to help with either, but "they helped [her] apply" to the Low-Income Home Energy Assistance Program (LIHEAP) for short-term assistance with her monthly electricity bills. For financially vulnerable women refugees, though, this short-term solution provides very little comfort. As several of the other women interviewed remarked, "[They] must still face their children" on a daily basis when they are food insecure for "days, sometimes weeks."

Two of the most salient experiences of African women refugees with the resettlement agencies related to limited job training and access to job opportunities. Several African women refugees expressed that resettlement agencies tended to focus their efforts on English-proficient and "job ready" refugees who happen to be "mostly men." In other words, these are refugees who are more likely to enable resettlement agencies to achieve the job entry quotas by which their performance is assessed and, by extension, their services funded. For example, English (i.e., Level 2: intermediate or higher) is required to participate in the formal job-training program offered by the agency. Unlike many of the African women refugees in this study, who arrived with little-to-no English and have limited childcare supports, recent "women refugee [arrivals] from Iraq and Southeast Asia," who have higher levels of English and more "childcare" supports, are more likely to access this limited job training, and they also have better success getting a job shortly after graduating this job-training program. For Iraqi refugees, this is partially due to not having lived in refugee camps before being resettled to the United States. Other refugees, such as Bhutanese refugees arriving from camps in Nepal, received basic English skills training before resettlement.

African women refugees who are "harder to employ" are put on TANF with the help of a resettlement agency, but with the understanding that they will participate in assigned work-related activities a certain number of hours per week. While well-intentioned, the resettlement agency places these women in "easy-to-access" or low-skilled job-related activities where upward mobility is limited. By way of example, one woman reported the following: "[Y]ou have to do 30 hours per week of voluntary work, but TANF is so few money. . . . Too much free work hours. And the voluntary work [involves] packing at the Safari Thrift Store. You can't really learn a job skill that you can use when you [are packing and cleaning shelves] at Goodwill stores."

Despite having successfully completed a formal job-training program, which is supposedly a gateway to employment for those with limited English or education, some women still struggled to find a job using the skills they learned. In fact, after the job training and despite also actively seeking employment, one woman commented that she was "unemployed for seven months." Thus, she not only exceeded the maximum eight-month eligibility period to access resettlement benefits but was also no longer under the umbrella of the resettlement agency. At the time of this study, this woman and her family were facing eviction, resulting in her having to rely to a small degree on a faith-based organization for food and clothing, but mostly on her community navigator, who helped with some immediate financial support. Following the interview, the first author connected her to some additional resources and provided some immediate resources, such as food and clothing for the children.

Refugee resettlement agencies are mandated to deliver myriad support to African women and other refugees. However, for most women, finding "good jobs that pay good money" using these support systems remains a huge problem. As low-income earners, women refugees from Africa struggle to provide for their families: "There are so many house bills to pay [in America] and most of the jobs that are available pay very little money."

Loan repayments. A significant barrier for African women refugees in the study was repayment of the loan from the UN International Organization of Migration (IOM) for the costs of travel to the United States. While interest-free, making repayments on the loan while they were trying to meet the basic needs of their families often posed a significant hardship. For the 20 women refugees presented in this chapter, most of whom are female heads of households, minimum-wage-earners, and food insecure, the price of freedom is not always free. In addition to the aforesaid stressors, the women's plane ticket (and those of their spouse, if any, and children under the age of 18 years old) from the refugee camp must be repaid.

The women are expected to begin incremental repayment of loans for plane tickets within six months of arriving in the United States. The total amount, which for large families can exceed $10,000 or even $20,000, is generally expected to be repaid to the U.S. government (specifically, the Bureau of Population, Refugees and Migration [PRM] for the funds it provided to IOM for refugee transportation) within 42 months (Sacco 2016). Many resettlement agencies have expressed support for the IOM loan program, positing that it provides an opportunity for refugees to build "good" credit. Unfortunately, good credit tomorrow is very little consolation for a refugee parent in poverty today. One woman elaborated, saying: "You know in America even if you don't have money, you still have to think about paying the loan because your credit will go down if you can't pay." Furthermore, she stated, "The "[resettlement] benefits" refugees receive "[is] not enough" even to cover living expenses like rent, let alone additional monthly travel loan payments. "My two [school-aged] sons work as dishwashers so they help me pay the rent, IOM, and Xcel [public utilities]. When I can't make . . . payment[s] I worry." Not only is this extremely overwhelming and "stressful," but if these women were to default on a payment, it would result in their sanctioning and/or severe penalty. Another woman's statement captures the concept of censure and penalty. To her, the United States "has very strict laws and we are not used to it. . . . [W]e were [repeatedly] told in orientation and by others [their case managers] that we must obey the laws [also referring to Child Protective Services]. Obey the laws is all we hear."

While much is known about the immense financial burden of the loan repayment upon many low-income refugee families postresettlement (Sacco 2016), a dearth of literature exists questioning and discussing both the legitimacy of these travel loans by host countries and refugees' postresettlement socioeconomic rights (Sacco 2016). Notably, only the United States, Australia, and Canada enforce this economic burden on resettled refugee families. Furthermore, the promissory note itself states that the federal government may use "all legal means to collect amounts past due" (as cited in Stacco, 1), including reporting the refugee to a credit bureau. As one women aptly described, "[R]efugee[s] don't know the American laws [our rights] . . . Here in America, it is not the same as in Africa—in Africa if you fail to have enough money you can ask family and the people in the village or refugee camp for help. . . . but here I found it to be different. They say the exact date and that is the date that [you have to pay] or you are charged interest. That is frustrating. . . . Sometimes it's like we are waiting for the police to come to our door." Ultimately, this undue economic burden of the travel loan does beg the question: Is the travel loan program as it exists today consistent with the humanitarian obligations of the United States to refugees?

Racism and discrimination in service provision. Given the history of peoples of African descent in the United States, it is not surprising that many women refugees from Africa revealed feeling marginalized and excluded from mainstream America. In fact, 85 percent of the women in this study articulated that the public discourse on African women refugees in the United States makes them look like "[we] are stupid . . . like we are nothing!" Women described feeling excluded in decision-making processes. Interestingly, some women thought that this lack of involvement was the reason resettlement agencies and service providers perceived them as lazy. One respondent expressed, "African women are not lazy; we can work. Tell them we need work that we can do, not pity!"

Another woman further explained: "We feel like there is a difference in the way African [women] refugees are treated. [Service providers] think that [we] are useless—we can't do anything because some of us don't have an education." On the other hand, "We want to go to school for education because we don't want to only work in housekeeping, you know. But we are told that we must go work in any job and learn English after work. It is hard. Who will look after our children?"

For some women, finding employment and navigating the system immediately postresettlement proved to be extremely challenging. One woman volunteered her experience when she arrived at the age of 18. She "had no family" living in the United States, nor did she have "any [prior work experience]." Eager to complete high school, which was interrupted by the war in Eritrea, she asked the resettlement agency if she could complete her schooling, instead. The agency expressed to her that "she [must] take care of [herself] . . . find work and make it on [her] own." This response resulted in her "[feeling] so bad" that she "never did go back to the [agency] for help. Being an African [woman] refugee isn't easy. They don't even try to understand us."

Another woman shared similar sentiments saying, "[She] was excited to leave Kakuma camp to come to America for a better life. Soon after we [her and her four school-aged children] arrived, we had no food for a month. I'm not sure why but I was told [by the agency] there was a problem with my Food Stamps. It was really difficult . . . We would just go to sleep with no food." However, "It was very important to be in the job-training because they [the agency] told us that we can get a job after the training. I sat in the [program name] job-training class all day, every day, and had no food to eat." After multiple attempts trying to resolve the issue, she said, "I [didn't] feel comfortable every time saying my problem to my case manager. I [didn't] like to feel like it's always me—the same person crying for my problem—it is not good. I want to ask for help once or twice, not always. . . . I am the type of person that usually does not ask for help unless, I am suffering, [then] I will run and say help me. . . . I don't want handouts. I work part-time at Safari Thrift store. It's not so good, but I have a job—what can I do?"

The women's statement invokes the concept of "us" and "them," which is ubiquitous in most racialized discourses. Their views expressed their feelings of invisibility and dependency on a "them" who wield enormous power to influence the fate of most women refugees from Africa. The multiple identities of race and ethnicity, gender, and class are interlocking components of most African women refugees' identities, placing them at the inferior end of the status continuum in everyday life in the United States and are often complicated through inaccessibility to support and resources.

Nine (45%) participants pointed out incidents of discrimination from fellow Africans (mostly from the same region, but from a different ethnic tribe/clan) when accessing services and resettlement benefits. Notably, "African male case managers" (made up of former refugees, but mostly voluntary immigrants) who were English-proficient and educated engaged in the most disturbing practices. The women talked about entrenched gender roles that continued to impact service delivery. Two women shared their story, saying, "[W]e have problems with the men from Africa working at [name of the resettlement agency]. You know, they . . . only take care of their own countries' refugee men . . . If you don't have a husband, they don't help. It is the same as life in the refugee camp and back home also. It's the same."

In addition to gender stereotypes, the women described how interethnic prejudices or political misconceptions (that existed in, for example, the DRC and Rwanda, and "gave rise to ethnic conflicts" and outright "warfare") were carried over to the United States. This also had a negative impact on service delivery for African women refugees from such countries. Ethnic case managers are meant to serve as cultural brokers between the recipient and the service provider. One participant described how some case managers still held on to deeply embedded ethnic and political discrimination and resentment, resulting in perceiving the woman recipient as the "enemy." For example, this woman and her case manager were both from the Congo, except one identified as ethnically "Hutu" and the other as "Tutsi." In Africa, the Hutu-Tutsi strife originated from class warfare, with the Hutus perceived to be cattle farmers and thus lower class, and the Tutsis having greater wealth and higher social status. The conflict between these two ethic groups became extreme and resulted in the 1994 Rwanda genocide (Umutesi 2006). The following statement characterizes one 29-year-old woman's experience of being pushed to the fringe and rendered invisible when working with her Congolese case manager: "My first eight months here, I never [saw or spoke] to my case manager ever. He just left me with my three children at my apartment. He did not tell or show me anything. I didn't know any English. I was confused and lonely . . . and [I am] the only African [and still am] in my apartment [building]."

Recalling this experience was emotional and traumatic for the participant. Instead of working in concert with the woman recipient, her case manager neglected to make available the mandated short-term or "welcome" provisions (e.g., SNAP and cash assistance), including her "social security card," after her arrival. He also failed to process the paperwork for her longer-term resettlement assistance, such as "job-training/English classes, childcare, and Medicaid." In her words: "I didn't even understand the phone system. Even if someone talked on the phone, I could not understand them. Really, nobody showed me how to adapt here."

Implications for Resettlement Practice

As is evident in the stories of the 20 women refugees that are presented in this chapter, their struggles to reach even a basic level of self-sufficiency were complex. These struggles were located at the intersection of personal experiences as a result of being women refugees from Africa, structural barriers that are faced by many women in the political economy, and systems that are set up to regulate or assist refugees in the United States.

The personal experiences of the women tell a story of past severe trauma that left them vulnerable to mental and at times physical impairments that cannot be overlooked in the resettlement services currently authorized by the U.S. government. Research on the impact of trauma on individuals and families points to the need to address traumatic stress symptoms in a holistic way that includes culturally responsive and integrated mental health, health, and social services that robustly (or centrally) attend to the trauma and its impact (Ostrander, Melville, and Berthold 2017). Clearly, for many of the women, 90 days of adjustment to a radically new society before commencing employment does not provide an adequate time for connecting to services, diagnosing health and mental health conditions, and sufficiently treating conditions that may negatively affect the ability to function adequately at work.

In addition to grappling with the effects of trauma, navigating resettlement and social service systems is a major challenge for the African refugee women participants, and many encountered refugee services that were not adequate. Arguably, several factors were at play: the lack of adequate federal funds appropriated for refugee services (Nawyn 2010); underfunded resettlement agencies (Geo-Jaja and Mangum 2007); an outdated *one-size-fits-all* approach to refugee resettlement; and refugee resettlement policy that prioritizes rapid economic independence for all newly arriving refugees, including women refugees (Haffejee 2016; Kramer 2011). Consequently, not only are resettlement agencies limited in the types of services they offer (Deacon and

Sullivan 2009) but women refugees must access several different agencies before acquiring all the services (e.g., Medicaid, SNAP, TANF) needed.

Very little research and literature has documented the fundamental role of navigators or cultural brokers in the process of refugee integration (Fielding and Anderson 2008). The use of cultural navigators by some health and social service agencies is a promising practice that facilitates the providers' increased awareness and sensitivity to the needs of the women refugees. It is important that these cultural navigators have a common language and background to the women refugees. Resettlement agencies could benefit by adopting the navigator model. For this model to be effective, however, resettlement agencies should enhance the role of navigators by providing them with additional training (e.g., community organizing, resource referral) and a salary commensurate with their job responsibilities. Wherever possible, navigators must be matched by gender and ethnic/tribal affiliation with the women refugees to avoid feelings of mistrust toward the service providers by the women, which typically would negatively impact women recipients.

Finally, U.S. refugee policy is unrealistic in regard to the expectation that all refugee adults can become self-sufficient within eight months, particularly for those who have experienced significant trauma with associated health and mental health consequences. The provision of TANF or SNAP as a minimal safety net is insufficient. For women refugees from Africa who do not have another income earner to help support them, we argue for a revised TANF policy that more adequately supports women refugees by recognizing the unique barriers they face and at a minimum gives them two years to build their language skills, exempts them from some of the activity requirements such as required volunteer time that does not support increased job skills or income, and promotes their access to health and mental health services.

References

Benson, Odessa Gonzalez. 2016. "Refugee Resettlement Policy in an Era of Neoliberalization: A Policy Discourse Analysis of the Refugee Act of 1980." *Social Service Review* 90, no. 3: 515–549.

Bhui Kamaldeep, Craig Tom, Mohamud Salaad, Warfa Nasir, Stansfeld Stephen A., Thornicroft Graham, and Paul McCrone. 2006. "Mental Disorders among Somali Refugees." *Social Psychiatry & Psychiatric Epidemiology* 41, no. 5: 400–408.

Craig, Tom, Jajua Peter, and Nasir Warfa. 2009. "Mental Health Care Needs of Refugees." *Transcultural Psychiatry* 8, no. 9: 351–354.

Crenshaw, Kimberlé, Gotanda Neil, Peller Gary, and Kendall Thomas. 1995. *Critical Race Theory: The Key Writings That Formed the Movement*. New York: New Press.

Deacon, Zermarie, and Cris Sullivan. 2009. "Responding to the Complex and Gendered Needs of Refugee Women." *Affilia* 24, no. 3: 272–284.

Delgado, Richard, and Jean Stefancic. 2000. *Critical Race Theory: The Cutting Edge*, 2nd ed. Philadelphia: Temple University Press.

Delgado, Richard, and Jean Stefancic. 2001. *Critical Race Theory: An Introduction.* New York: University Press.

East, Jean F. 1998. "In-Dependence: A Feminist Postmodern Deconstruction." *Affilia* 13, no. 3: 273–288.

Edin, Katherin, and Laura Lein. 1997. *Making Ends Meet: How Single Mothers Survive Welfare and Low-Wage Work.* New York: Sage.

Fielding, Angela, and Judi Anderson. 2008. "Working with Refugee Communities to Build Collective Resilience." *Association for Services to Torture and Trauma Survivors.* http://asetts.org.au/resources/Documents/collectiveresilenceweb.pdf.

Fineman, Martha Albertson. 2000. "Cracking the Foundational Myths: Independence, Autonomy, and Self-Sufficiency." *American University Journal of Gender, Social Policy & The Law* 8, January 1, 2000, 13. LexisNexis Academic: Law Reviews, EBSCOhost.

Fraser, Nancy, and Linda Gordon. 1994. "A Genealogy of Dependency: Tracing a Keyword of the US Welfare State." *Signs* 19, no. 21: 309–336.

Geo-Jaja, Macleans, and Garth Mangum. 2007. "Struggling at the Golden Door: International Refugees in Utah." Center for Public Policy and Administration, University of Utah.

Haffejee, Badiah. 2016. '"We Are Not Asking for Handouts!" Amplifying the Voices of African Women Refugees and Moving beyond Trauma towards Economic Self-Sufficiency: A Qualitative Inquiry." PhD diss., University of Denver.

Haffejee, Badiah, and Jean F. East. 2016. "African Women Refugee Resettlement." *Affilia: Journal of Women & Social Work* 31, no. 2: 232–242.

Haskell, Lori, and Melanie Randall. 2009. "Disrupted Attachments: A Social Context Complex Trauma Framework and the Lives of Aboriginal Peoples in Canada." *Journal of Aboriginal Health* 5, no. 3: 48–99.

Howard-Hamilton, Mary F. 2003. "Theoretical Frameworks for African American Women." *New Directions for Student Services* 104: 19–27.

Kniepp, Shawn. M. 2000. "Economic Self-Sufficiency: An Insufficient Indicator of How Women Fare after Welfare Reform." *Policy, Politics, & Nursing Practice* 1, no. 4: 256–266.

Kramer, Miriam. 2011. "Directors' and Participants' Perceptions of a Program Promoting the Economic Self-Sufficiency of Women with Refugee Status." Order No. 1495267. The University of Utah. https://pqdtopen.proquest.com/doc/879412451.html?FMT=ABS.

Martin, Daniel C., and James Yankay. 2012. "Refugees and Asylees: 2011." https://www.dhs.gov/xlibrary/assets/statistics/publications/ois_rfa_fr_2011.pdf.

Nawyn, Stephanie J. 2010. "Institutional Structures of Opportunity in Refugee Resettlement: Gender, Race/Ethnicity, and Refugee NGOs." *Journal of Sociology & Social Welfare* 37, no. 1: 149–168.

Office of Refugee Resettlement, ORR. 2012. "The Refugee Act of 1980." http://www.acf.hhs.gov/programs/orr/resource/the-refugee-act.

Opoku-dapaah, Edward. 2017. "'Ain't Making It in America': The Economic Characteristics of African Immigrants in North of African Immigrants in North Carolina, USA." *Journal of Immigrant & Refugee Studies* 15, no. 4: 406–427. doi:10.1080/15562948.2016.1234091.

Ostrander, Jason, Alysse Melville, and S. Megan Berthold. 2017. "Working with Refugees in the U.S.: Trauma-Informed and Structurally Competent Social Work Approaches." *Advances in Social Work* 18, no. 1: 66. doi:10.18060/21282.

Ott, Eleanor. 2002. "Get Up and Go: Refugee Resettlement and Secondary Migration in the USA." http://www.unhcr.org/pages/49c3646c125.html.

Refugee Act of 1980. 1980. Pub. L. No. 96-212, 94 Stat. 102.

Refugee Admissions Report. 2016. "Department of State Bureau of Population, Refugees and Migration." http://www.wrapsnet.org/admissions-and-arrivals/.

Refugee Admissions Report. 2017. "Department of State Bureau of Population, Refugees and Migration." http://www.wrapsnet.org/admissions-and-arrivals/.

Sacco, Steven. 2016. "Indebted Asylum: Why the Travel Loan Requirement for Refugees Is a Failure of the United States to Meet Its Obligations under the Convention on the Status of Refugees." *Journal of International Law*, April 11. https://www.law.gonzaga.edu/gjil/2016/04/indebted-asylum-why-the-travel-loan-requirement-for-refugees-is-a-failure-of-the-united-states-to-meet-its-obligations-under-the-convention-on-the-status-of-refugees/.

Smith, Jonathan A., Flowers Paul, and Michael Larkin. 2009. *Interpretative Phenomenological Analysis: Theory, Method, and Research*. London: Sage.

Sossou, Marie-Antoinette, Carlton D. Craig, Heather Ogren, and Michelle Schnak. 2008. "A Qualitative Study of Resilience Factors of Bosnian Refugee Women Resettled in the Southern United States." *Journal of Ethnic and Cultural Diversity in Social Work* 17, no. 4: 365–385.

Stiver, Irene P. 1991. "The Meanings of 'Dependency' in Female-Male Relationships." In *Women's Growth in Connection: Writings from the Stone Center*, edited by Judith Jordan, Alexandra G. Kaplan, Jean Baker Miller, Irene P. Stiver, and Janet L. Surrey, 143–161. New York: The Guildford Press.

Umutesi, Marie B. 2006. "Is Reconciliation between Hutus and Tutsis Possible?" *Journal of International Affairs* 60, no. 1: 157–171.

Zong, Jie, and Jeanne Batalova. 2017. "Refugees and Asylees in the United States." *Migration Policy Institute*, June 17, 2017. http://www.migrationpolicy.org/article/refugees-and-asylees-united-states.

CHAPTER THIRTEEN

Creative Arts Therapies with Refugees

Amber Elizabeth L. Gray

Not like the brazen giant of Greek fame,
With conquering limbs astride from land to land;
Here at our sea-washed, sunset gates shall stand
A mighty woman with a torch, whose flame
Is the imprisoned lightning, and her name
Mother of Exiles. From her beacon-hand
Glows world-wide welcome; her mild eyes command
The air-bridged harbor that twin cities frame.
"Keep, ancient lands, your storied pomp!" cries she
With silent lips. "Give me your tired, your poor,
Your huddled masses yearning to breathe free,
The wretched refuse of your teeming shore.
Send these, the homeless, tempest-tost to me,
I lift my lamp beside the golden door!"

Emma Lazarus, "The New Colossus," Inscription for
the Statue of Liberty (1883)

Introduction

The number of displaced people in the world is at an all-time high, as those caught in hostile environments across the globe flee persecution, violence, and uncertainty for the hope of a safer place to establish a new home. In 2014, the United Nations proclaimed that the number of refugees, asylum seekers, and internally displaced people worldwide had, for the first time in the post–World War II era, exceeded 50 million people (UNHCR 2015). By 2016, this number had swelled to 65.6 million, more than the population of the United Kingdom. The number was an increase of 300,000 on the year before, designating 1 in every 113 people on the planet as a refugee and indicating that someone, somewhere in the world is displaced every three seconds. In 2018, the number of displaced people on planet earth is a soaring 68.5 million; approximately 85 percent of those displaced are in developing countries, and more than half of them are children (UNHCR 2018).

From the preflight exposure to frightening and frequently life-threatening experiences, to the insecurity of flight and the often-humiliating challenges of resettlement, refugees live through extended periods of deeply unsettling, disorienting, and colossally life-changing experience. As interest in refugee mental health grows, it is incumbent upon those of us working with refugees at any phase of their experience of displacement to find ways to connect and support that are culturally and contextually responsive.

The creative arts have long been a universal voice for all aspects of human experience. The majority of the world is sociocentric, where collective and integrative healing processes are commonplace (Harris 2003). Rituals, rites of passage, celebrations, and family and communal gatherings often use creative processes and practices, such as dance, drumming, music, storytelling, art, and almost every creative form of expression imaginable, to support and invite healing, grieving, celebration, mourning, acknowledgment, and humanity. The creative arts provide a pathway to healing that may be particularly familiar and a safe way to engage global community members who are displaced by violence and persecution (Gray 2015a, 2015b). The arts offer us many avenues to give voice to a broad range of human experience—from the most unspeakable horror to the most celebrated joy—that no other form of communication and expression can. With the number of refugees and those displaced by human cruelty and environmental change steadily increasing, and the search for a place to land becoming more difficult and hostile, we need more imaginative and creative ways to connect across the pronounced divides of race, religion, ethnicity, political affiliation, gender, and all other fundamental aspects of our humanity. This chapter will explore the use of a variety of creative arts therapies with refugees, as well as elaborate why these approaches are particularly well-suited to addressing the impact of refugee trauma.

State of Traumatization Experienced by Refugees

Refugees are exposed to traumatic events that are life changing. The imprints that remain derive from physiological changes, or state-shifts, that initiate a cascade of biochemical and neurological changes that prepare the person exposed to danger to fight or flee, or, in the case of perceived life threat, to shut down (Gray 2018; Gray and Porges 2017). These physiological changes become the imprint of traumatization and are the basis of the affective and emotional responses one feels when facing danger (fear) or life threat (terror) in the moment of exposure. The overwhelming experience of fear or terror contributes to the potency of the imprint of the physiological state-shift that is ultimately in service of survival, and this can lead to a state of traumatization. Fear mobilizes us to defend ourselves or escape; shutting down immobilizes us so that we are less perceptible to the threat (Gray and Porges 2017). When there is no escape, the immobilization response actually prepares the body for death; for example, endorphins are released so that our pain tolerance increases, and we suffer less. In the moment of exposure, these more primitive survival strategies afforded us through our own evolution are what help us survive. Going onward, living in states of fear and terror does not support the states of safety that are essential to trust and meaningful relationship, a sense of belonging or connection, or a fulfilled sense of life (Gray 2015a). The physiological and emotional imprint can contribute to the person experiencing the same trauma reactions when triggered by any event or situation that reminds him or her of the original exposure. Vitality is often thwarted, and many refugees may recover from physical injuries and even find jobs and new friends in their new homes, but the sense of danger they continue to experience undermines their ability to have a robustly fulfilled life. This is what is meant by a state of traumatization, and it is for this reason that creative approaches to trauma treatment are essential to shift the refugee experience into one of inclusion, healing, restoration, and belonging (Gray 2015a).

The Creative Arts Therapies

The creative arts therapies, or CATS, recognize the creative process as fundamental to human development, relationship, and meaning-making (Gray 2015a). In the process of human development, children benefit from experiencing a balance between healthy structure and creative exploration. We need both. Dictionaries often define creativity with words like "the ability to create something new," "to innovate and begin anew." In this author's observation over two decades, survivors of trauma who continue to live in fear or terror most commonly have lost the ability or have a diminished ability to create or to perceive the world in creative ways. Another way to conceptualize being traumatized is being stuck in patterns arising from one's exposure moment of fear or terror. The full dimensionality of creative life can be reduced to duo- ("fight or flight") or uni- (shut down) dimensionality, so that survivors can lose a sense of purpose, vitality, and connection to things, people, and places that formerly mattered (Gray and Porges 2017). While this is not true for all survivors, it is true for many.

The majority of the world's refugees come from sociocentric cultures (Harris 2003), where a sense of self is defined more extensively and holistically than in the United States. The individualistic sense of self that defines the egocentric society of the United States can seem unusual to those who come from societies and cultures where family, community, ancestors, and even planets and the natural world are incorporated into a sense of self (Harris 2003). Sociocultural processes such as rituals and rites of passages are much more commonplace than psychotherapy and often integrate the arts: drumming, chanting, dancing, singing, playing music, and dramatic enactments. Poetry and art have been forces of expression, celebration, mourning, and documentation of all aspects of the human experience, from the most sublime to the mundane, since as long as humans have been known to exist.

In the context of psychotherapy in the Western and northern context, the primary categories of CATS include: art therapy, dance movement therapy, drama therapy, music therapy, and poetry therapy.

Art therapy (AT) is often described as a therapeutic process that allows clients to give form to their own state of internal chaos. It is defined as "an integrative mental health and human services profession that enriches the lives of individuals, families, and communities through active art-making, creative process, applied psychological theory, and human experience within a psychotherapeutic relationship" (American Art Therapy Association n.d.). Art therapy can be used as a powerful community intervention and to support a variety of treatment goals including: promoting self-awareness, insight, and self-esteem; resolving distress and conflicts; fostering emotional resilience; enhancing sensorimotor and cognitive functions and social skills; and further bringing about important ecological and societal transformation.

Dance/movement therapy (DMT) is an ancient form of physical release and expression that views the mind, body, and spirit as interconnected. Dance/movement therapy is defined as "the psychotherapeutic use of movement to further the emotional, cognitive, physical and social integration of the individual" (American Dance Therapy Association n.d.). DMT develops sensorimotor awareness and skills. It reconnects individuals with the core of our developmental progression, somatically and psychologically, because movement is a primary language for all humans, everywhere.

Drama therapy (DT) "is the intentional use of drama and/or theater processes to achieve therapeutic goals" (North American Drama Therapy Association n.d.). DT is an active approach that helps the client tell his or her story to solve a problem, achieve a catharsis, extend the breadth and depth of inner experience, understand the meaning of images, and strengthen the ability to observe personal roles while increasing flexibility between roles.

Music therapy (MT) "is the clinical and evidence-based use of music interventions to accomplish individualized goals within a therapeutic relationship by a credentialed professional who has completed an approved music therapy program" (American Music Therapy Association n.d.). Rhythm, also fundamental to DMT, is a core organizing principle of human life and is also an essential component of music therapies.

Poetry therapy (PT), which uses poetry "for healing and personal growth, may be traced back to primitive man, who used religious rites in which shamans and witch doctors chanted poetry for the well-being of the tribe or individual" (National Association for Poetry Therapy n.d.). Poetry therapy is the only one of the CATS that does not offer a certification credential. It combines writing with a variety of experiential processes and, in this author's experience, is one of the most "familiar" of the CATS for refugees.

An in-depth investigation of these therapies is not possible for this chapter, but each CAT is briefly defined and a sample activity or case based on actual work with refugees or asylum seekers is included to bring these powerful approaches to life.

Art Therapy

Art, as therapy, in this author's view, is one of the most initially accessible ways for refugees to begin to tell their story using nonverbal expression in a therapeutic or healing process. A premise of art therapy is that art offers an opportunity to begin with a blank, empty, or new landscape and create or re-create experience through the use of the elements of visual art: texture, color, image, symbol, shape (including sculpture), light, shadow, composition, and much more (King 2017).

Silencing is inherent to the human rights violations that many refugees are exposed to. The continuum of human language development begins with movement and evolves into the spoken word—with the metaphorical, imaginal, symbolic realm wedged between the two. Childhood, especially latency age from four or five years old to the beginning of puberty, is when the realm of the imaginal is core to communication, perception, and understanding. It is this author/clinician's observation that this intermediary symbolic realm is often the "relatively safest" place to begin communicating and expressing memories related to trauma. While current neuroscientific research clearly demonstrates the somatic nature of traumatic memory, working at the level of the body can be confronting and terrifying early in treatment, and verbalizing to share the trauma narrative—the unspeakable—can be impossible.

Candle Creation Art Therapy Process

Annie King, an art therapist and refugee youth counselor for Lutheran Family Services in Albuquerque, New Mexico, has developed and adapted many arts-based processes for her refugee clients. The idea for the candle art experiential activity shared in this chapter was developed by King in 2016 to offer at a World Refugee Celebration where she was asked to facilitate a large group art process. There are many things to consider in presenting an art process to large groups. Most important is the participants' experience. This particular event was held at a venue that had endless variables (such as no clear beginning or end time and the potential for 100 or more people coming to make art within a four-hour period). This made planning a challenge. With an overarching intention to offer an artistic process that was both interesting and appropriate for all ages, genders, artistic abilities, and cultures, this *candle creation* activity was born.

An important consideration is to create a process that will offer the opportunity for every participant to succeed, and for the large group art process, which could be intimidating, to be enjoyable and creative. The value of this process is as simple as the power of people creating an object of beauty and/or meaning, side by side, offering them a chance to connect, and exploring creatively in a shared space.

This arts therapy–based process supports connection, collaboration, and creation. Since the original use of this process in a large group setting, it has been adapted to be used in both small group and individual art therapy settings. This process was used in an Afghan refugee women's group and with individual refugee clients. It is appropriate for ages 12 and up (children as young as 8 can participate with close supervision and support) (King 2017).

CANDLE ART EXPERIENTIAL ACTIVITY

Supplies*:

- Seven-Day Candle
- Scissors
- Rulers, pencil sharpeners, erasers
- Pencils and colored pencils
- Markers
- Glue sticks, school glue, hot glue
- Diverse magazine images
- Paper, including white, colored, decorative, patterned, and printed
- Variety of stickers (universal symbols such as flowers, trees, animals, letters, seasons)

- Washi tape/decorative tape
- Variety of jewels and rhinestones, sequins
- Ribbon

*Please note that this is an elaborate material list and can be adapted depending on material availability and budget.

Preparation/ Directions: Create an "art buffet" of diverse, well-organized, and thoughtfully presented materials. Introduce the supplies and usage. Offer a number of examples unique to each type of supply (i.e., sequins, paper, stickers).

Introduce the exercise by sharing the following: "Today you will have the opportunity to decorate a candle to take home with you. Candles are used in numerous world cultures for many purposes. What do candles represent for you?" If they are using the exercise in a group, the facilitator may introduce it by saying, "We will begin our group by lighting a candle together."

For both the individual and group format, the facilitator can share, "Now you have the opportunity to create a candle with a special meaning. I will give you some instructions, but there are no rules. Create as you like with the intention you are holding. Be respectful and kind to each other in the art process. After I introduce you to the materials, you will have 45–75 minutes (depending upon the context) to decorate and create your candle. After that, we will gather to share our experiences."

Individual Therapy: In individual art therapy, this process can be used to evoke reflection, process, personal exploration, expression, and healing. The candle can be used to memorialize family members or friends who have died, to hold space for a missing family member, or to connect with a beloved they are separated from, all experiences that are common for refugees.

Group Therapy and Group Process Application: The facilitator may choose to light the candle and either invite the group (if it is already bonded or used to therapeutic processes) to create an intention or can state an intention for the group. The facilitator can light the candle to place in the center of the circle, or he or she can invite a group member to do so, or the group can choose someone to place the candle. Often in groups whose members share the same beliefs and traditions, their culturally referenced practices of leadership and holding space can inform who lights the candle.

Closing Questions and Process:

- Do you use candles in your daily lives?
- Do you use candles traditionally in your home, culture, or country?
- Please share something about the candle that you have made today.
- What did you learn?
- How did you feel while you made it?

The process for this activity can vary, depending upon the context in which the activity is offered (e.g., an ongoing therapy group; a one-time event), the willingness and/or ability of the group to engage in verbal processing, time, and many other variables. Some groups will answer the questions quite matter-of-factly, and others may offer metaphors or personal experiences, which offer rich opportunities to engage in a more therapeutic group process.

Dance/Movement Therapy

Dance/movement therapy is uniquely positioned at the convergence of CATS, somatic therapy, and neuroscience. With its emphasis on movement as a primary language and dance as the expression of that language, and the recognition that dance ranges from breath work to choreographed sequences of movement, DMT offers a range of nonverbal and verbal processes to work with those fleeing persecution whose reference for healing might be more somatically inclined and who are accustomed to the arts as a voice for healing and restoration. Dance for healing has been used for millennia in a broad cross section of countries and cultures. Australia's Aborigines have danced in community and ceremony, for healing and other sociocultural processes, for at least 40,000 years (Nadine Lee, personal interview, August 18, 2018). In many of the African countries where slaves were forcibly brought by colonizers to their own countries for labor, those dance and drum rituals and traditions followed them and exist today, albeit sometimes in altered forms. A strength of using DMT to work cross-culturally with populations who have been affected by mass violence and migration is the shared recognition of our body as a homeplace. In other words, no matter what one's cultural worldviews about home and place, our body is often perceived as a dwelling place for our spirit, soul, consciousness, or however the transpersonal aspect of the self is perceived.

Movement begins with breath; breath is what can control, quiet, diminish and expand, inspire, and create movement. For those reluctant to dance for cultural or other reasons, breath work and simple structured movement practices are important components of DMT for trauma that can facilitate the physiological shifts necessary to change psychological states, immediately and safely. In order to feel better, we cannot change with words or talking alone. Our thoughts, feelings, behaviors, perceptions, and actions are all literally rooted in our bodies. Changes in our biology and physiology are at the core of the trauma reaction. In order to change trauma-related beliefs or feelings, we have to promote physiological change, which means working at the level of the body (van der Kolk 2014). While the full scope of the physiological basis for DMT with refugee survivors of human rights violations is beyond the scope of this chapter, the following excerpt from a DMT case study with a refugee client of the author describes how resourcing, a fundamental component of somatic trauma therapy, is enhanced by DMT.

Resourcing through DMT

Resources are defined as "anything that helps a person maintain a sense of self and inner integrity in the face of disruption" (Diane Pool-Heller, personal interview with author, 1999). "Resourcing" is the term that describes the practice of assisting clients to recall, and reconnect to, anything that helped or helps them survive and, sometimes, thrive. It is fundamental to most somatic therapies.

This strength-focused approach acknowledges that survivors of traumatic events will need to process some aspects of their traumatic memories at some time (Gray In Press). Many clients describe the intensity of memories that are always "alive and well" in their bodies; remembering (except in cases of extreme shutdown or dissociation) is rarely the issue. While traumatic memory is rarely chronologically accurate, the potency of the shards of image and sensorimotoric-based implicit memory that reside in the body can make it too painful for survivors to talk about the past. A strong resource base gives survivors strength and a healing or positive experience reference point when trauma processing becomes uncomfortable or intolerable. Resources can be external (e.g., pets, a physical structure like a home or place of worship, clothing, or jewelry) or internal (e.g., pleasant sensations, feelings associated with positive emotions). Internal resources are likely to connect to implicit memory of the benevolent past. Often called body memory, these memories help clients integrate trauma memories into the broader context of their lives. In contrast to these body memories, the potency of the implicit trauma memories "grabs" the attention of the survivors; in many ways, PTSD and/or being traumatized is an attentional disorder that locks our attention in the past. It is generally considered optimal to begin trauma-focused therapy with attention to external resources, because identifying internal resources in a body that is equally filled with a minefield of trauma-related memory shards can trigger emotional and psychological reactivity.

Resources may be linked to or promote resiliency. Specific to the connection between resources and resilience, resilience has been defined as a process of "harnessing of resources to overcome adversity and sustain well-being" (Panter-Brick et al. 2018, 1803). Resilience can occur when someone is traumatized; it is often in states of traumatization that one's resilience becomes more obvious. A recent article on the complexity of resiliency summarizes Yehuda's perspective on this concept:

> My current definition of resilience as it applies to people would involve a reintegration of self that includes a conscious effort to move forward in an insightful integrated positive manner as a result of lessons learned from an

adverse experience. The idea of moving forward is an important component of resilience for me because this notion recognizes that some of the most resilient people, at least that I know, may have had or still have very severe PTSD that they struggle with every day. But they don't succumb to its negative effects. To me, resilience involves an active decision, like sobriety, that must be frequently reconfirmed. That decision is to keep moving forward. (Southwick et al. 2014)

A case example from this author's practice using a pseudonym demonstrates moving from external to internal resources with a refugee client who survived human rights abuses.

JEANNINA: A CASE EXAMPLE

Jeannina was a 53-year-old woman who fled her African home after a series of massacres followed by prolonged war that engulfed her community and country. She arrived in the United States alone, because her husband and three sons had been killed. One daughter already resided in the United States; the other remained behind in her homeland. Jeannina fled her country after the young soldiers who took her husband and sons away raped her repeatedly.

An intern at a torture treatment program assessed Jeannina, and after three intake sessions, the intern asked this therapist to take over. When asked anything about her past, benevolent or traumatic, Jeannina shut down. If probed, she would either remain dissociated, a clinical condition of being shut down to the point of "disappearing," or begin to emote intensely. The intern felt helpless and afraid of triggering Jeannina, hence her request that I take over.

While Jeannina would show up for every appointment, she would say very little. It is not uncommon that survivors of relational trauma will need considerable time to begin to trust the therapeutic relationship. When the assessment process involves any questioning that includes aspects of trauma history, the delicate balance of gathering information and establishing rapport can "make or break" the ongoing therapeutic process.

When clients keep showing up, it can indicate that trust is developing, and one of the skills the DMT therapist can employ is observation of subtle movement cues that indicate engagement. Movement, in this case, is not limited to gross motor movements; observing all aspects of a client's somatic presentation such as the way he or she dresses, the way the client greets the therapist, and the polyvagal-informed DMT and continuum movement (Gray and Porges 2017), and "markers of engagement" (i.e., shifts in posture, facial expressivity, vocal and body prosody [fluidity and variability in intonation and movement], mood and state, and gaze) can communicate what is unspoken but present in the growing relationship. These polyvagal-informed therapies are based on the integration of Dr. Porges's (2011) polyvagal theory with dance movement therapy's principles and theories.

As Jeannina continued to show up, but say very little, her nonverbal presence began to tell a story. Always on the lookout for resources to build into the early phases of therapy, this therapist noticed that Jeannina shifted from wearing the Western clothes she was given upon her arrival to the United States to wearing traditional African dresses. Her initial clinical presentation, from the perspective of DMT, was of a body shrunken in fearful withdrawal. Her kinesphere (or "personal space bubble") was retracted, and as this therapist has observed in many survivors of multiple rapes, her back was hyperconstricted and her belly was distended. She slumped in her chair. She did not make eye contact, except for a brief occasional moment, and it looked almost physically painful for her to lift her head. Her voice was monotonous when she spoke. On the third week of wearing traditional clothes, the dress she wore was particularly bright: a bold combination of yellow, oranges, gold, and red. Commenting on this very noticeable dress, the therapist noted that she had noticed the switch to traditional clothing and the unusually bright colors she wore today. With what sounded to this therapist as a little bit of pride, Jeannina sat up a little straighter and said, "Oh yes; my sister made this dress. She is one of the finest seamstresses in our region and sewed clothes for all the important people."

Early in treatment, it can be helpful to find external resources and to link them to internal resources, that is, how an individual expresses the thought or memory or experience of external resources (such as a church, or pet, or jewelry) in the body. The process for doing this is quite simple, and the following questions offer a template for this process:

Therapist: "It's a beautiful dress. I am curious how it feels to wear it today?"

Client: "It makes me feel my home"

Therapist: "Can you describe how it makes you feel your home?"

Client: "I can see and feel the African sun; the colors are of the sun."

> Therapist: "What does the African sun look like when you see it?"
>
> Client (with increased enthusiasm and engagement; sitting up straighter, more prosody in her voice and gesturing the rising and setting of the sun): "Oh, the African sun is big and yellow, and it rises up like this (gesturing) every morning. It tells me the day has begun. When it sets, it changes colors, and it is orange and red and goes to sleep quietly. The day is done and tomorrow is a new day."
>
> Therapist: "What does the sun feel like when it rises and sets?"
>
> Client: "It is warm. It is warm on my skin, my face, and I feel its light."
>
> Therapist: "Can we do this movement, and imagine the African sun rising, and feel the warmth?"

I asked Jeannina to show me the shape of the rising and setting sun because I saw that she had moved a little when describing it. Using her hands only, she opened them a little above her lap to show the sun coming up and then closed them in an almost prayer-like gesture to show the setting sun. I did this with her and then asked if we could make the shape and movement of the sun together.

We continued in this fashion, connecting the colors, images, memories, and movements of the African sun to her internal state. In the first session, she smiled a tiny smile and seemed to be more engaged in the conversation, as the markers of engagement became more visible. Over the following months, as this potent gesture became the practice that was our opening and closing ritual, Jeannina demonstrated and described a stronger sense of her body. This embodiment was evident in a restoration of markers of engagement, as evidenced by increased vocal and body prosody, increased facial expressivity, an increase in positive moods and socially engaged states (i.e., she was more conversational, increased physical contact such as hand shaking, and smiled and laughed more), and an ability to stay present (i.e., she no longer became intensely emotional or "disappeared" when describing both her benevolent and her traumatic history).

The discovery and ongoing practice of this ritual opened up the pathway to resourcing that served us throughout the rest of our work together. This became our regular opening, and closing, to all our sessions. Over time, we took this movement to the vertical dimension, rising out of the chair and standing, increasing her movement repertoire, which in DMT is a pathway to increasing emotional expressivity. The relationship between physiological state and emotional and psychological state is now well established (van der Kolk 2014). Movement shifts a person's physiological state because it engages his or her nervous system as an aspect of nonvolitional movement. Our shared opening and closing "dance" mimicking the sunrise and sunset held beneath the appearance of the movement itself implicit memories of her relationship to the daily sun's movements in her homeland. Each time we explored these movements, she described growing stronger because it reminded her of home and family and a rhythm that had defined her life before the violence that caused her to flee and to lose her family. Connecting to an external or exogenous rhythm can shift internal or endogenous rhythms, such as respiration and heart rate, thereby shifting physiological state (Gray and Porges 2017).

Resourcing through DMT is a subtle but profound process that enables a client to prepare for the difficult task of revisiting haunting memories and processing the loss, grief, and trauma that hold them captive to the past. Most survivors of relational trauma have endured losses of some sort; a loss of a sense of self is common, and for refugees and others who are displaced, the losses are very tangible, such as home, job, material belongings, and family members. When resources can be connected to some embodied sense of self, they can prepare clients for the restorative process. The restorative process refers to the simultaneous processing of trauma memories with ongoing resourcing, that is, connecting clients to what keeps them strong. The restorative process replaces the commonly used term "trauma recovery," as there is no true, full recovery. The therapist facilitates the process of the client restoring as much of what gives him or her meaning and a sense of belonging as possible.

Drama Therapy

Drama therapy offers refugees opportunities to imagine new possibilities. Using creativity, spontaneity, role-plays, and metaphor, drama therapy can create opportunities to move uncomfortable stories to past history, where they belong, and create new stories in the present. In her years of working with refugees, Drama Therapist Heidi Landis has had the opportunity to co-create, with colleagues, a drama therapy intervention named *Sobremesa Ensemble*. This name was created by the group Landis was working with in New York City at a center for newly arrived refugees who attended an ongoing drama therapy group. The group was made up of members from multiple Spanish- and French-speaking countries. *Sobremesa* is a Spanish word referring to the conversation at the table that continues after a meal is over and *ensemble* is the French word for together. During a time of sharing after the drama therapy session, the group decided to combine the words to reflect the experience they had shared and created together.

The timing of the creation of this intervention is important, as it was just before the Thanksgiving holiday. Holidays in the country of resettlement can be painful for those who have migrated to a new country (Heidi Landis, e-mail message to author, November 28, 2018). Immigration is never an easy option. Leaving people and places behind always comes at an excruciating price. As Warsan Shire, the British-Somali poet writes, in her poem *Home*, "No one leaves home unless home is the mouth of a shark" (Shire 2015). Clients of all ages have expressed great sadness and often confusion over the holidays (Heidi Landis, e-mail message to author, November 28, 2018). They are expected not only to understand what is happening around them but also to join the celebration, no matter their circumstances around language, finances, family situations, and traumatic experiences. This reality can exacerbate the feelings of loss they have for the celebrations and rites of passage they miss back home.

In this exercise, participants are asked to create a new holiday that celebrates the group, class, or community that they are currently in. After the creation of Sobremesa Ensemble, other groups have been asked to brainstorm qualities that make their group unique and use those to create a new group holiday—one that can be celebrated together through a drama therapy enactment to foster creativity, connection, and new role possibilities.

CASE EXAMPLE—CREATION OF SOBREMESA ENSEMBLE

It was the day before Thanksgiving break and Heidi Landis (e-mail message to author, November 28, 2018) describes working with a group of newly arrived immigrant teens in an international high school. The day had already been stressful, and there had been fights in the hallway and at lunch time, and the group was quieter than usual. Although Heidi was aware of the difficulties that her group members felt around this time of year, they were not wanting to engage it directly. She began the group with a check-in, asking each group member to tell about his or her favorite holiday. Many chose a holiday from their culture, and there was great delight in explaining the customs and often the food surrounding their holiday of choice. After a brief physical warm-up, the group was asked to think about the qualities they as a group community had in common. They started off slowly with things like "well there are nine of us" and "we are from many different countries." As the group started to think a bit more, they became more playful and the list grew to include: We are funny; we work hard, sometimes; we usually talk too much; we love gum; we are mostly respectful; we work together well; we are smart; and most of us are late to school. Using this list as a jumping-off point, the group was asked to use the list to create a group holiday—one that was just theirs that could celebrate their newly found community. They were to come up with a name and how they would celebrate. After some debate, the group named the holiday "Happy Smile Nine" day. Once the traditions were created, Heidi asked the group to choose characters that they might like to play in order to announce this holiday to the world. One student became a mayor, another a news reporter, another a store owner who would sell all the decorations that one would need for "Happy Smile Nine" day, and another a pop star who would create a celebratory song. As the group took on their new characters, the enactment began, with the mayor announcing to the world that a new holiday was created. It was announced that the holiday would be celebrated in the following way:

"Happy Smile Nine" Day Traditional Celebration Rituals

- You must eat nine different snacks from nine different cultures.
- You must sleep until 11:30.
- You must play games for at least 109 minutes or until you are happy and smiling.
- You must chew gum while playing games.
- You must work together with someone else from a different culture to cook a new dish to be shared at a large feast.

As the scenes played out, with various announcements about the holiday, storekeepers having holiday sales and families preparing to celebrate, the mood of the group shifted. After the group members came out of their roles, they spent some time in reflection, and the group commented that they felt excited about creating something that they all felt a part of. It led them to be able to really speak about how hard it was to be away from family and how confusing it was to try to be a part of celebrations that either did not mean much to them or were celebrated differently. They asked if they could actually celebrate "Happy Smile Nine" day at the school as a way to continue to create community. Barring the sleeping to 11:30 on a school day tradition, the principal said yes.

Music Therapy

Music therapy is another powerful approach. If one visits the remains of World War II concentration camps in Europe, one sees evidence of how the prisoners of those camps found ways to be creative, in service of their survival. Many examples of drawings, art, and music have been discovered and are on display at former camps; this author visited Auschwitz and bore witness to the many drawings and musical scores that were left by the prisoners. They are on display as evidence of the resiliency and fortitude of the human spirit and our call to survive and remain connected to life, even in terrible times.

Music therapy, like DMT, is both embodied and creative. Music, chanting, and rhythmic practices are core to many healing rituals around the world. There is an established evidence base for the benefits of music therapy for those living with depression (Gray 2011). Dr. Stephen Porges, noted researcher and developer of the polyvagal theory, writes:

> Music is intertwined with emotions, affect regulation, and interpersonal social behavior and other psychological processes that describe basic human experiences in response to environmental, interpersonal, and even intrapersonal challenges. These psychological processes shape our sense of self, contribute to our abilities to form relationships, and determine whether we feel safe in various contexts or with specific people. Although these processes can be objectively observed and subjectively described, they represent a complex interplay between our psychological experience and our physiology. (2011, 246)

Music can serve as a common denominator between a therapist and his or her refugee client. Music is truly a universal language; each and every culture has a relationship to sound, whether it is spiritual chanting, drumming, folk songs, or music played on a variety of ancient and modern instruments. Music's role in healing and restoration has been documented since ancient times.

The following case study from Brian Harris and colleagues of a young male refugee illustrates the power of music therapy in restoring communication and connection.

THE CASE OF ADNAN[1]

When I first met Adnan, he was 5 years old. A small boy with expressive blue eyes and messy blond hair, a local non-governmental organization referred him to the music therapy for delays in speech development, difficulties in socializing with his peers and concerns related to attachment and transition. I met with Adnan's mother, Sanela, prior to beginning treatment to learn about Adnan's history, including his family background. In our first encounter, Sanela appeared frightened and withdrawn. Her dark hair and skin contrasted with her son's light colouring. She held her body tightly to herself, lowered her head and made limited eye contact with me. She spoke in a soft, shaky voice about her son's difficulties, describing Adnan as very attached to her and having difficulty communicating and socializing with others. Sanela indicated that he relied heavily on her, and she felt the weight of this. In relation to his speech development, Adnan had seen a speech pathologist who could find no physiological reasons for his delay. Sanela's collapsed body posture, shaky vocal timbre, lack of eye contact and flat emotional affect appeared to indicate she was experiencing the effects of trauma. Understanding this likelihood was an important facet for my contextualization of Adnan's development.

My first meeting with Adnan took place in the Children's Room, a play space used to help children transition in and out of therapy. As I entered the room with a male interpreter, Adnan immediately stuck his chest out, put one hand on his waist, pointed to me and said in a low and forceful voice, 'You will not come near me!' He gave me the impression of a bird making himself appear larger out of fear. I instructed the interpreter to get down on the floor like I did, so we could make ourselves appear smaller and less threatening. During this session, the interpreter and I remained on the floor. I moved slowly and deliberately, engaging in independent play. I did not attempt to bring Adnan into the music therapy room at this time, waiting first to establish trust and to ease his difficulty in transition.

Eventually, Adnan was able to enter into my space. It became clear that the combination of separation from his mother and introduction of two strange men overwhelmed Adnan and would not make for a safe environment in which he could begin work. Therefore, in the second session, we invited Adnan's mother to join. This situation, however, was complicated due to her presumed trauma history and symbiotic relationship with Adnan. These complications impacted the clinical process, but it seemed necessary for Adnan to feel safe and aided his transition into therapy. Sanela's presence provided the security and familiarity he needed to enter into the session room. By the third session, with his mother joining, we were able to move into the music therapy room at the beginning of the session.

In this third session together, Adnan sat next to me at the piano, his mother beside us. After a brief hesitation, Adnan began to explore the piano keys. He played with a wide range of expression, greater than he had displayed outside the music, and examined the full range of notes and dynamics. He took my hands and made tonal clusters, screaming afterward as if to say, 'It hurts'. He began conducting me by looking at me intently to make sure I was following him. He raised his small hands and held them in mid-air, then slammed them down on the piano, watching to make sure I followed suit. Our hands produced a loud tonal cluster of sound. It had the auditory impact of an explosion. I instinctively kept my foot on the sustain pedal, allowing the sounds to continue resonating. As I did this, Adnan first looked at me and then stared away, as if absorbing the significance of the sound we had produced. He allowed for silence afterward.

Following the silence, he began to explore playful sounds and facial expressions. During this session and in following weeks, Adnan repeated this sequence of alternating between loud sounds and silences. It is worth noting that during the first eight sessions, Adnan did not move from the piano to explore other instruments or parts of the room. This consistency and predictability seemed important to his development of trust and sense of safety with the sound environment and with me as a therapist. Though I saw the limits of not being able to work with his family and the community system, I was moved to be a witness to his growth. By witnessing and accepting the magnitude of his expression, I was able to help him move this experience into a state of play, and to develop a context within which containment of and transition beyond his trauma associations were also possible.

The creation of sound described in the study with Adnan illustrated a musical representation of a traumatic experience. In his daily life, Adnan had great difficulty with transitions. He experienced anxiety with endings and beginnings, particularly when these involved separating from his mother. Adnan also appeared frozen in certain aspects of his development. This freeze was likely related to the developmental trauma he had experienced as a result of his heavily traumatized environment (van der Kolk 2005). In music therapy, Adnan used the frame of the piano and containment of the music to create his expression of this experience. Importantly, although this range of expression outside of music may have been retraumatizing, Adnan was able to make sense of it inside the music. In this case, music acted as a safe container in which to re-examine prior and recurring traumatic experiences, allowing broken boundaries to become framed, and frozen developmental states to become mutable. By creating a safe environment for Adnan's expressions, music and the therapeutic relationship helped Adnan move towards a healthier social and emotional development and gave him a stronger and more effective 'voice' for his expressions. As Adnan transitioned to his daily life after the music therapy sessions, he began to generalize these areas of growth to experiences with family and with community systems.

Over the nearly two-year course of work with Adnan, he demonstrated significant changes in his health and development. His transition to other instruments and expressions in music therapy became linked to a growing ease with other transitions in his life. Additionally, his speech improved as he began to vocalize various emotions in his sessions. Adnan's capacity to develop a trusting relationship in therapy also served as a model for reframing his relationship with his mother.

The case of Adnan illustrates music therapy's ability to promote Adnan's state-shifting from fear, and frozenness, to play and meaningful engagement with both his mother and the therapist. Music as therapy can draw the silenced voice out into the world without the burden of choosing words to create the coherent narrative that traumatic memory erases. Music is as universal as breath; it differs per country, and culture, but through rhythm, sound, melody, harmony, and the myriad other components of music that inspire emotion and connection, the wounds of developmental and war trauma can be healed. Music therapy offered Adnan a space to express his most uncomfortable feelings in the context of safe relationship, with his therapist, which enabled him to strengthen his relationship with his mother.

Poetry Therapy

Poetry therapy represents the oldest and most common use of an art form to support the restorative process. The silence that commonly accompanies and defines the states of traumatization often experienced by those surviving egregious human rights abuses can contribute to a sense of being completely isolated and alone. This isolation may be the most difficult aspect of their suffering, for human beings are "wired" to connect and be in relationship (Porges 2011).

Shanee Stepakoff, a poetry therapist and clinical psychologist who has worked with refugees and survivors of torture for many years, writes that psychotherapeutic "methods that rely on the creative utilization of language are particularly salient for survivors of ethnopolitical traumatic loss. Most survivors do not readily find words to describe their experiences and emotions, particularly not in the early stages of recovery. In addition, larger sociocultural and political forces discourage—and even actively suppress—the verbal narration of the violations they have endured" (Stepakoff and Ashour 2011, 22).

In order to promote movement along the continuum of human language, from the forcibly silenced nonverbal to the spoken word, giving refugee clients an opportunity to express through written word in the context of a safe, caring relationship "paves a pathway for reconnection with self and restoration of the capacity to connect with other human beings" (Stepakoff and Ashour 2011, 22). Poetry therapy is a formal academic and professional discipline, primarily used in the United States, with growing use elsewhere, that recognizes the transformative power of literature in ancient cultures, such as Arabic culture.

Two common ways of working with poetry in therapy are receptive (working with an existing poem) and expressive (creating one's own poem) (Stepakoff and Ashour 2011). A passive poetry therapy practice could utilize a poem suggested by the client or the therapist. In one example, a client from the Middle East who had sustained serious injuries to his spine during torture had focused on this pain for most of his treatment. It was very challenging for him to focus on anything positive or resourcing. Eventually, after several months of therapy that focused on somatic and dance therapy practices to reduce pain, he began to share stories from his home country. The horror of what he had suffered there caused him to shun his home initially. When he began sharing some of his earlier, happier history, he remembered some of his favorite poets and writers from back home. Following a session in which he described both his and his mother's torture, which he was forced to witness, he brought in prose by a favorite mystical author. The piece told the story of a flute whose beautiful music was created by the cutting of a branch from its tree, and the subsequent hollowing of the wood. The flute's music was its mourning for what it had lost.

After relating this poem to his own torture, and metaphorically connecting his suffering to a meaningful cultural resource, he decided he wanted to write his own poem. Drawing a line from another poem he loved, we used an expressive technique where he chose his favorite line ("When the flute speaks") and shared its meaning with the therapist. In a subsequent session, requested by the client who said, "I want to write my own story," the phrase was used as a cue. The client chose to write a poem instead of a story, and the therapist and client co-created the poem named "When the Flute Speaks" to tell his own story, in his own words.

This expressive technique is done by inviting the client to bring in a poem, or read or listen to a poem chosen by the therapist (passive), and then reflect and share the meaning, emotions, and sensation of the poem with the therapist. For this client, the therapist requested a line from the story of the flute, and the line he chose was "When the flute speaks." To create the poem, the therapist recited this line and either held up a single finger, to request the client to say a word, or an entire hand (all five fingers), to invite the client to offer a phrase, to complete a phrase that relates to "when the flute speaks." This is the poem the client wrote:

When the Flute Speaks.
When the flute speaks, I soften.
When the flute speaks, join life.
When the flute speaks, I feel the snake dance.
When the flute speaks, it complains to go back to what it once was.
When the flute speaks,
Sweetness,
Mourning,
Emptiness,
Sweetness.
When the flute speaks,
It brings calm to the soul.

Conclusion

The creative arts, from ancient cave paintings to modern rap music, chronicle the human journey. Each of the refugee clients described in this chapter, whether as individual clients or in group therapy, benefited from creative arts therapy as part of their healing and restoration. Whether to resource and connect a client to his or her strengths or foster connection through metaphor, shared experience, and meaning, the painful challenges of resettlement and the suffering caused by traumatization following violent displacement were made more endurable through CATS. Once referred to as "adjunct" or "alternative" therapies, CATS are now gaining credence as promising and even best practice treatment for trauma. Neuroscientific research, growing evidence bases in each of the CATS, the very cross-cultural nature of this work, and increased awareness that talk therapies are simply not enough to meet the undescribable, unutterable reality of traumas resulting from war, political violence, and human rights abuses, all converge in strong support of CATS to promote restorative processes with refugees and asylees. CATS are adaptable to the myriad of cultures that comprise refugee and asylum-seeking communities; they may be more familiar to the healing and sociocultural processes that many refugees are accustomed to. CATS provide safety and containment through a strong theoretical base and structured practices and activities and are naturally adapted to individual, family, group, and community work. Personal development is supported by a healthy balance of structure and creative exploration. To restore this creative process, treatment must engage creativity. As a species, we might be seen to be the result of a creative process of survival. From this perspective, CATS are a therapeutic approach that promote social engagement, human connection, and more familiar and nurturing environments for growth and healing. Perhaps, CATS are even in service of evolution.

Note

1. Reprinted with permission from B. Harris, M. Gonsalves, S. Katz, C. Kenny, D. Price, and P. Nolan, "Music Therapy for Children and Families with Mass Trauma Exposure," in *Music Therapy and Trauma: Bridging Theory and Clinical Practice*, 1st ed., ed. K. Stewart (New York: Satchnote Press, 2010), 203–228.

References

American Art Therapy Association. n.d. "About Art Therapy." https://arttherapy.org/about-art-therapy/.

American Dance Therapy Association. n.d. "What Is Dance/Movement Therapy?" https://adta.org/wp-content/uploads/2015/12/What-is-DanceMovement-Therapy.pdf.

American Music Therapy Association. n.d. "What Is Music Therapy?" https://www.musictherapy.org/about/musictherapy/.

Gray, Amber Elizabeth. 2011. "Expressive Arts Therapies: Working with Survivors of Torture." *Torture* 21, no. 1: 39–47. https://irct.org/assets/uploads/Expressive_art_therapies_Torture1-2011.pdf.

Gray, Amber Elizabeth. 2015a. "Dance/Movement Therapy with Refugee and Survivor Children: A Healing Pathway Is a Creative Process." In *Creative Interventions for Traumatized Children*, 2nd ed., edited by Cathy A. Malchiodi, 169–190. New York: The Guilford Press.

Gray, Amber Elizabeth. 2015b. "The Broken Body: Somatic Perspectives on Surviving Torture." In *Therapists Creating a Cultural Tapestry: Using the Creative Therapies across Cultures*, edited by Stephanie L. Brooke and Charles E. Myers, 170–190. Springfield, IL: Charles C. Thomas.

Gray, Amber Elizabeth. 2018. "Roots, Rhythm, Reciprocity: Polyvagal-Informed Dance Movement Therapy for Survivors of Trauma." In *Clinical Applications of the Polyvagal Theory: The Emergence of Polyvagal-Informed Therapies*, edited by Stephen W. Porges and Deb A. Dana, 207–226. New York: Norton Books.

Gray, Amber Elizabeth. In Press. "Body as Voice: Restorative Dance/Movement Psychotherapy with Survivors of Relational Trauma." In *The Routledge International Handbook of Embodied Perspectives on Psychotherapy: Approaches from Dance Movement and Body Psychotherapies*, edited by Helen Payne, Sabine Koch, and Jennifer Tantia. London: Routledge Publishers.

Gray, Amber Elizabeth, and Stephen Porges. 2017. "Polyvagal-Informed Dance Movement Therapy: Dance/Movement Therapy with Children Who Shut Down. Restoring Core Rhythmicity." In *What to Do When Children Clam Up in Psychotherapy: Interventions to Facilitate Communication*, edited by Cathy A. Malchiodi and David A. Crenshaw, 102–136. New York: Guildford Press.

Harris, David Allen. 2003. "Cross-cultural Intervention: Viewing Therapy through the Lens of Culture." Presentation at the Rocky Mountain Survivors Center, January. Denver, Colorado.

King, Annie. 2017. "Seeking Refuge: Restoring Belonging after Large Scale Loss with Refugee Survivors of War." Presentation at the 8th Annual Expressive Therapies Summit, October 12–15, 2017. New York.

Lazarus, Emma. 2005. "The New Colossus." In *Emma Lazarus: Selected Poems: (American Poets Project #13)*, edited by John Hollander , 58. New York: The Library of America.

National Association for Poetry Therapy. n.d. "History of NAPT." https://poetrytherapy.org/index.php/about-napt/history-of-napt/.

North American Drama Therapy Association. n.d. What Is Drama Therapy? http://www.nadta.org/what-is-drama-therapy.html.

Panter-Brick, Catherine, Kristin Hadfield, Rana Dajani, Mark Eggerman, Alastair Ager, and Michael Ungar. 2018. "Resilience in Context: A Brief and Culturally Grounded Measure for Syrian Refugee and Jordanian Host-Community Adolescents." *Child Development* 89, no. 5: 1803–1820. doi: 10.1111/cdev.12868.

Porges, Stephen W. 2011. *The Polyvagal Theory: Neurophysiological Foundations of Emotions, Attachment, Communication, Self-Regulation.* New York: W.W. Norton.

Porges, Stephen W. In Press. *Music Therapy & Trauma: Insights from the Polyvagal Theory.* In *Symposium on Music Therapy & Trauma: Bridging Theory and Clinical Practice,* edited by K. Stewart. New York: Satchnote Press. https://pdfs.semanticscholar.org/ae81/423342b0b7e2eb2f0d97eb09b5b19c60de54.pdf.

Shire, Warsan. 2015. "Home." http://seekershub.org/blog/2015/09/home-warsan-shire/.

Southwick, Steven M., George A. Bonanno, Ann S. Masten, Catherine Panter-Brick, and Rachel Yehuda. 2014. "Resilience Definitions, Theory, and Challenges: Interdisciplinary Perspectives." *European Journal of Psychotraumatology* 5. doi: 10.3402/ejpt.v5.25338.

Stepakoff, Shanee, and Lina Ashour. 2011. Reading and Writing: Working with Traumatic Grief among Iraqi Refugees in Jordan. *The Forum: The Quarterly Publication of the Association for Death Education and Counseling: Special Issue on Expressive Therapies in Thanotology* 37, no. 1: 22–23.

UNHCR. 2015. *Annual Global Trends 2014,* June 18, 2015. https://www.unhcr.org/statistics/country/556725e69/unhcr-global-trends-2014.html.

UNHCR. 2018. *Figures at a Glance,* June 19, 2018. https://www.unhcr.org/figures-at-a-glance.html.

van der Kolk, Bessel. 2005. "Developmental Trauma Disorder: Toward a Rational Diagnosis for Children with Complex Trauma Histories." *Psychiatric Annals* 35: 401–408.

van der Kolk, Bessel. 2014. *The Body Keeps the Score: Brain, Mind and Body in the Healing of Trauma.* New York: Viking Press.

CHAPTER FOURTEEN

Future Directions to Promote the Rights of Refugees and Asylum Seekers

S. Megan Berthold and Kathryn R. Libal

Substantive structural change is required to address the widespread assaults to the well-being and dignity of refugees and asylum seekers documented throughout this book (Ostrander, Melville, and Berthold 2017). Little lasting or meaningful transformation for the majority of forced migrants will occur without changing institutions, laws, and systems and building public support among those who may feel indifferent or even hostile to refugees and asylum seekers. This concluding chapter highlights a number of avenues and mechanisms for such systemic transformation that employs a wide array of stakeholders. These include clinicians, public health workers, social workers, teachers, lawyers, policy makers, other professionals, and ordinary members of society, including refugees and asylum seekers themselves. Cooperation and coalition building between each of these constituencies can more effectively promote the rights of refugees and asylum seekers in domestic and global contexts.

A number of contributors to this book have made a case for human rights–based approaches that build capacity for substantive advocacy, legal, and policy change. Only through collective action to challenge unjust policies and practices is such a change possible. In this brief chapter, we provide several examples of ways to become engaged on these issues at universities and in communities.

Human Rights–Based Approaches: Building Capacity for Advocacy and Social Change

A human rights–based approach to clinical work with refugees is important and necessarily requires practitioners to be equipped to bridge the divide between micro and macro practice (Androff and McPherson 2014; Berthold 2015). Much work remains for clinicians to have the capacity to do so. Strengthening their understanding of the right to rehabilitation (Berthold and Libal 2016) and using relevant human rights instruments and mechanisms (Androff 2016; McPherson 2018) are essential ingredients in this process. As Yamin (2008) argues, however, the question of a human rights–based approach to health must be addressed by first taking the suffering of all human beings seriously. This would call for a fundamental shift in our approaches to rights and to health in theory and practice, something radically different from the dominant individually oriented approach to public health and clinical medicine prevalent in many societies. Yamin (2008) stresses that what is needed is accountability and frameworks that support accountability. This is relevant beyond the realm of health for all domains of rights. Consonant with the codes of ethics for health and social service professions, fostering human dignity and flourishing, regardless of citizenship status or cultural or national identities, is critical to this work. And, as Humphries (2004) underscores, merely developing skills for anti-oppressive practice at the micro level will not bring about the necessary change to eliminate the conditions producing human rights violations that immigrants, refugees, and asylum seekers face.

Forced migration is a global phenomenon, and solutions must address the interconnectedness of contributing factors beyond and across borders, while also developing policies to protect the rights of refugees, asylum seekers, and migrants at local and national levels. The processes to craft global compacts on refugees and safe migration (UN Global Compact on Refugees 2018; UN Global Compact on Safe, Orderly, and Regular Migration 2018) and the inclusion of migration in the UN Sustainable Development Goals are the most visible recent international mechanisms to highlight the necessity of developing global solutions. The New York Declaration for Refugees and Migrants (UN General Assembly 2016) calls for a "multi-stakeholder, whole-of-society" approach. This entails involving "national and local authorities, international organizations, international financial institutions, regional organizations, regional coordination and partnership mechanisms, civil society partners, including faith-based organizations and academia, the private sector, media and refugees themselves" (2016, Annex 1, para. 2).

We must focus efforts to combat antimigrant and refugee policies and practices at local, national, regional, and global levels. In doing so, voices at all levels matter. The more stakeholder voices reaching all possible venues and persons in positions of influence and power on these issues, the better. Those on the front lines working with migrants have made a difference in providing expert opinions in court cases regarding the impact of family separation on the well-being of children, testimony in legislative hearings, and research findings to support policy advocacy (LaFaute and Coene 2018; Linton, Griffin, and Shapiro 2017; Miller 2018; Zayas and Bradlee 2014).

Constituent groups often seek to influence the actions and votes of elected policy makers. Civil society actors (such as community groups, nongovernmental organizations, labor unions, indigenous groups, charitable organizations, faith-based organizations, professional associations, and foundations) have also mobilized and have had a formal and powerful role in providing testimony and advocacy reports to UN Committee bodies charged with monitoring states regarding various human rights issues. For example, the U.S. National Consortium of Torture Treatment Programs (NCTTP) has made progress regarding the right to rehabilitation for torture survivors. The NCTTP received training and consultation from the U.S. Human Rights Network (USHRN), a nationwide network of individuals and grassroots groups that furthers the building of leadership and capacity to strengthen the culture and movement for human rights within the United States, facilitate collective action, and hold authorities accountable.

The USHRN organized many civil society actors to contribute reports (called *shadow reports*) and in-person testimony in Geneva, Switzerland, to the UN Committee against Torture (CAT) at the time that it was doing a formal periodic review of how well the United States was upholding its obligations under the UN Convention against Torture (UN General Assembly 1984). The National Consortium of Torture Treatment Programs (2014) developed a Shadow Report response to the U.S. Report in preparation for the U.S. review before the UN Committee against Torture (CAT) held in November 2014. The NCTTP Shadow Report was submitted and excerpts presented on November 11, 2014, to the UN Committee against Torture. It focused on Article 14 (The Right to Rehabilitation) of the Convention against Torture. Along with other members of civil society, a delegation of three members of the NCTTP's Executive Committee (including Piwowarczyk and Riley, contributors to this volume, and Mary Lynn Everson) met with the UN Committee against Torture. Other civil society actors spoke against U.S. police brutality and the treatment of Guantanamo detainees as torture. The UN Committee against Torture incorporated some of the points from these shadow reports and testimony in its concluding observations and recommendations (UN Committee against Torture 2014). Mobilizing and advocacy can matter. In addition, Dr. Piwowarczyk, NCTTP president, delivered brief testimony on the right to rehabilitation of torture survivors on November 11, 2014, at the time of the U.S. periodic review to the U.S. Government Delegation.

As the example of NCTTP's advocacy discussed earlier shows, developing awareness of and capacity for advocacy and institutional change to realize the rights of refugees and asylum seekers is predicated on creating multifaceted networks of support. This is important not only for those whose rights may be violated or otherwise denied but also for those working in solidarity with refugees and asylum seekers. The New York Declaration calls specifically on civil society partners—including those in academia and the private sector—to participate in this process. Indeed, to counter movements in the Global North that seek to radically restrict access to refugees, asylum seekers, and migrants (largely from the Global South), innovative approaches to advocacy must be developed. One means of doing so is to use digitally based networking for training, information sharing, and organizing, such as efforts by the Migrant Rights Network in the United Kingdom or the European Network of Migrant Women. Participating in research networks, such as the newly established Policy, Politics, and Culture: EU Migration and Integration Network, provides another forum for translating research into practice (see also Salehyan 2018).

Such advocacy efforts are often not as visible to grassroots constituents, let alone refugees and asylum seekers themselves. Thus, more systematic and sustained effort is needed to develop bridges between scholars and practitioners, who conduct research on the experiences of asylum seekers and refugees or have direct insights related to their experiences based on practice, and those who play key roles in shaping programs and policies at local, national, or international levels. As the backlash against refugees, asylum seekers, and other migrants has developed in recent years, translating research and practice findings to broader publics has become all the more critical. In the United States, for example, weak public awareness of the refugee resettlement program made it much easier for the Trump administration to curtail the program. Absent recognized Congressional or other public figures championing resettlement, as well as limited public involvement in resettlement, it has become an easy target to effectively dismantle (see Chapter 4).

Challenging Unjust Policies and Practice

Gaining knowledge of domestic laws and policies and international human rights law that impact forced migrants is a necessary first step for those seeking to challenge unjust policies and practices. This content should be systematically integrated into professional curricula broadly across multiple disciplines. Clinical practitioners in many fields, for example, should be on alert for health and mental health effects of unjust and inhumane policies and laws and assess and treat them accordingly. In addition, health and social service practitioners need to be aware of eligibility criteria for various benefits as well as the implications of using such benefits and alterative options when making treatment or care plans. Community-based social workers, public health and mental health practitioners, and allied professionals must understand and be prepared to work in coalition to address the limits of social welfare supports for refugees and asylum seekers in their workplaces. Importantly, they could use their own relative positions of power (at least compared to refugees and asylum seekers) to develop innovative advocacy networks to create reform at local, state or provincial, and national levels to address de facto and dejure exclusions of refugees and asylum seekers from social supports. To the extent that asylum seekers and refugees can participate as well in shaping advocacy efforts, without jeopardizing their status, such efforts better align with rights-based approaches to change.

Knowledge sharing among professionals working across disciplines is critical to further the movement to combat injustices and ensure the rights of migrants. One such example of a statewide coalition comprised of immigration attorneys, historians, and social work and human rights faculty, practitioners, and students is the Connecticut Coalition for Migrant Families and Children (CCMFC). The CCMFC has been meeting at least quarterly since 2015 to share information, cross-train, host continuing professional and public education events, organize and advocate against unjust laws and governmental practices that harm migrants, and support coalition members engaged in lawsuits to promote migrant rights. One of the CCMFC members successfully prosecuted the federal government (*J.S.R. v. Sessions* and *V.F.B. v. Sessions*) in the case of the 9-year-old boy from Honduras and the 14-year-old girl from El Salvador described earlier in this book (see Chapter 10). A U.S. district court judge ruled that the forcible separation of these children from their parents at the U.S.-Mexico border was unconstitutional, granted the parents parole, and reunited the families (Altimari 2018). One of the most notable aspects of the coalition's work is the information sharing among practitioners that takes place both in person and through Internet-based networking. The coalition is able to quickly respond to requests for support at a state level and, often overlooked, provides a sense of solidarity and collective purpose to members.

A Call to Action: On Ways to Become Engaged at Universities and in Communities

Scholars and practitioners have a responsibility to share insights from their research with broader publics than those reached by peer-reviewed journal articles or academic books. Several authors in the book engage in media work. S. Megan Berthold, for example, shares insights on trauma-informed work with torture survivors for national public radio audiences and, with colleagues, presents regularly to community groups and practitioner associations both in the United States and globally (Where We Live 2015, 2018). Harding and Libal (2017) sought to draw attention to underexamined aspects of the January 2017 executive order on "Protecting the Nation from Foreign Terrorist Entry into the United States" (identified as the "Muslim ban" or "refugee order" in news analysis). Harding and Libal also participated in direct legislative advocacy related to Iraqi refugee resettlement and humanitarian support in the past, in an effort to influence political leadership in Congress. Other avenues at the community level include innovative means of preparing teachers and volunteers in community organizations to work with refugees from varied experiences or backgrounds through creative games (Lam 2018) or participatory dialogue fostered through collective celebrations or other community events (De Mello 2017). Recent studies have shown, however, that combatting racism and xenophobia through targeted pro-immigrant or pro-refugee campaigns may be more challenging than expected (Deardorff Miller 2018). Scholars in a collaborative global project encourage challenging racist or xenophobic prejudice among "frontline" public and private sector workers in an array of institutions that address the rights and needs of refugees and asylum seekers (Pocock and Chan 2018).

Another means of raising awareness of the experience of forced migration is to conduct engaged or service-learning classes in which students collectively carry out research and participate in advocacy related to a particular asylum case or support a persecuted scholar. The Scholars at Risk (SAR) Program, an international human rights advocacy organization housed at New York University, supports professors creating such courses at their local universities and also hosts student interns with SAR (Scholars at Risk n.d.). These types of courses are being offered not only in the United States but also at other universities worldwide.

There are many avenues available to us all to volunteer or contribute to organizations that are advocating and fighting legal battles against illegal or unconstitutional practices that harm migrants. In the United States, by becoming a member of the American Civil Liberties Union (ACLU), one can support the ACLU's Immigrants' Rights Project, which is working to promote and protect the civil liberties and rights of immigrants and prevent or prosecute discrimination against them. Issues the ACLU is litigating include: illegal detention practices, the denial of the constitutional right to due process for every migrant, abuses by Immigration and Customs Enforcement and the U.S. Border Patrol agents, and anti-immigrant discriminatory local and state laws including those that racially profile (ACLU n.d.). The Refugee and Immigrant Center for Education and Legal Services (RAICES) is an example of a nonprofit delivering low-cost and pro-bono legal services to refugees and immigrant children and families in South and Central Texas. RAICES facilitates an Action Network, which empowers organizations and individuals to engage in progressive activism. Individuals can get involved in advocacy and outreach work with RAICES or, through its Accompaniment Program, in solidarity work with those challenged with deportation proceedings.

While interpreting in court, health, and social service settings calls for trained and certified professional interpreters (Juckett and Unger 2014), others with language skills may be able to volunteer to provide interpretation, translation services, or to be a language partner to newly arrived migrants struggling to communicate. Refugee resettlement agencies and grassroots immigrant rights groups stress the need for fostering language skills across the life span. Given the limited budgets and resources of many refugee and immigrant-serving nongovernmental organizations, developing programs to provide sustained language support through trained volunteers is vital. Secondary schools, universities, faith-based organizations, and other community groups are critical partners in such efforts. Most refugee-serving NGOs in the United States, Canada, Germany, and other countries resettling large numbers of refugees offer opportunities for such engagement (see, e.g., Hindy 2018; U.S. Committee for Refugees and Immigrants n.d.).

The human rights concerns of refugees and asylum seekers that the contributors have outlined in this book have been part of a scholarly dialogue on the roles of social workers, health professionals, and lawyers to redress injustices experienced for decades in the United States, Canada, and Europe. More than 15 years ago, Beth Humphries (2004) called on social workers to "begin to act collectively and in solidarity with those affected and impoverished by reactionary policies, rather than in fragmented, commercialized and exploited situations" (105). Humphries concluded: "Surely it is time for social workers to find that combination of genuine caring for people in big trouble, with the informed anger and rage to galvanize them into action against manifest injustice" (2004, 105). Extending our view beyond a social work audience, we hold that such collective action is necessary now more than ever. Now is the time to harness and direct all of our talents and resources toward promoting a more just and humane world for all, regardless of immigration status and national origin.

References

Altimari, Daniela. 2018. "Judge Rules Separation of Immigrant Children Living in Connecticut from Their Parents Is Unconstitutional." *The Hartford Courant,* July 14, 2018. http://www.courant.com/politics/hc-pol-judge-rules-detention-unconstitutional-20180714-story.html.

American Civil Liberties Union. n.d. "Immigrant Rights." https://www.aclu.org/issues/immigrants-rights.

Androff, David. 2016. *Practicing Rights: Human Rights-Based Approaches to Social Work Practice.* New York: Routledge.

Androff, David, and Jane McPherson. 2014. "Can Human Rights-Based Social Work Practice Bridge the Micro/Macro Divide?" In *Advancing Human Rights in Social Work Education*, edited by Kathryn R. Libal, S. Megan Berthold,

Rebecca L. Thomas, and Lynne M. Healy, 39–56. Alexandria, VA: Council on Social Work Education.

Berthold, S. Megan. 2015. *Human Rights-Based Approaches to Clinical Social Work Practice*. New York: Springer U.S.

Berthold, S. Megan, and Kathryn Libal. 2016. "Migrant Children's Rights to Health and Rehabilitation: A Primer for US Social workers." *Journal of Human Rights and Social Work* 1, no. 2: 85–95. doi:10.1007/s41134-016-0010-3 (Erratum, *Journal of Human Rights and Social Work*, Published online July 6, 2016. doi:10.1007/s41134–016–0015-y).

De Mello, Sonia. 2017. *Digesting the Disaster: Understanding the Boom of Refugee Food Entrepreneurship in the Face of Increasing Xenophobia*. Bachelor of Arts Thesis, Scripps College. https://scholarship.claremont.edu/cgi/viewcontent.cgi?referer=https://www.google.com/&httpsredir=1&article=2150&context=scripps_theses.

Deardorff Miller, Sarah. 2018. *Xenophobia towards Refugees and Other Forced Migrants*. World Refugee Council Research Paper No. 5—September 2018. World Refugee Council. https://www.worldrefugeecouncil.org/sites/default/files/documents/WRC%20Research%20Paper%20no.5.pdf.

Harding, Scott, and Kathryn Libal. 2017. "The Trump Administration's Covert Strategy for Ending Refugee Resettlement." *Truthout*, February 23, 2017. http://www.truth-out.org/news/item/39584-the-trump-administration-s-covert-strategy-for-ending-refugee-resettlement.

Hindy, Lily. 2018. *Germany's Syrian Refugee Integration Experiment*. The Century Foundation. September 6, 2018. https://tcf.org/content/report/germanys-syrian-refugee-integration-experiment/?session=1.

Humphries, Beth. 2004. "An Unacceptable Role for Social Work: Implementing Immigration Policy." *British Journal of Social Work* 34: 93–107.

Juckett, Gregory, and Kendra Unger. 2014. "Appropriate Use of Medical Interpreters." *American Family Physician* 90, no. 7: 476–80.

LaFaute, Dirk, and Gily Coene. 2018. "'Let Them In!' Humanitarian Work as Political Activism? The Case of Maximilliaan Refugee Camp in Brussels." *Journal of Immigrant and Refugee Studies*, doi: 10.1080/15562948.2018.1430283.

Lam, Michelle. 2018. "'We Can't Paint Them with One Brush': Creating Opportunities for Learning about Refugee Integration." *Refuge* 34, no. 2: 103–112.

Linton, Julie M., Marsha Griffin, and Alan J. Shapiro. 2017. "Detention of Immigrant Children." *Pediatrics* 139, no. 5: e 20170483.

McPherson, Jane. 2018. "Exceptional and Necessary: Practicing Rights-Based Social Work in the USA." *Journal of Human Rights and Social Work* 3, no. 2 (Spring): 89–98.

Miller, Devin. 2018. "AAP a Leading Voice against Separating Children, Parents at Border." *AAP News*, June 14, 2018. http://www.aappublications.org/news/2018/06/14/washington061418?utm_source=TrendMD&utm_medium=TrendMD&utm_campaign=AAPNews_TrendMD_0.

National Consortium of Torture Treatment Programs. 2014. "Shadow Report. Article 14: The Right to Rehabilitation." Prepared for the United States' Review before the United Nations Committee against Torture, November 2014. http://www.ncttp.org/INT_CAT_CSS_USA_18541_E.pdf.

Ostrander, Jason, Alysse Melville, and S. Megan Berthold. 2017. "Working with Refugees in the United States: Trauma-Informed and Structurally Competent Social Work Approaches." [Special Issue]. *Advances in Social Work* 18, no. 1: 66–79.

Pocock, Nicola, and Clara Chan. 2018. "Refugees, Racism, and Xenophobia: What Works to Reduce Discrimination?" *Our World*, June 20, 2018. https://our-world.unu.edu/en/refugees-racism-and-xenophobia-what-works-to-reduce-discrimination.

Salehyan, Idean. 2018. "Conclusion: What Academia Can Contribute to Refugee Policy." *Journal of Peace Research*. Online early view https://doi.org/10.1177/0022343318812975.

Scholars at Risk. n.d. "Student Advocacy Seminars." https://www.scholarsatrisk.org/actions/student-advocacy-seminars/.

UN Committee against Torture. 2014. "Concluding Observations and Recommendations of the Committee against Torture with Respect to the U.S. Government's Third-Fifth Periodic Report (November 2014)." CAT/C/USA/CO/3–5. https://www.state.gov/documents/organization/234772.pdf.

UN General Assembly. 1984. Convention against Torture and Other Cruel, Inhuman or Degrading Treatment or Punishment, United Nations, Treaty Series, vol. 1465, p. 85. http://www.refworld.org/docid/3ae6b3a94.html.

UN General Assembly. 2016. New York Declaration for Refugees and Migrants: Resolution/Adopted by the General Assembly, October 3, 2016. A/RES/71/1. https://www.refworld.org/docid/57ceb74a4.html.

UN Global Compact on Refugees. 2018. https://www.unhcr.org/events/conferences/5b3295167/official-version-final-draft-global-compact-refugees.html.

UN Global Compact on Safe, Orderly, and Regular Migration. 2018. https://www.un.org/pga/72/wp-content/uploads/sites/51/2018/07/migration.pdf.

U.S. Committee for Refugees and Immigrants. n.d. "Volunteer." https://refugees.org/get-involved/volunteer/.

Where We Live. 2015. "If We Torture, What Makes Us Different from Those We Condemn?" by John Dankosky and Betsy Kaplan. January 16, 2015. http://wnpr.org/post/if-we-torture-what-makes-us-different-those-we-condemn.

Where We Live. 2018. "When It Comes to Trauma, Who Helps the Helpers?" by Carmen Baskauf and Lucy Nalpathanchil. September 25, 2018. http://www.wnpr.org/post/when-it-comes-trauma-who-helps-helpers.

Yamin, Alicia Ely. 2008. "Will We Take Suffering Seriously? Reflections on What Applying a Human Rights Framework to Health Means and Why We Should Care." *Health and Human Rights* 10, no. 1: 45–63.

Zayas, Luis H., and Mollie H. Bradlee. 2014. "Exiling Children, Creating Orphans: When Immigration Policies Hurt Citizens." *Social Work* 59, no. 2: 167–175.

Index

Note: Page numbers followed by an *italicized t* or *f* refer to a table or a figure, respectively.

Accompaniment Program, 342
Acculturation, 161, 190, 272, 280, 281, 282
Action Network, 342
Additional Protocol I (ICRC 1977), 110
Adjudicatory bias, 27–28
Admissions ceiling, 20, 21–22, 32, 94n2, 290–291
Admissions targets, 75, 81
Advisory Committee on Family Residential Centers (Department of Homeland Security), 209
Advocacy efforts, 8, 11, 31, 76, 246, 276, 280, 283, 285, 337, 338–341; human rights, 342; legal, 185; legislative, 92, 342; priorities for, 204, 222, 238; social justice, 195; state-level, 93
Affordable Care Act (ACA), 241
Afghanistan: asylum seekers from, 64, 117; migrants and refugees from, 3, 21, 82, 94n3, 101, 102, 112–113, 115t, 133, 319; return of refugees to, 64, 112–113
Africa, asylum seekers and refugees from, 94n2, 143, 166–171, 185, 187, 277, 278, 290–293, 323. *See*

also African women refugees; *individual African countries by name*
African women refugees: dependence on community navigators, 303–304; and economic self-sufficiency, 294–296; family situations of, 296; lack of practical assistance for, 309–310; language proficiencies of, 296, 300–301, 303, 305–306; lived experiences of, 290, 292, 296–297; need for culturally responsive services, 304–305; policy barriers to self-sufficiency, 302–310; postmigration themes, 296–297; problems with food insecurity, 307; problems with loan repayments, 306–308; problems with racism and discrimination, 308–309; qualitative study of, 293; resettlement in Colorado, 291; resettlement problems, 302–310; trauma and its impact, 298–300; trauma experiences and war, 297–298; workplace barriers to self-sufficiency, 300–302
Aguirre-Aguirre v. INS, 40n25
Ahistoricism, 292
Al Shabab, 65

Albania, refugees from, 185

Algeria, postconflict communities in, 161

Al-Hussein, Zeid Ra'ad, 211

Alternative für Deutschland (AFD) party, 3

American Baptist Churches v. Thornburgh, 28–29

American Civil Liberties Union (ACLU), 2, 49, 207–209, 214, 215, 342; Immigrants' Rights Project, 342; lawsuit against ICE, 212–213

American dream, 302

American Psychiatric Association, 138, 272

Amnesty International, 74

Anemia, 239

Anthropology, 8

Anti-immigrant rhetoric, 85, 113

Anti-immigration sentiment, 3

Antimigrant policies, 338

Anti-refugee sentiment, 3, 147

Anti-Semitism, 78

Anxiety and Anxiety disorders, 161, 186, 232, 242

Aquarius (rescue ship), 2

Arendt, Hannah, 4, 103

Art therapy (AT), 9, 10, 184, 186, 317, 318–321; candle creation art therapy process, 318–320

Asia. *See* Central Asia; East Asia; South Asia; Southeast Asia

Asian Association of Utah (AAU), 91–92

Assisted Voluntary Return (AVR), 63–64

Asylees, 205. *See also* Asylum seekers

Asylum policies, 3, 8; exclusionary 2–3; restrictive, 3, 102

Asylum process: access to asylum, 34–37; adjudication in Austria, 118–119; adjudicatory bias, 27–28; adjudicatory structure for asylum and withholding applications, 23–25; appeal of decision, 119;

asylum office (affirmative applications), 23–24; in Austria, 113; barriers to, 40n25; Board of Immigration Appeals and Federal Courts of Appeal, 24–25; and the burden of proof, 109; changes to interpretation of standards, 76; credible fear interview, 27; decrease in asylum grants, 64; deportation without hearing, 45; disparities in decision making, 25, 40n27; gender-related persecution, 29; hearings, 247; immigration court (defensive applications), 24; impact/ influence of hearings and their outcomes, 195; limiting of requests, 101–102; and the question of effectiveness, 111; and the question of fairness, 111; requirement to remain in Mexico, 34–35; restrictions on, 76; risk assessment, 118; "well-founded fear of persecution" standard, 22–23, 26, 28–29, 35, 40n25, 41n42, 61, 75, 109, 139–140, 159, 205, 222

Asylum Reception Center, 116–117

Asylum seekers: effects of detention on, 48–54; experience of trauma, 118; with HIV, 165; interdiction and forcible return of, 40n25; language difficulties, 118; legal protection for, 18; legal representation for, 30–31; media images of, 1; moral obligation to help, 6; processing, 8; prosecution of for "illegal" entry, 36; quota system for, 114; reasons for seeking asylum 279; refugees as, 104; restrictions of, 340; resulting from mass displacement, 100; rights of, 5, 9, 11, 111, 337–343; support for, 2; and welfare laws, 76, 78, 119, 222, 241. *See also* Deportation; Detention; Immigrants; Refugees; Refugees and immigrants by country of origin; Refugees and immigrants by country of refuge

Attachment relationships, 236, 249, 298

Attorneys. *See* Lawyers

Australia: isolationist policies in, 102; refugees in, 165

Austria: asylum laws in, 119; asylum seekers and migrants in, 117–120, 118*f*, 165; border security in, 102; immigration policies in, 102, 113; rights of migrants in, 9

Autism spectrum disorder (ASD), 277

Ayloush, Jussam, 2

Bail (bond), 56

Bail for Immigration Detainees (BID), 50

Bates, John, 215

Belgium, 2

Bell, Derrick, 291–293

Bellevue/NYU Program for Survivors of Torture (PSOT), 9; cross-discipline supervision at, 186; culturally driven support groups, 185–186; group sessions 183; practical considerations for group interventions with forced migrants, 190–195; rationale for group interventions with forced migrants, 187–190; service provision model, 184–185; setting and organization, 183–186

Berthold, S. Megan, 341

Bhabha, Jaqueline, 6

Bhutan, 149

Bilateral agreements, 112–113

Board of Immigration Appeals (BIA), 24–25

Boehnlein, James, 133, 134

Bond check-ins, 56

Border security, 101, 102, 104, 121

Border wall, 35

Bosnia: asylum seekers and refugees from, 132, 139, 149–150, 185

Boston Center for Refugee Health and Human Rights, 162

Brexit vote, 3

Brook House, 54

Buddhist refugees, 137, 139, 187

Bullying, 245

Bureau of Population, Refugees and Migration (PRM), 81, 307

Burma (Myanmar), refugees/immigrants from, 102, 104, 132, 134, 150

Bush, George H.W., 26

Bush, George W., 76; administration's approach to immigration, 62

Caal Maquin, Jakelin Amei Rosmery, 2

Cabo Verde, 19

Cambodia: postconflict communities in, 161; refugees from, 81, 133, 135, 136, 138, 142–147, 149–150, 151; war in, 5

Canada: asylum seekers in, 41n41; diversity in, 263, 268, 280–281, 284–285; hate crimes in, 269; immigrants and refugees in, 263–264, 278; immigrants from, 42–43n64; injustices in, 343; mental health services, 10, 265–267, 269–271, 283–285; migration to, 11; multiculturalism legislation in, 264; refugee and mental health policies, 10; refugee resettlement in, 33; Syrian refugees in, 22; UACs from, 206. *See also* Cultural Consultation Services (CCS)

Canadian Charter of Rights and Freedoms, 267

Canadian Immigration Act (1976), 264

Canadian Task Force on Mental Health Issues Affecting Immigrants and Refugees, 265

Candle creation art therapy process, 318–320

Capacity building, 116, 196, 338–340
Carey, Bob, 211
Caribbean, immigrants and refugees
    from, 21, 62–63, 94n2, 278
Cartagena Declaration, 110
Carter, James Earl "Jimmy," 75;
    approach to immigration, 80
Case for Diversity (Mental Health
    Commission of Canada), 263
Case managers, 9, 131, 140, 152, 302,
    303, 304, 307, 308–310
Cash assistance, 293–294, 295, 310
Catholic Charities of Louisville, 87
Catholic Community Services
    (CCS), 91
Center for Constitutional Rights, 185
Center for Human Rights &
    Constitutional Law, 49, 213
Center for Victims of Torture, 196
Center on Immigration and Child
    Welfare, 248
Central America: conditions causing
    migration, 5; migrants and refugees
    from, 5, 30, 37, 41n44, 58, 64, 74,
    102, 132, 149, 215, 221, 233;
    military dictators in, 5; return of
    refugees to, 64
Central Asia, refugees from, 94n2
Central Europe, refugees from, 80. See
    also Europe; European Union (EU)
Ceremonies, 164, 165
Chad, 33
Charitable giving, 77
Charter Affirming the Values of State
    Secularism and Religious Neutrality
    and of Equality between Women
    and Men, Providing a Framework
    for Accommodation Requests, 268
Charter for Compassion, 88
Chaverra v. ICE et al., 52
Child development, 236–238; practice
    recommendations, 238–239
Child hunger, 241
Child migrants, 2, 10, 154; abuses and
    neglect of, 207–215, 233, 243, 248;
being lost by Department of Health
    and Human Services, 209–210; and
    child development, 236–239;
    contexts for leaving homeland,
    232–233; continued risk of danger
    and trauma after leaving homeland,
    233; continuum of care for, 250;
    cross-cultural treatment of, 154; in
    dangerous refugee camps, 234;
    dangers en route to U.S., 233–234;
    deportation of, 206; in detention, 47,
    49, 57–59; developmental delays in,
    237–238; early intervention
    supports for, 237; education for, 119,
    241, 244–246; effect of massive
    trauma on, 154; experiences during
    the Obama administration, 207–
    209; experiences during the Trump
    administration, 209–215;
    exploitation of, 233; family
    dynamics, 247–249; forms of
    immigration relief for, 206; health
    and well-being of, 231–232,
    235–236, 239–242, 249; human
    rights abuses of, 221; as immigrants,
    2, 10, 100; international
    mechanisms for protection, 216;
    international treaties, standards,
    and principles relevant to the
    protection of, 217–219t; legal
    representation for, 31; mental health
    of, 242–244; orphaned, 79;
    protecting the rights of, 216,
    221–222; as refugees, 30, 154, 315;
    rights of, 202–204, 207–208;
    school-based interventions for, 246;
    screening for disease, 239; seeking
    asylum, 234; sexual abuse of, 49,
    207, 208, 211, 213, 220–221, 240;
    in Sierra Leone, 244; statistics
    regarding, 205; stressors upon entry
    into U.S., 234–235; support for,
    223; targeting parents and family
    members of, 37; trafficking of, 205,
    206–207, 210, 212, 233;

unaccompanied children (UACs), 59, 64, 100, 203, 205, 206–207, 221; undocumented, 206, 234; in the U.S., 2, 10; U.S. safeguards of rights, 220–221; violations of the rights of, 247; as vulnerable population, 233. *See also* Child psychiatry; Child soldiers; Refugees

Child Protective Services, 307

Child psychiatry: clinical vignette, 277; consultation process, 271–273; in Montreal, 270–277; special considerations in consultation, 273–274; special considerations in treatment, 274–277. *See also* Children, mental health of; Psychiatry

Child soldiers, 234

Child welfare, 247–248

Childcare costs, 305

Children. *See* Child migrants; Child soldiers

China, 263

Chinese Exclusion Act, 78

Chinese Exclusion Case, 18

Christian organizations, 84, 86. *See also* Faith communities

Christian refugees, 32, 139

Church of Jesus Christ of Latter-day Saints, 92–93

Citizenship, 102, 148

Civil Rights Movement, 291

Civil society, 76, 93, 116, 121–122, 207, 338, 339, 340

Clark v. Martinez, 61

Clinicians: challenges faced by, 9, 143, 155, 160, 174–177; cultural competence of, 195, 269; resilience of, 175; use of spiritual approach by, 166; therapeutic collaboration with trauma survivors, 177; training of, 194; working with child migrants, 232, 236, 238, 241–242, 243, 248, 271. *See also* Therapists

Clinton, Hillary, 3–4

Club House model, 146–147

Cognitive behavioral therapy (CBT), 166, 188, 244, 276

Collective trauma resolution, 164. *See also* Refugee trauma; Trauma

Collyer, Michael, 63–64

Committee on the Protection of the Rights of All Migrant Workers and Members of Their Families, 216

Committee on the Rights of the Child, 216

Common European Asylum System (CEAS), 110, 111, 118

Community groups, 86, 89

Community integration, 87

Community navigators, 10, 303–304, 306, 311

Community networks, 10. *See also* Group sessions

Community Psychiatry, 147. *See also* Psychiatry

Community sponsorship, 85–86

Community support, 87

Compassion, 175, 177; self-, 194

Compassion fatigue, 176

Concentration camps, 328–329

Congo. *See* Democratic Republic of Congo (DRC)

Connecticut: refugee resettlement in, 9; voluntarism in, 77, 84, 85–87, 93n4

Connecticut Coalition for Migrant Families and Children (CCMFC), 341

Convention Against Torture and Cruelty (CTC), 105, 339

Convention for the Elimination of all forms of Discrimination against Women (CEDAW), 105

Convention for the Elimination of all forms of Racial Discrimination (CERD), 105

Convention for the Protection of All Persons against Enforced Disappearance (ICPED), 105

Convention for the Rights of the Child (CRC), 105, 216

Convention on Refugee Problems, 110

Convention Related to the Status of the Stateless Persons, 104

Convention Relating to the Status of Refugees, 5, 19–20, 74, 104, 108, 264; as human rights instrument, 109; and the principle of nonrefoulement, 110

Cooper, Holly, 210

CoreCivic, 53, 54

Corrections Corporation of America (CCA), 53

Council on Arab and Islamic Relations, 2

Counternarratives, 292

Creative arts therapies (CATS), 8, 10, 271, 315, 316–318, 334; art therapy, 9, 10, 184, 186, 317, 318–321; dance/movement therapy, 317, 321–326, 333; drama therapy, 10, 317, 326–328; music therapy, 10, 317–318, 328–332; poetry therapy, 10, 317, 318, 332–333

Creativity, 316, 326

Critical legal studies, 291

Critical race theory (CRT), 291–293, 295; and economic self-sufficiency, 294–296

Critical theory, 291

CSSS de la Montagne—CIUSSS West Central Montreal health care network, 270

Cuba, 21, 74, 94n3

Cultural brokers, 309, 311

Cultural competence, 195, 266

Cultural Consultation Services (CCS; Jewish General Hospital), 262, 270, 277–285; vignette, 282–283

Cultural formulation, 274, 279

Cultural identity, 338

Cultural knowledge, 93

Cultural navigators, 10, 311. *See also* Community navigators

Cultural psychiatry, 10, 284

Culture, 10; egocentric, 317; as interpersonal, dynamic function, 195; sociocentric, 317

Culture brokers, 270, 273, 276, 279, 284

Customs and Border Protection (CBP), 205, 211, 212, 213; child migrant policies, 221; detaining of unaccompanied children by, 206

Cutler, David, 147

Czech Republic, 108

Czechoslovakia, 74

Dance/movement therapy (DMT), 10, 317, 321–326, 333; case example, 323–326; resourcing through, 322–323, 326

Deferred Action for Childhood Arrivals (DACA) program, 206, 215, 235

Deleted family units, 211, 214

Dementia, 138, 150–515

Democratic Republic of Congo (DRC): migration from, 5; refugees from, 165, 291, 296, 309; return of refugees to, 64; war in, 5, 309

Denmark, 102

Department for Foreign Citizens and Asylum Seekers (BFA), 118

Department of Health and Human Services (DHHS), 94n3, 209; Office of Refugee Resettlement (ORR), 81

Department of Homeland Security (DHS), 2, 23, 24, 29, 36–37, 56, 57, 58, 211, 233; Advisory Committee on Family Residential Centers, 209; Office for Civil Rights and Civil Liberties (CRCL), 208; Office of Inspector General, 49; U.S. Citizen and Immigration Services (USCIS), 81

Department of Justice (DOJ), 24, 31, 36–37

Department of Psychiatry (Oregon Health & Science University), 132, 135

Dependency, 294–296

Deportation, 3, 7, 9, 44–45, 62–65, 76, 118, 203, 235, 343; of children, 206; cost of, 63; fear of, 283; of Somalis, 64–65; threat of, 278; in the U.S., 45. *See also* Asylum seekers

Deportation nation, 62

Depression, 138, 142, 147, 161–162, 168, 232, 278, 283, 328; association with trauma and torture, 161

Derivative asylees, 205

Designated Countries of Origin, 267

Detainees: conscripted as laborers, 54; mistreatment of, 48; self-harm by, 49; special needs of, 57–60

Detention, 9, 29–30, 44–45; alternatives to, 55–57; as cause of psychiatric disorders, 48–49; of children, 47, 49, 57–59; cost of, 56; as deterrent, 41n45, 48; effects of, 48–54; expansion of, 36, 38; facilities for families, 30; of families, 209; as gateway to deportation, 48, 55, 62; illegal practices in, 342; indefinite, 46; medical care in, 53; purpose of, 47; in the U.K., 45–47; in the U.S., 45–47; use of private contractors for, 52–53; vulnerable people in, 49–50, 57–60. *See also* Asylum seekers

Detention centers, 213; Brook House, 54; Buffalo Federal Detention Facility, 57; deaths in, 51–52; increasing numbers of, 58; medical care in, 51; run by private contractors, 52–53; sexual abuse in, 49, 100, 213; use of detainee labor in, 54; Yarl's Wood, 58

Detention Watch Network, 56

Diagnostic and Statistical Manual: 3rd edition, 138; 5th edition, 272, 279

Discrimination, 262, 301; in service provision, 308–309

Dislocation, 192

Displaced Persons Act (1948), 80

Diversity, 280–281

Division of Social and Transcultural Psychiatry. *See* McGill University Division of Social and Transcultural Psychiatry

Domestic law, 18, 19

Dominican Republic, 104

Drama therapy (DT), 10, 317, 326–328; case example, 327–328; celebration rituals, 328

DRC. *See* Democratic Republic of Congo (DRC)

Dublin III Agreement, 111, 119

Due process rights, 76

Duvalier, Jean-Claude, 25–26

East Asia, 94n2, 278

Eastern Europe, 80. *See also* Europe; European Union (EU)

Education: about sexual and reproductive health, 241; for child migrants, 119, 241, 244–246; community-engaged, 246; culturally tailored, 246; informed by resettlement experiences, 246; multisystematic, 246; for refugees, 117

Educators, 8

El Salvador, migrants and refugees from, 5, 21, 28–29, 232, 341

Electronic Benefits Transfer (EBT), 302

Electronic monitoring, 55–56

Ellsworth, A. Whitney, 74

Embodiment, 325, 328

Empathetic strain, 155

Employment, 93

Employment Equity Act (Canada), 263

English language. *See* Language
  instruction; Language proficiency
Environmental refugees, 104
Eritrea, refugees from, 291, 296
Ethiopia: postconflict communities in,
  161; refugees from, 132, 139,
  149–150, 152, 296; refugees in, 6
Ethnic cleansing, 102
Ethnic identities, 269
Ethnic interest groups, 76
Ethnic mental health counselors, 9,
  131, 133–138; Arabic-speaking,
  135; Bosnian, 136; Cambodian,
  136, 147; Ethiopian, 136; Farsi-
  speaking, 136; Indochinese, 145;
  Mien, 136, 147; Nepalese, 136;
  Russian-speaking, 136; Somalia,
  135; Vietnamese, 135, 140, 147
EU-Afghanistan Agreement, 112–113
Europe: Central, 80; Eastern, 80;
  forced migration in, 101;
  immigration policies, 9; injustices
  in, 343; legal and social policy
  issues, 8; migration to, 11; refugee
  crisis in, 1, 5; refugee policies, 1;
  refugees from, 80, 94n2. *See also*
  European Union (EU)
European Convention on Human
  Rights, 110
European Council on Refugees and
  Exiles, 112
European Network of Migrant
  Women, 340
European Social Charter (ESC), 111
European Union: bilateral migration
  agreements, 112–113;
  externalization of borders, 102; and
  the forced migration crisis, 102;
  human rights laws, 110–111;
  immigration law in, 46, 119;
  migration to, 113, 114; refugee
  laws, 110, 111; refugees in, 104;
  return of refugees by, 64. *See also*
  Europe
European Union charter, 111

European Union (EU) Returns
  Directive, 46
EU-Turkey Agreement, 112
Executive Office of Immigration
  Review (EOIR), 24
Executive orders: Border Security and
  Immigration Enforcement
  Improvements, 34–37, 42–43n64;
  Enhancing Public Safety in the
  Interior of the United States, 34–37;
  of President George H.W. Bush, 26;
  of President Trump, 6–7, 18;
  Protecting the Nation from Foreign
  Terrorist Entry into the United
  States ("Muslim Ban"), 6, 18, 22,
  32–34, 38n1, 291, 342; reducing
  refugee admissions, 77; restrictive,
  241; Resuming the USRAP with
  Enhanced Vetting Capabilities, 33;
  of Truman (expediting admissions
  of refugees from Europe), 79–80
Expedited removal policy, 26–27, 35
Expressive arts, 186
Extortion, 233
Eye movement desensitization
  reprocessing (EMDR), 166, 244

Faith: engaging with faith practices,
  170–171; listening to the testimony
  of, 169–170; and loss, 170;
  testimony and personal history
  with, 170; and trauma, 164–166
Faith leaders: protest in support of
  immigrants, 2; supporting refugees
  and immigrants, 8
Faith-based communities, 84, 93
Faith-based institutions, 76, 85–86
Families: deleted family units, 211,
  214; involvement in psychiatric
  care, 269, 271–276; mixed-status,
  235, 238; reunification of, 21, 107,
  214, 222; separation of at the
  border, 2, 7, 65, 101, 203, 211–213,
  232, 236, 338–339, 341
Family dynamics, 247–249

Family networks, 10
Family Reunification Directive, 111
Family therapy, 276
Federal Courts of Appeal, 24–26
Feminist studies, 291
Fisher, Greg, 88
Flores Settlement, 59, 203, 213, 220, 221
Flores v. Reno, 59, 203, 213, 220
Folklore, 8
Food insecurity, 241, 305, 307
Food Stamps/SNAP, 295, 308, 310, 311
Forced conscription, 234
Forced displacement, 290
Forced exile, 192
Forced labor, 205
Forced migration, 1, 3, 4–8, 89, 195, 337; bilateral agreements and national migration platforms, 112–113; challenge of defining, 103–105; and the EU migration framework, 110–112; and the EU response, 113; in Europe, 101; and European Union human rights laws, 110–111; experience of, 342; global scope of, 182; hardships of, 89; and international human rights laws, 105–108; and international humanitarian laws, 110; international legal framework and emergent trends, 101–103; international refugee laws, 108–110; legal challenges, 105–110; resulting from conflict, 102; resulting from ethnic cleansing, 102; resulting from natural disasters, 102; resulting from protracted emergencies, 102; and the rights of migrants, 107; solutions to, 338. *See also* Migration
Foreign policy, 93
Fourteenth Amendment (US Constitution), 7
Fourth Geneva Convention, 110

France: detention practices in, 46; refugees in, 101
Freedom of Information Act (FOIA), 208
FRONTEX, 101–102

Gang violence, 76, 232
Gee, Dolly, 213, 214
Gender equality, 268
Gender stereotypes, 309
Gender-based violence (GBV), 76, 233, 278, 282, 291, 297. *See also* Rape; Violence
Gender-related persecution, 41n41, 76, 266
Genocide, 78, 309
GEO Group, 52, 54, 56
George, Chris, 85–86
Germany: acceptance of refugees, 3; asylum application status of refugees, 115; border security in, 102; deportation of refugees from, 112; education and employment for the effective integration of migrants, 114–117; opposition to refugee policies, 3; pro-immigration discourse in, 114; refugees from, 79; refugees in, 101; return of refugees from, 64; rights of migrants in, 9; Syrian refugees in, 22
Global Compact for Safe, Orderly and Regular Migration (GCM), 2, 4, 107–108, 121–122, 204
Global Compact on Refugees (GCR), 4, 107, 122
Global Framework for the Comprehensive Refugee Response Framework (CRRF), 107
Global North, 1; moral obligation of, 6
Global refugee crisis, 290
Globalization, 1
Government Accountability Office (GAO), 233
Government benefits, 295

GPS monitoring, 56
Grassroots movements, 121, 215, 339, 343
Great Depression, 78
Greece, refugees in, 111, 112
Green cards, 237
Group process application, 320
Group sessions, 183–197, 244; activity groups, 190–191; clinical efficiency and sustainability, 189–190; culturally driven, 185; culturally syntonic interventions, 187–188; defining goals and format, 190–191; defining target population, 191–192; group rules/norms, 193–194; group selection criteria, 192–193; impact/influence of asylum hearings, 195; and normalization, 188–189; Orientation Groups, 185; practical considerations, 190–195; at PSOT, 185–186; psychoeducational, 190; and reduction of isolation, 188; role of the facilitator, 194; support groups, 191; therapy and trauma-focused groups, 191; with torture survivors, 195–197; training and use of co-facilitators, 194–195
Group therapy, 9, 10; art therapy as, 320. *See also* Group sessions
Guantanamo detention center, 26, 339
Guatemala, refugees from, 2, 5, 21, 28–29, 139
Gulf Coast Jewish Family and Community Services, 196

Haiti: asylum seekers from, 25–26, 40n25; human rights violations in, 26; refugees from, 21, 37–38, 94n3, 104
Hannum, Hurst, 74
Harris, Brian, 328
Hart-Celler Act (Immigration and Nationality Act 1965; Hart-Celler Act), 80

Hate crimes, 269
Healing: as active process, 186; in community, 188, 189, 190, 191, 196; and the creative arts, 334; dance for, 321; facilitated by artistic expression, 186; impediments to, 281; interdisciplinary approach to, 196; music for, 328; promotion of, 244, 275; rituals for, 172, 329; self-, 162; and spirituality, 160, 162, 164, 168, 172–174, 176–177; from torture, 183, 184
Health care benefits, 295
Health care services, 9, 10; access to, 311; human rights-based approach to, 338
Health professionals, 8; role of, 343. *See also* Ethnic mental health counselors; Mental health practitioners; Physicians
Herbert, Gary, 90
History, revisionist, 292
HIV/AIDS, 240
Holocaust, 103, 105
Home visits, as alternative to detention, 56
Homeland Security Act (2002), 207
Honduras, refugees and immigrants from, 29, 202–203, 232, 341
Hong Fook Mental Health Association, 269
Hoover administration, approach to immigration, 78
Hope and Grace Foundation, 184
Hope Border Institute, 212
Human rights, 1, 3, 8, 11, 122, 267; abuses of, 21, 185, 192, 196, 234, 242–243, 332; of child migrants, 202–204, 221; and forced migration, 4–8; fundamental, 105; international, 6, 8; of refugees and asylum seekers, 338–340, 343; and the right to migrate, 103; violations of, 26, 318, 321
Human Rights First, 184

Human rights laws: international, 105–108, 340; lack of enforceability of, 107

Human rights organizations/groups, 77, 184

Human Rights Watch, 60

Human trafficking: by asylum seekers, 119; among migrants, 100; of children, 205, 206, 210, 212, 233; victims of, 59–60

Humanitarian agencies, 79

Humanitarian aid, 107

Humanitarian laws, 6, 8, 107; international, 110

Humanitarian parole, 36, 80, 247

Humanitarian policies, 93

Humanitarian protection, 104

Humphries, Beth, 343

Hungary: closing of borders to refugees, 113; refugees from, 74; withdrawal from GCM, 108

Hypertension, 186

Hypervigilance, 235

"I Was a Stranger" program (LDS church), 93

identity: American, 77; Canadian, 264; in the clinical interview, 279; cultural, 269; and faith, 165, 171; formation of, 282; national, 338; process of, 274–275, 281; professional, 175; of refugees, 103; religious, 269

Ilori v. SSHD 2017, 50

Immigrant, refugee, ethnocultural, and racialized (IRER) groups, 265, 266, 269, 270

Immigrants: criminalization of, 62, 76; definition of, 204–205; effects of detention on, 48–54; illegal, 2, 17, 45; integration through education and employment, 113; interfaith protest in support of, 2; legal, 17; permanent legal status, 18; social benefits for, 102; support for, 7; unauthorized, 65–66n1; undocumented, 76, 102; unwanted, 102. *See also* Asylum seekers; Migrants; Refugees; Refugees and immigrants by country of origin; Refugees and immigrants by country of refuge

Immigration: Bush (George H.W.) approach to, 26; Bush (George W.) approach to, 62, 76; Carter (Jimmy) approach to, 75, 80; decrease in quotas, 3; Hoover administration approach to, 78; Obama (Barack) approach to, 3, 6, 21, 22, 36, 41n45, 62, 82, 83, 85, 94n2, 94n3, 207–209, 290, 291; open policies, 102; Reagan (Ronald) approach to, 25–26; restrictions on eligibility, 2–3. *See also* Deportation; Migration; Trump, Donald J.; Trump administration

Immigration Act (1917), 78

Immigration Act (1924), 79

Immigration and Customs Enforcement (ICE), 24, 76, 212, 235, 238, 245; abuses by, 342; ACLU lawsuit against, 212–213; additional officers, 36

Immigration and Nationality Act (1952; McCarran-Walter Act), 80

Immigration and Nationality Act (1965; Hart-Celler Act), 80

Immigration and Nationality Act (INA), 45, 75

Immigration and Refugee Board (Canada), 264

Immigration court (defensive applications), 24

Immigration laws, 8; in the EU, 46, 118, 119; in the U.S., 215; violation of, 47–48, 55. *See also* Migration laws

Immigration policies, 3, 8, 9; annual goals for, 74; in Canada, 264; during the Carter administration,

75; in the EU, 113; in Europe, 121; of exclusion, 90; international legal framework and emergent trends, 101–103; polarization of, 94n1; politicization of, 7–8; restrictive, 6, 76, 78, 82, 93, 101, 102; targeting parents and family members of child migrants, 37; in the U.S., 3, 8, 17, 76, 85, 121, 195; visa ban targeting Muslims, 18. *See also* Refugee policies

Immigration quotas, 79, 80, 101, 114

In-Canada Asylum Program, 264

India, refugees in, 163

Indigenous peoples, 221

Individualism, 317

Indochina, refugees from, 139. *See also* Cambodia; Laos; Vietnam

Indochinese Psychiatric Program, 132, 155–156n1. *See also* Intercultural Psychiatric Program (IPP)

Indochinese/Intercultural Socialization Center (ISC), 131, 146–147, 156n2; benefits of, 149–150; closing of 150; scope of clinical and rehabilitation activities, 148–149; treatment goals of groups, 148

Infra (interdiction and forcible return of asylum seekers), 40n25

INS v. Cardoza-Fonseca, 40n25

INS v. Stevic, 40n25

Integrated Refugee and Immigrant Services (IRIS), 85–86

Intercultural Psychiatric Program (IPP), 9, 131, 155; administrative structure, 132; age and country/language of origin of current patients, 139t; background and origin of, 132; case examples, 143–144; characteristics of patients, 138–140; clinic development, 133; current psychiatric, neurocognitive, and medical diagnoses of patients,

141t; how the system of care works, 140–142; Intercultural Socialization Center, 144–150; ongoing developments, 133–134; roles of ethnic mental health counselors, 135–138; roles of psychiatrists, 134–135; Torture Treatment Center of Oregon, 150–154; treatment approach, 142–143

Intercultural Socialization Center. *See* Indochinese/Intercultural Socialization Center (ISC)

Interim Federal Health Program (IFHP; Canada), 267

Internally displaced populations (IDPs), 104, 162, 315

International compassionate city, 88

International Convention for the Protection of the Rights of Migrant Workers and Families (ICPRMW), 105

International Covenant for Civil and Political Rights (ICCPR), 105

International Covenant for Economic, Social, and Cultural Rights (ICESCR), 105

International Displacement Monitoring Center (IDMC), 113

International law, 18, 19; and detention of children, 59; human rights, 105–108, 340; humanitarian (IHL), 75, 110; and nonrefoulement, 64; regarding child migrants, 203

International Organization of Migration (IOM), 5, 63, 79

International Refugee Assistance Program (IRAP), 76

International Rescue Committee (IRC), 91

Interpretative Phenomenological Analysis (IPA), 293

Interpreters, 9, 192, 244, 250, 273, 279, 284, 304–305, 330, 343

Intersectionality, 292

IQ network, 116

Iran: refugees from, 33, 94n1, 132, 133, 139, 150; refugees in, 6

Iraq: asylum seekers and refugees from, 3, 33, 76, 82, 94n3, 101, 113, 115t, 117, 132, 139, 161, 162, 306; war in, 5, 82, 85

ISC Socialization Scale, 149, 152–153

Islamophobia, 301

Isolationism, 6, 78, 102

Israel, withdrawal from GCM, 108

Italy: border security in, 102; refugees in, 101, 111

Jackson, Robert, 25

Jesuit Refugee Service, 48–49

Jewish General Hospital (Montreal), 262, 270, 283

Jewish organizations, 84, 86. *See also* Faith communities

Jewish refugees, 78–79, 103

Job placement, 293

Job-training, 77, 93, 114, 116, 117, 148–149, 293, 305–306, 308, 310

J.S.R. v. Sessions, 247, 341

Kanstroom, Daniel, 62

Kelly, John, 212

Kennedy, Edward, 25

Kentucky: refugee resettlement in, 9; voluntarism in, 77, 84, 87–90, 93n4; as Wilson/Fish state, 84, 87–88

Kentucky Office for Refugees (KOR), 87, 88

Kenya, refugees in, 165

Kidnapping, 233

King, Annie, 318

Kinzie, J. David, 132, 134, 155–156n1

Konigsteiner Key, 114

Kurdi, Alan, 85

"La Famille Africaine," 185–186

Landis, Heidi, 326

Langeloth Foundation, 184

Language instruction, 77, 114, 120, 145, 184, 244–245, 293

Language proficiency, 89, 246, 296. *See also* Refugees by language

Laos: refugees from, 81, 135, 138, 145–147, 149, 150; war in, 5

Latin America: refugees from, 21, 94n2, 278; refugees in, 110

Law, 8; domestic, 18, 19; European Union, 46, 110–111, 119; human rights, 105–108, 340; humanitarian, 6, 8, 107, 110; immigration, 8, 46–48, 55, 118, 119, 215; international, 18, 19, 59, 64, 75, 105–108, 110, 203, 340; migration, 103–104; welfare, 119. *See also* U.S. refugee law and policy

Law students, 57, 65

Lawful Permanent Resident (LPR), 17–18, 237

Lawyers, 8, 65, 215; immigration, 152; role of, 343

Leaders' Summit on Refugees, 6

Lebanon, refugees in, 6

Legal advocacy groups, 185

Legal aid, 56–57

Legal counseling and consultation, 119, 283

Legal organizations, 215

Legal representation, 30–31, 119

Leung, Paul, 133, 134

Libya, refugees from, 33, 94n1, 291

Lloyd, E. Scott, 211

Loan repayments, 306–308

Long-Term Residents Directive, 111

Louisville, Kentucky, as international compassionate city, 88

Low-Income Home Energy Assistance Program (LIHEAP), 305

Lutheran Family Services, 318

Magdas Hotel (Vienna), 120

Malaysia, psychiatric treatment for Aborigines in, 135

Malnutrition, 239, 240, 241

Market justice, 294

Marrakesh Compact on Migration, 220

McCarran-Walter Act (Immigration and Nationality Act of 1952), 80

McGill University Division of Social and Transcultural Psychiatry, 10, 262, 268

Meaning-making, 171–172, 277, 316; reciprocal, 172

Medicaid, 296, 310, 311

Medical care, 133, 150–151, 267

Medical Certification for Disability Exception, 134

Médicins Sans Frontières (MSF), 2, 112

Memory, 38, 324; body, 322; implicit, 322; loss of, 299; trauma-related, 322; traumatic, 186, 318, 322, 332

Mental Health Commission of Canada (MHCC), 263, 265–266; *Case for Diversity*, 263, 266, 269, 285; *Changing Directions, Changing Lives: The Mental Health Strategy for Canada*, 265; *Improving Mental Health Services for Immigrant, Refugee, Ethno-cultural and Racialized groups: Issues and Options for Service Improvement*, 265; Science Advisory Committee, 266; *Supporting the Mental Health of Refugees*, 266

Mental health counselors, 186; Cambodian, 147; ethnic, 131, 133–138; Mien, 147; Vietnamese, 147

Mental health issues, 57; anxiety disorders, 161, 186, 232, 242; depression, 138, 142, 147, 161–162, 168, 232, 278, 283, 328; Post-traumatic stress disorder (PTSD), 50, 138, 142, 143, 150, 151, 161–162, 168, 232, 261, 283, 322; risk factors for, 266

Mental health practitioners, 186, 341. *See also* Clinicians; Ethnic mental health counselors; Therapists

Mental health services, 8, 10, 261–262, 300; access to, 311; in Canada, 265–267, 269–271, 283–285; CCS vignette, 282–283; for child migrants, 242–244; cultural considerations in, 10; cultural consultation service (CCS), 277–282, 283–285; language-specific and ethno-specific, 269–270; proximity-based collaborative child psychiatry, 271–277; transcultural, 10

Meritocracy, 292, 302

Merkel, Angela, 3, 114

Mexico: asylum seekers remaining in, 34–35; immigrants from, 78; refugees from, 5; UACs from, 206

Michel, Charles, 2

Middle East, refugees from, 83, 278, 333

Mien refugees and immigrants, 143, 145–147, 149–150

Migrant camps, on Nauru Island, 102

Migrant caravan, 2

Migrant crisis, 65

Migrant Rights Network, 340

Migrants: attitudes of employers toward, 116; Indigenous peoples as, 221; integration of, 118; internally displaced, 104; irregular, 104; loss of family and community networks by, 10; media images of, 1; missing or dead, 35, 101; official response to, 11; as "other," 8; traumatized, 10; voluntary return of, 63–64. *See also* Immigrants; Refugees; Refugees and immigrants by country of origin; Refugees and immigrants by country of refuge

Migration: as adaptation, 103; by asylum seekers, 5; to Europe, 113; as fundamental freedom, 103; global politics of, 1–2; reasons for, 1; rights-based approach to, 9; and the role of state government,

103–104; secondary, 91. *See also* Forced migration; Immigration

Migration and Refugee Assistance Act, 80

Migration governance, 105; international human rights framework for, 105, 106–107*t*

Migration laws, 103–104. *See also* Immigration laws

Migration policies, 2; in Europe, 9; Mexican, 221; regional and global, 121–122

Migration Policy Institute, 4, 33

Migration protection categories: humanitarian protection status, 104; subsidiary protection status, 104

Migration theories, 104

Migration trauma, 280

Miller, Stephen, 2

Montreal Children's Hospital, 270

Mood disorders, 161

Moral compass, 163

Multicultural Mental Health Resource Centre, 266

Multiculturalism, 264

Music therapy (MT), 10, 317–318, 328–332; case example, 329–331

Muslim Ban (Travel Ban), 6, 18, 22, 32–34, 85

Muslim organizations, 84, 86. *See also* Faith communities

Muslim refugees, 76, 90–91, 137, 139, 144, 162, 291

Myanmar (Burma), migrants/refugees from, 102, 104, 132, 134, 150

Myth making, 164

Nafsiyat, 270

Narrative, 8, 108, 221, 318, 332; alternate, 277; collective, 274, 275; counter-, 292; cultural, 274; about deportation, 235; hopeful, 282; personal, 163; social, 274; use in therapy, 276; torture, 169, 171; traumatic, 177, 283; in the U.S., 302

National Capacity Building Project, 196

National Consortium of Torture Treatment Programs (NCTTP), 151, 152–153, 161–162; advocacy of, 339–340; Executive Committee, 339

National Partnership for Community Training, 196

National Referral Mechanism (NRM), 60

National security issues, 113; and the detention process, 29–30

National sovereignty, 103, 109, 113

Nationalism, 3, 6

Nationality laws, 79

Near East/South Asia, refugees from, 83, 94n2, 263, 278, 282–283

Nepal, refugees from, 134, 150, 165

Neuroscience, 321

New Americans, 91

New Americans Taskforce Welcoming Plan, 91

New York Declaration for Refugees and Migrants, 107, 220, 338, 340

New York Summit on Refugees, 6

New York University School of Medicine, 183

Newland, Kathleen, 4

Nicaragua, refugees from, 5

Nigeria, asylum seekers from, 50, 117

Noncitizens, "public charge" grounds for deportation, 7

Nongovernmental organizations (NGOs), 113, 119, 121, 343

Non-political crime, 40n25

Nonrefoulement, 19, 40n25, 61, 64, 110

Normalization, 188–189

North Korea, immigrants/refugees from, 33, 94n1

Norway, migrants/refugees to, 64, 101

Norwegian Refugee Council, 113

Obama, Barack: approach to immigration, 3, 6, 36; approach to refugees, 83, 290; increasing the admissions ceiling, 22; security checks for Syrian refugees, 21; summit of leaders on refugees, 82

Obama administration: approach to immigration, 41n45, 62, 94n2, 94n3; approach to refugee resettlement, 82, 85; approach to refugees, 94n3, 291; experiences of child migrants under, 207–209

Office for Civil Rights and Civil Liberties (CRCL; Department of Homeland Security), 208

Office for New Americans, 91, 92

Office of Refugee Resettlement (ORR), 59, 80, 81, 150, 151, 152–153, 184, 206–207, 210, 211, 232, 233

Official language minorities, 266

Open Society Foundation, 184

Operation Streamline, 211, 212

Oregon Health & Science University, 131, 134

Oregon Office of Vocational Rehabilitation, 148

Oregon State Mental Health Division, 132, 135

Organization for the African Unity (OAU), 110

Pakistan: asylum seekers/refugees from, 117, 165; refugees in, 6

Palestine, postconflict communities in, 161

Parasympathetic nervous system, 186

Parole hearing, 56, 57

Pence, Mike, 85, 90

Pereira v. Sessions, 62

Persecution, homophobic, 9, 185, 192, 278

Personal Responsibility and Work Reconciliation Act (1996), 294

Persons of concern, 104

Philanthropic organizations, 184

Physicians, 186, 271. *See also* Health professionals

Physicians for Human Rights, 50

Plyer v. Doe, 245

Poetry therapy (PT), 10, 317, 318, 332–333

Pol Pot regime (Cambodia), 136, 138, 150, 151

Poland: closing of borders to refugees, 113; refugees from, 74; withdrawal from GCM, 108

Policy, Politics, and Culture: EU Migration and Integration Network, 340

Political science, 8

Polyvagal theory, 324

Porges, Stephen, 328

Postmigration stressors, 262, 272, 278, 307

Postracial society, 302

Post-traumatic stress disorder (PTSD), 50, 138, 142, 143, 150, 151, 161–162, 168, 232, 261, 283, 322; association with trauma and torture, 161

Prejudice: combating, 223; interethnic, 309; xenophobic, 342

Primary care physicians (PCPs), 134

Prison Rape Elimination Act (PREA), 220–221

Pro-immigration discourse, 114

Prophetic witness, 173–174

Proximity-Based Collaborative Child Psychiatry and Community Mental Health Care Team, 284

PSOT. *See* Bellevue/NYU Program for Survivors of Torture (PSOT)

Psychiatric care: age and country/language of origin of current patients, 139t; and burnout, 155; Club House model, 146–147; cost of, 131–132; evidence-based practice, 196; group sessions, 137–138; group therapy, 144–149; holistic view, 184; interdisciplinary philosophy of, 184;

outcomes of, 131–132; patient characteristics, 138–140; psychospiritual approaches, 172; psychotropic medicines, 142, 154, 185, 187, 214; for refugees, 9, 131–132; resilience-focused, 184; therapeutic and healing modalities, 173; trauma-informed practices, 165, 182–183, 244, 276, 341; use of ritual and ceremony in, 165, 172. *See also* Clinicians; Group sessions; Indochinese/Intercultural Psychiatric Program (IPP); Therapists

Psychiatric illnesses, 150; mood disorders, 161. *See also* Depression; Post-traumatic stress disorder (PTSD); Psychosis

Psychiatrists, 9; role of, 134–135

Psychiatry: community, 147; cultural, 10, 284; hospital-based, 10. *See also* Child psychology

Psycho-educational orientation groups, 9

Psychoeducators, 271

Psychological distress, 48–49, 161; caused by forced migration, 182

Psychologists, 271

Psychology, 8

Psychopathology, 162; Resilience Scale, 162

Psychopharmacology, 185

Psychosis, 147, 151

Psychosocial rehabilitation, 149, 153

Psychosocial treatment, 9. *See also* Group sessions

Psychospiritual approaches, 172–173

Psychotherapy, 9, 11, 317

Psychotropic medicine, 142

Public charge doctrine, 76, 78, 119, 222, 241

Public health, 8, 237, 267, 284

Public health practitioners, 337, 341

Public welfare, 295

Public-private partnerships, 77

Qualification recognition, 114, 116

Quebec: historical and cultural context, 268–269; medical care for refugees in, 267

Quota system, 79, 80, 101, 114

Racial discrimination, 240

Racial equity, 292

Racial profiling, 342

Racism, 10, 262, 280, 281, 292, 294, 301, 308–309, 342

Rape, 140, 143, 155, 208–209, 233, 282, 323. *See also* Gender-based violence (GBV)

Reagan, Ronald, 25–26

Reception and Placement Program (R & P Program), 83–84

Refugee Act (1980), 9, 19–25, 37, 74, 75, 80, 81, 293; applications at the border or from within the U.S., 22–25; asylum applications, 22–23; U.S. Refugee Admissions Program, 20–22; withholding of removal, 22–23

Refugee and Humanitarian Resettlement Program (Canada), 264

Refugee and Immigration Center for Education and Legal Services (RAICES), 342

Refugee camps, 234, 291, 293, 296; Moria (Lesbos, Greece), 100; sexual victimization in, 100

Refugee Cash Assistance, 84

Refugee Convention (1951), 37

Refugee crisis, 5

Refugee Education and Training Center, 91

Refugee policies, 3; admissions ceiling, 93; antimigrant, 338–339; as barriers to self-sufficiency, 302–310; challenging unjust policies and practice, 340–341; politicization of, 7–8; and public welfare, 295; unrealistic expectations of, 310–311; ways to become engaged, 341–343. *See also* Immigration policies; U.S. refugee law and policy

Refugee policy, 294; in the U.S., 293–294

Refugee Protocol, 19–20

Refugee Protocol (1967), 37

Refugee quotas. *See* Immigration and Nationality Act (1965; Hart-Celler Act)

Refugee resettlement, 5, 8, 9, 33; using agencies, 343; changes by Trump administration, 76–77; in Colorado, 291; community involvement in, 94; community sponsorship/cosponsorship of, 94; federal funding for, 92; implications for practice, 310–311; problems with, 302–310; programs for, 75–76, 93; restrictions on, 8, 102; role of federal agencies in, 81; and the Trump administration, 340; in the U.S., 34. *See also* Refugee resettlement organizations (RROs); U.S. refugee resettlement program

Refugee resettlement organizations (RROs), 83–84; in Connecticut, 85

Refugee Resettlement Program, 81

Refugee Services Office, 92

Refugee trauma, 9, 10, 150, 153, 163, 315–316; and child migrants, 235. *See also* Trauma

Refugees: admission of, 8, 81; admission targets for, 75, 81; advocacy for, 280, 285, 338–340; arrivals by fiscal year (2016–2018), 83*t*; cash assistance for, 293–294, 295, 310; from collectivist cultures, 183; community sponsorship/ cosponsorship of, 85–87; deaths of upon return to home countries, 64; definition of, 204–205; in developing countries, 5; economic independence for, 294; education

for, 117; empowerment of, 10; environmental, 104; evaluation of, 279; expedited removal policy, 26–27; faith and resilience in, 162–164; goal of self-sufficiency for, 86, 87; group activities for, 144–149; history of trauma, 138; housing for, 93, 120, 277, 302–303, 305; humanitarian concerns, 20–21; hunger strikes by, 100; identity of, 103; increasing numbers of, 315; legal perspectives, 8; images of, 1; moral obligation to help, 6; and the national interest, 20; official response to, 11; opposing responses to, 1; as pioneers, 90; priority processing categories, 20; protection for, 18–20, 38, 57, 103–104, 107–108; public attitudes toward, 1; regional prioritizing, 83; restrictions of, 340; resulting from mass displacement, 100; rights of, 6, 9, 11, 107–108, 109, 111–112, 307–308, 337–343; safe spaces for, 120, 121; security checks for, 21, 33; self-sufficiency as goal of, 75, 77, 81, 84; social inclusion of, 9; social networks of, 86; social policy perspectives, 8; social welfare supports for, 341; state aid to, 5–6; suicide attempts by, 51–52, 100, 102; support for, 2, 7, 93; trauma experienced by, 315–316; "trophy," 28; as victims of trafficking, 59–60; vulnerability of, 100; well-being of, 8, 9, 11. *See also* African women refugees; Asylum seekers; Immigrants

Refugees and immigrants by country of origin: Afghanistan, 3, 21, 64, 82, 94n3, 101, 102, 112–113, 115*t*, 117, 133, 319; Africa, 10, 21, 94n2, 143, 166–171, 185, 187, 277, 278, 290–291, 292–293, 323; Albania, 185; Bhutan, 149; Bosnia, 132, 139,

149–150, 185; Cambodia, 81, 133, 135, 136, 138, 142–147, 149–150, 151; Canada, 42–43n64; Caribbean, 21, 62–63, 94n2, 278; Central America, 5, 30, 37, 41n44, 58, 64, 74, 102, 132, 149, 215, 221, 233; Central Asia, 94n2; Central Europe, 80; Chad, 33; China, 263; Cuba, 21, 74, 94n3; Czech Republic, 108; Czechoslovakia, 74; Democratic Republic of Congo (DRC), 165, 291, 296, 309; Designated Countries of Origin, 267; Dominican Republic, 104; East Asia, 94n2, 278; Eastern Europe, 80; El Salvador, 5, 21, 28–29, 232, 341; Eritrea, 291, 296; Ethiopia, 132, 139, 149–150, 152, 296; Europe, 94n2; Germany, 79; Guatemala, 2, 5, 21, 28–29, 139; Haiti, 21, 25–26, 37–38, 40n25, 94n3, 104; Honduras, 29, 202–203, 232, 341; Hungary, 74; Indochina, 139; Iran, 33, 94n1, 132, 133, 139, 150; Iraq, 3, 33, 76, 82, 94n3, 101, 113, 115t, 117, 132, 139, 161, 162, 306; Laos, 81, 135, 138, 145–147, 149, 150; Latin America, 21, 94n2, 278; Libya, 33, 94n1, 291; Mexico, 78; Middle East, 83, 278, 333; Mien, 143, 145–147, 149–150; Myanmar (Burma), 102, 104, 132, 134, 150; Near East/South Asia, 83, 94n2, 263, 278, 282–283; Nepal, 134, 150, 165; Nigeria, 50, 117; North Korea, 33, 94n1; Pakistan, 117, 165; Poland, 74; Russia/USSR, 21, 132, 138, 149–150; Sierra Leone, 185; Somalia, 21, 33, 64–65, 94n1, 132, 139, 143–144, 149–150, 152, 165, 291, 296, 301–302; South America, 132, 149; Southeast Asia, 74, 80, 278, 306; Sri Lanka, 162; Sudan, 102, 165, 291, 296; Syria, 3, 5, 21, 22, 32–34, 85, 89–90, 91, 94n1, 101, 102, 112, 113, 115t, 116–117, 242, 264; Tibet, 163, 185, 187; Venezuela, 5, 33, 94n1, 102; Vietnam, 80–81, 133, 134, 135, 138, 139, 145–147, 149–150; Yemen, 33, 94n1, 102

Refugees and immigrants by country of refuge: Australia, 165; Austria, 117–120, 118*f*; Canada, 11, 22, 33, 41n41, 263–264, 278; European Union, 104, 113, 114; Germany, 3, 22, 101, 114–117; Greece, 111, 112; India, 163; Kenya, 165; Latin American countries, 110; Sweden, 64, 101, 161; Turkey, 5, 6, 101, 112; United Kingdom, 101, 165; United States, 3, 9, 11, 101, 290–291

Refugees by language: Arabic-speaking, 85, 132; Farsi-speaking, 132, 150; Francophone African, 185; Spanish-speaking, 132

Refugees by religion: Buddhist, 137, 139, 187; Christian, 32, 139; Jewish, 78–79, 103; Muslim, 76, 90–91, 137, 139, 144, 162, 291

Regional Program for the Settlement and Integration of Asylum Seekers (PRAIDA), 270

Rehabilitation, right to, 338, 339

Release on own recognizance, 56

Religious accommodation, 268–269

Religious values, 90, 281

Removal: voluntary or forced, 62–63. *See also* Deportation

Repatriation, 62. *See also* Deportation

Reporting, as alternative to detention, 55

Research networks, 340

Resettlement programs. *See* Refugee resettlement

Resilience, 9, 261, 266; among refugee children, 249; among refugees and asylum seekers, 160–162; demographic factors, 162; economic factors, 162; and faith, 162–164;

and gender, 162; promotion of, 272; and recovery from trauma, 160–166; and resourcing, 322–323; role of, 162; social factors, 162; spiritual frameworks for, 174, 177; and spirituality, 160–162; vicarious, 159

Resourcing, 322–323, 326

Restrictionism, 76, 102

Returns Directive, 111

Revisionism, 292

Riley, Crystal, 145, 146–147, 156n2

Rites of passage, 10–11, 317, 327

Rituals, 10–11, 164, 165, 317, 328; dance and drum, 321

Robin Hood Foundation, 184

Rohingya, as migrants, 102, 104

Roma, as refugees, 139

Rudd, Amber, 59

Russia (U.S.S.R.), refugees from, 21, 132, 138, 149–150

Rwanda genocide, 309

Saarland, Syrian refugees in, 116–117

Sabraw, Dana M., 213, 214

Sale v. Haitian Centers Council, 40n25

Salt Lake Community College, 91

Sanctuary cities, 7, 37

Sanctuary jurisdictions, 36–37

Schengen space, 102

Schey, Peter, 213

Scholars at Risk (SAR) program, 342

Secular values, 268

Securitization, 102, 104, 113, 121–122

Self-care, radical, 174–175

Self-compassion, 194

Self-esteem, 163, 189, 317

Self-forgiveness, 177

Self-help initiatives, 77

Self-respect, 189

Self-sufficiency, 10, 77, 81, 84, 86, 87, 297; barriers to, 10; from a critical race theory lens, 294–296; difficulties involved in achieving,

310–311; economic, 77, 290, 294–296

September 11, 2001, terrorist attacks, 76, 82, 185

Service organizations, 147

Sessions, Jeffrey, 76

Sexism, 10

Sexual abuse, 49, 207, 208, 211, 213, 220–221, 240

Sexual health, 240

Sexual slavery, 205

Sexual victimization, 100, 192

Shadow Reports, 339

Sheehan Disability Scale, 140, 149, 152–153

Shengen Agreement, 122

Shengen space, 122

SHERPA Research Program, 270

Shire, Warsan, 327

Sierra Leone: refugees from, 185; war-exposed youth in, 244

Silencing, 318

Smugglers and smuggling, 119, 233

Sobremesa Ensemble, 326; creation of, 327–328

Social capital, 295

Social change, 338–340

Social connections, 93

Social inclusion, 8, 9, 122, 262, 316

Social isolation, 144–145, 188, 245

Social justice advocacy, 195

Social media, 1

Social networks, 86, 295

Social service agencies, 140, 186, 271, 273–274, 277, 293–294, 338, 340

Social stigma, 187, 238, 241, 249, 269, 274, 282

Social ties, 244

Social welfare, 294

Social workers, 8, 65, 341; role of, 343

Socialization groups, 144–150

Sociocultural processes, 10

Socio-faith networks, 165

Sociology, 8

Somalia: refugees from, 21, 33, 64–65, 94n1, 132, 139, 143–144, 149–150, 152, 165, 291, 296, 301–302; return of refugees to, 64

Somatic therapy, 321, 333

Somatic trauma therapy, 321

Somatoform disorders, 161

South America, refugees from, 132, 149

South Asia/Near East: immigrants and refugees from, 83, 94n2, 263, 278, 282–283

South Sudan, refugees from, 102

Southeast Asia, refugees from, 74, 80, 278, 306

Southeast Asian refugee crisis, 80

Special Immigrant Juvenile Status, 206

Special Immigrant Visa Program, 82, 94n3

Spiritual practices, 275

Spiritual testimony, 177

Spirituality, 9, 160, 165; and recovery from trauma, 160–166; and resilience, 160–162, 174, 177

Sri Lanka, refugees from, 162

State neutrality, 268

Stateless persons, 104

Stepakoff, Shanee, 332

Stigma. *See* Social stigma

Storytelling, 164

Student visas, 17

Subsidiary protection, 104

Substance abuse programs, 91

Sudan, refugees from, 102, 165, 291, 296

Supplemental Nutritional Assistance Program (SNAP), 296

Survivors of Torture (SOT) grant, 151, 152

Sweden: approach to immigration, 56; migrants and refugees in, 64, 101, 161

Syria: asylum seekers from, 117; forced conscription of children in, 234; refugees from, 3, 5, 21, 22, 32–34, 85, 89–90, 91, 94n1, 101, 102, 112, 113, 115t, 116–117, 242, 264; war in, 85

T visa, 206

TANF. *See* Temporary Assistance to Needy Families (TANF) program

Teachers, preparing to work with refugees, 342

Telephonic monitoring, 56

Temporary Assistance to Needy Families (TANF) program, 10, 84, 92, 294, 295, 296, 304, 306, 311

Terrorism, 45; 9/11 attacks, 76, 82, 185; in Paris, 85

Testimony therapy, 165, 166, 169, 172

Theology, 8

Therapists: challenges of working with trauma survivors, 174–177; and radical self-care, 174–175; as spiritual witness, 172–174. *See also* Clinicians

Therapy groups. *See* Group sessions; Group therapy

Third individuation, 281

Third-country solutions, 107

Tibet, refugees from, 163, 185, 187

Tigar, Jon, 215

Torture, 9, 140, 142, 150, 151, 155, 163–164; and cardiovascular disease, 154; of children, 213, 234, 242; at Guantanamo, 339; Tola's experience, 166–171

Torture survivors, 154, 159, 192, 195, 333; Albanian-speaking, 185; English-speaking, 185; faith and resilience in, 162–164; female, 185; French-speaking African, 187; Fulani-speaking, 185; mental health of, 161–162; rehabilitation for, 339; trauma-informed work with, 341; treatment programs, 9, 152–153, 323. *See also* Bellevue/NYU Program for Survivors of

Torture (PSOT); Torture Treatment
    Center of Oregon
Torture Treatment Center of Oregon
    (TTCO), 131, 140, 151; conclusion,
    155; experiences of refugees and
    asylum seekers in treatment in the
    US, 151–152; outcomes of IPP
    model, 152–154; reflections on cost
    of care, 152; research associated
    with, 154; teaching associated
    with, 153–154; treating torture
    survivors, 150–151
Torture Victims Relief Act, 150, 184
Tourist visas, 17
Trafficking in Persons Unit, 60
Trafficking victims. See Human
    trafficking
Transactional Records Access
    Clearinghouse (TRAC), 40n27
Transcultural psychiatry, 8, 271–277
Trauma, 138, 278; and cardiovascular
    disease, 154; cognitive impact of,
    299; developmental, 331; effect on
    children, 154, 235–236; effects of,
    330; emotional impact of, 299;
    exposure of migrant children to,
    242; and faith, 164–166; impact of,
    298–300, 310; impact on children,
    242–243; and the lived experiences
    of women refugees, 297–300; and
    meaning-making, 171–172;
    physical impact of, 299; relational,
    323; Tola's experience, 166–171;
    vicarious, 174. See also Refugee
    trauma
Trauma survivors: group
    interventions for, 183; holistic view
    of, 184; psychiatric care for, 177
Trauma syndrome, 142
Traumatic loss, 332
Traumatic memories, 318, 322, 332;
    processing of, 186. See also Memory
Travel ban, 85. See also Muslim Ban
Travel loan program, 306–308
Trudeau, Justin, 3

Truman, Harry S., 79
Trump, Donald J., 2, 6; anti-
    immigration platform of, 3;
    approach to deportation, 64;
    approach to immigration, 38, 57;
    approach to refugees, 76–77,
    82–83, 90; ban on Syrian refugees,
    22; refugee policies of, 85. See also
    Executive orders
Trump administration: antimigrant
    policies of, 222; approach to
    immigration, 57–58, 62, 94n2, 102,
    203; approach to immigration
    relief, 206; approach to refugees,
    291, 340; experiences of child
    migrants under, 209–215; and the
    private prison industry, 53; and
    refugee resettlement, 76–77, 93,
    340; use of alternatives to
    detention, 56; use of private
    detention facilities by, 53; zero
    tolerance policy, 7, 46–47, 49, 59,
    65, 76, 101, 102, 211, 232
TTCO Symptom Checklist, 140
Turkey: asylum seekers in, 101;
    refugees in, 5, 6, 101, 112; as safe
    third country, 112

U visa, 206
Uganda, asylum seekers from, 185
UN Committee against Torture
    (CAT), 339
UN International Organization of
    Migration (IOM), 306–307
UN Sustainable Development
    Goals, 88
Unaccompanied children (UACs), 59,
    64, 100, 203, 205, 233; care and
    custody of, 206–207; education for,
    245–246; as at-risk populations,
    221. See also Child migrants
Unaccompanied Refugee Minor
    Program, 233
Undocumented children (UDCs), 234.
    See also Child migrants

UNHCR (United Nations High Commissioner for Refugees), 4

Union of Soviet Socialist Republics (USSR/Russia), refugees from, 21, 132, 138, 140–150

United Kingdom: Brexit vote, 3; deportation practices in, 9, 62–63; detention practices in, 9, 45–47, 51, 54, 55, 58–59, 59–60; mistreatment of detainees in, 48–49; refugees in, 101, 165; use of detention as deterrent, 48

United Nations, and human rights, 5

United Nations Convention on the Protection of the Rights of All Migrant Workers and Members of Their Families, 108

United Nations High Commissioner for Human Rights (UNHCHR), 211, 222

United Nations High Commissioner for Refugees (UNHCR), 4, 5–6, 20–21, 33, 57, 75, 108

United Nations Leaders' Summit on Refugees, 6

United Nations Protocol Relating to the Status of Refugees, 108, 264

United Nations Sustainable Development Goals, 338

United Nations Voluntary Fund, 184

United States: antimigrant policies in, 338–339; deportation policies and practices, 9, 62; detention practices in, 9, 45–47, 51–58, 60; failure to ratify the U.N. Convention on the Rights of the Child, 216; and the forced migration crisis, 102; human rights violations in, 6, 10; humanitarian and foreign policy in, 93; immigration law in, 8; immigration policies, 2, 17, 195; injustices in, 343; legal and social policy issues, 8; legal protection for refugees, 18–20; migration to, 11; mistreatment of detainees in,

48–49; as "nation of immigrants," 77–78; opposing the Global Compact on Safe Migration, 121; politicization of immigrant and refugee policy, 7–8; refugee crisis in, 5; refugee policies, 1, 293–294; refugee resettlement in, 3, 9, 101; refugees and immigrants in, 290–291; responsibility for forced migration, 5; reversal of refugee admission practices, 3; status of refugees and asylum seekers, 8; support for immigrants and refugees in, 7; use of detention as deterrent, 48; withdrawal from GCM, 108. *See also* Trump, Donald J.; Trump administration

United States Citizenship and Immigration Services (USCIS), 21

United States National Consortium of Torture Treatment Programs (NCTTP), 339

Universal Declaration of Human Rights, 4, 105

University of Saarland, 116

Unreturnables, 61

U.S. Border Patrol, abuses by, 342

U.S. Citizen and Immigration Services (USCIS), 81

U.S. citizens (USCs), 17–18

U.S. Customs and Border Protection (CBP), 27

U.S. Human Rights Network (USHRN), 339

U.S. Immigration and Customs Enforcement (ICE), 2

U.S. International Refugee Assistance Program (IRAP), 75–76

U.S. Refugee Admissions Program, 20–22

U.S. refugee law and policy: 1980 Refugee Act, 9, 19–25, 37, 74, 75, 80, 81, 293; 1980 to the end of the Obama administration (January 2017), 20–31; barriers to protection and critiques of the process, 25–31; Border Security and Immigration Enforcement Improvements, 34–37; Enhancing Public Safety in the Interior of the United States, 34–37; January 2017 to the present, 32–37; protection from foreign terrorists ("Muslim Ban"), 32–34. *See also* Refugee policies

U.S. refugee resettlement program: background, 74–77; centrality of volunteers in, 84; history of (after Vietnam War), 80–81; history of (resettlement of refugees 1880–1975), 77–80; overview, 81–83; at state and local levels, 83–84. *See also* Refugee resettlement

U.S. State Department, Bureau for Population, Refugees, and Migration, 81

USRAP, 38

Utah: refugee resettlement in, 9; voluntarism in, 77, 84, 90–93, 93n4

Utah Department of Workforce Services, 91, 92

Utah State University, 91

Vandalism, 88

Venezuela, 19; refugees from, 5, 33, 94n1, 102

Vera Institute of Justice, 212

V.F.B. v. Sessions, 247, 341

Vicarious resilience, 159. *See also* Resilience

Vicarious trauma, 174. *See also* Trauma

Victims of Child Abuse Act (VCAA), 220

Vietnam, refugees from, 80–81, 133, 134, 135, 138, 139, 145–147, 149–150

Vietnam War, 5, 80, 87

Vietnamese Depression Scale, 154

Violence: against child migrants, 223; domestic, 29; gender-based (GBV), 76, 233, 278, 279, 282, 291, 297–298; nondirect, 242; postmigration, 281; sexual, 192, 234, 298. *See also* Rape; Torture; Trauma

Vocational Education and Training System (VET), 116

Voices of color, 292

Voluntarism, 9, 89, 342–343; agencies, 79; in Connecticut, 77, 84, 85–87, 93n4; in Kentucky, 77, 84, 87–90, 93n4; by local businesses, 148; and refugee resettlement, 92; in Utah, 77, 84, 90–93, 93n4. *See also* Volunteers

Voluntary departure, 63–64

Voluntary resettlement agencies (VOLAGs), 77, 79, 81, 86

Volunteering and Civic Life in America, 92

Volunteers, 121; community members/individuals, 148, 149; local clubs, 148; preparing to work with refugees, 342; students, 149; in U.S. refugee resettlement, 84. *See also* Voluntarism

Vulnerable populations, 233

Wagner, Steven, 209

War on Drugs, 5

Welcoming cities, 7

Welfare laws, 119

White self-interests, 292

William Wilberforce Trafficking Victims Protection Reauthorization Act (2008; TVPRA), 221

Wilson/Fish states, 84, 87–88

Windrush scandal, 62–63

Withholding of removal, 40n25

Women and girls: from Africa, 10, 185; cultural roles of, 136; in detention,

57, 57–58; and domestic violence, 29; education for, 244; marginalization of, 301, 308; Muslim, 301–302; oppression of, 295; pregnant, 57–58; as refugees, 10, 30, 293, 295–296; resettlement of, 291; self-sufficiency of, 10; subjugation of, 295; as victims of gender-based violence (GBV), 76, 233, 278, 279, 282, 291, 297–298; as victims of sexual violence, 192, 234, 298. *See also* African women refugees; Rape
World War II, 78–79, 105

Xenophobia, 3, 42–43n64, 102, 195, 342

Yarl's Wood, 58
Yemen, refugees from, 33, 94n1, 102
Yoga groups, trauma-informed, 9–10, 184, 186
Youth Mental Health (YMH) teams, 271

Zadvydas v. Davis, 61
Zero tolerance policy, 7, 46–47, 49, 59, 65, 76, 101, 102, 211, 232
Zolberg, Aristide, 77–78
Zoley, George, 52

About the Editors and Contributors

Editors

S. Megan Berthold, PhD, LCSW, is an associate professor and the director of Field Education at the University of Connecticut's School of Social Work. She has worked with diverse refugee and asylum-seeking survivors of torture, war traumas, human trafficking, and other traumas since the mid-1980s in the United States (including at the Program for Torture Victims in Los Angeles) and in refugee camps in the Philippines and on the Thai-Cambodian border. She has conducted National Institute of Mental Health-funded research, examining the prevalence of mental and physical health consequences among Cambodian refugee genocide survivors. Berthold has served as the cochair of the National Consortium of Torture Treatment Programs' Research and Data Committee for the past 11 years. Her community-based participatory research in Cambodian refugee communities across the United States has contributed to building community capacity to conduct research to address their health disparities. She has testified extensively as an expert witness in U.S. Immigration Court and published widely on refugee issues. Berthold coauthored *Achieving the Impossible Dream: How Japanese Americans Obtained Redress* (1999), coedited *Advancing Human Rights in Social Work Education* (2014), and authored *Human Rights-Based Approaches to Clinical Social Work* (2015). The National Association of Social Workers selected Berthold as the 2009 National Social Worker of the Year.

Kathryn R. Libal, PhD, is an associate professor of social work and human rights at the University of Connecticut and director of the Human Rights Institute. She received her doctorate in cultural anthropology at the University of Washington. Her scholarship has addressed women's and children's rights movements in Turkey, international nongovernmental organizational advocacy on behalf of Iraqi and Syrian refugees, and the localization of human rights norms and practices in the United States. She is currently conducting a collaborative qualitative study on the politics and practices of voluntarism and refugee resettlement in the United States. She coedited *Human Rights in the United States: Beyond Exceptionalism* (2011) and coauthored *Human Rights-Based Community Practice in the United States* (2015). She also was lead editor of *Advancing Human Rights in Social Work Education* (2014). She serves on the editorial board of the *Journal of Human Rights and Social Work* and directs an interdisciplinary human rights program, the Human Rights Institute, at the University of Connecticut.

Contributors

Adeyinka M. Akinsulure-Smith, PhD, received her doctorate in counseling psychology from Teachers College, Columbia University. She is currently a tenured professor in the Department of Psychology at the City College of New York and at the Graduate Center of the City University of New York. Akinsulure-Smith is a senior supervising psychologist at the Bellevue/NYU Program for Survivors of Torture in New York City. Her areas of professional interest include the experiences of forced migrants, trauma and human rights abuses, and multicultural issues.

Carol Bohmer, LLM, PhD, a lawyer and sociologist, is a visiting scholar in the Government Department at Dartmouth College and a teaching fellow at King's College, London. She has worked in the area of law and society, examining the way legal and social institutions interact, with particular emphasis on the role of gender in law. Her current research interests are in the field of immigration and asylum. She is the coauthor with Amy Shuman of *Rejecting Refugees: Political Asylum in the 21st Century* (2007) and *Political Asylum Deceptions: The Culture of Suspicion* (2018).

Jean F. East, PhD, MSW, is professor emerita at the University of Denver, Graduate School of Social Work. East has over 40 years of practice experience in the Denver community. Her research is based on the implementation of an empowerment model with women who are financially vulnerable, combining trauma and clinical work with advocacy and community organizing. She recently published *Transformational Leadership for the Helping Professions: Engaging Head, Heart and Soul* (2019).

Rayanne Elias, MD, is a resident in psychiatry at the University of Toronto with an interest in Social and Transcultural Psychiatry. Elias teaches psychiatry to medical students and residents in Toronto and abroad in Addis Ababa, Ethiopia. She engages in outreach to provide psychiatric care to individuals from diverse cultural backgrounds in Northern Ontario and Nunavut.

Grace Felten, MSW, is a doctoral candidate in the School of Social Work at the University of Connecticut. She began her career working for the Jane Goodall Institute, focusing on community service at the local and international level. She obtained her MSW at the University of Connecticut, along with an interdisciplinary graduate certificate in human rights and specializations in the areas of international social work and women, children, and families. Felten completed her fieldwork at the United Nations, representing the International Association of Schools of Social Work on UN NGO advocacy committees focused on migration, human trafficking, sustainable development, poverty, and the rights of women and girls. She continued her fieldwork with the Global Network of Women Peacebuilders, advocating for the implementation of UN Security Council Resolutions on women, peace, and security. Her research interests include the gendered experience of forced migration, volunteering/community service, reproductive health, community mobilization to support refugee resettlement, global health, and child/early marriage.

Kathleen Flinton, MAR, MSW, LICSW, is a senior consulting clinician and clinical supervisor at the Boston Center for Refugee Health and Human Rights at Boston Medical Center, and a lecturer and the director of the Postgraduate Certificate in the Treatment of Trauma at the Boston University School of Social Work. She holds a BA from Vassar College, an MSW from Simmons School of Social Work, and an MAR from Yale Divinity School. Flinton has over 20 years of experience in working with survivors of trauma. Her area of expertise is in cross-cultural trauma treatment, with a specialization in working with refugees and asylum seekers. In her role at the Boston Center for Refugee Health and Human Rights, Flinton provides training and supervision on mental health treatment to survivors of torture, trafficking, war, and human rights abuses. In her position at Boston University School of Social Work, she teaches courses across the trauma sequence and in immigrant and refugee practice. Flinton has postgraduate training in EMDR, sensorimotor psychotherapy, and maternal mental health. In addition to clinical supervision and teaching, Flinton has a private practice, working with survivors of torture, and has served as an expert witness in federal immigration court.

Amber Elizabeth L. Gray, MPH, MA, LPCC, BC-DMT, is an internationally recognized expert in refugee mental health and torture treatment. Amber established New Mexico's Refugee Mental Health program, the first of its kind in the United States, in 2007 and coordinated the program for seven years. She was the clinical director at the Rocky Mountain Survivors Center; clinical advisor for the Center for Victims of Torture, and past president of the Board of Directors for the Torture Abolition and Survivors Support

Coalition (TASSC) International. She currently directs Restorative Resources Training and Consulting and the Kint Institute Program for the Creative Arts and Trauma Treatment. Gray regularly trains health and mental health professionals and paraprofessionals in her trauma and resiliency framework and Restorative Movement Psychotherapy, a therapeutic approach that integrates the creative arts, somatic therapies, and mindfulness into refugee mental health. She is the 2010 recipient of the American Dance Therapy Association's Outstanding Achievement Award and a 2016 nominee for the Barbara Chester award.

Jaswant Guzder, MD, is a professor of psychiatry, McGill University, and former head of child psychiatry at the Jewish General Hospital. She was a codirector of the Cultural Consultation Service of the Jewish General Hospital from its inception. From 1980 to 1984, she worked in Mumbai, India, as a psychiatric consultant and psychoanalyst. Guzder's current research interests include cross-cultural training, global health project work, and child trauma issues.

Badiah Haffejee, PhD, MSW, is an assistant professor at Elizabethtown College, Department of Social Work. She is a macro social worker, specializing in the integration process of newly resettled refugee families in the United States. Her research focuses on the effects of trauma (such as war, refugee camp experiences, gender and sexual violence, and poverty), institutional barriers (i.e., refugee policy, racism, discrimination, and Islamophobia), and the role of resiliency in mitigating these barriers for refugee families in the United States.

Scott Harding, PhD, is an associate professor and codirector of the PhD Program in the School of Social Work, University of Connecticut. He is coauthor of *Counter-Recruitment and the Campaign to Demilitarize Public Schools* (2017) and *Human-Rights Based Approaches to Community Practice in the United States* (2015). He has participated in several multiyear qualitative research projects related to war and its effects. His current collaborative research on the politics of refugee resettlement in the United States examines the role of volunteers and community members in response to changes in U.S. refugee policy. Harding is a board member of Integrated Refugee and Immigrant Services (IRIS), was executive director and policy coordinator for the California Homeless Housing Coalition, and is a former editor of the *Journal of Community Practice*.

Ghayda Hassan, PhD, is a clinical psychologist and professor of cultural clinical psychology at the University of Quebec at Montreal (UQAM). Hassan believes that we cannot develop expertise in any specific cultural group, but rather that clinical cultural psychology is more about a clinical stance, a "way of being," "a way of being with the other," and an approach to "meaning making within the context of an encounter with the other." Her clinical and research activities focus on the interplay of culture, identity, mental health, and violence in a variety of clinical and community settings.

G. Eric Jarvis, MD, MSc, is an associate professor of psychiatry and director of the Cultural Consultation Service at the Jewish General Hospital. His clinical work involves the psychiatric evaluation and treatment of immigrants and refugees with psychotic disorders. His current research interests include the relation between psychosis and culture, language barriers in psychiatric services, and the process of cultural consultation. Jarvis also writes about the history of psychiatry.

J. David Kinzie, MD, FACPsych, received his MD degree from the University of Washington. Following an internship, he worked as a general physician in Vietnam and Malaysia during the Vietnam War. After finishing his psychiatric residency at the University of Washington and a Fellowship in Transcultural Psychiatry at the University of Hawaii, he taught medicine at the University of Malaya and the University of Hawaii before coming to the Oregon Health & Science University (OHSU) in 1976. He has held several positions within the Department of Psychiatry at OHSU, including training director, director of Clinical Services, and vice-chair. In 1977, Kinzie founded the Indochinese/Intercultural Psychiatric Program (IPP) and served as its director for about 15 years. Kinzie has worked for over 40 years with refugee psychiatric patients and continues to see patients several days a week at the IPP. He has published numerous research articles and book chapters in this field and has given presentations on various facets of refugee psychiatric work across the United States and in many foreign countries. He is a distinguished fellow of the American Psychiatric Association and a fellow of the American College of Psychiatry.

Alysse M. Loomis, PhD, LCSW, has extensive clinical practice experience working with children and adults impacted by trauma. This includes forensic evaluations for individuals seeking asylum as well as children and families impacted by immigration policies. Loomis is an assistant professor at the University of Utah College of Social Work. She is actively involved in conducting research to support trauma-impacted populations, including refugees and young children. She has worked on community-based participatory research projects with refugee populations in Connecticut, including work on the impact of social isolation on physical and mental health in Cambodian refugees and conceptual work on the need for culturally and structurally competent social work practice with refugee populations. Loomis has conducted trainings for schools and mental health agencies on working with traumatized youth and is an endorsed Infant Mental Health Specialist, IMH-E® (III), and a member of the Connecticut Association for Infant Mental Health and the International Society for Traumatic Stress Studies.

Toby Measham, MD, MSc, is an assistant professor, Department of Psychiatry at McGill University, and a member of the Divisions of Social and Transcultural Psychiatry and Child Psychiatry. Her clinical and research interests include transcultural child psychiatry and the development of collaborative community-based mental health–care services for children and their families. She is training director for Psychiatry Resident Training at the Montreal Children's Hospital.

Richard F. Mollica, MD, MAR, is the director of the Harvard Program in Refugee Trauma (HPRT) of Massachusetts General Hospital and Harvard Medical School and professor of psychiatry at Harvard Medical School. In 1981, Mollica cofounded the Indochinese Psychiatry Clinic (IPC). Over the past two decades, HPRT and IPC have pioneered the mental health care of survivors of mass violence and torture. HPRT/IPC's clinical model has been replicated throughout the world. Mollica has published over 160 scientific articles and is the author of *Healing Invisible Wounds: Paths to Hope and Recovery in a Violent World* (2006) and a new book, *A Manifesto: Healing a Violent World* (2018). He has received numerous awards for his work. In 1993, he received the Human Rights Award from the American Psychiatric Association. In 1996, the American Orthopsychiatry Association presented him with the Max Hymen Award. In 2001, he was selected as a Fulbright New Century scholar. Under Mollica's direction, HPRT conducts training, policy, and research activities for traumatized populations around the world. HPRT's screening instruments are considered a gold standard in the field and have been widely translated into over 30 languages. HPRT's scientific work has helped place mental health issues at the center of the recovery of postconflict societies. Mollica and his team over the past 30 years have cared for over 10,000 survivors of extreme violence worldwide. Through his research, clinical work, and trainings, he is recognized as a leader in the treatment and rehabilitation of traumatized people and their communities.

Karen Musalo, JD, Bank of America Chair in International Law, is a professor of law and the founding director of the Center for Gender and Refugee Studies at U.C. Hastings College of the Law. Musalo is recognized as a national authority on refugee and asylum issues. She is lead coauthor of *Refugee Law and Policy: An International and Comparative Approach* (5th edition), as well as numerous reports, book chapters, and articles. She has contributed to the evolving jurisprudence of asylum law through her extensive scholarship, as well as her litigation of landmark cases, including *Matter of Kasinga*, the first landmark decision recognizing that women who flee gender-based harms may qualify for asylum. Musalo has received numerous awards for her pioneering legal work, including an honorary Doctor of Humane Letters from Lehman College in 2012. In 2014 she was named the Bank of America Foundation chair in International Law in recognition of her cutting-edge engaged scholarship and litigation, which has positively impacted so many refugees from around the world.

Lucie Nadeau, MD, MSc, is an associate professor, Department of Psychiatry at McGill University, and a member of the Divisions of Social and Transcultural Psychiatry and Child Psychiatry. She works as a child psychiatrist in Montreal community-based settings and at the Montreal Children's Hospital and the Jewish General Hospital and as a child psychiatry consultant in Inuit communities of Nunavik. Her research focuses on collaborative care in youth mental health and wellness, both in Montreal's multiethnic neighborhoods and in Indigenous communities.

Fernando Ona, PhD, MPH, LCSW, is a clinical associate professor of public health and community medicine at Tufts University and a student of theology at Boston University. His research, in part, has focused on refugees and asylum seekers who are survivors of torture.

Linda Piwowarczyk, MD, MPH, is the director and cofounder of the Boston Center for Refugee Health and Human Rights (BCRHHR) and an assistant professor of psychiatry at the Boston University School of Medicine. She first began working with refugees in 1993, as a Fellow in International Psychiatry at the Indochinese Psychiatry Clinic. Since 2002, Piwowarczyk has served on the Executive Committee of the National Consortium of Torture Treatment Programs and was first elected NCTTP president in 2011. She is the recipient of the Sarah Haley Memorial Award for Clinical Excellence from the International Society for Traumatic Stress Studies, the Local Legends Award from the National Library of Medicine, and co-awardee, with BCRHHR colleagues, of the Kenneth B. Schwartz Compassionate Honorable Mention Caregiver Award. A Distinguished Fellow of the American Psychiatric Association, recipient of the 2018 Humanitarian Award from Open Avenues Foundation, Piwowarczyk has presented on the topic of torture locally, nationally, and internationally and has published several articles in various medical journals.

Marciana Popescu, PhD, is an associate professor at Fordham University, Graduate School of Social Service. Prior to this appointment, Popescu taught at universities in the United States and Europe and worked in international development with international organizations and UN agencies since 1995. Over the last 10 years, she conducted study tours, taking Fordham graduate students to the Dominican Republic, Peru, and Haiti, focusing primarily on human rights violations, statelessness, postdisaster displacement, and forced migration, on the one hand, and microcredit initiatives and women's empowerment, on the other. In 2016 she was awarded a Fulbright scholarship and spent five months in Austria/Europe studying migration policies and their impact on refugees, with a focus on women asylum seekers and refugees. She was a visiting scholar in Germany, Saarland University (March 2018) and coedited (with Kathryn Libal) a special issue of *Advances in Social Work*, focusing on immigrants and refugees, published in September 2018. More recently, Popescu was nominated by her university for an Andrew Carnegie fellowship (November 2018) for a study that focuses on innovative employment and entrepreneurship initiatives for women refugees in the United States. Popescu continues her research on forced migration and teaches master's and doctoral-level courses, focusing on rights-based policy practice, international nonprofits, international social development, and women's rights. In 2018 she received a Fulbright Specialist award (2018–2021), focusing on program and curriculum development in the area of migration and human security.

Crystal Riley, MA, received her MA degree in clinical psychology from George Mason University. Following clinical work in mental health facilities in Virginia and Illinois, she has been affiliated with the Intercultural Psychiatric Program (IPP) at the Oregon Health & Science University (OHSU) for the last 32 years as a qualified mental health professional, program manager, supervisor, and researcher. At the IPP, Riley helped to develop and served as manager of three clinical refugee programs: the Indochinese/Intercultural Socialization Center, the Torture Treatment Center of Oregon, and the Intercultural Child Psychiatric Program. Since 2000, Riley has been involved in the work of the National Consortium of Torture Treatment Programs, serving for the last eight years as the NCTTP's vice-president, and for the last 11 years, as chair of its Research & Data Committee. Riley has developed an extensive research project with NCTTP members that has OHSU Institutional Review Board oversight. The project has collected data to date on approximately 17,000 torture survivors who have come for treatment to NCTTP centers across the United States.

Cécile Rousseau, MD, MSc, is a professor, Department of Psychiatry at McGill University, and is the director of the Transcultural Psychiatry Service in Montreal community-based services. She has worked extensively with immigrant and refugee communities, developing specific school-based interventions and leading policy-oriented research. Presently, her research focuses on the evaluation of collaborative mental health care models for youth in multiethnic neighborhoods and on intervention and prevention programs to address youth radicalization.

Amy Shuman, PhD, is a professor of folklore and narrative and a faculty member of the Mershon Center for International Security at the Ohio State University. With Carol Bohmer, she has coauthored *Political Asylum Deceptions: The Culture of Suspicion* (2018) and *Rejecting Refugees: Political Asylum in the 21st Century* (2007) as well as many articles. With Bridget Haas, she is the coeditor of a forthcoming book *Technologies of Suspicion and the Ethics of Obligation in Political Asylum*. She is the recipient of a Guggenheim Fellowship.

Hawthorne E. Smith, PhD, received his doctoral degree in counseling psychology (with distinction) from Teachers College, Columbia University. He is currently an associate clinical professor in the Department of Psychiatry in the New York University School of Medicine. Smith directs the Bellevue/NYU Program for Survivors of Torture in New York City. His areas of professional interest also include the experiences of forced migrants, trauma and human rights abuses, and multicultural issues.

8-8-19